"This insightful book elevates design methodologies into a systemic framework, providing leaders with the practical tools needed to integrate planetary boundaries, geopolitical risk, and technological advances into modern decision-making."
—JENNIFER GARDNER, Director, Stanford Doerr School of Sustainability

"An essential guide for leaders shaping the future—where scaling AI is not just a technical act but a moral and systemic evolution in human wisdom and empathy."
—DEEPTI PAHWA, Distinguished Scholar Stanford GSB, MIT Media Lab: AI Ventures

"This unique book brings design thinking back to its original purpose: solving the world's wicked problems and charting a course for a new era of designing exclusively for humanity."
—Fraunhofer Institute for Industrial Engineering IAO

"This bold and essential blueprint calls on leaders to move beyond human-centered design, providing the transformative framework needed to address today's 'wicked problems' through systemic, regenerative, and life-centered action."
—CHIP FLETCHER, Dean, School of Ocean and Earth Science and Technology, University of Hawaii at Manoa Honolulu

Explore more transformative books by Michael Lewrick, delving into design's profound impact on business, innovation, and personal growth.

Lewrick
Design Thinking and Innovation Metrics
Powerful Tools to Manage Creativity, OKRs, Product, and Business Success
ISBN: 978-1119983651

Lewrick
Design Thinking For Business Growth
How to Design and Scale Business Models and Business Ecosystems
ISBN: 978-1119815150

Lewrick, Link, Leifer
The Design Thinking Toolbox
A Guide to Mastering the Most Popular and Valuable Innovation Methods
ISBN: 978-1119629191

Lewrick, Link, Leifer
The Design Thinking Playbook
Mindful Digital Transformation of Teams, Products, Services, Businesses and Ecosystems
ISBN: 978-1119467472

Lewrick, Thommen, Leifer
The Design Thinking Life Playbook
Empower Yourself, Embrace Change, and Visualize a Joyful Life
ISBN: 978-1119682240

DESIGN THINKING FOR HUMANITY

DESIGN THINKING FOR HUMANITY

PRACTICAL TOOLS AND METHODS
TO BUILD RESILIENCE
FOR A BETTER FUTURE

MICHAEL LEWRICK

ILLUSTRATIONS
NHU NHU NGUYEN

WILEY

THE DESIGN THINKING FOR HUMANITY WHEEL

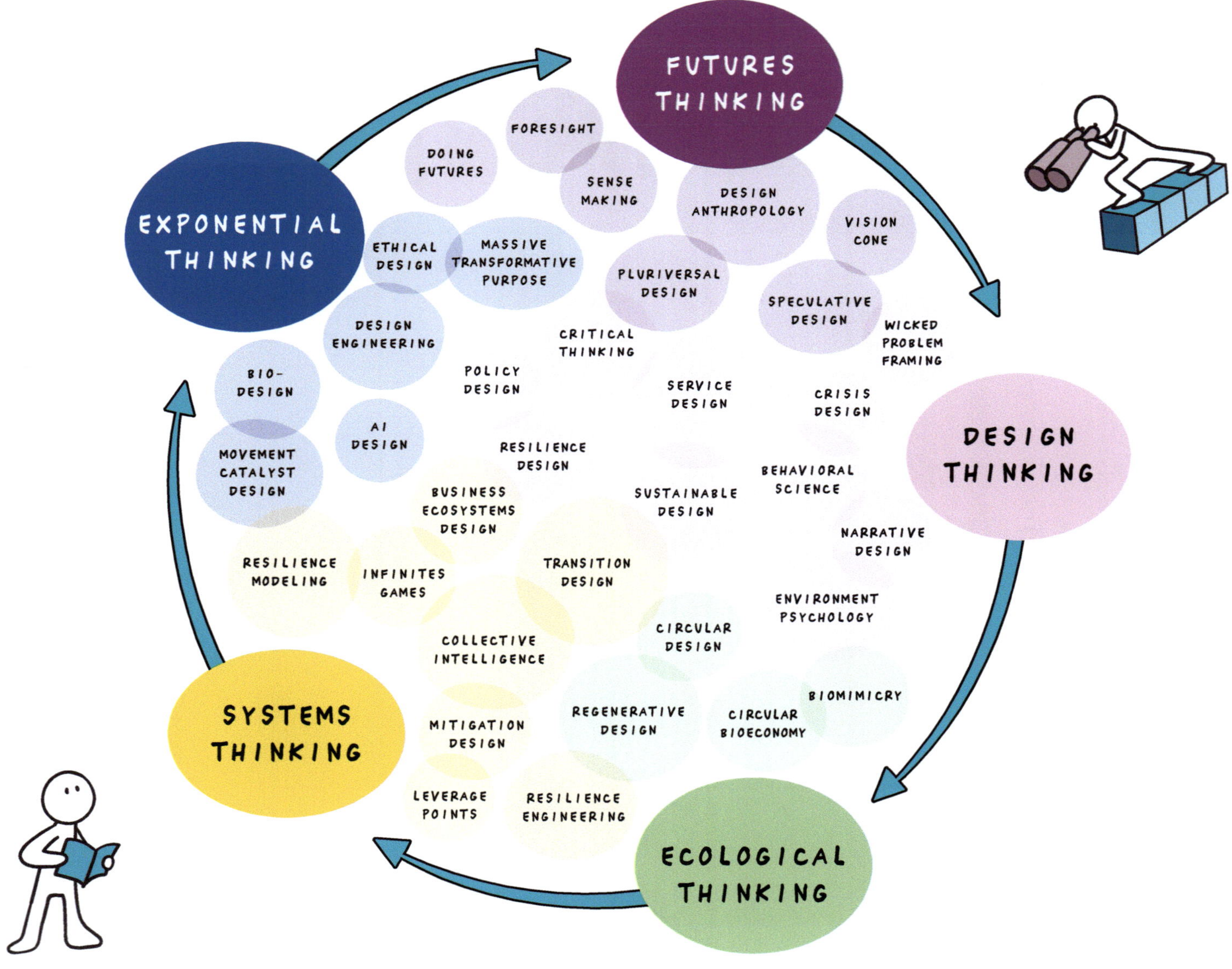

From Business Growth to Global Impact

The Wiley Design Thinking series has explored various facets of design thinking, from the foundational principles outlined in *The Design Thinking Playbook* and the practical methods presented in *The Design Thinking Toolbox*, to the business-focused strategies of *Design Thinking for Business Growth* and the crucial metrics explored in *Design Thinking and Innovation Metrics*. Building upon this foundation, *Design Thinking for Humanity* expands the toolkit and methodologies of the series, shifting the focus from primarily customers and business concerns to the creation of a more resilient and equitable world for everyone.

Preface: A Conversation on Systemic Evolution

A book about fundamental change demands a preface that is equally dynamic. Instead of a traditional foreword, I have chosen a more engaging format: **a focused dialogue with one of the greatest minds steering the methodology beyond the corporate sphere**.

I am honored to introduce **Jeanne Liedtka, professor emeritus at the Darden School of Business** and a leading expert on applying design thinking to complex social and governmental challenges. Given her expertise in **Design Thinking for the Greater Good**, my conversation focuses on the necessary strategic and systemic evolution of the practice. I asked Jeanne five powerful questions about moving design thinking from individual solutions to profound, collective achievement.

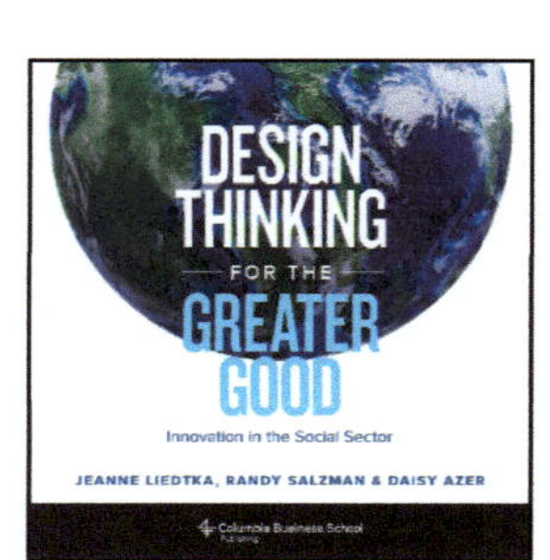

1. From User-Centric to Life-Centric:
Traditional design thinking often emphasizes deep empathy with the user. From your perspective, where does this classic "user-centric" approach fail when we try to address planetary-scale problems?

Jeanne Liedtka: "The 'Human-Centered' label can become a spotlight that blinds us to the larger context. It focuses intensely on an individual's immediate needs but ignores the systemic impact, the environmental cost, and the long-term consequences. To address planetary problems, **we must expand our empathy to include this broader context**. We have to move from solving exclusively for the user alone to solving for the user within an entire ecosystem. We must consider the needs of the environment and future generations, not just the person standing in front of us today."

2. Designing Beyond the Product:
Many leaders struggle to see policy and governance as something "designable," viewing them instead as rigid constraints. How should they change their mental model to apply design thinking beyond just products?

Jeanne Liedtka: "The challenge is to see policy or strategy as a prototype rather than a rigid plan. **An experimental approach is critical in a complex and uncertain world**. We would like to be able to test governance structures just like we test a new toaster. If we don't prototype policy, we remain blind to unintended consequences until it is too late. Leaders must shift their design target. We are no longer just designing products; we are designing 'platforms for participation' and 'ecosystems of value' that allow society to thrive. Of course, this is much easier to advocate than to practice, and we have a lot to learn about how to conduct experiments on policies rather than products."

3. Agency over Prediction:

A core tension in strategy is the difference between predicting the future and 'prototyping' it. Why do you believe that relying on standard prediction is dangerous for modern leadership?

Jeanne Liedtka: "In a world of change, prediction is a trap. Leaders love it because the illusion of certainty it offers feels safe, but working from single point prediction is just about the most dangerous thing you can do. The true value of futures thinking isn't about getting the specific forecast right; it is about acknowledging the often scary realization that the future is not already out there waiting to happen—it something we invent, and our agency matters. **Without a clearly articulated 'preferable future,' a strategic intent, organizations are just drifting**—letting technology and market forces dictate their destiny."

4. Experimentation as Risk Reduction:

A major barrier to systemic innovation is the fear of uncertainty. How can change agents convince risk-averse executives to embrace this experimental mindset?

Jeanne Liedtka: "Large organizations are not designed to deal well with uncertainty. They are designed for predictability and control. In an environment that offers far less of both of these than leaders would like to admit, we have to help leaders reframe what 'risk' actually means. The biggest risk today is ignoring the reality around us or doing nothing or doing the wrong thing efficiently. We need to demonstrate that small, low-fidelity **experiments are not risky; they are risk reduction strategies**. They allow us to learn fast and cheaply before making massive commitments."

5. Measuring Systemic Health:

In a data-obsessed world, traditional return on investment (ROI) often fails to capture systemic value. What is the most effective metric for tracking the success of complex, regenerative initiatives?

Jeanne Liedtka: "We are obsessed with what we can easily count, but the things that matter most—resilience, trust, ecological health—are hard to count. We have to get better at combining 'hard data' with 'thick data,' the stories that give the numbers meaning. Instead of just quarterly output, **we should measure the learning velocity and the adaptability of the system**. That is the true indicator of whether you are building a resilient future."

> The era of incremental design is over. Design Thinking for Humanity is not a suggestion; it is the necessary framework for this century's greatest challenge: creating resilience and prosperity that is shared by all—humanity and the planet.

Jeanne Liedtka: "As you embark on the strategic transformation detailed in these pages, **I encourage you to approach the systemic complexity with profound humility, unwavering curiosity, and a relentless bias toward action**. May this book from Michael provide you with the wisdom, the tools, and the collective courage required to architect the thriving future we know is possible. Go forth and design the greater good."

Lead with Vision:

Inspire, Empower, Transform.

- Champion Design Thinking for Humanity across all levels.
- Foster a culture of courage, empathy, and long-term vision.
- Prioritize both people and the planet.

Design Sustainable Offerings:

Reimagine, Reduce, Restore.

- Expand empathy beyond the user to include non-human stakeholders.
- Create solutions that optimize for the well-being of the entire web of life.
- Make sustainable the new standard, accessible and desirable for all.

Build Thriving Ecosystems:

Connect, Collaborate, Create.

- Forge multi-stakeholder partnerships for shared value creation.
- Design regenerative systems that prioritize circularity and resource efficiency.
- Orchestrate networks where value flows fairly to all participants.

THE DESIGN THINKING FOR HUMANITY MINDSET

WWW.DESIGN-HUMANITY.COM

Empower Individuals:

Engage, Educate, Enable.

- Inspire sustainable lifestyles and informed consumer choices.
- Foster a sense of shared responsibility and empower individuals to drive change.
- Facilitate proactively collective actions of empowered individuals.

NEW MINDSET.
NEW PARADIGM.
BETTER SOLUTIONS.

Future-Proof Your Business:

Adapt, Innovate, Thrive.

- Integrate circular and regenerative practices into business models.
- Leverage exponential technologies to solve wicked problems at scale.
- Prioritize long-term value creation over short-term optimization.
- Embed ethical guardrails to ensure technology serves humanity and the planet.

Drive Regenerative Impact:

Restore, Replenish, Revitalize.

- Move beyond do no harm to create verifiable, net-positive impact for the planet.
- Actively restore social and ecological systems through circular and biomimetic design.
- Focus on healing the biosphere, not just minimizing the footprint.

How to get the most out of the book

The following elements make it easier to find your way in the book:

The frameworks presented in this book are designed as flexible guides rather than rigid blueprints, empowering you to tailor strategies to their unique contexts for the creation of enduring resilience and a thriving future.

Various known and new tools and procedural models will be presented. You will find an overview of all the tools, methods, and frameworks on the first page. Remember that this map is not the territory; use these tools, but do not mistake the process for the outcome.

At the end of each logical section, the content is reflected upon and summarized.

Selected templates are available for download as PDF templates. Premium templates, with a detailed description for the application shown on the template, are available in the online store: **www.dt-toolbook.com/shop**

Follow the Journey: To bridge the gap between theory and practice, this book follows a single, continuous design challenge—**The Living Soil Mandate**—from vision to scale.

The **speculative case study** moves from a high-level futuristic vision of regenerative agriculture to a tangible, user-centric solution for a farmer named Javier. As the challenge progresses, the narrative explores how to scale this solution using artificial intelligence while strictly ensuring that the outcome actively heals and regenerates the ecosystem. This ongoing narrative serves as a practical anchor, demonstrating how abstract concepts translate into on-the-ground innovation.

The case study is **structured into five distinct segments**, strategically positioned between the introduction of each lens and its corresponding toolbox. The primary objective is not to present a flawless, finalized solution, but to illustrate the practical application of a selection of tools for each specific lens. The iterative development of Javier's challenge demonstrates how to wield the tools of **futures, design, ecological, systems, and exponential thinking** to drive systemic impact. This approach necessitates looking beyond the tools themselves to understand the rigorous process of their integration.

The case study initiates on page 63 and continues through the subsequent lenses on pages 69–75, 137–140, 198–203, 237–241 and 277–279, culminating with all results documented in the Resilience Blueprint on pages 280–281.

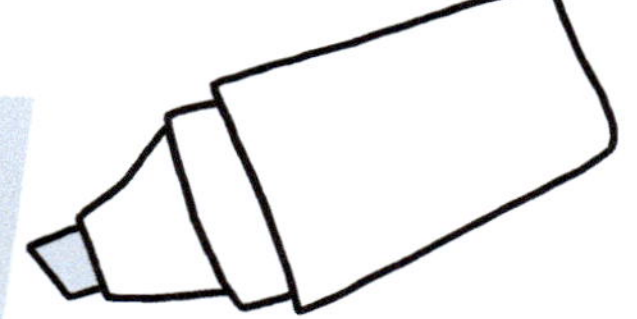

Contents

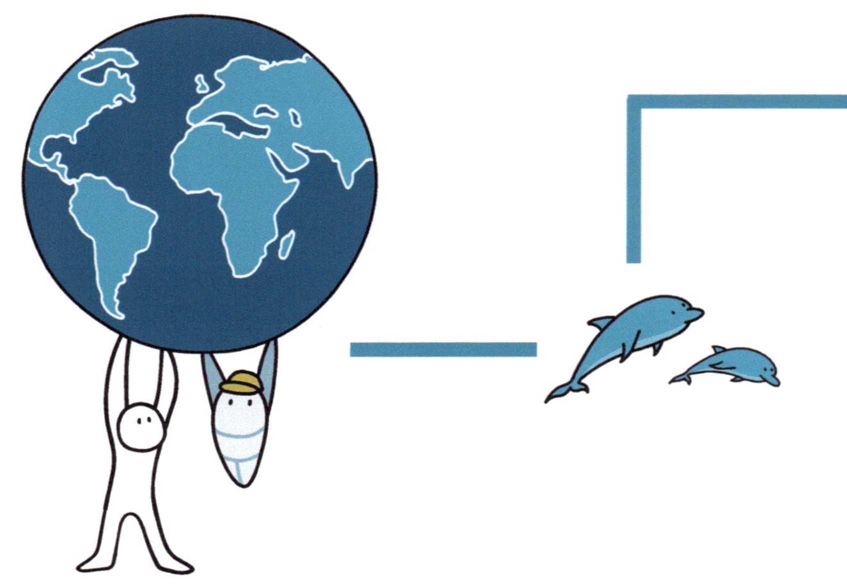

Futures Thinking — 54

Design Thinking — 120

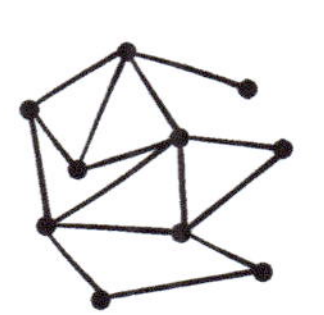

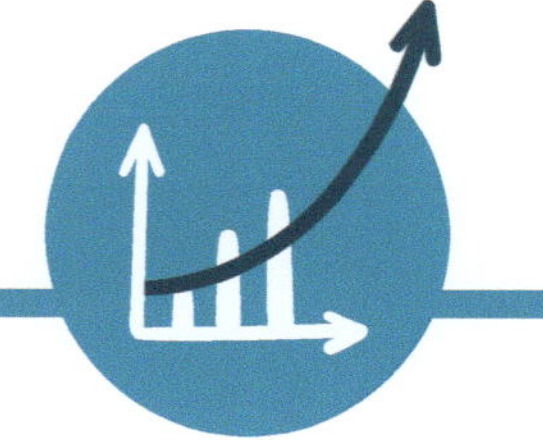

Motivation for This book

Michael Lewrick, PhD | MBA, defines the cutting edge of business ecosystem design and exponential innovation. For more than two decades, he has helped multinational organizations and high-growth startups solve their most complex challenges. As the founder of **Lewrick & Company**, Michael acts as a strategic catalyst. He equips leaders with the mindsets required to lead transformation in an era of accelerating change. He is an award-winning thought leader and the lead author of the global bestselling publications on design thinking and exponential change. His latest work expands this toolkit. It provides the essential frameworks for aligning technological power with ecological health to secure long-term business viability.

Accelerate your impact. Reach out via LinkedIn or lewrick.ch to engage Michael for executive advisory, expert panels, and keynotes.

> *Design Thinking for Humanity is a moral imperative. We must intentionally **shape a future** where innovation **serves all life**. It cannot serve only the privileged few or the bottom line.*

Traditional design **optimizes for the individual**. Design Thinking for Humanity **elevates our gaze**. It fosters solutions that tackle **systemic challenges**. It builds **resilience for generations**.

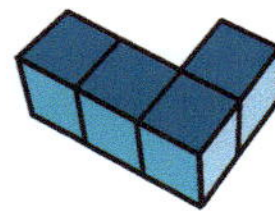

Linear thinking cannot solve **wicked problems**. We need the empathetic lens and iterative tools of design thinking. These tools allow us to **navigate complexity**. We must co-create solutions that are **viable, desirable, and sustainable**.

Technology offers immense potential. But it **requires direction**. Design Thinking for Humanity ensures innovation **remains human-centered**. It is the framework for **harnessing exponential power responsibly**.

We must move **beyond incremental improvement**. This mindset empowers us to envision a new future. Creativity is not just about profit. It is about **architecting a world** where **all beings thrive**.

I have carried a deep inner belief for years. I knew this book needed to be written. The timing is finally right. We have reached a critical threshold where our technological power matches our systemic fragility. This specific moment demands a new and rigorous response.

We live in an age defined by paradox. Humanity possesses exponential technologies like AI, synthetic biology, and quantum computing. These tools offer unprecedented potential to solve climate change and eradicate poverty. They promise a new era of planetary abundance. Yet we simultaneously face accelerating existential risks. Ecological collapse and profound social inequality threaten the very foundations of our civilization.

The fundamental question defining our time is not what we can build, but why and how we choose to build it.

This gap between exponential potential and linear wisdom is the most significant design failure of our era. For decades, design thinking has been the engine of human-centric innovation. It prioritized the user/customer and solved problems with empathy. However, its success has exposed a primary limitation. Its empathy is often linear and isolated.

We have trained a generation of innovators to scale. We have failed to train them to pause and assess. Traditional design focuses on the immediate user and often overlooks long-term systemic consequences. These planetary impacts are amplified when a solution scales. The moment a solution scales exponentially, its impact often outgrows its original ethical container.

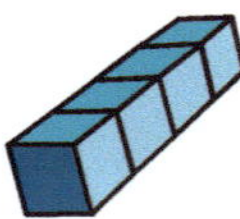

The challenge is not technological. It is methodological. We do not need better code. We need a better framework for deciding where and why that code is deployed. The strategic mandate for the next decade is clear. We must evolve design thinking from a practice of isolated optimization to a practice of systemic regeneration.

This conviction is the genesis of this book. Design Thinking for Humanity is not a philosophy. It is the essential upgrade. We live in a world defined by compounding complexity where relying solely on intuition is insufficient. We need a disciplined process. We need a framework capable of mediating the immense velocity of the exponential curve with deep wisdom. This holistic approach is required for long-term survival.

This methodology tackles complexity head-on. It translates the high conceptual load of systems, ecological, and futures thinking into a set of simple and usable tools. The goal is not to paralyze innovation teams. It is to provide a clear path forward. We integrate these lenses without sacrificing the core human-centered principles that make design thinking effective. The individual needs of customers are not ignored. They are expanded to encompass the health of their community, their environment, and future generations.

For decades, we designed for efficiency, and in doing so, we made our world fragile. Design Thinking for Humanity is the blueprint for the next era: shifting our focus from optimizing short-term profits to architecting long-term resilience.

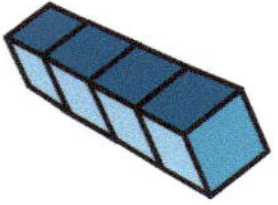

The core of this framework begins with a new mindset (see pages 11–12) to address the human root causes of our challenges. It rests on the integration of five distinct disciplines. These are **futures thinking, design thinking, ecological thinking, systems thinking, and the responsible application of exponential technologies**. These lenses provide essential guidance for viewing challenges through a comprehensive perspective.

This book provides the philosophy and the necessary inner shift. It outlines the disciplined process and practical tools required to move beyond incremental improvement to create 10x impact. I extend my sincere wish that everyone studying this book finds inspiration. I hope you drive the profound and transformative change necessary to architect a future of genuine and equitable abundance. This architectural shift marks the end of purely industrial extraction and the beginning of a new historical epoch: **The Age of Resilience**.

—Michael Lewrick

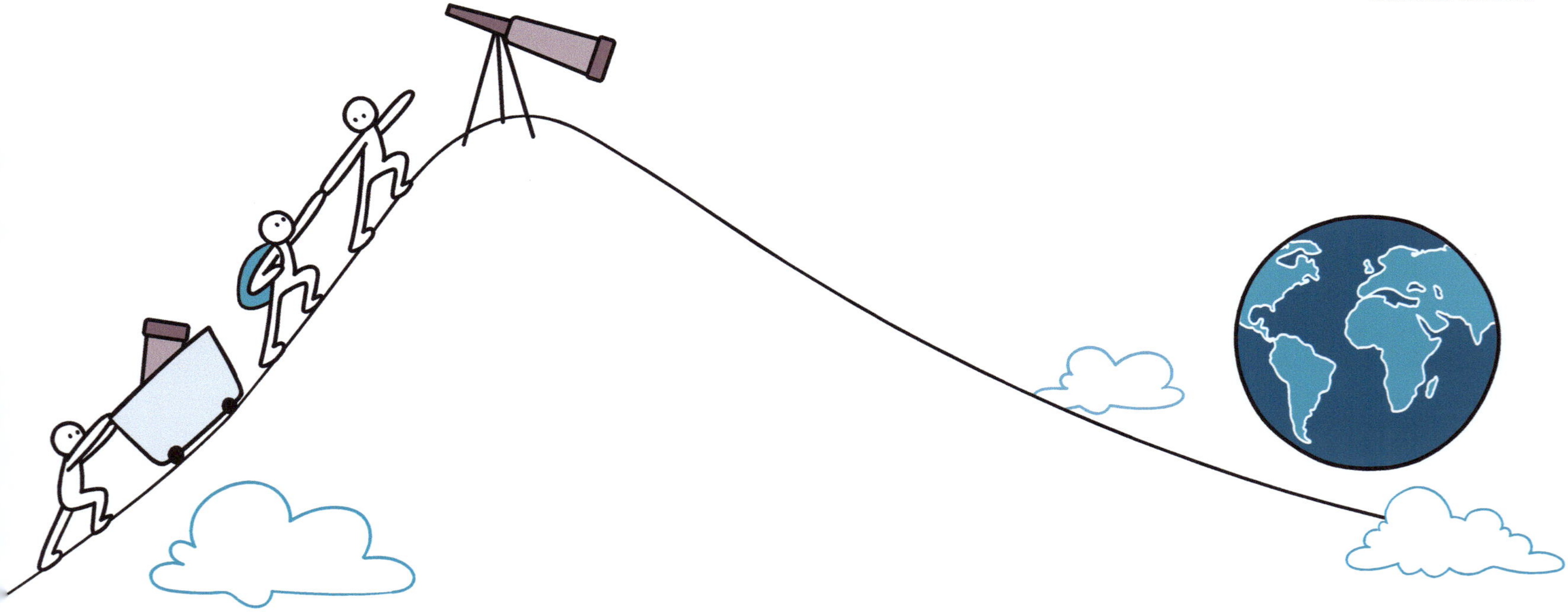

The Age of Resilience

18TH–19TH CENTURY	1870–1914	1980–2010	2010–2020	NOW
Steam engine	Oil, electricity, steel, combustion engine	Computers, Internet	Mobility, artificial intelligence, cloud, big data, digitalization, IoT, blockchain	Convergence of human ingenuity, ecological intelligence, and AI to restore planetary balance

TIME

Setting the Scene for a Global Movement

Collaboration is the cornerstone for a global movement. This may sound simplistic, but it is true. Only concerted effort by individuals working alongside businesses, educators, and politicians effects the necessary changes to restore planetary equilibrium. Simultaneously, we must cultivate a fundamentally different approach to human interaction.

We must evaluate individuals as unique entities, transcending the limits of categorization. This collaborative movement requires us to actively question the status quo, challenge ingrained assumptions, and seek innovative solutions that address root causes.

The Finite Planet

We operated for too long under the assumption that Earth's resources are infinite. A view from space reveals the truth: we have only this small, finite sphere and its limited resources.

We must accept that we are all in this together. We and everything around us form a complex, interconnected system. The root causes of current phenomena are multifaceted and interwoven.

Understanding these complex systems is the greatest challenge facing every human. It encompasses societal trends, economic power, beliefs, commerce, and politics. Some relationships are direct and obvious; the majority remain indirect, slow-acting, and often invisible.

Nearly everything we design, build, and implement is driven by profitability metrics. We often insufficiently consider the impact on people, the environment, and waste generation. This profit focus leads us to neglect the well-being of many, externalizing costs onto society and the planet.

We optimize for short-term gains at the expense of long-term sustainability and the equitable distribution of benefits and burdens. This requires understanding interconnected factors and anticipating unintended consequences. We must design solutions that address immediate needs and contribute to the long-term health of our planet and its inhabitants.

This is a shift: optimize for the flourishing of the entire system, not for isolated metrics.

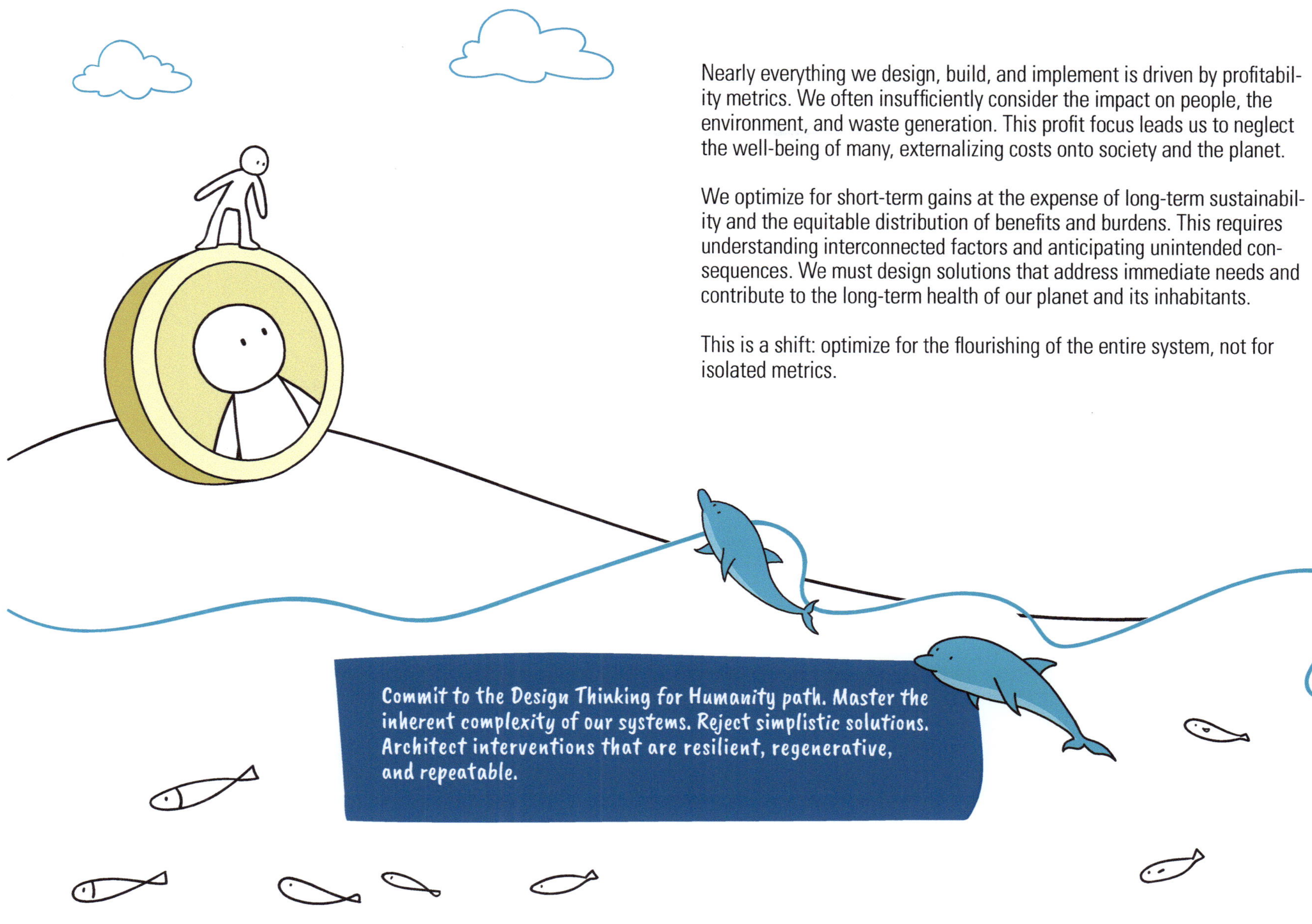

A global movement demands convergence, not just a single method. To build resilience, we cannot rely on empathy alone. We must fuse design thinking's human-centric focus with futures thinking's long-term vision and ecological thinking's planetary boundaries. Siloed approaches crumble under the weight of modern complexity. Only a unified framework provides the clarity needed to navigate our exponential future.

The Fifth Industrial Revolution as a Catalyst: This convergence is powered by a new era of human-machine collaboration. We are not just using technology for efficiency; we are using exponential thinking to accelerate regeneration.

AI as Partner: From AI-driven drug discovery to optimizing bio-fuels, intelligent agents allow us to model complex ecosystems and solve problems at a speed and scale previously impossible.

Systemic Synergy: By integrating systems thinking, we ensure these powerful technologies do not operate in silos. We design robust ecosystems where data, resources, and value flow seamlessly between stakeholders, AI, and the environment.

The Result: We move away from generic solutions to localized, community-driven initiatives that are globally connected and technologically empowered.

A brief definition of all five lenses can be found in the Key Concepts section on page 39. While each lens can be applied as a standalone approach, the effort to combine them creates the systemic impact required to navigate modern complexity and achieve global regeneration.

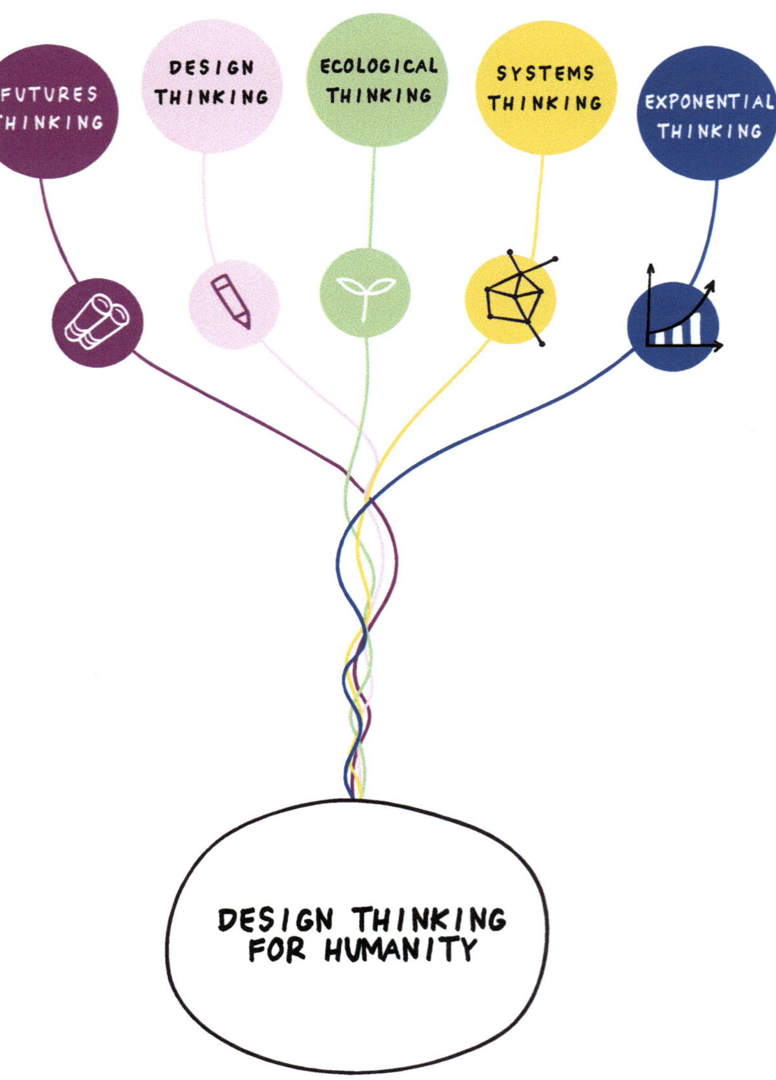

Bridging the Gap

Creating a sustainable future requires breaking down silos. We must embrace interdisciplinary collaboration and work together across sectors, AI systems, and nations. This is the only way to address our complex challenges. We must actively build the transition.

A deep chasm separates us from the regenerative future we desire. We cannot simply leap across; we must construct a bridge strong enough to carry all of humanity. Concerted action unlocks the potential of technology, creating a world where both humanity and the planet thrive.

The Design Thinking for Humanity mindset integrates futures, design, ecological, and systems thinking with responsible exponential technologies to address complex global challenges and build resilience.

Acknowledge that our planet's finite resources and understand that all elements on Earth form a complex, interconnected system, demanding a holistic view of societal, economic, and environmental factors.

Innovation teams should shift from a sole focus on profitability to valuing impact on people, the environment, and waste, optimizing for the long-term health and well-being of the entire system, not just short-term gains.

A global movement requires concerted collaboration among individuals, businesses, educators, and politicians to restore planetary equilibrium and foster improved human interaction.

DESIGN THINKING ESSENTIALS

The Cognitive Shift

Design thinking is not merely a toolbox. It is a **fundamental cognitive shift**. This section serves as a foundation for newcomers and a strategic recalibration for practitioners. We must move beyond the misconception that this is just a workshop method. It is a rigorous discipline. It requires a deep exploration of the problem space before any solution is attempted. This **mindset** does not just generate ideas. It sparks the **radical innovations** necessary to navigate our current era of exponential change. We place human needs and values at the core.

However, we now view these needs through a wider lens. We *Accept Complexity* in all our challenges. We champion *Radical Collaboration* across disciplines to break down silos. We rely on a *Culture of Prototyping* and a strong *Bias Toward Action*. We do not debate in boardrooms. We *Show, Don't Tell*. We confront wicked problems with empathy and curiosity. We remain *Mindful of the Process*. This disciplined flexibility allows us to navigate uncertainty and architect solutions that are not just desirable, but sustainable and resilient.

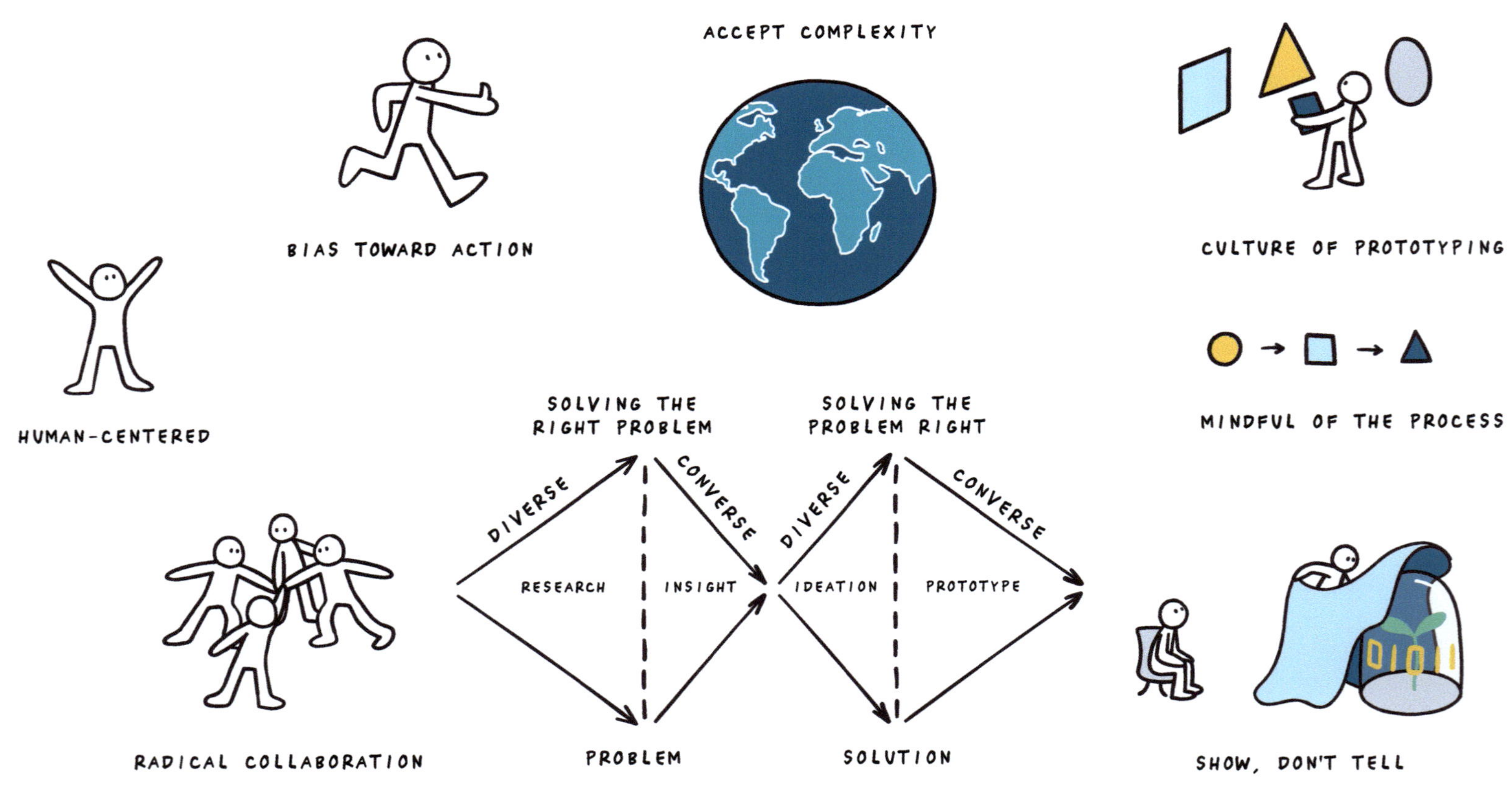

Teams engaged in design thinking operate within a structured yet flexible process designed to guide their activities from ambiguity to clarity. This process is often viewed at two levels. At the macro level, it is represented by frameworks like the Double Diamond (illustrated on the left). The first phase of this framework explores the **problem space** to ensure the team is tackling the right challenge, while the second phase explores the **solution space** to ensure the team is creating the right solution. At the micro level, this journey is navigated through five to six iterative steps (illustrated on the right), which commonly include understanding the user context, observing behaviors, defining a clear point of view, generating ideas, creating tangible prototypes, and rigorously testing them with customers/users.

The fuel for this process is a dedicated, **interdisciplinary team**, as true innovation rarely happens in a silo. Bringing together diverse perspectives, such as those from engineering, business, social science, and design, is essential for understanding the multifaceted nature of complex problems and for generating a richer spectrum of potential solutions. This collaboration thrives in an environment that allows for **free thinking, learning, and creativity**, where psychological safety empowers team members to challenge assumptions and share nascent ideas without fear of failure.

Design thinking is an engine of continuous learning powered by rapid iterations. Teams apply the appropriate tools for the situation, moving through the micro-steps not in a rigid, linear fashion, but in a fluid cycle of "thinking" and "doing." They create low-fidelity prototypes to make ideas tangible, test them to gather feedback, and use those learnings to refine their point of view and generate better ideas. This iterative loop of prototyping and testing is repeated relentlessly. **The goal is to progressively de-risk the innovation process and converge upon a powerful problem-solution fit**, where the final solution deeply and elegantly resonates with the real-world needs of the people it is designed to serve.

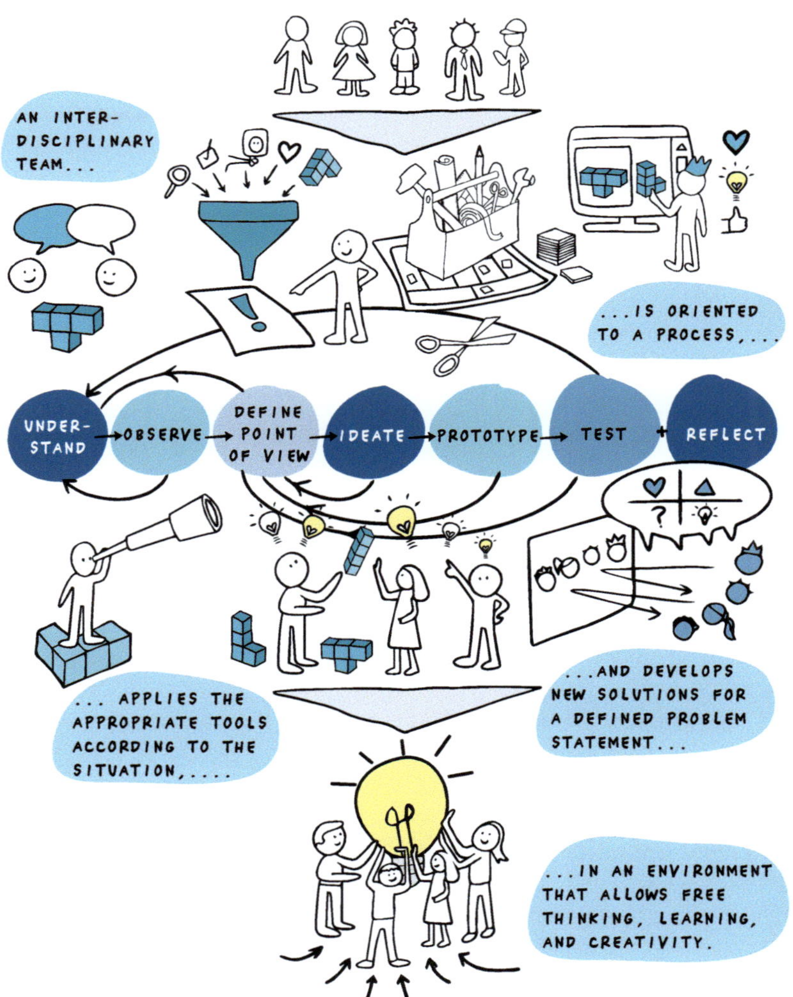

The Critical Decision Point

Design thinking excels at navigating the unknown through deep observation. Teams explore problem spaces, synthesize insights, and refine "How Might We" questions to uncover needs. This focus is often too narrow. It optimizes for a single user within a relatively stable system. This approach fails when facing the complex, interconnected "wicked problems" of our time.

A purely human-centered approach is insufficient. To design responsibly for the 21st century, we must evolve our practice. We must expand empathy from the user to the entire system and consider our creations' long-term consequences. Shift from solving contained problems to fostering resilient, adaptable ecosystems. Transform our perspective from human-centered to Design Thinking for Humanity.

Two Trajectories: Every team eventually faces the critical decision point illustrated on page 33. When we confront a complex challenge, we must choose between two distinct trajectories:

- **The Traditional Path (Lower Curve):** Focus strictly on human-centric product-market fit. It often ignores the wider system.

- **The Design Thinking for Humanity Path (Upper Curve):** Reframe the situation to be human and planet-centric. Leverage futures, exponential, and systems thinking to optimize for Systemic Resilience.

The New Definition of Success

Taking the upper path redefines success. We no longer settle for simple market acceptance. We optimize for systemic resilience. We create solutions that allow both society and the planet to thrive long-term. This is the new standard.

DESIGN THINKING

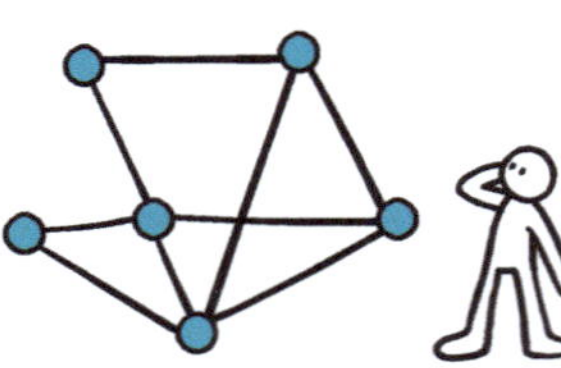

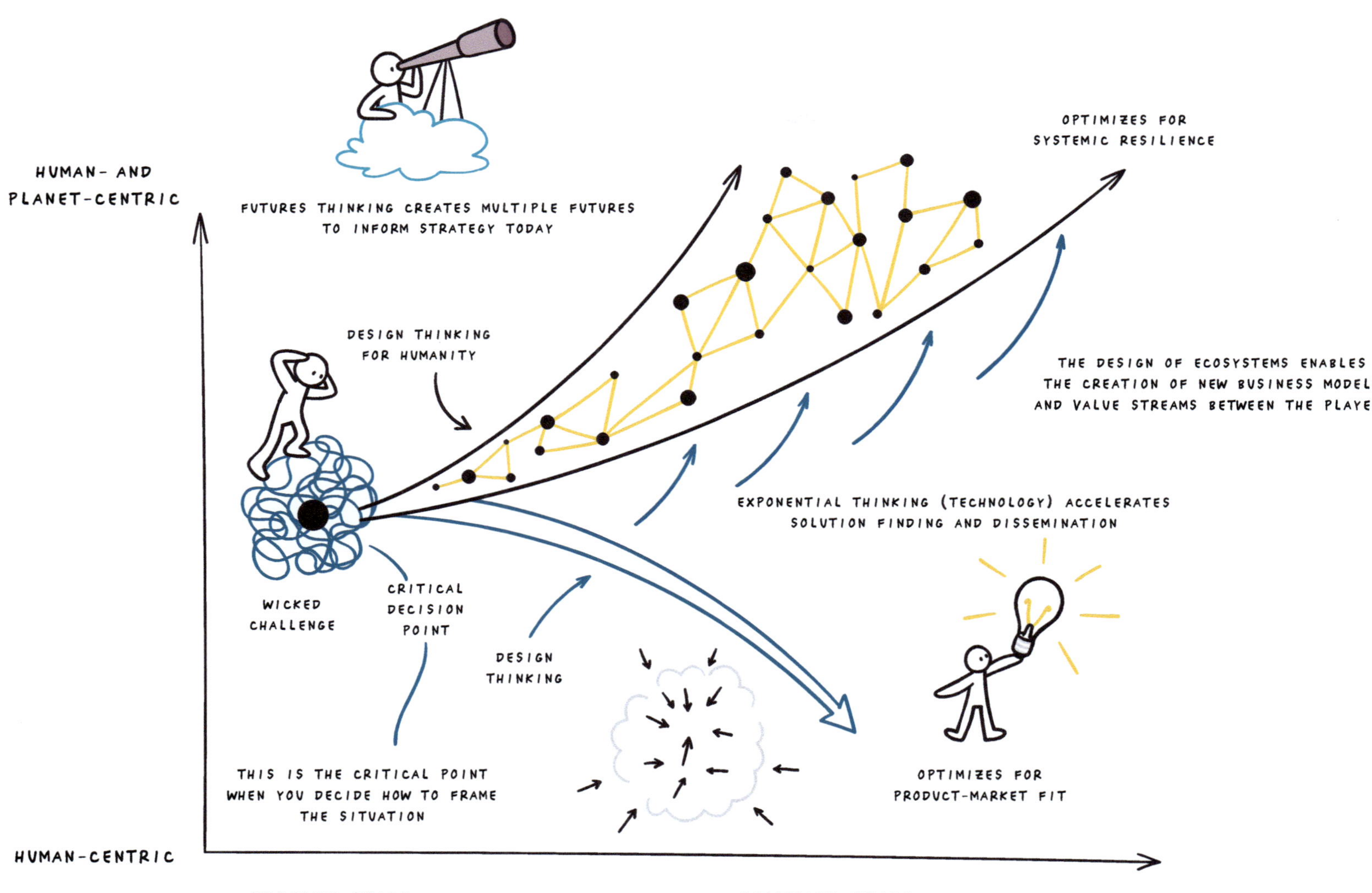

HUMAN- AND PLANET-CENTRIC
HUMAN-CENTRIC
FUTURES THINKING CREATES MULTIPLE FUTURES TO INFORM STRATEGY TODAY
OPTIMIZES FOR SYSTEMIC RESILIENCE
DESIGN THINKING FOR HUMANITY
THE DESIGN OF ECOSYSTEMS ENABLES THE CREATION OF NEW BUSINESS MODELS AND VALUE STREAMS BETWEEN THE PLAYERS
EXPONENTIAL THINKING (TECHNOLOGY) ACCELERATES SOLUTION FINDING AND DISSEMINATION
WICKED CHALLENGE
CRITICAL DECISION POINT
DESIGN THINKING
THIS IS THE CRITICAL POINT WHEN YOU DECIDE HOW TO FRAME THE SITUATION
OPTIMIZES FOR PRODUCT-MARKET FIT
PROBLEM SPACE
SOLUTION SPACE

Design thinking is a mindset focused on deeply understanding people's needs and values. It employs an iterative process of exploring problems, generating ideas, prototyping, and testing solutions.

Fuel the process with empathy and radical collaboration across diverse teams. The goal is to create desirable, feasible, and viable solutions to complex challenges.

Champion "learning by doing" and relentless adaptation based on direct feedback. Apply this approach universally—from crafting innovative products, services, and experiences to shaping ecosystems and robust business models.

Embrace the evolved paradigm. By integrating systems, futures, and exponential thinking, design thinking transforms from a product creation method into a framework for shaping a resilient and equitable world.

THE FRAMEWORK

WHY? HOW? WHAT?

Why Design Thinking for Humanity?

Our world is currently out of balance. We face a convergence of ecological, social, and technological crises that linear problem-solving can no longer address. To survive and thrive, we must fundamentally shift our approach. We must stop extracting short-term value and start generating long-term resilience.

Our core motivation is simple yet profound. We seek to empathize with and enhance the quality of life for all living things, both today and for generations to come. This requires resilience. We must cultivate the capacity to adapt, persevere, and innovate in the face of constant adversity.

> "We, the people of the earth, must build and enhance the resilience of human society so that as the environment and climate change, humans will continue to exist."
>
> —Don Norman, author of *Design for a Better World*

The Shared Responsibility

To achieve this resilience, we must bring our Earth back into balance. This mission extends beyond human needs to encompass all living systems that contribute to our well-being. It leverages every available lever, from behavioral change to exponential technology, and demands the shared responsibility of makers, leaders, and citizens alike.

This requires us to evolve from human-centered design to Design Thinking for Humanity. While the original mindset solved user/customer problems and achieved market fit, this new paradigm serves a higher purpose. It expands our empathy to include the health of the ecosystems upon which we all depend.

Design must serve humanity as a whole. We prioritize solutions that benefit both people and the planet to ensure a thriving future for all. We actively consider long-term consequences and refuse to optimize for individual convenience at the expense of collective survival.

The Shift from Spotlight to Floodlight

Standard human-centered design places the user/customer in a spotlight; the environment remains in the dark. This narrow focus optimizes for the individual and ignores the broader system. This creates a disconnected reality where products exist in a vacuum. We must break this silo.

Design Thinking for Humanity transforms the ecosystem from a passive backdrop into a critical stakeholder. We solve for systemic health rather than simple user friction. Our definition of the customer/user expands beyond the person paying or clicking. We serve the complex web of relationships between people, nature, and technology.

To succeed in this new paradigm, we **master three critical shifts:**

- **Deepen the Human-Planet Relationship.** Stop viewing nature merely as a resource to extract. Develop a holistic understanding of our impact. We recognize that human well-being is inseparable from planetary health.
- **Strengthen Your Futures Imagination.** Move beyond prediction. Conceptualize and chart bold pathways to realize unprecedented possibilities for a resilient future.
- **Integrate Ecological Thinking.** Make ecological integrity a core constraint of the innovation process. Ensure solutions are Planet-Centric and regenerative by design.

What Is Design Thinking for Humanity?

Design Thinking for Humanity is not just a mindset. It is a disciplined operating system for the 21st century. It requires us to open our eyes to interconnected challenges. We must understand every angle to weave solutions that resonate with life itself. We do not settle for incremental improvements. We reimagine what is possible. We utilize the **Design Thinking for Humanity Wheel (see page 8)**. These five lenses are chosen carefully. Together they form the comprehensive framework required to tackle the intricate challenges of our world.

Used individually, each lens is valuable. Used together, they are transformative. **This synergistic integration unlocks the potential to move beyond isolated solutions**. It allows us to recognize the profound interconnectedness of human, social, technological, and ecological systems. We cannot rely on code alone to leverage AI responsibly. We must integrate Systems Thinking to understand societal impact. We must apply Ecological Thinking to ensure regenerative outcomes. We design proactive and positive change. **We do not simply fix the problems created by the industrial past**.

[Design Thinking for Humanity is a holistic mindset that integrates human empathy, ecological integrity, and systemic awareness. It empowers innovators to leverage exponential technologies not just for growth but to build resilient solutions that regenerate the planet and secure a thriving future for all.]

Key Concepts:

Futures Thinking: Anticipating and exploring multiple plausible futures to inform present-day decisions and design. This involves identifying trends, envisioning alternative scenarios, and proactively shaping desired outcomes to build long-term resilience and adaptability.

Design Thinking: Empathizing with people to deeply understand their needs, challenges, and desires. This forms the foundation for generating creative solutions that are human-centered and deliver real value.

Ecological Thinking: Recognizing the interdependence of humans and nature, and designing solutions that promote harmony and balance between social and ecological systems. This approach seeks to minimize negative impacts and create regenerative outcomes.

Systems Thinking: Analyzing complex problems within their broader context to identify underlying causes and leverage interconnected relationships. By taking a long-term perspective, systems thinking enables the design of solutions that address root causes and create lasting change.

Exponential Thinking: Adopting a nonlinear mindset to leverage accelerating technologies for rapid, global scale restorative impact. This approach seeks audacious breakthroughs and 10X improvements while maintaining alignment with deep ethical intent and collective human values.

Beyond Robustness and Resilience

We often mistake resilience for simple robustness. Robustness is merely the ability to resist change and maintain the status quo. In a world of accelerating disruption and interconnected crises, however, rigid systems eventually break. **We need a fundamental shift in how we design our organizations and ecosystems**. We must move from trying to control uncertainty to building the capacity to navigate it effectively.

Resilience is commonly defined as the ability to "bounce back" after a shock. While valuable, this is merely a baseline requirement. If a system was already vulnerable, returning to that previous state is not a success. True resilience requires more than recovery. It demands the capacity to adapt, evolve, and transform in response to deep challenges.

Our ambition reaches higher: we aim for an exponentializing state (see illustration on page 41). This is where a system does not just survive a shock but grows stronger because of it. An exponentializing system uses volatility as fuel for innovation, leveraging disruption to accelerate learning and turn potential disasters into catalysts for systemic improvement.

This state represents the ultimate win-win-win scenario. It ensures humanity, the economy, and the planet thrive together, even in turbulent times. We must intentionally weave five specific attributes into the DNA of every solution we create. The five attributes of an exponentializing system are our design criteria for an evolutionary future.

Five Attributes of an Exponentializing System

1. Embrace Radical Diversity
Diversity is the ultimate source of adaptive capacity. We must cultivate biodiversity in ecosystems and cognitive diversity in teams. This provides the rich palette of options needed to solve unforeseen problems.

2. Build Intelligent Redundancy
Efficiency is brittle; redundancy is insurance. We must move beyond hyper-optimization to create robust networks with multiple pathways for critical resources like food, energy, and data.

3. Nurture Mindful Connectivity
We must act as weavers. Design for the healthy flow of information and resources, but create "firewalls" to prevent the rapid spread of shocks or misinformation. The system must be connected, but not dangerously over-coupled.

4. Design for Equity
Inequality is a systemic risk. A system that benefits only a few is inherently unstable. We must design solutions that are accessible and just, building the deep social trust required for collective action during crises.

5. Embed Adaptive Learning
Static systems fail. We must design feedback loops that allow the system to sense change, learn from failure, and transform itself in real time.

From Recovery to Evolution

We must aim higher than simple recovery. While a resilient system bounces back to its original state, an **exponentializing** system bounces forward. It treats challenges, volatility, and uncertainty not as threats but as fuel for accelerated learning and innovation.

This state represents the peak of systemic health. As illustrated here, this approach transforms disruption into opportunity. Like a muscle that grows stronger with resistance, an exponentializing system thrives on stress. **This state represents the ultimate win-win-win**, where the organization, society, and the planet do not just survive the shock. They evolve and prosper because of it.

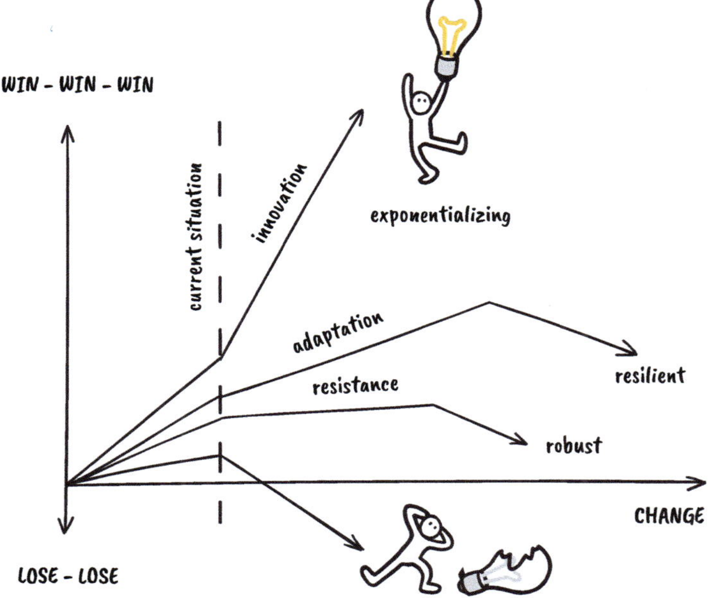

We are not just aiming to survive; we are pushing for a win-win-win future. That is how we truly become resilient and grow stronger with every challenge.

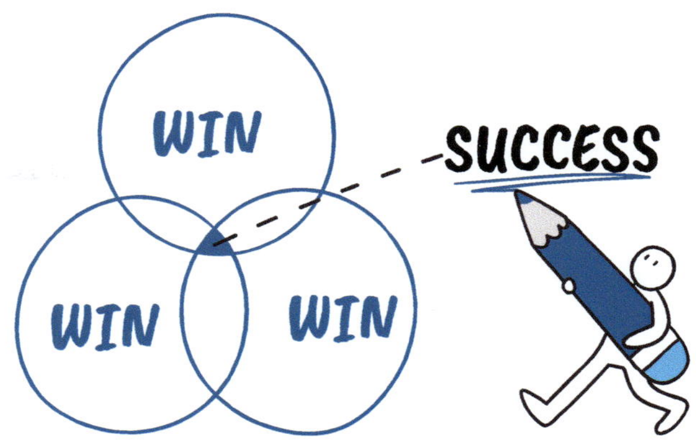

Understanding System Responses

Decay (Lose-Lose)
=> The System Collapses.
It cannot withstand the shock and deteriorates, leading to negative outcomes for all stakeholders. This is the default path of fragile, extractive systems.

Robust (Win-Lose/Status Quo)
=> The System Resists.
It absorbs the shock without breaking but remains static. It prioritizes stability over evolution, often protecting the status quo at the expense of necessary change.

Resilient (Win-Neutral/Bounce Back)
=> The System Recovers.
It withstands the shock and returns to its original state. While valuable, it essentially restores the previous vulnerability, preparing only to survive the same shock again.

Exponentializing (Win-Win-Win/Bounce Forward)
=> The System Evolves.
It thrives on the shock, using the disruption as a catalyst to accelerate innovation and regenerate capacity. It emerges from the crisis stronger, more equitable, and more vibrant than before.

How to Apply It to Create Impact

Creating meaningful impact with Design Thinking for Humanity requires a **transdisciplinary approach**. While the framework encompasses the necessary disciplines, a critical gap exists in education and capabilities. Teams tackling these complex challenges require a working understanding of diverse fields, ranging from politics and ethics to behavioral science and exponential technologies. No single discipline can address these multifaceted tasks alone; **a true fusion of expertise is essential**. To succeed, these diverse teams must first establish a common language. We must translate specific jargon into shared meaning to prevent misalignment.

Transformative breakthroughs emerge when diverse viewpoints intersect with collective reasoning. This approach goes beyond simply combining existing knowledge. It leverages the **complementary strengths of human imagination and AI's generative capabilities**. Exploring the tensions between human intuition and machine recall creates the cognitive conditions necessary for novel, high-impact solutions to emerge.

Orchestrating Transdisciplinary Impact

Increased collaboration between intelligent technologies and leaders from all sectors is vital. Design Thinking for Humanity belongs in the learning agenda of all students. These are the future leaders across every discipline. Simultaneously, the incentives driving decision-makers require critical examination. The prevailing paradigm often prioritizes short-term gains. We must shift the focus to long-term actions that yield sustainable benefits. This is crucial even if the visible impact takes years to materialize.

To work in a truly transdisciplinary way, the classic design thinking process must evolve. The well-known "double diamond" is extended with a crucial preliminary phase guided by futures thinking. This initial "future space" allows organizations to explore scenarios and define a clear vision before framing a specific problem.

Fixing this planet is not just the right thing to do, it is the only thing to do. Re-creating it is a pipe dream; preserving it is our imperative—a core principle of Design Thinking for Humanity.

Synchronizing Strategic Horizons

The five disciplines do not operate in isolation. They form a deeply interconnected system that creates a dynamic model for innovation. We must move beyond using single tools to navigating a continuous cycle of strategic thinking that guides our work from the immediate to the visionary. Escaping the gravity of the present is our most urgent challenge. We cannot build a regenerative future by optimizing for the next quarter. **We must anchor our work in a horizon of 10 or 20 years to identify root causes.** This long view empowers us to define a preferable future that respects planetary boundaries. Only by looking far ahead can we ensure that our solutions today do not become the problems of tomorrow.

Bridging the Present and the Preferable

We intersect four key lenses: design, systems, exponential, and futures thinking, to bridge the gap between the probable future we expect and the preferable future we must create. This synchronizes immediate actions (1–5 years) with mid-term scaling (10 years) and long-term vision (20+ years). We do not just solve today's problems; we reverse-engineer our strategy from the future. **The futures thinking chapter (pages 54–119)** provides the essential tools and methodologies to navigate and align work across all these horizons.

Notice the outer circle. Ecological thinking acts as the non-negotiable context. It is not merely a separate lens but the foundation through which all others must be viewed. This defines the planetary boundaries within which every solution, regardless of its time horizon, must operate. We **must embed ecological thinking deep into the algorithms we develop and spread**. This ensures that the immense scale of technology is directed exclusively toward regenerative outcomes.

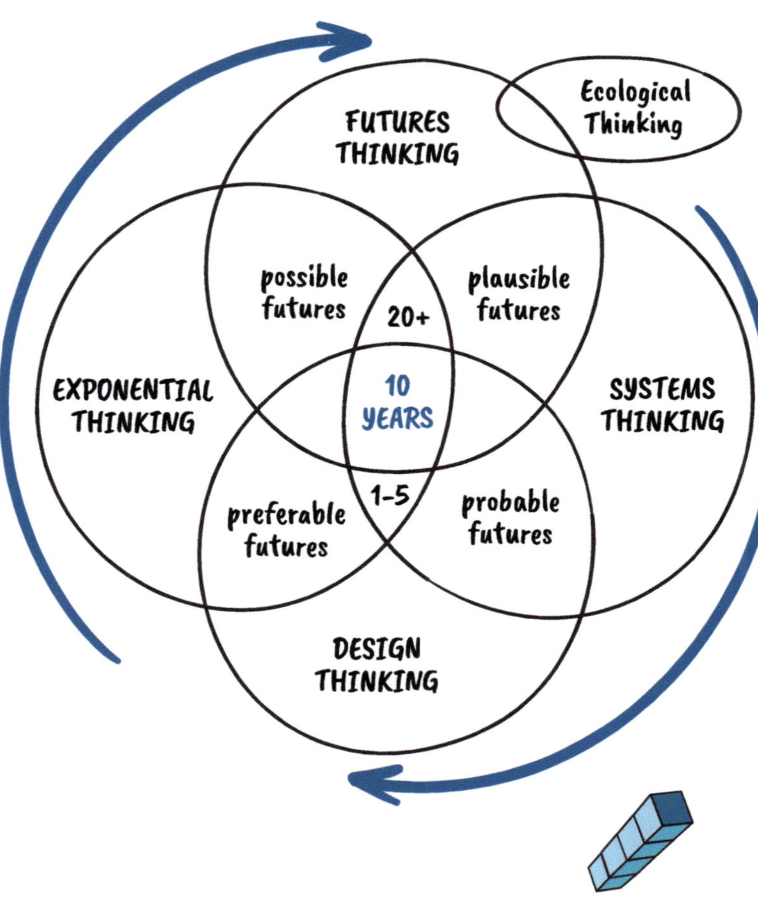

Designing Narratives for Systemic Change

Merely slapping "green" or "responsible" labels on a product is no longer enough. We must apply design principles to the narrative itself, treating the story as a prototype to be tested and refined. Iterate until the message connects deeply with human values and showcases benefits that extend far beyond a simple marketing slogan. By articulating threats and benefits clearly, we transform passive observers into active participants.

To mobilize this participation, we must **bridge the gap between complex science and daily life**. Rigorous data often alienates non-specialists, so we must translate metrics into compelling visualizations that illustrate real-world implications. Focus on the human element. Show exactly how changes directly affect lives, communities, and the planet we inhabit.

However, a new narrative requires a new definition of success. Models grounded solely in pure economics fail to capture reality. **We must transform our measurement systems to encompass a broad spectrum of criteria beyond profit (see Regenerative Ecological Metrics, page 192)**. Quantify progress in health, environmental sustainability, fairness, and societal well-being. If we do not measure these values, we cannot design for them.

The danger of poor translation is best illustrated by the **1.5°C trap**. To a scientist, this number represents a catastrophic tipping point. To the general public, it often sounds like a slightly warmer afternoon. This is the failure of data without narrative. Stop communicating in abstract degrees. Start communicating in tangible consequences like flooded cities, dried-up farms, and the loss of the places we love.

WHAT DIFFERENCE DOES A WARMING OF 1.5°C MAKE ANYWAY?

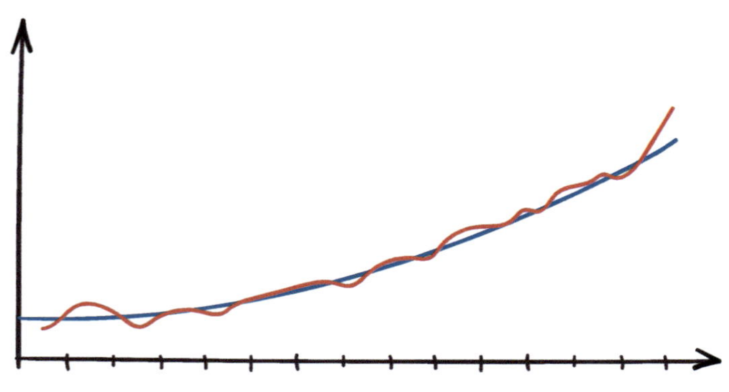

Global temperature increase since pre-industrial baseline

Leadership and Principles

Leadership today operates in a landscape defined by rapid disruption and deep global interdependence. To succeed, leaders must pivot away from rigid, legacy models and embrace a mindset of continuous adaptation. This new reality demands a fundamental **transition from static management to dynamic stewardship**, requiring a dual focus on immediate agility and long-term systemic resilience. There are many roles to consider, and the following are two examples.

Enterprise and Startups

Corporate leadership must shift from command-and-control structures to a **focus on adaptability and holistic resilience**. Instead of relying on simple prediction, these leaders prioritize early sensing and scenario planning to navigate ambiguity. By empowering decentralized, interdisciplinary teams, they foster an agile culture that balances short-term responsiveness with long-term stability, ensuring the organization thrives amidst complexity.

Government and Policy

In the public sector, leaders must embrace "futures thinking" to anticipate evolving social and economic contexts rather than merely reacting to them. This requires dismantling silos in favor of lean, horizontal collaboration across all levels of governance. By balancing immediate political imperatives with long-term planetary needs, **these leaders cultivate diverse, transparent partnerships** and invest in a future-ready workforce to drive sustainable, equitable policy.

However, equally important is the **resilient commonwealth**, which has to actively transition from being passive beneficiaries to engaged co-creators, sharing the responsibility for driving these systemic changes from the bottom up.

All tools presented in this book support the process from strategy to action for the different roles and associated challenges.

Summary of the
DESIGN THINKING FOR HUMANITY PRINCIPLES

To guide this systemic transformation, we adhere to a set of core tenets. These principles harmonize human innovation with ecological integrity and ethical responsibility.

Embrace Design's Profound Responsibility

Recognize design as a powerful force shaping our world. Wield it with unwavering ethical awareness. Question the purpose and potential impact of every project. The choice to participate carries the responsibility to be informed. We must "do no harm" to people or the planet.

Cultivate Awareness and Transparency

Champion open information and empower informed decision-making. Strive to create awareness among users, customers, and teams about the broader context and consequences of design choices. Foster a culture of transparency that enables responsible action.

Design for the Ecosystem

Look beyond the immediate product or service; understand its intricate place within a larger system. Proactively consider unintended consequences. Strive to design solutions that minimize negative impacts and contribute to the overall health and resilience of the interconnected human and natural world.

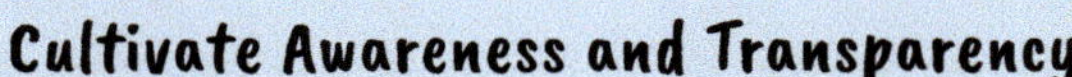

Strive for Elegant Reduction

Resist the urge to solve problems by adding layers of complexity. Instead, aim for elegant simplicity, recognizing that complex systems increase the risk of unintended outcomes. Discuss necessary complexity from unnecessary clutter, remembering that true simplicity serves, not oversimplifies, reality.

Center Humanity in a Planetary Context

Understand that designing for a better planet is inherently designing for the well-being of all living things. Foster diverse and inclusive teams, actively valuing different perspectives and remaining conscious of personal biases. Generate solutions that are equitable and truly serve human needs within ecological limits.

Embody Radical Optimism

Acknowledge the significant challenges ahead, but approach them with unwavering optimism and a belief in the power of human ingenuity. Embrace the discomfort of change; actively seek the multitude of possibilities for innovative solutions that benefit both our planet and society. Foster a mindset that sees opportunities where others see only obstacles.

Leverage Exponential Technologies for Scalable Impact

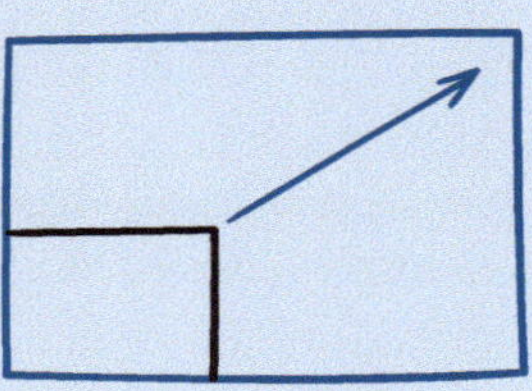

Recognize the transformative potential of exponential technologies, such as AI, biotechnology, and renewable energy, to amplify the impact of Design Thinking for Humanity. Actively explore and integrate these technologies to scale solutions efficiently and effectively, addressing global challenges with the speed and reach necessary for meaningful, lasting change.

The Resilience Blueprint Canvas

The canvas supports the documentation of all activities over the entire design cycle. It unifies purpose and future context; win-win-win value for humans, planet, and society; and systemic and scalable implementation into one strategic view. **The tool is described in detail on pages 296–297.**

Purpose & Future Context

MASSIVE TRANSFORMATIVE PURPOSE
What is the single, audacious, and inspiring purpose that drives this entire endeavor?

PREFERABLE FUTURE
What does the world look like in 20+ years if this project is a profound success?

SYSTEMIC CHALLENGE
What is the core "wicked problem" this initiative is designed to address?

COSTS
What are the financial, resource, and potential negative externality costs of implementing the solution?

Win-Win-Win

VALUE PROPOSITION(S)
HUMANS   PLANET   SOCIETY

Value for People:
How does this solution create tangible, meaningful value for the individuals and communities it serves? What deep human needs does it fulfill?

Value for the Planet:
How does this solution actively regenerate the ecosystems it touches? What is its net-positive ecological impact?

Value for Society:
How does this solution build social equity, community resilience, and collective well-being?

OBJECTIVES AND KEY METRICS
How will we measure our progress toward creating value for people, the planet, and society?

Systemic & Scalable Implementation

KEY INTERVENTIONS AND SOLUTIONS
What are the core products, services, policies, or platforms that will deliver the "win-win-win" value?

ECOSYSTEM OF PARTNERS
Who are the critical actors in our collaborative ecosystem required to make this solution a reality?

RESPONSIBLE PATH TO SCALE
How will this solution leverage exponential trends to create impact at a scale that matches the size of the problem, and what are the key ethical guardrails that will ensure this is done responsibly?

BENEFITS
What are the quantifiable benefits for all stakeholders involved?

DOWNLOAD TOOL
www.design-humanity.com/en/resilience-blueprint

Design Thinking for Humanity is a transformative mindset that aims to create "win-win-win" situations where society, the environment, and the economy can thrive together, rather than at each other's expense.

The tools and methods address behavioral change by creating new narratives and using profound storytelling to make a preferable future feel real and achievable.

New leadership models are required in both the public and private sectors to champion this long-term, holistic, and collaborative approach to innovation.

Design Thinking for Humanity is a call to action, empowering us with the principles and frameworks to move beyond just solving problems to proactively designing a more resilient and sustainable world for all.

IMPACT CHECKLIST

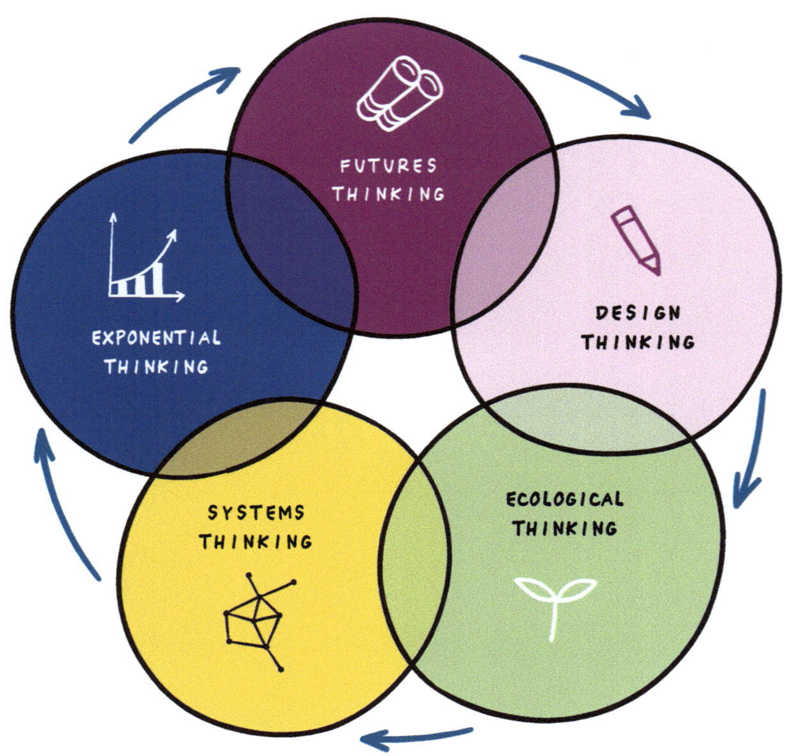

This checklist is designed to guide practitioners in developing solutions that are not only human-centered but also future-proof, ecologically sound, systemically informed, and capable of generating exponential impact.

Your Teams' Strategic Compass

The following checklist provides a first orientation for what to consider when applying the Design Thinking for Humanity framework. These questions are not exhaustive but rather serve as a strategic compass. They are designed to help you and your team quickly diagnose a project, idea, or strategy, assessing its alignment with the core principles of creating a more resilient and sustainable future. Think of this checklist as a tool for reflection, prompting the critical conversations necessary to move from abstract theory to concrete, responsible action.

By thoughtfully answering these questions, you will begin to see where your efforts are strong and, more importantly, where they need to be strengthened. The checklist will help you identify the areas that require more attention, deeper empathy, and greater creativity. Use it as a starting point for the intentional work ahead. It is the first step in a continuous process of inquiry and adaptation, guiding you as you begin the challenging but essential work of designing for a thriving, win-win-win world.

1. Futures Thinking

Objective: Envision and prepare for multiple possible futures to ensure long-term relevance and resilience of solutions (see pages 55–88).

Have you defined a compelling "preferable future" that is ambitious enough to inspire a movement?

☐ Yes   ☐ Partly   ☐ Not yet

Have you mapped the potential unintended consequences of your solution for the next generation?

☐ Yes   ☐ Partly   ☐ Not yet

Is your strategy resilient enough to thrive in a world of unexpected shocks and "black swan" events?

☐ Yes   ☐ Partly   ☐ Not yet

Objective: Apply the design thinking mindset to deeply understand the problem needs, generate creative solutions, and iterate based on real-world feedback (see pages 121–164).

Have you moved beyond a single user's needs to build deep, systemic empathy for the entire community and the planet?

☐ Yes   ☐ Partly   ☐ Not yet

Is your "How Might We" question aimed at a true leverage point, or are you still just addressing a surface-level symptom?

☐ Yes   ☐ Partly   ☐ Not yet

Are you actively prototyping and testing not just your solution but your core, underlying assumptions about the problem itself?

☐ Yes   ☐ Partly   ☐ Not yet

Objective: Understand and respect the interconnectedness of our solutions with natural systems, aiming for regenerative and sustainable outcomes (see pages 167–216).

Does your solution actively regenerate the ecosystems it touches, or does it merely do "less harm"?

☐ Yes   ☐ Partly   ☐ Not yet

Have you designed your business model for circularity, eliminating the concept of "waste" from the beginning?

☐ Yes   ☐ Partly   ☐ Not yet

Does your narrative inspire a genuine shift toward more sustainable behaviors, or does it just label the old way "green"?

☐ Yes   ☐ Partly   ☐ Not yet

Objective: Analyze and understand complex interdependencies within the problem space to identify high-leverage intervention points (see pages 219–261).

Does your business model create a clear "win-win-win," where a healthier planet and a more equitable society are direct drivers of your success?

☐ Yes   ☐ Partly   ☐ Not yet

Have you designed the collaborative ecosystem of partners required to bring your systemic solution to life?

☐ Yes   ☐ Partly   ☐ Not yet

Have you considered how your solution will shift power dynamics, and have you designed for equity and fairness from the start?

☐ Yes   ☐ Partly   ☐ Not yet

5. Exponential Thinking

Objective: Develop solutions that are scalable, transformative, and capable of generating disproportionately large positive impact (see pages 263–300).

Is your solution designed to leverage exponential trends to create impact at a scale that truly matches the size of the challenge?

☐ Yes   ☐ Partly   ☐ Not yet

Have you established clear ethical guardrails to ensure your solution is scaled responsibly and serves humanity's best interests?

☐ Yes   ☐ Partly   ☐ Not yet

Is your purpose framed as a "Massive Transformative Purpose" that is powerful enough to unite and mobilize a global community?

☐ Yes   ☐ Partly   ☐ Not yet

FUTURES THINKING

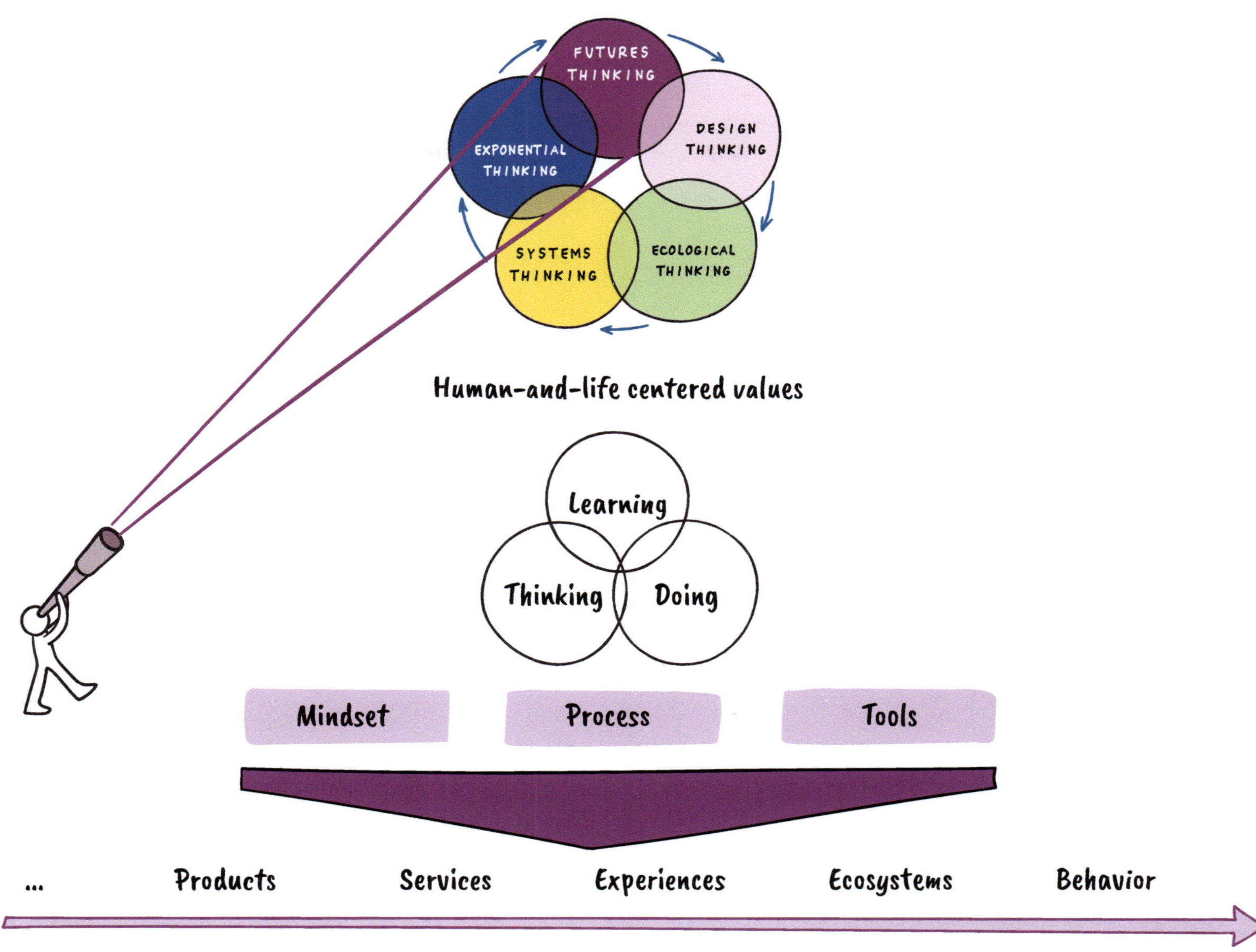

FUTURES THINKING
EXPONENTIAL THINKING
DESIGN THINKING
SYSTEMS THINKING
ECOLOGICAL THINKING
Human-and-life centered values
Learning
Thinking
Doing
Mindset
Process
Tools
... Products Services Experiences Ecosystems Behavior
THE SPECTRUM OF POSITIVE, RESILIENT CHANGE WE AIM TO CREATE.

Doing Futures and Foresights

Futures thinking encourages exploration of possibilities through the strategic use of "what if…" and "imagine that…" questions, fostering a future-oriented mindset. These imaginative exercises allow us to **envision optimistic preferable futures**, identify potential pathways to achieve them, and inspire action toward creating a better world. However, futures thinking, as a starting point for Design Thinking for Humanity, goes beyond the desirable future. It blends insights, foresights, and futures studies with practices from psychology, all filtered through the lens of the design thinking mindset.

This iterative process involves developing artifacts of the future and exploring various possible opportunities through a dynamic interplay of discovery and decision-making. Futures thinking is not about predicting the future. It is about illuminating the potential, often unexpected, implications of today's problems. This illumination empowers individuals, policymakers, and organizations to proactively shape all imaginable futures, the so-called "possible" futures. The focus shifts from predicting what will happen to exploring what might happen, given various observed factors. It includes even events that current research would not (yet) be able to explain.

[Design thinking in combination with futures thinking is a proactive, iterative process that starts with "what if" and "imagine that" scenarios to explore possible futures, not to predict them but to illuminate the implications of present-day problems and inspire action toward creating positive impact on both people and the planet.]

From Prediction to Possibility

Many organizations, when planning for the future, focus on prediction. This approach is suitable only for narrow questions where all parameters are known and static, allowing for a single, precise forecast. However, in an era of exponential change, most critical challenges involve numerous unknowns, making any single prediction an unreliable guide. Futures thinking, therefore, requires a fundamental shift in perspective: we must move from the assumed certainty of a single **predicted future** to an exploration of the full range of **possible futures**. This means embracing uncertainty and preparing for a diverse set of outcomes rather than a single, predetermined path.

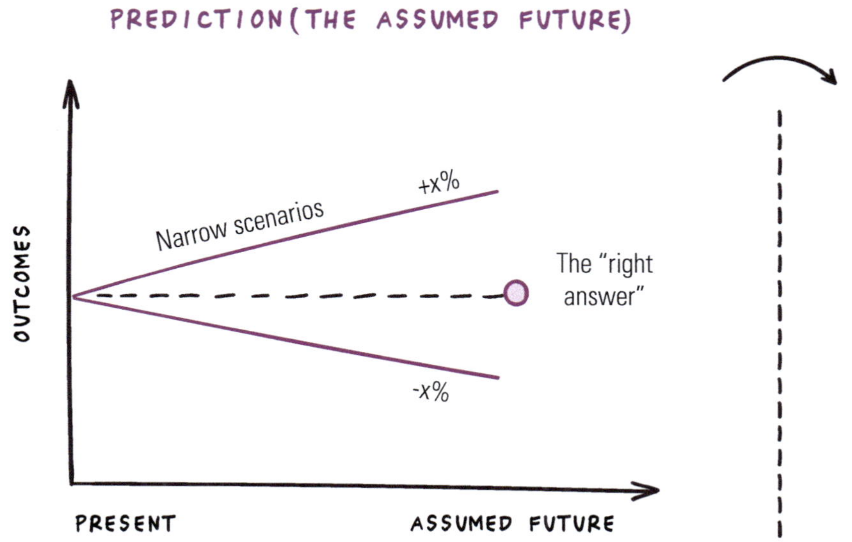

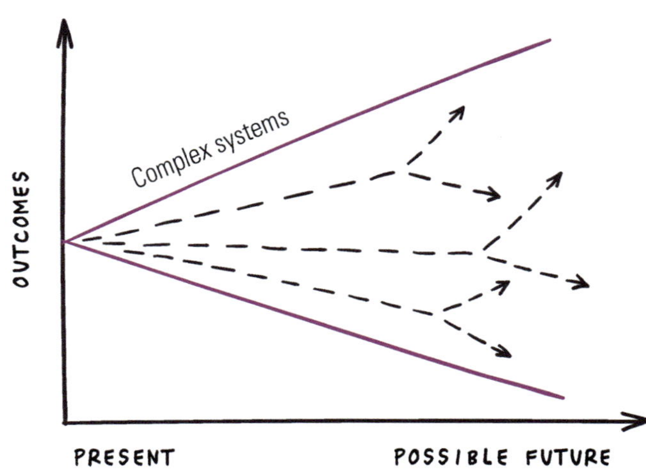

- Seeks a single "right" answer

- Assumes all parameters are known and static

- Best suited for narrow, stable scenarios

- Navigates multiple unknowns and complex systems

- Explores a broad range of plausible outcomes

- Builds resilience and adaptability for diverse possibilities

Embracing Uncertainty: Black Swans and Butterflies

Small events trigger massive consequences in our highly interconnected world. We often call this the butterfly effect. We must navigate this unpredictability. We recognize the different types of knowledge and ignorance we face. We use the following framework to audit our honest position. It breaks these down into four categories to assess what we truly know.

The **Strategic Awareness Framework (see page 59)** identifies our certainties first. These situations occur where External Evidence Exists and We Feel Certain (**Known Knowns**). We have facts and evidence on hand here. We contrast these with identifiable risks. Here External Evidence Exists but We Feel Uncertain (**Known Unknowns**). We are aware of risks like market shifts or new regulations but cannot predict their specific impact. We actively plan for these foreseeable uncertainties.

The more challenging categories force us to look deeper. Hidden biases represent assumptions where We Feel Certain but External Evidence is Missing (**Unknown Knowns**). Our mental models fail us here. We believe we understand a situation when we actually lack the data. We finally face the true surprises. These black swan events lie where External Evidence is Missing and We Feel Uncertain (**Unknown Unknowns**). They exist outside our current experience. We admit this category exists. We take the first step toward building genuine resilience against future shocks.

The Strategic Awareness Framework

<table>
<tr><td></td><td>External Evidence Exists (known)</td><td>External Evidence Missing (unknown)</td></tr>
<tr><td>WE FEEL CERTAIN (known)</td><td>Descriptor: Certainties

Core Idea: The facts and evidence we currently possess.

Strategic Stance: Leverage and build upon this established knowledge.</td><td>Descriptor: Hidden Biases & Blind Spots

Core Idea: The unconscious assumptions and flawed mental models that make us believe we understand a situation when we do not.

Strategic Stance: Challenge assumptions and actively seek diverse, outside perspectives to reveal these blind spots.</td></tr>
<tr><td>WE FEEL UNCERTAIN (unknown)</td><td>Descriptor: Identifiable Risks

Core Idea: The risks and variables we know exist but cannot fully predict.

Strategic Stance: Actively plan and prepare for these foreseeable uncertainties.</td><td>Descriptor: Unforeseeable Disruptions

Core Idea: The "black swan" events that are impossible to predict because they lie outside our current experience.

Strategic Stance: Build genuine, systemic resilience to be able to adapt and transform in the face of true surprise.</td></tr>
</table>

Acknowledging these different forms of uncertainty is the first step toward building genuine resilience against future shocks. This leads to a fundamental principle for innovators and leaders:

The goal is not just to prepare for the risks we know, or to withstand the shocks we can imagine, but to build a system that grows stronger from the surprises we cannot.

This principle pushes us beyond mere resilience. While a resilient system is designed to withstand disorder and bounce back to its original state, an **exponentializing** system is one that actually gains strength from shocks, volatility, and uncertainty. Just as human muscles grow stronger from the stress of exercise, an exponentializing system (see pages 40–41) is designed not just to endure the unpredictable but to thrive because of it.

Applying the Vision Cone

The Vision Cone visualizes the entire landscape of what lies ahead. It moves outward from the certainty of the present day through expanding layers of uncertainty. This helps us categorize and make sense of the full spectrum of possibilities. This is not a tool for prediction. Instead, the cone acts as a framework for exploration to ensure strategic conversations remain imaginative and well-grounded. Understand the different layers to move beyond reacting to obvious trends and proactively shape the future you desire.

The Vision Cone forms the foundational framework for many tools in this toolbox (see Futures Thinking Toolbox, pages 76–117). It provides the canvas upon which we paint all subsequent futures and foresight work. Activities like Horizon Scanning and PESTLE Analysis gather the signals and trends that populate the different layers of the cone. The Probability/Impact Matrix then helps us prioritize these signals. We identify which ones have the power to push us toward or away from a specific future. The cone gives these disparate pieces of information a home and a context.

Once we map the landscape, the Vision Cone becomes a powerful engine for ideation and strategy. We build the most compelling stories for Scenario Planning by exploring the tensions between different plausible futures within the cone. Use Creative Mash-Ups and the Futures Wheel to generate innovations that are resilient across multiple possible futures, not just the most probable one. **The Vision Cone ensures creative work stays tethered to reality and responds directly to the full spectrum of what lies ahead**.

The Vision Cone connects the future back to the present. Identify a "preferable future" within the cone first. Then use tools like Backcasting and Future -Ready Roadmapping to chart a course from that desired destination back to the actions we must take today. This transforms foresight from a passive academic exercise into a dynamic, actionable strategic practice. It provides a clear answer to this question: Knowing what is possible, what should we do now to build a better world?

- Map the full spectrum of possibilities to define a clear "preferable future" that serves as your strategic North Star.

- Avoid the trap of a single "projected future" by exploring the full spectrum of plausible and possible futures to understand all risks and opportunities.

- Identify systemic tensions between different futures to reveal the barriers you must overcome.

- Connect your preferable future to the present by using tools like Backcasting to map the necessary steps, policies, and innovations required.

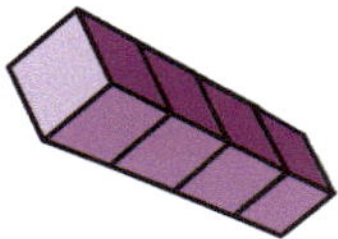
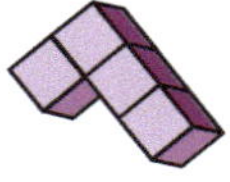

The Vision Cone

The Vision Cone serves as a powerful tool for Design Thinking for Humanity practitioners. It allows us to explore the full spectrum of potential futures intentionally rather than being limited to a single projected path. We diverge from immediate assumptions about what the future will be. This opens up space **to consider all possible futures, ranging from plausible to preferable**. However, "preferable" means more than just organizational preference.

It represents a future that optimizes human well-being, equity, and ecological regeneration. This comprehensive exploration ensures our solutions remain robust and adaptable. They truly resonate with diverse needs and evolving societal landscapes. **This ultimately leads to more impactful and sustainable innovation**.

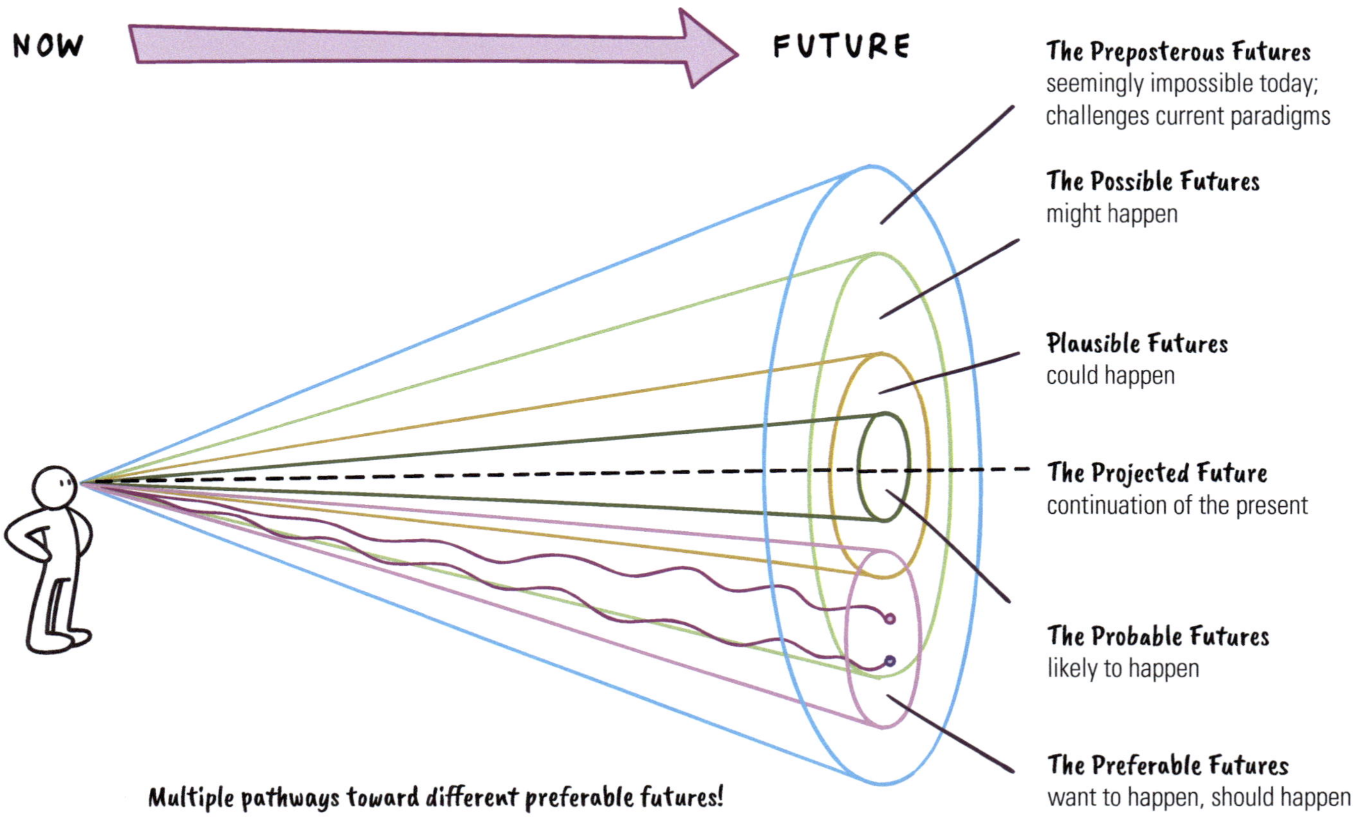

Multiple pathways toward different preferable futures!

Futures thinking in the context of Design Thinking for Humanity is the appropriate paradigm because it:

- **Enables us to explore a range of possible futures.** We look at organizations, products, services, and processes beyond immediate needs to consider long-term impacts and possibilities.

- **Facilitates the evaluation of these possible futures.** This allows us to ascertain which futures are most desirable for humanity and the planet. We understand the underlying values and principles that make them so.

- **Supports us to identify strategic decisions and actions.** We increase the likelihood of achieving those desirable outcomes. We shift from reactive problem-solving to proactive future-building.

- **Bridges the gap between understanding deep human needs and envisioning long-term possibilities.** Design thinking understands the needs; futures thinking envisions the possibilities. This ensures that design solutions are both relevant and sustainable.

- **Allows us to reveal the potential, often unexpected, implications of current problems.** Rather than predicting the future, we empower ourselves to address problems in ways that contribute to a more positive and resilient future.

Futures thinking has become an integral part of Design Thinking for Humanity. It paves the way for quality long-term thinking. Design thinking provides the foundation for understanding deep human needs and exploring appropriate problem spaces. Futures thinking injects an essential forward-looking perspective.

**Futures Studies
(The Academic Foundation)**

**Futures Thinking
(The Mindset)**

**Foresights
(The Analytical Practice)**

The Future Is Unpredictable, Not Predetermined

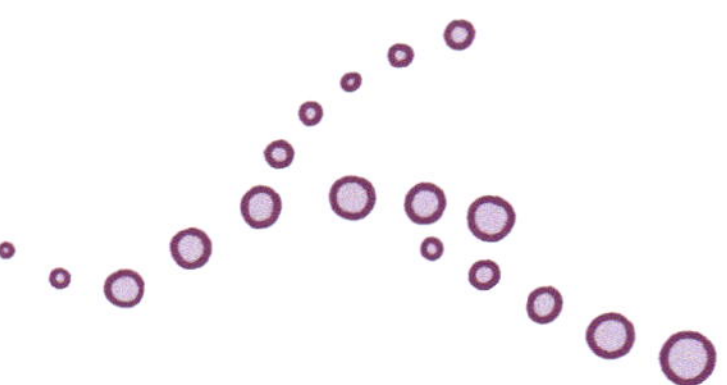

The Future Is Plausible, Not Singular

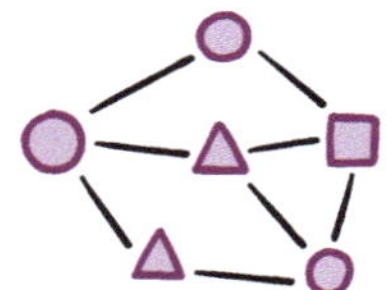

Individual and Collective Choices Shape the Future

Understanding Potential Futures Empowers Present-Day Action

Creating **possible** future worlds

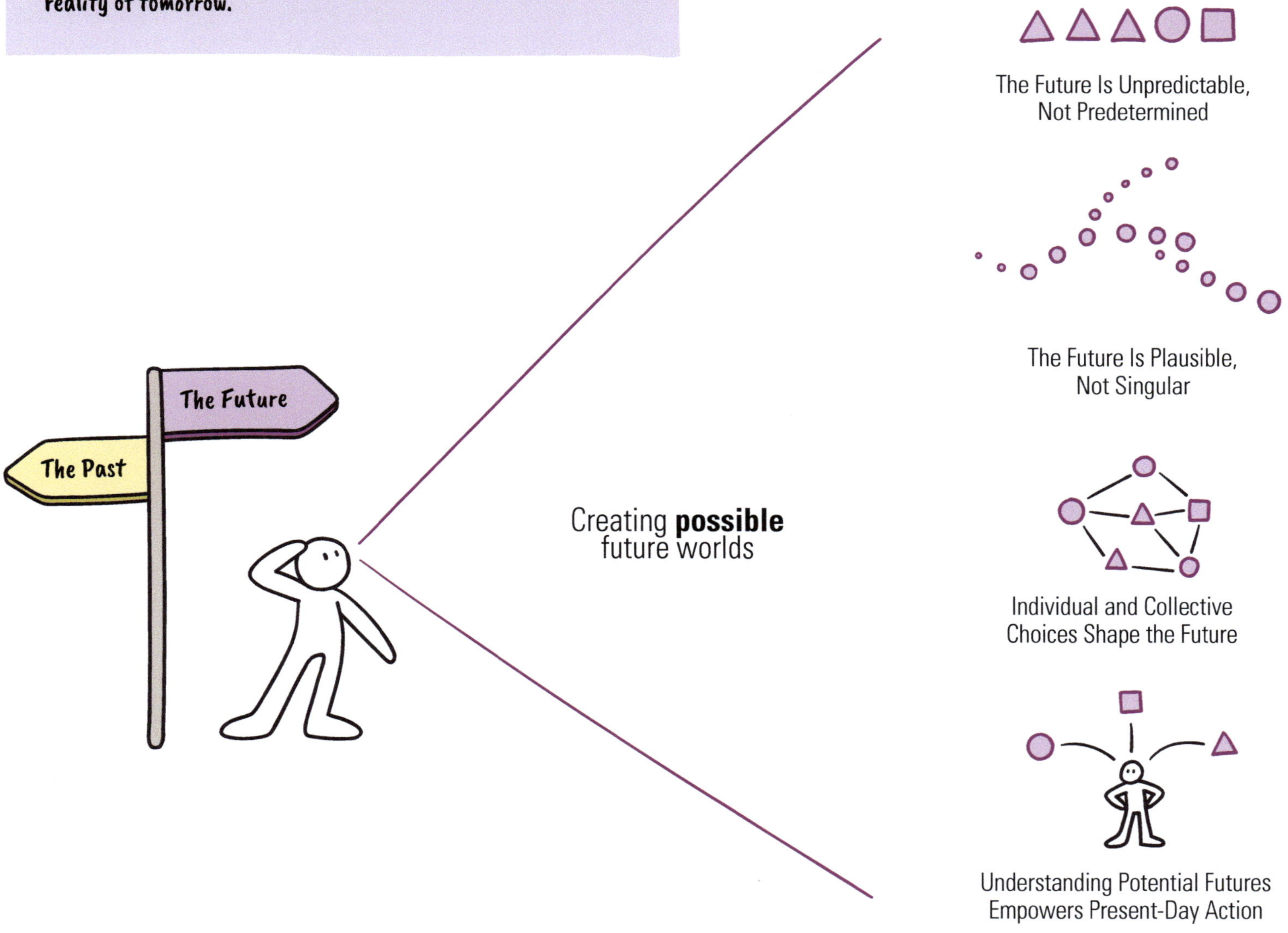

Facilitating Future-Oriented Design

Facilitating future-oriented design is the practical art of guiding a team from long-term, abstract possibilities to concrete, present-day action.

The facilitator acts as the steward of the Future-Forward Design Process (see page 65). They create a structured yet flexible environment where teams safely explore potential futures, challenge their own assumptions, and build a shared, resilient vision. This requires skillfully managing the inherent uncertainties and human biases that challenge foresight work.

The facilitator guides the team through the five phases of the process, intentionally creating conditions for both divergent and convergent thinking. In divergent phases, such as Futures Immersion & Empathy, the facilitator fosters expansive, imaginative exploration. They apply specific tools from the toolbox to encourage the team to question mental filters and conceive truly novel futures. This moves the team beyond the "predicted future" that often limits innovation.

In convergent phases, such as Future Framing & Problem Definition, the focus shifts to guiding the team toward clarity and commitment. The facilitator synthesizes vast amounts of information and identifies emerging patterns. **While AI collaborators can analyze data, the human facilitator remains the crucial sensemaker.** They interpret ambiguity, weigh complex ethical and cultural nuances, and help the team build a shared, meaningful understanding.

Decision-makers in traditional settings tend to focus on 'the predicted future' that unfold gradually from current patterns.

A core responsibility is creating an environment of profound psychological safety. Exploring potential futures, especially disruptive or dystopian ones, can provoke anxiety. The facilitator must create a safe space where participants confront these challenges without fear. By acknowledging emotional responses and framing exploration as a creative exercise, the facilitator transforms potential resistance into a powerful source of insight.

The facilitator orchestrates a team's journey into the future. By applying the right tools at the right time and holding the team accountable to the work's principles, **they transform foresight from a passive academic exercise into a dynamic engine for creating a more resilient and thriving future**.

Facilitators' Actions!

- Facilitate transdisciplinary workshops that bring together diverse experts from science, design, and the humanities to co-create novel solutions.

- Build collaborative networks by actively connecting enterprises, policymakers, and communities to drive shared, real-world impact.

- Coach new leadership mindsets that prioritize long-term resilience over short-term gains and empower decentralized teams to respond to change.

- Design and integrate Design Thinking for Humanity into all learning agendas to build the skills and capabilities needed to initiate massive change.

Traditional innovation processes often trap us in the present. They optimize for current user needs but ignore the approaching waves of disruption. **To architect a resilient future, we must change our starting point**. We cannot simply iterate on what exists today. We must anticipate the context of tomorrow and define where we are going before we decide what to build. This approach ensures that we do not stop at an abstract vision. We conclude with a real strategic pathway that bridges the gap between our future ambition and today's execution.

The core of the Future-Forward Design Process is the **integration of futures thinking and design thinking.** This combination enables us to explore future possibilities and effectively address today's challenges. In the Foresight phase, we do not empathize with a user yet; we empathize with the future. We scan for signals and map scenarios to define a preferable future. **This vision becomes the North Star**. We reverse-engineer solutions that are not just desirable for users today but resilient and sustainable for the decades to come.

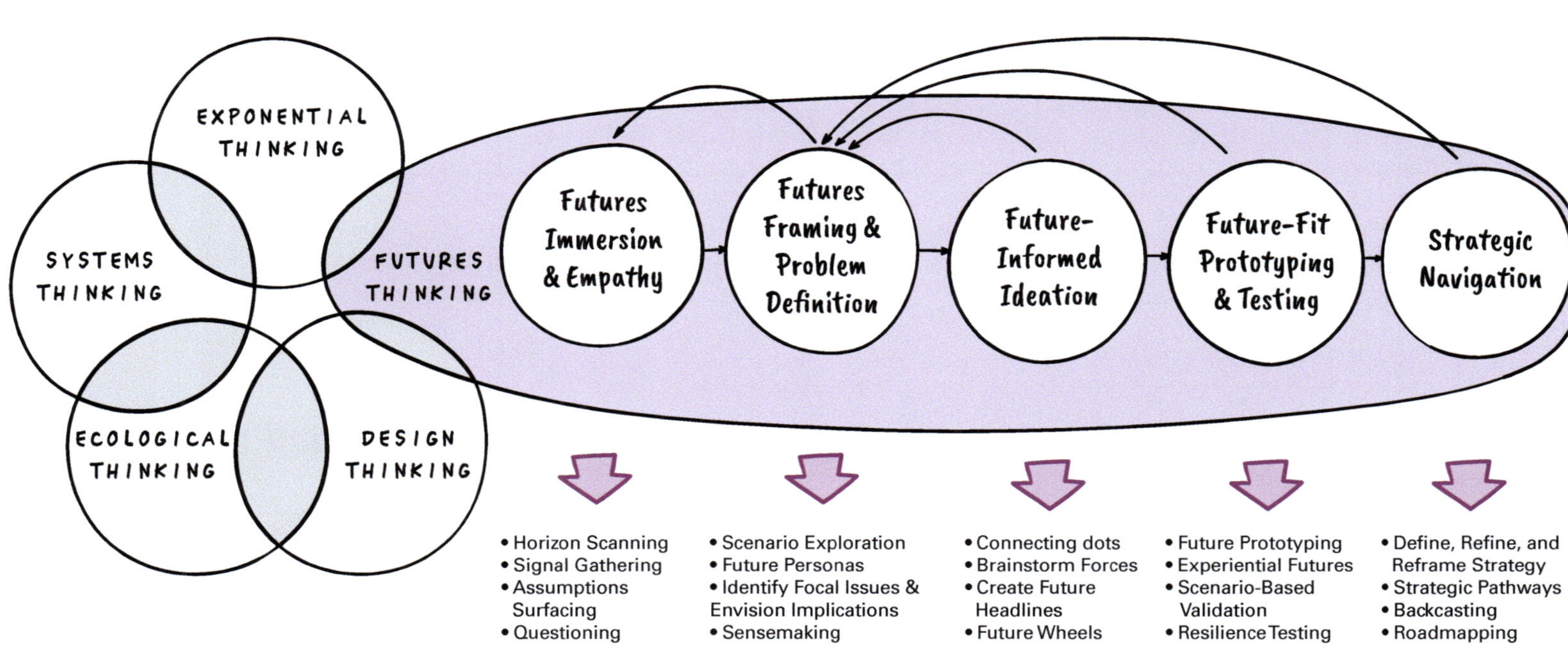

We navigate the transition from foresight to execution through five strategic phases. This framework ensures we do not get lost in the abstraction of the future or the myopia of the present. Each step requires a specific mindset and a dedicated set of tools (see pages 76–117) to ensure that our long-term vision translates into immediate, impactful action.

Phase 1: Futures Immersion & Empathy

This initial phase involves a thorough investigation into signals, trends, human behaviors, and needs. It requires a deep analysis to uncover underlying biases, unquestioned assumptions, established systems, and the core values or pervasive myths that shape a worldview. By illuminating these foundational layers, a more nuanced and realistic picture of potential futures is constructed, moving beyond simplistic or overly optimistic projections.

Phase 2: Future Framing & Problem Definition

Building upon this foundational understanding, the next phase synthesizes these insights. It involves a careful examination of emerging trends, observed disruptions, and ongoing transformations related to a specific focal issue. This stage emphasizes pattern recognition and developing a deeper comprehension of the forces at play, which helps to frame human-centered problems within a future context.

Phase 3: Future-Informed Ideation

This phase applies various ideation techniques and powerful "what if" questions to enable divergent thinking. By leveraging the insights gathered from the future framing stage, a wide range of innovative solutions can be generated. These solutions are not only relevant for today but are also designed to be adaptable to various potential future scenarios.

Phase 4: Future-Fit Prototyping & Testing

The diverse scenarios explored in earlier stages become the basis for this phase. "Prototypes" are constructed that reflect different potential future worlds and the artifacts that might exist within them. This approach allows concepts to be tested against multiple alternative future scenarios, gaining valuable insights into their resilience and desirability.

Phase 5: Strategic Navigation

Finally, the insights gained from exploring these future possibilities are translated into actionable strategies and visions for the present. This translation process guides the creation of preferred outcomes and helps build resilience against the inherent uncertainties of the future, ensuring all solutions are both robust and forward-looking.

Futures thinking methods adapt to any challenge. Do not limit them to a single context. **Use this versatile framework to address the full spectrum of issues**. Scale your approach from complex, global "wicked problems" down to focused national and local initiatives. At the global scale, tackle deeply interconnected challenges like climate change, societal polarization, or the human-AI relationship. Apply the long-term, holistic perspective of futures thinking to anticipate cascading consequences across systems. Design truly resilient interventions rather than temporary fixes.

Futures thinking applies fractal principles to challenges of varying scope.

Global Scale: Tackle quintessential wicked problems like climate change, societal polarization, or the future of the human-AI relationship. These interconnected challenges require a long-term, holistic perspective to anticipate cascading consequences and design truly resilient interventions.

National Scale: Drive initiatives like public health and well-being improvement. Move beyond reactive health-care systems to envision proactive "health-care" models. Explore future scenarios for personalized medicine and design interventions that encourage preventative behaviors. Create resilient infrastructures adaptable to demographic shifts or pandemics.

Local/Community Scale: Enhance urban resilience. Cities can explore the future of local food systems, urban mobility, or community connection. Engage citizens in collaborative processes to envision a preferable future. Leaders co-create initiatives like community garden networks, modular transport systems, or digital platforms that foster local bonds.

When addressing a global challenge like climate change and its cascading crises, begin with deep, systemic empathy for diverse impacts on communities and ecosystems. **Reframe broad challenges into specific, actionable problems**. Design circular economy models for specific industries or develop resilient water management systems for vulnerable regions. Ideate and prototype radical solutions that integrate new technologies, policy shifts, and behavioral changes. Maintain a long-term view to ensure environmental and social sustainability.

The focal points for this work vary as widely as the challenges themselves.

Specific Company: Focus on the "Future of Employee Engagement and Well-Being in an AI-Driven Hybrid World." Use foresight to design human-centric organizational models.

Industry Level: Tackle "Achieving True Circularity in Manufacturing." Use scenario planning to map required technologies, supply chains, and business models.

Startup Level: Focus on "Building Trust and Ethical AI" in a niche product. Use foresight to anticipate and mitigate potential user harm in applications like personalized mental health tools.

Journey Through the Five Lenses: The Living Soil Mandate

Bring concepts to life with a practical design challenge. Follow **the Living Soil Mandate** through the upcoming chapters. Design a global regenerative model that makes topsoil health the primary success metric by 2050. Apply tools from all five disciplines to build a scalable solution. **Review the summarized results in the Resilient Blueprint on page 280.**

Futures Thinking (pages 69–75): Setting the Direction

Exploring the future landscape of agriculture and economics. This phase involves scanning for weak signals, building four distinct future scenarios (from "Regenerative Abundance" to "The Great Dust Bowl"), and identifying a clear, "preferable future."

Key Tools Applied:
Horizon Scanning
Scenario Planning & the 2x2 Matrix
Creative Mash-Up

Design Thinking (pages 137–141): Grounding the Vision in Human Needs

Transforming the long-term vision into a human-centered solution. This involves creating a Future Persona (Javier, the farmer), framing a Wicked Problem, ideating the "Carbon Harvest" platform, and testing it for ethical consequences.

Key Tools Applied:
Future Persona
Wicked Problem Framing
Ethical Consequences Scanner

Ecological Thinking (pages 198–201): Designing for Regeneration

Ensuring the solution is not just sustainable but actively regenerative. This involves analyzing the solution's material footprint and designing its business model and behavioral nudges to be in harmony with natural systems.

Key Tools Applied:
Life Cycle Assessment (LCA) Simplified
The Doughnut Economics Model
Sustainable Behavior Design

Exponential Thinking (pages 277–279): Scaling for Global Impact

Designing the strategy to scale the solution globally. This involves understanding the technological growth curves, creating a purpose-driven movement, and ensuring the scaled solution remains ethically aligned and socially beneficial.

Key Tools Applied:
The 6 Ds of Exponentials
Massive Transformative Purpose (MTP)
Movement Catalyst Design

Systems Thinking (pages 237–241): Architecting the Ecosystem

Moving from a single solution to designing the entire collaborative network. This involves mapping the feedback loops that drive the system, identifying leverage points, and creating the "win-win-win" business ecosystem that connects farmers, corporations, governments, and the planet.

Key Tools Applied:
Causal Loop Diagramming (CLD)
Leverage Points Analysis
"Win-Win-Win" Business Ecosystem Canvas

Part 1

A Speculative Case Study:

Applying Futures Thinking

This case study demonstrates how futures thinking serves as the initial, critical step in tackling a complex, systemic challenge. Before designing solutions, we must first deeply understand the landscape of tomorrow. We use foresight not to predict what will happen but to uncover the weak signals and megatrends that point toward what could happen. This exploration grounds our subsequent design work in reality rather than assumption.

The overarching goal for our case study is both ambitious and essential.

The Living Soil Mandate

Our objective within this challenge is to design a new global economic and agricultural model that makes the regeneration of the world's topsoil the primary measure of agricultural success, ensuring long-term food security, reversing climate change, and restoring biodiversity by 2050.

The first step in tackling this grand challenge involves a deep immersion into the present landscape to understand the forces at play. Scan for signals of change, understand long-term megatrends, and engage with diverse perspectives through deep inquiry.

Collecting and Clustering Weak Signals

Futures thinking prompts us to scan the "fringes" of society to identify weak signals of potential future change. Observe unusual developments to gain insights into emerging trends that might eventually impact our design domain.

- Ambiguous and subtle: These signals are not yet mainstream or obvious.
- Potentially significant: They carry the seed of major disruption or opportunity.
- Require interpretation: They demand that we connect the dots to see patterns.

- What unconventional things are happening globally today?
- What forces are driving these developments?
- Why are these signals intriguing, and what future implications might they hold?
- How could these seemingly disparate signals potentially apply to the domain we are designing within, revealing unexpected opportunity areas?

Weak Signals (Small Selection):

A consortium of food companies invests in a satellite platform to monitor soil carbon levels in real time.

A new "soil microbiome" health test for farms becomes commercially available.

A fashion brand launches a clothing line made from fibers grown using regenerative agricultural practices.

The government of a small nation officially includes "Natural Capital" in its national accounting.

A popular health documentary links human gut health directly to the soil health where food is grown.

Clustering into Potential Driving Forces:

- **The Soil-Health Nexus:** A growing scientific and public understanding of the direct link between soil health, human health, and climate stability.

- **Verifiable Regeneration:** The emergence of new technologies that can transparently and affordably measure ecological outcomes like soil carbon.

- **The Bio-Economy:** A shift toward agricultural products being seen as the feedstock for everything from fashion to construction materials.

- **New Economic Models:** The exploration of economic models that account for the value of nature.

Understanding Megatrends

Weak signals do not exist in a vacuum. They serve as early indicators of the profound, long-term shifts reshaping our world. Understand these megatrends. They act as the fundamental drivers shaping the plausible futures we might inhabit. Frame our challenge against powerful megatrends like accelerating climate change, increasing global food insecurity, and the growing crisis in public health related to diet.

Some megatrends started 10.000 BCE and others, like the increase risks to humanity, in the 1970s.

Level of confidence   High 🟢 Medium 🟡 Low 🔴

Engaging Experts with Hybrid Questions

To deepen our understanding, we must engage with a diverse range of experts, from scientists and economists to community activists and indigenous leaders. Hybrid interviews, which blend structured and unstructured questions, are a potent technique for this.

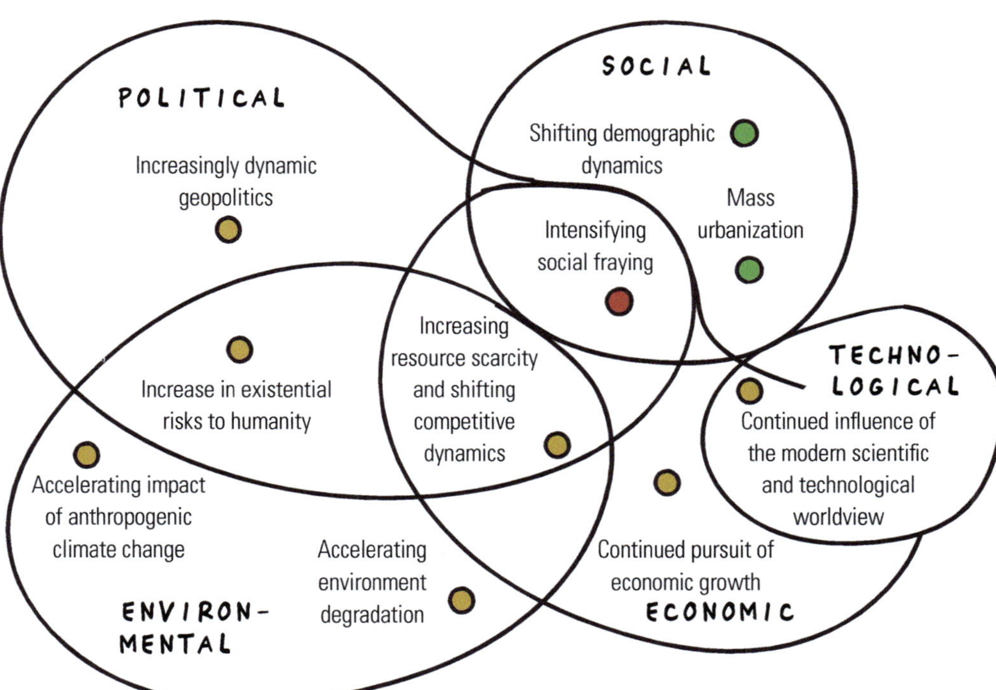

Example of Powerful Questions for an Expert on Planetary Balance:

- **Farsighted:** "If you could speak with an oracle from 2050, what three things would you want to know about the state of the world's soil?"

- **Optimistic Scenario:** "If humanity were to successfully regenerate the majority of its agricultural soils by 2050, what would be true of our food systems?"

- **Pessimistic Scenario:** "If our soils were to continue to degrade, what might be the single most catastrophic, unforeseen consequence?"

- **System Constraints:** "What is the single most powerful force that is currently preventing the widespread adoption of regenerative agriculture?"

- **Leverage Points:** "What is the single most important intervention we could make in the next five years to accelerate the transition to a soil-first food system?"

Next, build a set of distinct, plausible future scenarios upon this foundational understanding. Treat them not as predictions but as narratives. Use them to stress-test strategies and identify robust pathways toward the goal.

Scenario 1: "Regenerative Abundance" (Optimistic): A global awakening to the soil crisis leads to a massive, coordinated shift. Regenerative agriculture becomes the global norm, driven by a combination of strong policy, consumer demand, and technological breakthroughs. Food is abundant, nutritious, and a primary tool for carbon sequestration.

Key Drivers: Strong political will; widespread consumer awareness; breakthroughs in soil science and monitoring technology.

Economic Model: A regenerative, circular bio-economy where farmers are rewarded for ecological outcomes (carbon sequestration, biodiversity) as well as for food production.

Challenge: Scaling regenerative practices globally and ensuring an equitable transition for all farmers.

Scenario 2: "The Techno-Food System" (Centralized Efficiency): Soil degradation is largely ignored. Instead, humanity turns to large-scale, industrial, lab-grown food and synthetic biology to feed the population. While efficient, this system is highly centralized, is energy-intensive, and creates unforeseen health and ecological consequences.

Key Drivers: Belief in a purely technological salvation; powerful corporate actors in the biotech space; reactive rather than proactive policy.

Economic Model: A highly centralized, patent-driven food-tech industry. Traditional agriculture becomes a niche, premium market.

Challenge: Unforeseen ecological side effects, loss of biodiversity, and the social and ethical dilemmas of a world disconnected from its natural food systems.

Scenario 3: "Local Havens, Global Famine" (Adaptive): Global food systems collapse due to widespread soil degradation and climate shocks. In response, resilient local communities create self-sufficient, regenerative "food havens." However, there is widespread famine and conflict in regions that were unable to adapt.

Key Drivers: Geopolitical fragmentation; collapse of global supply chains; strong community leadership and local innovation.

Economic Model: A network of decentralized, self-sufficient, and highly resilient local food economies.

Challenge: Lack of global coordination on larger issues and significant inequality between the resilient "havens" and the collapsed regions.

Scenario 4: "The Great Dust Bowl" (Pessimistic): The "business-as-usual" of degenerative industrial agriculture continues, leading to catastrophic soil erosion, widespread desertification, and a permanent decline in global food production capacity.

Key Drivers: Political inertia; powerful vested interests in the chemical-industrial agriculture complex; failure to act on scientific warnings.

Economic Model: A degenerative, increasingly fragile, and resource-constrained agricultural economy, leading to chronic food shortages and price volatility.

Challenge: Widespread human suffering, mass migrations from uninhabitable regions, and the potential for a large-scale collapse of civilization.

With a rich view of the potential futures, we can now move to ideation. A creative mash-up is an excellent tool for synthesizing diverse signals and uncovering entirely new opportunity areas.

Example Mash-Up for Planetary Balance

Intersection of Signals:

- AI-powered, real-time soil health monitoring
- A new social media platform based on verifiable contributions
- The legal concept of "natural capital" in national accounting

Novel User Need:
A way for farmers to be directly and transparently rewarded for the ecological value they create (like sequestering carbon or increasing biodiversity), not just for the volume of crops they produce.

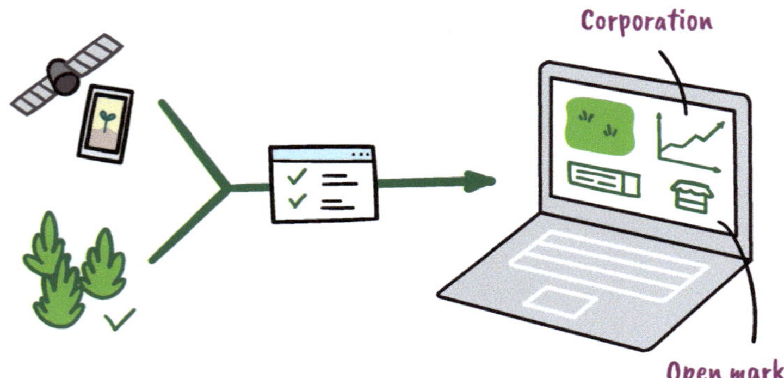

New Product/Experience (The Mash-Up)

The "Carbon Harvest" Platform:
A global digital platform where farmers can use verifiable, real-time data from soil sensors and satellites to issue "regeneration credits." These credits, representing sequestered carbon and increased biodiversity, can then be sold on an open market to corporations and individuals, creating a direct financial incentive for regenerative practices.

Phases 4 & 5: Future-Fit Prototyping & Strategic Navigation

Before we can build a full strategy, we must assess our readiness to navigate toward our preferable future. The following questions are a powerful tool for testing the readiness of our scenarios and the solutions we have designed for them.

Powerful Questions for Assessing Scenario Readiness:

- **Human:** How do we ensure these future scenarios genuinely serve human needs and enhance well-being across all demographics? What new skills or mindsets will humans need to thrive in this future?

- **Planet:** How do these future scenarios impact the environment? How can we ensure that our future choices contribute to ecological regeneration, rather than depletion?

- **Knowledge:** What critical information is missing to navigate this future effectively? How will we generate, share, and utilize new knowledge to adapt and innovate?

- **Tools:** What technologies and infrastructures are required to realize this future? Are the existing tools adequate, or do we need to invent or adapt new ones?

- **Rules:** What policies, regulations, and ethical frameworks need to be established to support this future and ensure fairness and accountability?

- **Networks:** What new collaborations and partnerships need to be forged to build and sustain this future? How will we foster trust and effective communication across diverse stakeholders?

From Scenarios to Strategy

Finally, we use the four scenarios to build a robust and adaptive strategy for the "Carbon Harvest" platform.

- **"No-Regret Moves":** What strategic actions are a good idea in all four scenarios?

- **Investment in low-cost, verifiable soil sensors:** This is valuable whether the future is regenerative or techno-utopian.

- **Building a powerful, farmer-centric educational platform:** Empowering farmers with knowledge is a resilient strategy in any future.

By investing in low-cost, verifiable soil sensors and a powerful, farmer-centric educational platform from the outset, the "Carbon Harvest" platform is positioned to thrive in a world of either "Regenerative Abundance" or a more fragmented future.

"Contingent Strategies":

- **If** we see early signals that the "Regenerative Abundance" scenario is emerging (e.g., major governments begin to subsidize soil carbon), **then** we will rapidly scale our market-making function.

- **If** we see early signals that the "Techno-Food System" is emerging (e.g., massive investment in lab-grown food), **then** we will pivot to position our platform as a premium "natural food" verification system for a niche, high-value market.

The goal of futures thinking is not to generate a single "correct" prediction of what will happen. It is a rigorous process designed to expand our awareness of what could happen. By exploring a diverse range of possible futures, we build the resilience to navigate uncertainty and the agency to shape the outcomes we desire. Traditional strategy often fails because it treats the future as a linear extension of the past. In contrast, strategy built on futures thinking uses the future as a laboratory to test assumptions and prototype resilience.

Traditional Strategy vs. Futures Thinking

FEATURE	TRADITIONAL STRATEGY	FUTURES THINKING IN STRATEGY
Perspective	Focuses on optimizing the status quo	Focuses on systemic transformation
Method	Relies on historical data and linear trends	Scans for weak signals and disruptive shifts
Horizon	Solves for immediate competitive advantage	Solves for long-term planetary health
Response	Reactive adjustment to market forces	Proactive design of a preferable future

> "The value of Futures Thinking isn't getting the forecast right. It is about realizing that the future is something we invent."
> —Jeanne Liedtka

Three Pillars of Future-Forward Strategy

1. Developing Strategic Agency
We must stop viewing the future as a destination that happens to us. Futures thinking provides the tools to move from passive observation to active participation. When we articulate a "preferable future," we create a North Star that guides every decision we make today.

2. Prototyping Systems, Not Just Products
Every strategy is a hypothesis. By using futures thinking, we can prototype these hypotheses against different scenarios to uncover unintended consequences. This allows us to stress-test governance, policy, and business models—ensuring they align with regenerative principles before they are deployed into the real world.

3. Activating the Living Soil Mandate
The process concludes by translating high-level futures thinking into a **real strategic pathway**. This is the foundation of the **Living Soil Mandate Strategy**. It ensures that our long-term vision for planetary health is embedded into the core "soil" of the organization. We bridge the gap between current operations and the systemic resilience required for humanity and the planet to thrive.

Futures Thinking Tools

Extend your gaze beyond the present to design for a thriving future within the Design Thinking for Humanity framework. Actively engage with potential tomorrows. Design thinking tools inspire tangible outcomes like products, services, and new business models. They help navigate ambiguity with optimistic confidence. Futures thinking offers a vital, complementary perspective.

Aim for inspiration on a grander scale. Think expansively about opportunities that may materialize in the coming years. Explore potential futures to inform strategy for tomorrow and make it robust against inherent uncertainty. Embrace the ambiguity of envisioning what lies ahead. Foster pragmatic humility as you navigate the realm of possibilities.

Integrate these powerful tools seamlessly into design thinking initiatives. Enrich understanding and expand creative horizons to create regenerative solutions. Move beyond reacting to current challenges. Proactively shape a desirable future for both people and the planet. Use the selection of futures thinking tools outlined on the following pages.

Futures Thinking Toolbox

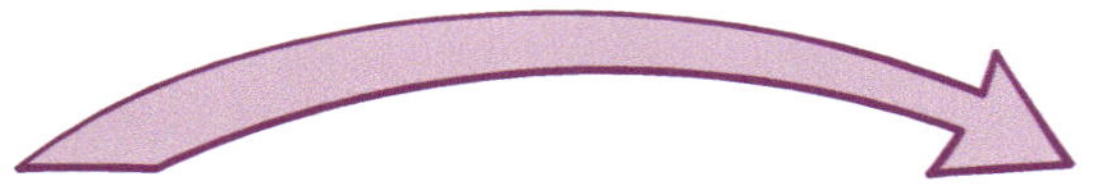

Horizon Scanning:

This systematic process involves actively looking for early signals of change, emerging trends, and potential disruptions across various domains (PESTLE). It helps us to identify weak signals that might grow into significant forces shaping the future.

Stakeholder Analysis & Mapping:

Identifying and understanding the perspectives, power, and interests of different stakeholders is vital in futures thinking. This helps to uncover diverse viewpoints, potential conflicts, and opportunities related to emerging trends and future scenarios. Tools like power-interest grids and stakeholder journey maps can be valuable here.

PESTLE Analysis

This tool provides a framework to scan the macro-environment using six domains: political, economic, social, technological, legal, and environmental. It helps teams identify large-scale drivers of change and understand the broader context in which they operate, moving their perspective beyond immediate internal challenges.

Unconscious Bias Model/Analysis:

Recognizing and understanding cognitive biases (like confirmation bias, anchoring bias, etc.) that can skew our perception of the present and future is crucial. Tools like the Unconscious Bias Model help to identify and mitigate these biases in futures thinking activities, leading to more objective observations.

Ladder of Inference:

This tool helps to surface assumptions and interpretations made when observing data and forming conclusions. By understanding where we jump to conclusions, we can revisit our observations and ensure our understanding of the present (and thus potential futures) is based on more solid ground.

Causal Layered Analysis (CLA):

CLA encourages a deeper exploration of issues beyond surface-level trends. It involves four layers: the litany (superficial news), systemic causes, social discourse/worldview, and myth/metaphor. Unpacking these layers reveals deeper cultural and historical underpinnings that influence how we perceive and shape the future.

Scenario Planning & the 2x2 Matrix:

A classic foresight technique that uses the most critical uncertainties (identified through a 2x2 impact/uncertainty matrix) to build a set of distinct, plausible stories about the future.

Probability/Impact Matrix:

This tool helps prioritize identified trends or potential future events based on an assessment of their likelihood of occurrence and the magnitude of their potential impact. By visually mapping these elements, it allows us to focus attention and resources on the most critical uncertainties.

Pattern Recognition:

This involves actively looking for recurring themes, connections, and relationships among the diverse signals and trends identified during environmental scanning. It is about making sense of seemingly disparate pieces of information to uncover deeper underlying patterns that might indicate significant future shifts.

Sensemaking:

This is the process of interpreting ambiguous or complex information to develop a coherent understanding of its implications for the future. It involves framing, contextualizing, and narrating the identified patterns and trends to create meaning and inform subsequent futures thinking activities like scenario building.

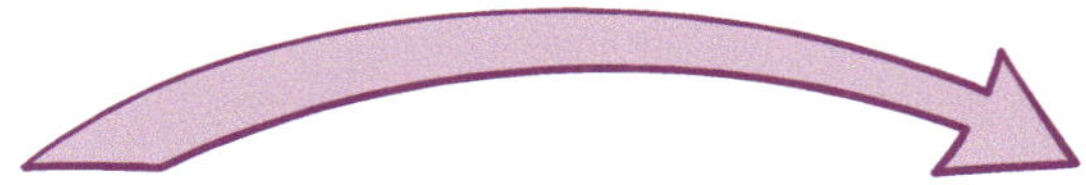

Futures Wheel

This tool is a structured brainstorming method used to explore the cascading, ripple-effect consequences of a future trend or event. By mapping out the direct (first order), indirect (second order), and subsequent (third order) impacts, teams can uncover hidden opportunities, risks, and unexpected areas for innovation that are not immediately obvious.

Creative Mash-Up

This tool sparks innovation by forcing the combination of two or more unrelated concepts. In a futures context, it involves taking a core human need from the present and "mashing it up" with a speculative future technology or trend. This structured collision of ideas helps teams break free from conventional thinking and generate unique, future-ready solutions.

Future Headlines

This tool uses storytelling to drive ideation by challenging a team to write a compelling news headline from a desired future. By first defining a successful future outcome as a tangible headline, the team can then work backward to brainstorm the specific products, services, or social shifts that would need to exist for that headline to become a reality.

Object from the Future

This tool makes a future scenario tangible by challenging a team to design and prototype a physical or digital artifact from that specific future. Whether it is a food packaging label from a world without plastic or a user interface for a service that does not yet exist, creating an "object from the future" is a powerful way to generate and test ideas in a hands-on, experiential way.

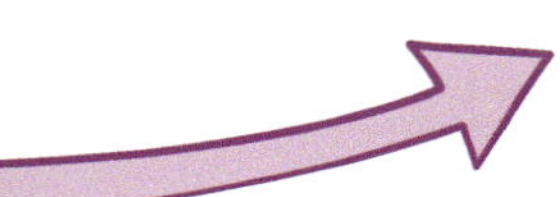

Experiential Futures

This tool moves beyond just describing a future to creating an immersive experience that allows people to "feel" it. By creating tangible "artifacts from the future" or staging interactive scenarios that simulate a future environment, it allows stakeholders to test and react to a future concept in a deeply human and insightful way.

Wind Tunneling

This tool is a powerful method to test the resilience of a current strategy, product, or idea. The concept involves metaphorically placing your idea in the "wind tunnel" of each of the future scenarios you have built to see how it performs—assessing whether it thrives, adapts, or breaks under different future conditions.

Future Role-Playing

This tool explores the human and social dynamics of a potential future by having participants act out a specific situation within that scenario. By assigning personas and a context, it is an incredibly effective way to uncover the unforeseen social norms, conflicts, and human experiences that a new technology or system might create.

Backcasting

This tool reverses the traditional planning process. Instead of forecasting forward from the present, it starts with a clear vision of a desirable future and then works backward in time to identify the necessary policies, milestones, and actions that must be taken to connect that future to the present.

Future-Ready Roadmapping

This tool is used to create a dynamic and adaptive strategic roadmap. Unlike a rigid, linear plan, it identifies multiple potential pathways, key decision points, and "signpost indicators" to monitor. This allows a strategy to evolve and be adjusted as the future unfolds and new information becomes available.

Horizon Scanning

...systematically search for early signals of change and potential disruptions on the horizon before they become mainstream.

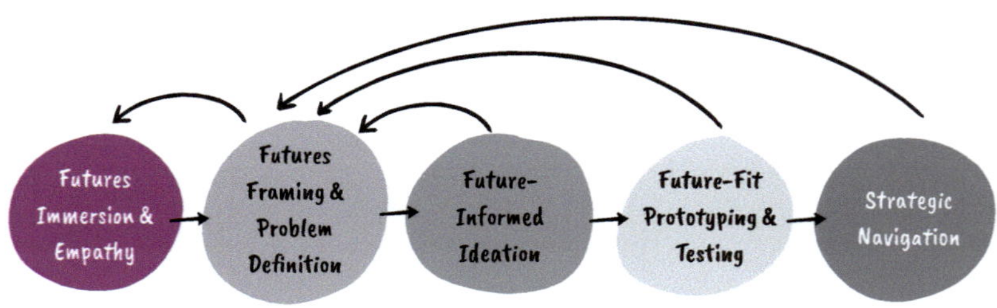

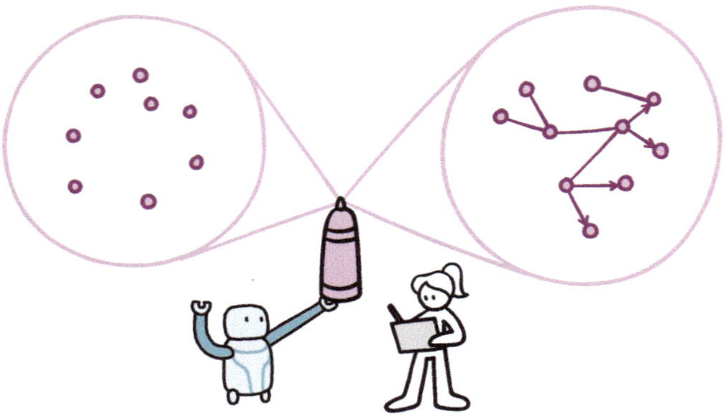

What you can do with the tool:

- Identify emerging trends and weak signals that could grow to have a significant future impact.
- Move beyond reacting to current events by proactively anticipating future developments.
- Broaden the team's perspective and challenge assumptions about what is possible or impossible.
- Gather the raw material (signals, trends, drivers of change) that will serve as the direct input for tools like **Pattern Recognition (see page 96) and the Probability/Impact Matrix (see page 94)**.
- Build a more dynamic and forward-looking awareness of the external environment.

Expert Tips

Look to the Fringes
Meaningful change rarely starts in the mainstream. To find truly novel signals, look to the "fringes," including the artists, the activists, the niche subcultures, the radical scientists, and the early-stage startups. These spaces often reveal the future first.

Curate, Do Not Just Collect
The goal is not to create an exhaustive library of everything that is happening. The real skill is in curation, which is the first step toward sensemaking. A small collection of powerful, relevant signals is far more valuable for identifying patterns than a large, noisy archive.

Make It a Continuous Practice
Habit Horizon Scanning is most effective when it is a continuous, ongoing practice, not a one-time project. Encourage a "scanning mindset," constantly looking for signals of change and bringing them back to the team. This builds a dynamic and resilient organizational awareness.

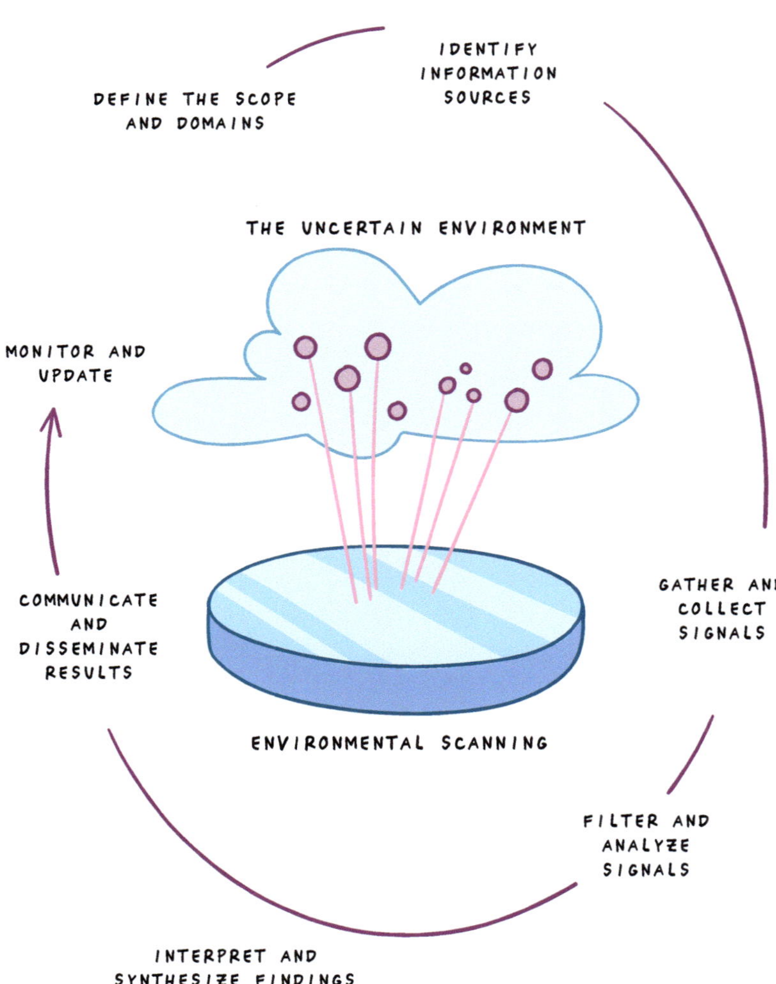

=> See **Exponential Trends Scanning (see page 286)** as a specialized variation of this tool.

Horizon Scanning is a structured process for looking beyond the immediate and familiar to identify potential future developments. It involves actively searching for signals of change across a broad landscape, often using the **PESTLE Analysis framework (see page 84)** to ensure a comprehensive scan.

Step 1: Define the Scope and Domains
First, define the scope of your scan. What is the central topic or question you are investigating? Then, identify the key domains to scan for signals. A common framework is PESTLE (Political, Economic, Sociological, Technological, Legal and Environmental), or sometimes applied as STEEP (Social, Technological, Economical, Environmental, and Political).

Step 2: Gather Signals
Systematically gather information from a wide variety of sources. Look for "weak signals," the small, early indicators of a potentially significant change not yet widely recognized. Include sources such as academic journals, patent filings, niche blogs, art projects, social media trends, and expert interviews. Collect a diverse portfolio of signals.

Step 3: Document and Assess
Document each signal clearly, noting its source and potential implications. A simple method is to use a "signal card" for each piece of information. As a team, you can then begin an initial assessment:
- Is this signal novel?
- Does it have the potential to grow?

This step turns raw data into a curated library of potential future drivers.

Stakeholder Analysis & Mapping

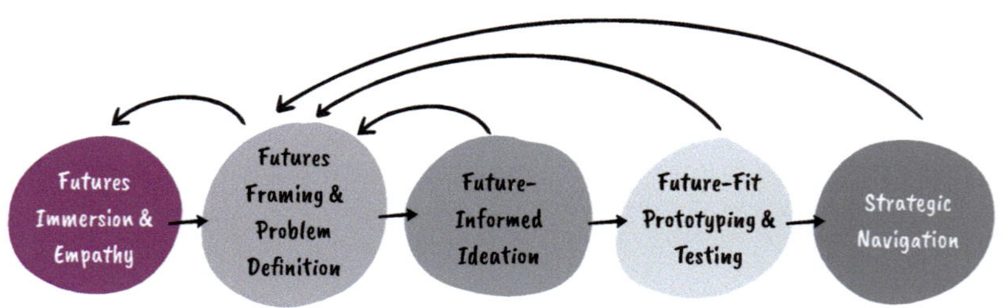

I would like to...

...identify all the actors and forces involved in our challenge and visualize their relationships and influence.

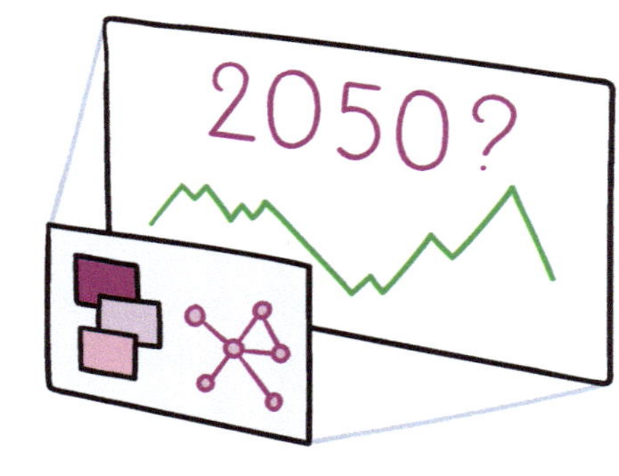

What you can do with the tool:

- Determine which stakeholders have the most power to shape future trends and outcomes related to the area of focus.
- Identify key players, including those who may be overlooked, such as non-human stakeholders (e.g., a river, a forest) or future generations.
- Understand the complex network of relationships, power dynamics, and interdependencies.
- Anticipate potential conflicts, uncover opportunities for collaboration, and identify leverage points for systemic change.
- Provide a solid foundation for building human- and life-centered solutions that consider the entire system.

Expert Tips

Give a Voice to the Voiceless
When mapping challenges related to humanity and the planet, make a deliberate effort to represent stakeholders who cannot speak for themselves. Create a persona or a set of needs for "The Ocean" or "A Future Child." This ensures that their interests are considered in the solutions you develop.

Map Flows, Not Just Connections
Elevate the map by visualizing the flows between stakeholders. Use arrows to show the direction of money, data, resources, and influence. This often reveals the underlying power dynamics and systemic incentives that are not immediately obvious and serves as a direct input for the Multi-stakeholder Value Network Mapping tool (see page 250).

Use It as a Living Document
A systems map is not a one-time exercise. It is a living document that should be updated as you learn more throughout the future thinking process. Revisit the map after building scenarios or prototypes to see how the relationships and power dynamics might shift in different futures.

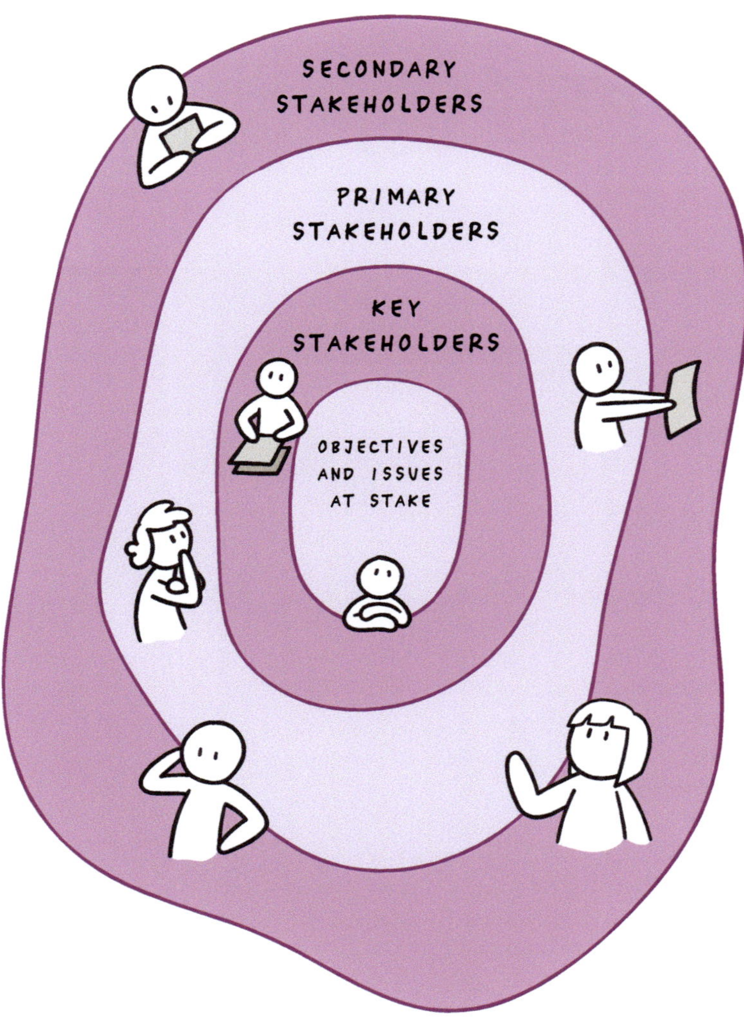

=> See **Systemic Empathy Map (see page 148)**, as stakeholder mapping is the direct prerequisite for it.

A Stakeholder & Systems Map is a visual representation of all the actors and elements connected to a particular challenge. It moves beyond a simple list to show the dynamic relationships between them.

Step 1: Brainstorm all Stakeholders

Starting, for example, with the output of a **Wicked Problem Framing (see page 152)** session, the team brainstorms all possible stakeholders. Think broadly. Include users, customers, internal teams, partners, regulators, and the community. Crucially, for a "for Humanity" approach, also include non-human or abstract stakeholders like "the planet," "local ecosystems," "future generations," or "public trust."

Step 2: Position and Map Relationships

Place your central challenge in the middle of a large canvas. Begin to position the identified stakeholders around it. You can group them by proximity or category (e.g., internal, external, public). Use lines and connectors to visualize the relationships between them. Use different line styles to represent different types of connections (e.g., solid for direct influence, dotted for indirect, lightning bolt for conflict).

Step 3: Analyze the System

With the map visualized, analyze the system as a team.
Ask key questions:
- Who holds the most influence?
- Where are the strongest alliances?
- Where are the points of tension or conflict?
- Are there any stakeholders who are isolated?
- What are the flows between them (e.g., money, data, resources)?

This analysis transforms the map from a simple diagram into a powerful strategic tool.

PESTLE Analysis

...conduct a broad scan of the macro-environmental forces that could shape our future.

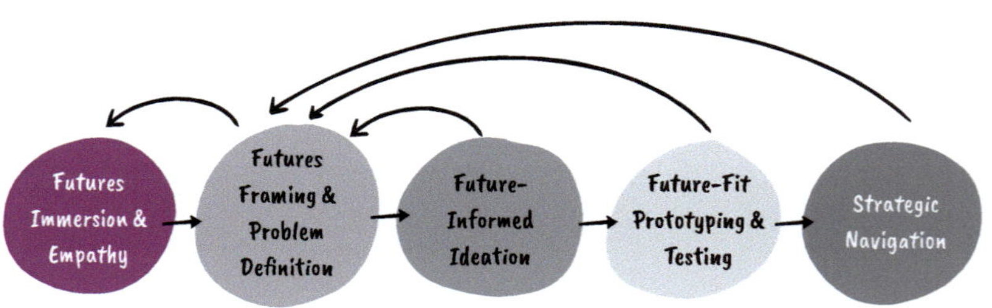

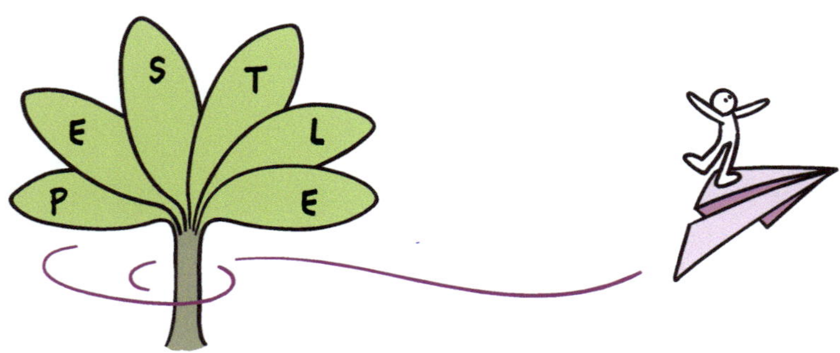

What you can do with the tool:

- Provide a structured framework for a comprehensive environmental or horizon scan.
- Ensure a balanced analysis by prompting the team to look beyond their immediate area of expertise.
- Identify large-scale drivers of change that could create future opportunities or threats.
- Understand the external context in which your organization or challenge operates.
- Gather a rich set of signals and trends to use as direct input for tools like **Pattern Recognition (see page 96)** and the **Probability/Impact Matrix (see page 94)**.

Expert Tips

Look for Interconnections

The real power of a PESTLE analysis comes not from the individual lists but from understanding the interconnections between the domains. Ask your team: how might a technological shift (e.g., AGI) create a new political challenge (e.g., job displacement policy)? These intersections are where complex future scenarios emerge.

Think Globally and Locally

When brainstorming drivers, remember to think at multiple scales. A driver can be a global geopolitical shift, a national policy change, or a local community value. Capturing this diversity will create a much richer and more realistic picture of the external environment.

Use It as a Living Framework

Treat PESTLE as a dynamic framework rather than a static, one-time exercise. Revisit it periodically to update your understanding of the macro-environment. A quick PESTLE review every six months can help your team stay attuned to the evolving landscape and avoid strategic blind spots.

P	POLITICAL
E	ECONOMIC
S	SOCIAL
T	TECHNOLOGICAL
L	LEGAL
E	ENVIRONMENTAL

PESTLE is an acronym that stands for Political, Economic, Social, Technological, Legal, and Environmental. It serves as a mnemonic to guide a comprehensive scan of the external macro environment.

Step 1: Define the Focal Question
Start with a clear question or topic at the center of your analysis. This could be a broad area like "The Future of Global Supply Chains" or a specific challenge like "Building Resilient Urban Water Systems."

Step 2: Brainstorm Drivers for Each Domain
Working as a team, brainstorm the key trends, signals, and potential future events for each of the six PESTLE domains:

Political: What is happening with government policies, geopolitical shifts, political stability, or trade regulations?

Economic: What are the key trends in economic growth, inflation, employment, or market dynamics?

Social: What are the shifts in demographics, cultural values, lifestyles, and consumer behavior?

Technological: What are the emerging technologies, new materials, or scientific breakthroughs on the horizon?

Legal: What changes in legislation, regulations, or legal frameworks could have an impact?

Environmental: What are the critical issues related to climate, ecosystems, resource availability, and sustainability?

Step 3: Analyze and Prioritize
Once the canvas is populated, discuss the most significant drivers that have been identified. The team can then use a tool like the **Probability/Impact Matrix (see page 94)** to prioritize these drivers and determine which ones warrant a deeper analysis.

Unconscious Bias Model/Analysis:

I would like to...

...identify and acknowledge the hidden mental shortcuts and stereotypes that automatically influence my perception and decisions.

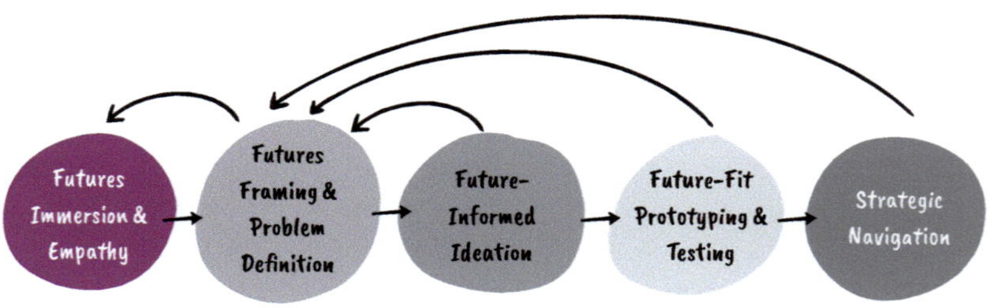

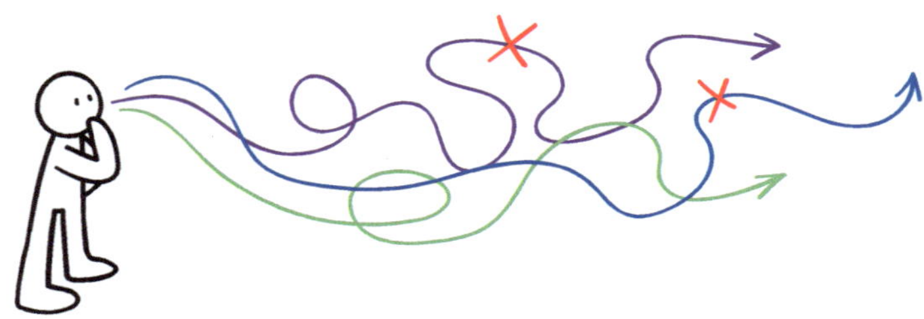

What you can do with the tool:

- Become aware of the cognitive biases that shape your interpretation of people, signals, and data.
- Foster a more inclusive and objective team environment by recognizing and mitigating stereotypes.
- Make more deliberate and fair decisions by understanding the subconscious filters you apply.
- Improve the quality of your empathy work by recognizing how your own biases can color your understanding of others.
- Lay the groundwork for more rigorous analysis by first addressing the "noise" in your own thinking.

Expert Tips

Create a Bias Checklist
Before starting a major analysis or ideation session, have the team quickly review a short checklist of the most common biases (Confirmation, Anchoring, Availability, etc.). This simple act primes everyone's awareness and makes it more likely that biases will be caught in the moment.

Diversify Your Inputs
The best way to fight bias is to diversify your sources of information. If all your signals come from the same industry reports or news outlets, your perspective will be inherently biased. Make it a rule to intentionally scan sources from different cultures, disciplines, and unconventional "fringes" of society.

Appoint a Devil's Advocate
For important decisions, formally assign one team member the role of "devil's advocate." Their job is to constructively argue against the group consensus, expose potential biases, and stress-test the team's reasoning. This makes challenging assumptions a formal part of the process, not an act of criticism.

- **Confirmation Bias**
  The tendency to favor information confirming existing beliefs can lead futures thinking practitioners to overlook signals that contradict their preferred future scenarios.

- **Availability Bias**
  Relying on easily recalled information might cause futures thinking to overemphasize recent or dramatic events, neglecting less obvious but potentially more impactful trends.

- **Anchoring Bias**
  Over-relying on initial pieces of information can skew future projections, even if that initial data is not the most relevant or accurate.

- **Optimism Bias**
  The tendency to overestimate positive outcomes and underestimate negative ones can lead to overly rosy future scenarios and a lack of preparedness for challenges.

- **Hindsight Bias**
  Believing past events were predictable can create a false sense of understanding future inevitabilities, hindering the exploration of truly novel possibilities.

- **Groupthink**
  The desire for harmony within a futures thinking team can suppress dissenting opinions and limit the consideration of diverse and challenging future perspectives.

- **Affinity Bias**
  The tendency to favor people or ideas that are similar to our own can lead to a narrow exploration of future possibilities, overlooking diverse perspectives and potentially disruptive trends.

- **Confirmation Bias**
  In futures thinking, this can manifest as seeking out and valuing only those signals and data points that reinforce pre-existing assumptions about the future, while dismissing contradictory information.

Unconscious bias refers to the automatic mental associations we make often based on stereotypes without our conscious awareness. The goal of this analysis is not to eliminate bias entirely because that is an impossible task. Instead, the objective is to become aware of these associations and mitigate their influence on our futures thinking work.

Step 1: Identify Common Biases
The first step is to build a shared vocabulary by familiarizing the team with common cognitive biases that affect foresight. These include confirmation bias, the tendency to favor information confirming existing beliefs; availability bias, relying on easily recalled information; and anchoring bias, over-relying on the first piece of information offered..

Step 2: Question First Impressions
When encountering a new idea, signal, or piece of data, consciously pause and question the team's gut reaction. Ask: "What is our immediate interpretation here? What past experiences or assumptions might be driving that initial reaction?" This deliberate pause interrupts the automatic thinking process.

Step 3: Actively Seek Alternative Perspectives
Mitigate bias effectively by deliberately engaging with different viewpoints. Actively seek out data that contradicts an initial hypothesis. Involve people from diverse backgrounds, roles, and cultures in the conversation to challenge the team's dominant perspective and uncover blind spots. A powerful way to structure this critical reflection is to apply the **Ladder of Inference (see page 88)** to deconstruct how the team is forming its conclusions.

Ladder of Inference

I would like to...

...deconstruct my thinking process, making my path from observation to conclusion transparent and open to challenge.

What you can do with the tool:

- Visualize the often-invisible mental steps that lead from data to action.
- Pinpoint the exact moments where assumptions and biases enter your reasoning process.
- Resolve team disagreements by tracing conclusions back to the specific data and interpretations they are based on.
- Improve strategic conversations by focusing them on evidence rather than on competing, unsubstantiated beliefs.
- Foster a culture of clear thinking and evidence-based reasoning within your team.

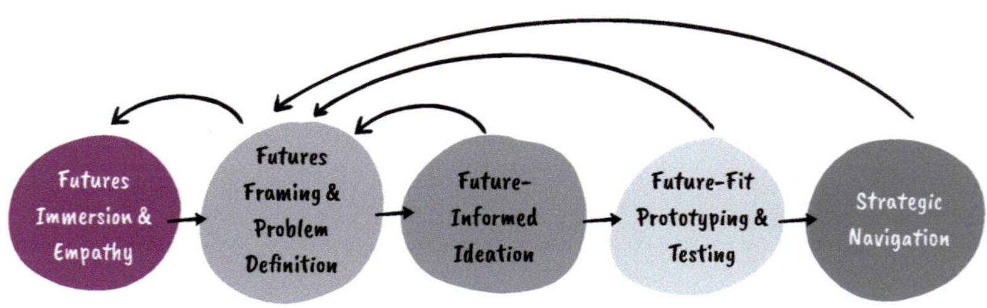

Expert Tips

Practice Walking Back Down
The most powerful use of this tool is to deconstruct an existing belief. When a strong conclusion is reached, start at the top of the ladder and walk back down. Ask: "What belief led to this action? What assumption was made? What data was focused on, and what was ignored?" This practice builds critical self-awareness.

Share Your Ladder with the Team
This tool is essential for Radical Collaboration (see page 126). In discussions, practice saying, "The data I am focusing on is X, and I am interpreting it to mean Y, which leads me to believe Z." This creates immense clarity and allows the team to build upon each other's reasoning, not just their conclusions.

Use It as a Listening Tool
When a team member presents an argument, try to map their reasoning onto the ladder. This helps to listen more deeply and to ask more precise, clarifying questions, such as, "It sounds like an assumption is being made that X is true. Can that be explored further?"

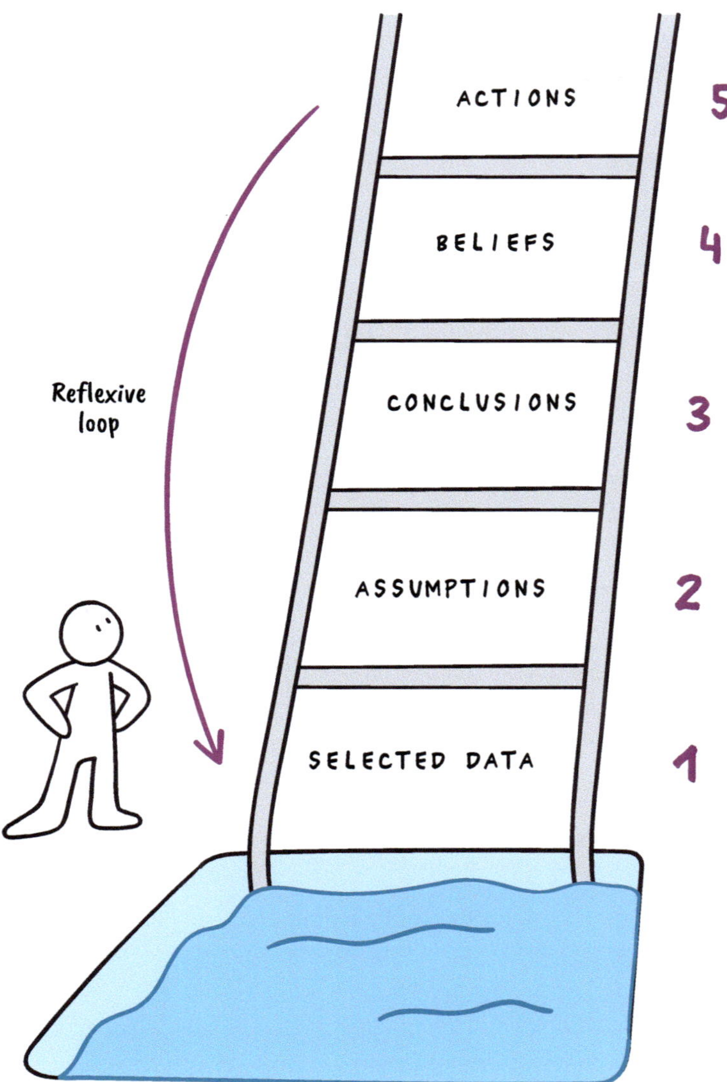

The Ladder of Inference is a model that illustrates how we move from a piece of data to a final action. By consciously walking up the rungs, we can reveal the leaps of logic and hidden assumptions that shape our decisions.

Step 1: Observe Reality and Select Data

At the bottom of the ladder is the vast pool of observable reality. From this, a small subset of data is selected for attention, often based on inherent biases and past experiences.

Step 2: Add Meaning and Make Assumptions

Movement up the ladder occurs by interpreting the selected data and assigning it a personal or cultural meaning. Based on that meaning, assumptions are then made to fill in any gaps.

Step 3: Draw Conclusions and Take Action

Finally, conclusions are drawn from these assumptions, which solidify into beliefs. These beliefs drive the resulting actions. This process creates a "reflexive loop," where beliefs at the top of the ladder influence which data is selected next time at the bottom.

Step 4: Descend the Ladder for Better Futures Thinking

To improve futures thinking, the ladder must be consciously descended by questioning conclusions about the future. The following questions can be addressed by a team:

- What future conclusions have been reached?
- How were the initial signals interpreted?
- Which signals were the primary focus?
- What underlying assumptions are being made about the future?
- What crucial signals might be missing?

This reflective process helps identify **biases (see page 86)** and builds more robust and nuanced perspectives on potential futures.

Causal Layered Analysis (CLA)

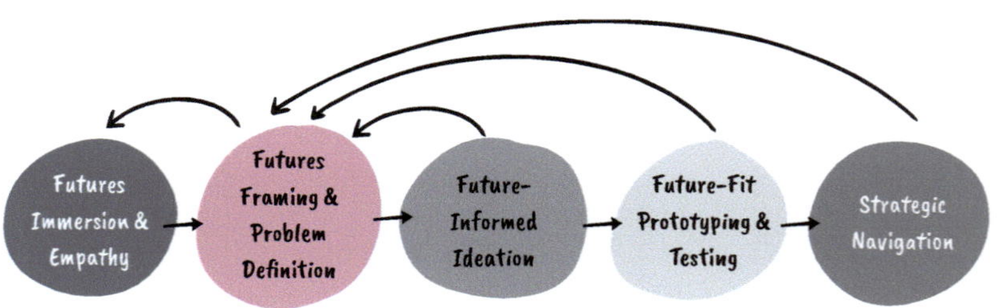

I would like to...

...move beyond surface-level problems and understand the deeper systemic, cultural, and mythic drivers that shape our future.

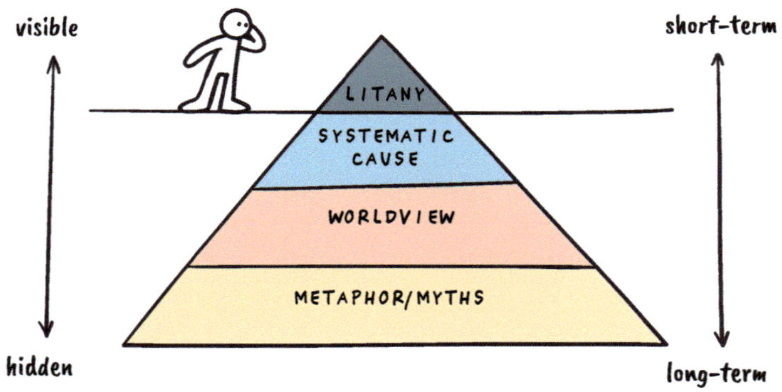

What you can do with the tool:

- Go beyond treating symptoms to identify the root causes of complex challenges.
- Expose the underlying worldviews, assumptions, and myths that limit conventional thinking and hinder transformative change.
- Develop richer, more profound future scenarios that challenge the status quo rather than just extending current trends.
- Identify deeper leverage points where interventions can have a more lasting and meaningful impact for humanity and the planet.
- Facilitate a more holistic understanding of a problem, leading to more innovative and systemic solutions.

Expert Tips

Go Beyond the Obvious
The real power of CLA is in digging below the surface. Do not stop at the systemic causes that are easy to identify. Push the team to question the underlying Worldview and the foundational myths that hold those systems in place.

Challenge the Core Myth
For challenges related to humanity and the planet, actively identify and challenge the core myth of human separation from nature. Question the worldview that prioritizes endless growth over ecological well-being.

Build a New Narrative
Use CLA not just as an analysis tool but also as a creative one. Once the old story has been deconstructed, use that insight to build a new and more resilient narrative, such as "humanity as a steward within a living system," and design the preferable future envisioned.

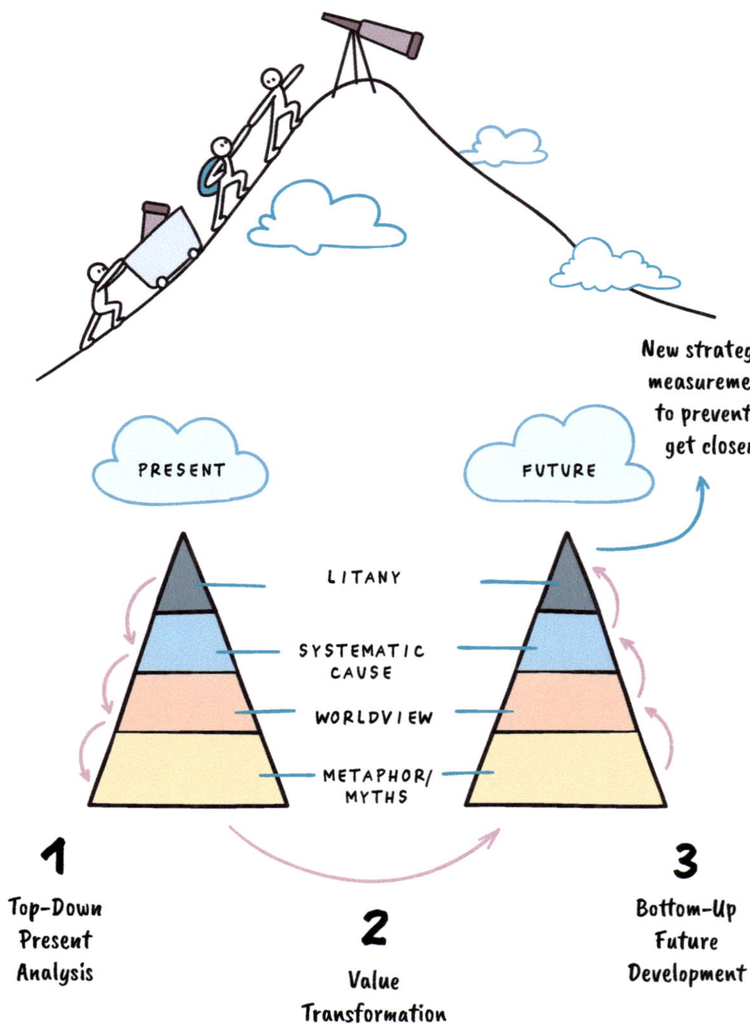

This new litany can then serve as the direct inspiration for a **Future Headline (see page 104).**

The power of Causal Layered Analysis lies in its dynamic, three-step process. It guides us to deconstruct the present down to its core, transform the foundational narrative, and then reconstruct a new, preferable future from the bottom up.

Step 1: Deconstruct the Present

The first step is to analyze the current issue by moving down through the four layers of the "Present" pyramid. This process of deconstruction helps to reveal the hidden drivers behind the obvious problems. The layers are:

- **Litany:** The surface level of the issue, for example the daily headlines, data, and events we see and hear
- **Systemic Cause:** The social, economic, and political structures that create the litany
- **Worldview:** The cultural and ideological assumptions that justify the systems
- **Metaphor/Myths:** The deep, unconscious stories that shape our collective worldview

Step 2: Transform the Core Narrative

This step involves a "value transformation" where we challenge the limiting myth or metaphor at the base of the "Present" pyramid and replace it with a new, empowering one for the "Future." For example, a metaphor of "the economy as a machine" might be transformed into "the economy as a garden" to prioritize regeneration over pure output.

Step 3: Reconstruct a Preferable Future

With a new foundational myth in place, we begin the creative process of "Bottom-Up Future Development." We build upwards through the "Future" pyramid:

- The new **Myth** inspires a new **Worldview**.
- This new worldview allows for the design of new **Systems**.
- These new systems ultimately produce a new, more desirable **Litany** of outcomes.

Scenario Planning & the 2x2 Matrix

I would like to...

...navigate an uncertain future by creating a set of distinct, plausible stories that prepare our organization for a range of possibilities.

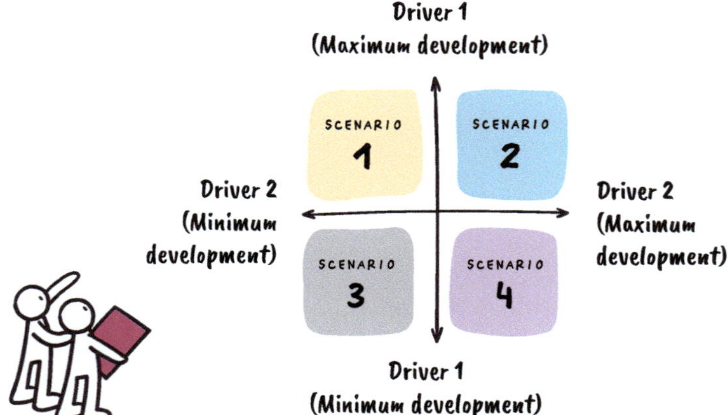

What you can do with the tool:

- Identify the most critical uncertainties that will shape the future landscape.
- Challenge "official future" thinking and expose organizational blind spots by forcing the exploration of different pathways.
- Develop more robust and resilient strategies that can be stress-tested using **Wind Tunneling (see page 110)**.
- Communicate complex future possibilities to stakeholders in a compelling, narrative format.
- Build a shared language and facilitate strategic conversations about how to prepare for long-term change.

Expert Tips

Make Your Scenarios Human
Do not let the scenarios remain abstract lists of trends. Populate each future world with "Future Personas" (see page 144). How would a specific person, such as a farmer, a city-dweller, or a community leader, experience life in this scenario? This grounds the foresight work in human reality.

Test for Resilience, Not for Accuracy
Do not aim to predict which scenario is "correct." Find real value by testing current strategies against all four of them. A truly resilient solution is viable, or at least adaptable, across multiple possible futures.

Explore the Unthinkable Quadrant
The most insightful strategic conversations often emerge from the most counter-intuitive or "unthinkable" scenario. Do not dismiss this quadrant. Pushing a team to prepare for this unexpected future is a powerful way to identify hidden assumptions and build true anti-fragility (see exponentializing, pages 40–41).

THE FUTURE OF MOBILITY?

RENEWABLE

Regulated Renaissance
- Public & Shared Transit Dominates: Cities invest heavily in high-speed rail, integrated public transport, and autonomous shared vehicle fleets.
- Strict Emissions & Zoning Laws: Urban centers have zero-emission zones, and personal car ownership is heavily taxed and restricted.

Automated Paradise
- Corporate Tech Dominance: Large technology companies operate vast fleets of autonomous, electric vehicles, competing for subscribers.
- Personalized Mobility-as-a-Service (MaaS): Individual travel is hyper-personalized with subscription models offering everything on demand.

HIGH REGULATION

LOW REGULATION

Eco-Gridlock
- Legacy Systems Endure: Cities struggle to maintain aging public transport systems while enforcing strict congestion charges.
- High Cost of Personal Mobility: Fuel taxes are extremely high, and internal combustion engine vehicles face significant tolls.

Tech-Fueled Chaos
- Hyper-Individualism Reigns: Personal ownership of fossil-fuel vehicles remains the norm, leading to extreme urban sprawl and congestion.
- Fragmented Innovation: New mobility services compete fiercely in a deregulated market, creating a chaotic and inefficient system.

FOSSIL-FUEL

Scenario Planning is a classic foresight technique that uses a structured process to transform high-level uncertainty into a set of powerful and practical narratives for strategic exploration.

Step 1: Identify and Prioritize Drivers of Change
Begin by brainstorming the key forces and trends identified during **Horizon Scanning (see page 80)** and **PESTLE Analysis (see page 84)**. Then, plot these drivers on a **2x2 Matrix** based on two factors: their potential **Impact** and their level of **Uncertainty**. The drivers that land in the top-right quadrant (High Impact, High Uncertainty) are your "critical uncertainties."

Step 2: Build the Scenario Framework
From the prioritized list, select the top two most critical uncertainties to form the axes of your scenario framework. The endpoints of each axis should represent two plausible extremes. For example, for the future of mobility, the axes could be "Level of Regulation" (High vs. Low) and "Dominant Energy Source" (Fossil-Fuel vs. Renewable). This creates a grid with four distinct and equally plausible future worlds.

Step 3: Develop the Scenarios
Bring the four quadrants to life by writing a compelling narrative for each one. Give each scenario a memorable name to make it tangible. The story should describe what that future world looks and feels like, what has happened to get there, and what its key characteristics are. These narratives can be further enriched by creating **Future Personas (see page 144)** who live within each scenario.

Probability/Impact Matrix

I would like to...

...prioritize a list of trends, signals, or potential future events to focus our attention on the most critical factors.

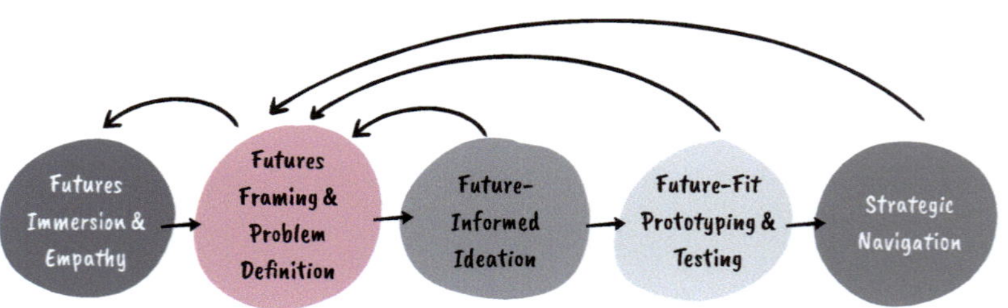

What you can do with the tool:

- Systematically assess a wide range of potential future events or trends.
- Distinguish between events that are merely interesting and those that are strategically critical.
- Create a clear, visual map for prioritizing risks and opportunities.
- Build team alignment on which uncertainties require the most attention and resources.
- Provide a rational basis for strategic decisions about where to focus deeper futures thinking activities.

Expert Tips

Focus on the "Wild Cards"
Teams often focus exclusively on high-probability events. However, the most transformative strategic insights often come from the "High Impact/Low Probability" quadrant. These are the potential wildcards. Dedicate specific time to explore these events, as they represent the kinds of disruptions that traditional planning often misses.

Define Your Scales First
Before plotting, align as a team on what "High Impact" or "Low Probability" means in a specific context. Does "High Impact" mean a significant change in human well-being or a major ecological disruption? Defining the scales up front prevents confusion and ensures a more consistent evaluation.

Use This as an Input for Scenarios
The Probability/Impact Matrix is the perfect precursor to Scenario Planning (see page 92). The "High Impact/Low Probability" events are the critical uncertainties. These prioritized factors should be used as the axes for a scenario framework to ensure the stories about the future are focused on the drivers that matter most.

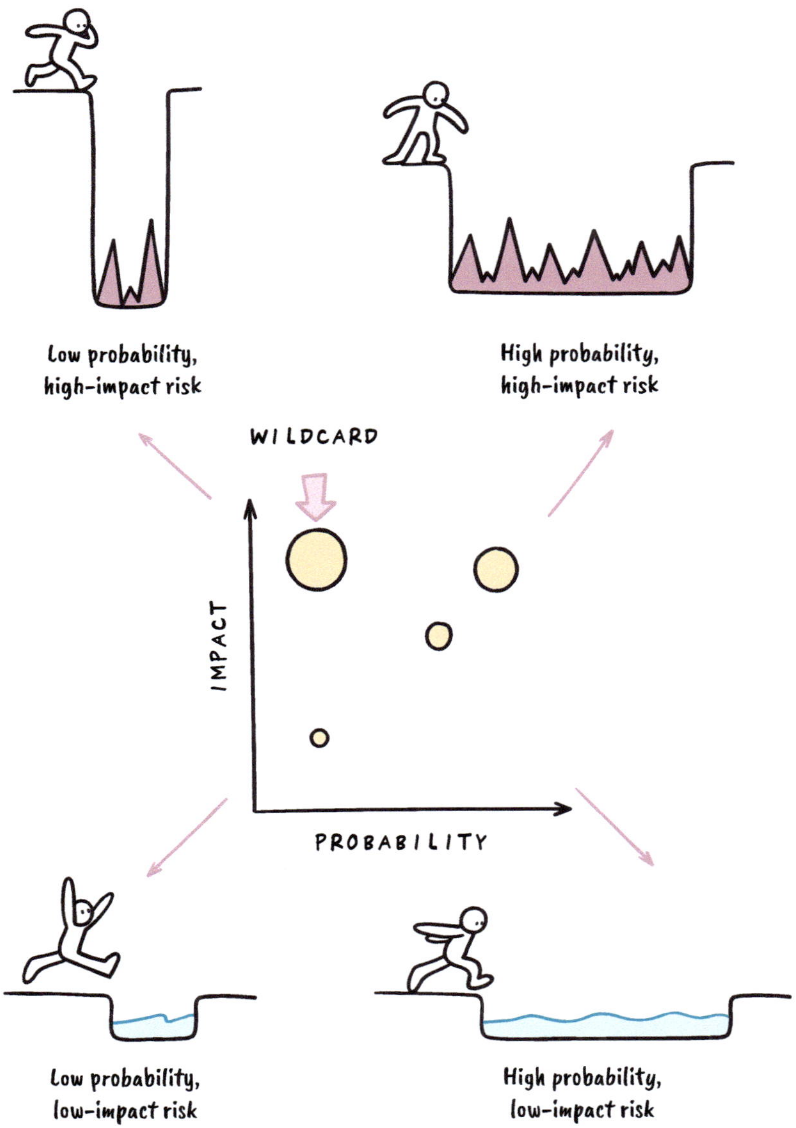

The Probability/Impact Matrix is a fundamental tool for sorting through the noise of the future. It helps a team move from a long list of possibilities to a focused set of high-priority items that warrant further investigation.

Step 1: Brainstorm Potential Events and Trends

As a team, generate a comprehensive list of potential future events, signals, or trends relevant to the topic. The source of these should be the outputs from a **Horizon Scanning (see page 84)** or **PESTLE Analysis (see page 80)** activity. Aim for quantity at this stage.

Step 2: Assess Probability and Impact

For each item on your list, assess two key dimensions:

- **Probability:** How likely is this event or trend to occur within your defined timeframe (e.g., on a scale from Low to High)?
- **Impact:** If it were to occur, what would be the magnitude of its impact on your organization, project, or community (e.g., on a scale from Low to High)?

Step 3: Map the Items onto the Matrix

Place each item onto the 2x2 matrix according to its assessed probability and impact. This will visually sort your list into four distinct quadrants.

Step 4: Prioritize and Define Action

Categorize the items mapped onto the matrix into clear strategic groups.

- **High Impact/High Probability:** Critical priorities that require immediate strategic planning.
- **High Impact/Low Probability:** "Wildcards" or potential "black swans" that need to be monitored and considered in scenario planning.
- **Low Impact/High Probability:** Nuisances that may require monitoring or minor adaptation but are not strategic priorities.
- **Low Impact/Low Probability:** Items that can be safely ignored for now, freeing up mental and strategic resources.

Pattern Recognition

I would like to...

...make sense of diverse and seemingly disconnected information by identifying meaningful themes, connections, and relationships.

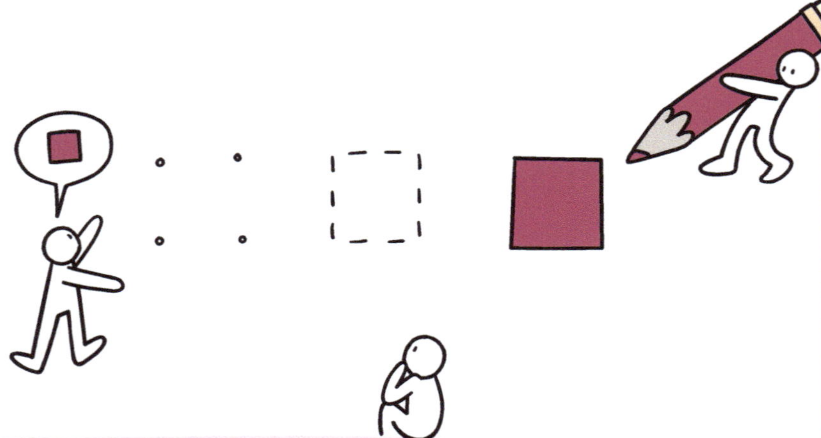

What you can do with the tool:

- Transform a chaotic collection of individual signals and trends into a set of coherent, underlying patterns.
- Uncover deeper systemic shifts that are not obvious from any single piece of information.
- Move from simply collecting data to generating genuine foresight about where the world is heading.
- Create a solid foundation for more advanced foresight activities, such as **Causal Layered Analysis (see page 90) and Scenario Planning (see page 92)**.
- Build a shared understanding within a team about the key dynamics shaping the future.

Expert Tips

Look for Tensions and Contradictions
Patterns are not always simple trends. Some of the most valuable insights come from identifying tensions in the data. Exploring the dynamic between conflicting signals is often more insightful than analyzing either one in isolation.

Combine, Do Not Just Categorize
Avoid simply putting signals into neat boxes. Discover emergent patterns by creating novel connections between seemingly disparate pieces of information. Ask, "What is the relationship between this technological trend and that social value shift?"

Visualize Your Patterns
Do not let patterns remain as text on a page. Create a visual "pattern map" or "constellation diagram" that shows how the signals connect into larger themes. This makes the relationships easier to understand, communicate, and use for building scenarios.

EXAMPLE: CLUSTERING SIGNALS FOR THE "FUTURE OF FOOD"

Signal A: A startup successfully 3D-prints a nutritionally complete, plant-based steak.

Signal B: A report shows rising consumer demand for food supply chains traced via blockchain.

Signal C: A popular documentary criticizes the environmental and ethical costs of industrial animal farming.

Signal D: Venture capital funding for cellular agriculture (lab-grown meat) has tripled in the past year.

Signal E: A social media trend involves influencers sharing their personal "food carbon footprint" scores.

Signal F: Gene-editing technology is being used to create hyper-efficient, drought-resistant crops.

Cluster 1: The Bio-Convergence of Food
This pattern connects the signals related to the technological reinvention of food production.
=> **Included Signals: A, D, F**
=> **Nascent Pattern:** Technology is fundamentally reshaping what food is and how it is made, moving production from the farm to the lab.

Cluster 2: The Rise of the Conscious Consumer
This pattern connects signals related to a shift in consumer values and awareness.
=> **Included Signals: B, C, E**
=> **Nascent Pattern:** Consumers are increasingly making purchasing decisions based on ethical, environmental, and health-related data, not just on taste or price.

Pattern recognition is the essential process of synthesis that turns the raw information from **Horizon Scanning (see page 80)** into strategic foresight. It involves a systematic search for connections and recurring themes among the collected signals.

Step 1: Immerse in the Data
Gather all the signals, trends, and data points the team has collected and display them in a shared space, such as a physical wall or a digital whiteboard. Allow the team time to individually and collectively immerse themselves in the information without immediately trying to find answers.

Step 2: Cluster and Theme
Begin to group related items together. Look for affinities, direct connections, or recurring ideas. These initial groupings are the nascent patterns. Give each cluster a descriptive name or theme that captures its essence, for example, "Decentralization of Trust" or "The Rise of Regenerative Materials."

Step 3: Articulate the Pattern
For each major cluster, articulate the deeper pattern it represents. A pattern is more than just a summary; it is an insight into a significant, underlying shift. Describe what is happening, why it is happening, and what its potential implications are. This transforms a simple collection of signals into a powerful piece of strategic intelligence.

Sensemaking

I would like to...

...interpret ambiguous, complex information and patterns to create a coherent and shared understanding of what the future might hold.

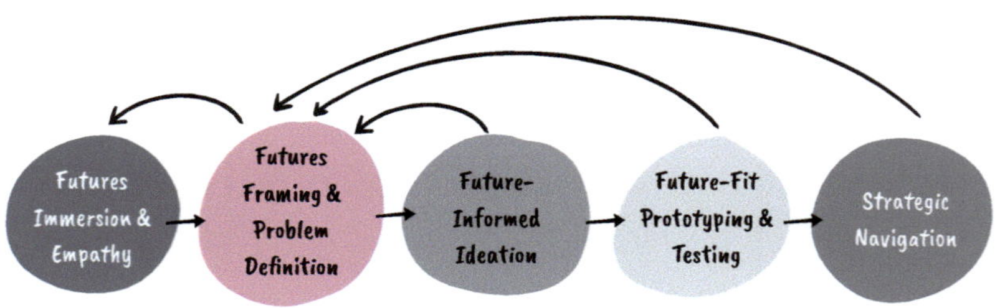

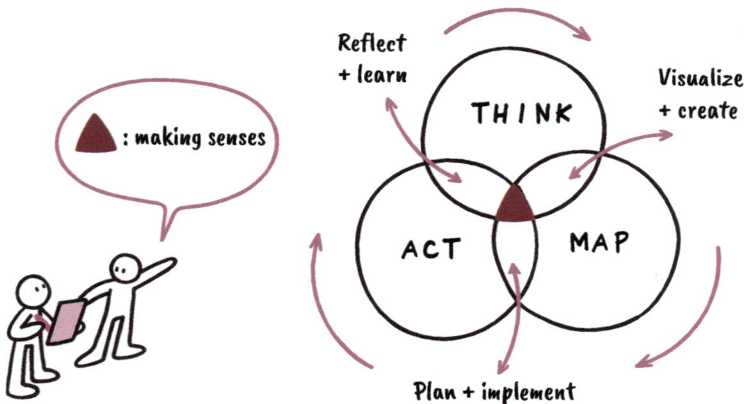

What you can do with the tool:

- Transform complex data and abstract patterns into meaningful strategic narratives.
- Frame and contextualize foresight work to ensure its relevance and impact.
- Move from simply identifying "what" is happening to understanding the deeper "so what?" for an organization and community.
- Create the essential bridge between the analysis from **Pattern Recognition (see page 96)** and the creative work of **Scenario Planning (see page 92)**.
- Align a team around a shared story of the future, enabling more effective and coordinated strategic action.

Expert Tips

Make It a Dialogue, Not a Monologue

Sensemaking is a collaborative act. Avoid having a single person or a small group create the "official" interpretation. Use workshops and interactive sessions where the entire team can contribute to building the narrative together. The best insights often emerge from the dialogue and debate.

Combine, Do Not Just Categorize

There is rarely a single, correct interpretation of a complex future pattern. Encourage the team to explore multiple plausible meanings. What if this trend is not a threat but an opportunity? What if two conflicting patterns are actually two sides of the same coin? This builds strategic flexibility.

From Sensemaking to Storytelling

The output of sensemaking is a powerful story. Turn this story into a tangible artifact, such as a short presentation, a visual map, or a one-page summary. Storytelling is the most effective way to communicate the complex implications of foresight work and to align decision-makers around a shared vision of the future.

Sensemaking is the critical process of creating shared meaning from the patterns you have identified. It is less a single action and more a collaborative effort to narrate and contextualize complex information, turning foresight into insight.

Step 1: Frame the Narrative

Start with the key patterns and themes identified during **Pattern Recognition (see page 96)**. For each one, begin to construct a narrative by asking: What is the story here? How did this pattern emerge, and where might this be leading? Frame the information in a way that is relevant to the core challenge.

Step 2: Contextualize the Meaning

Place the narrative into a broader context. How does this story connect to the needs of the stakeholders, the goals of the organization, or the well-being of the planet? This step ensures the interpretation is not just an interesting observation but a strategically relevant insight.

Step 3: Articulate the Implications

The final step is to clearly articulate the "so what." Based on the narrative, what are the key implications, challenges, and opportunities for the future? This creates a clear and compelling understanding that can directly inform the development of scenarios, strategies, and new ideas.

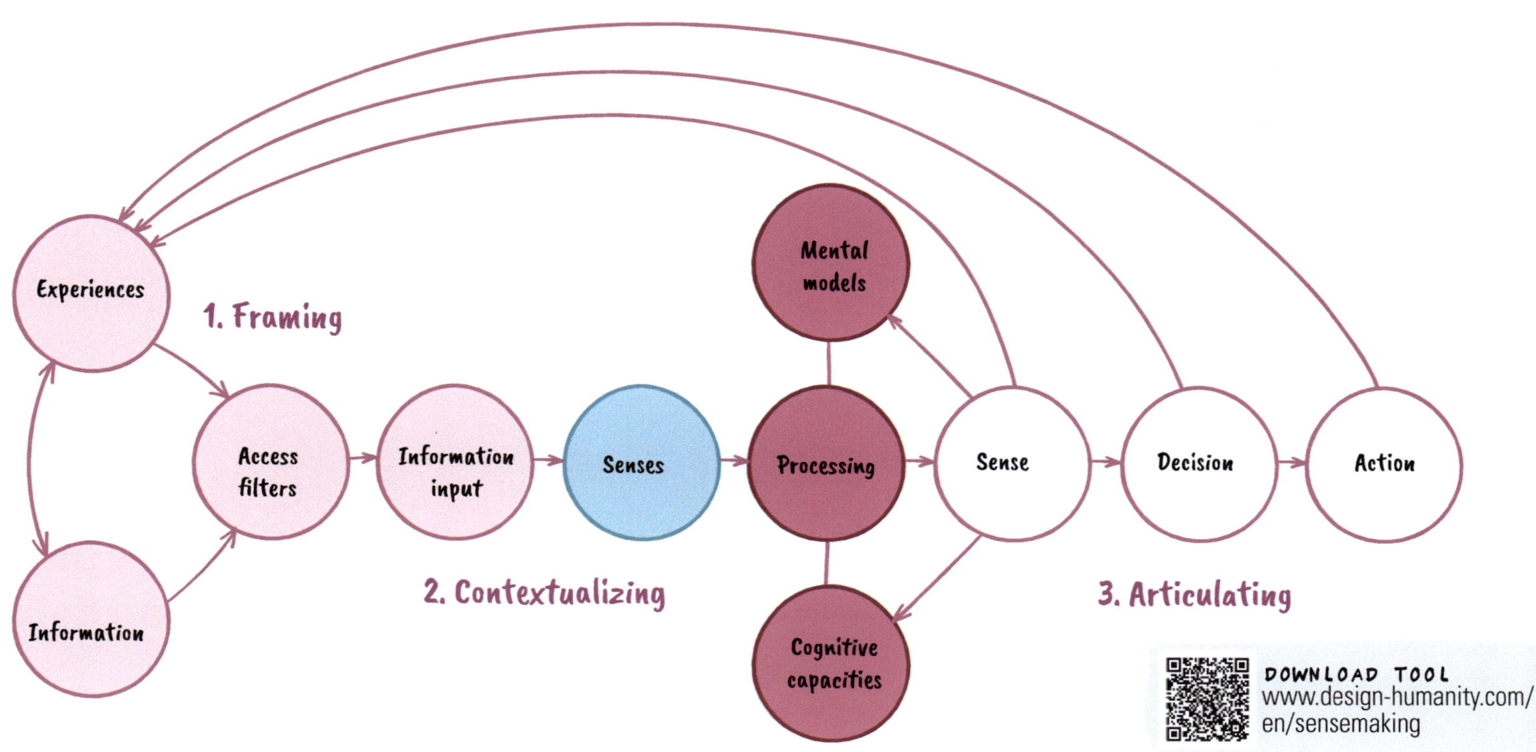

Futures Wheel

I would like to…

…systematically explore the direct and indirect consequences of a future change to uncover hidden opportunities and risks.

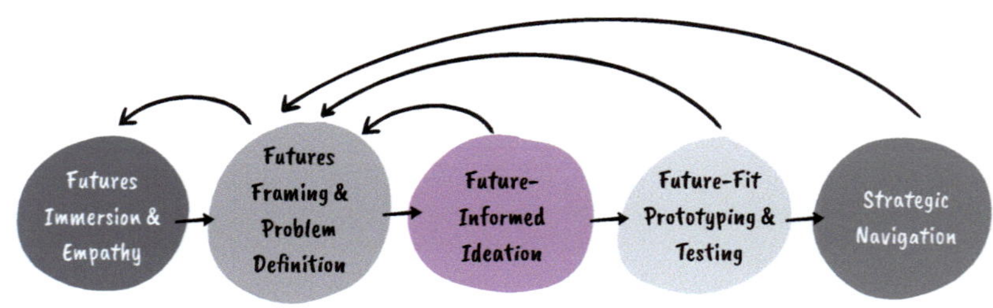

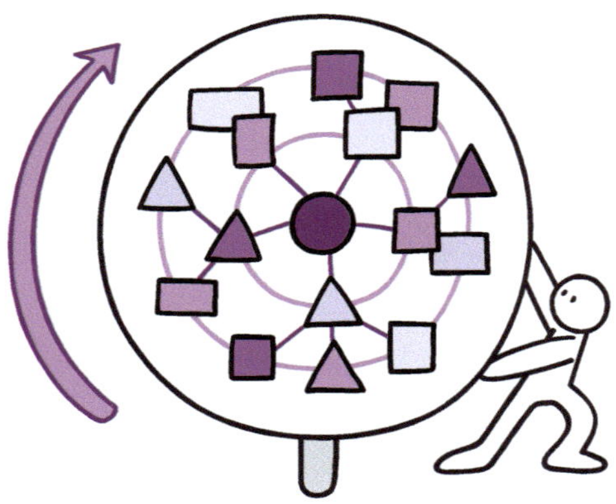

What you can do with the tool:

- Move beyond first-order thinking to map the cascading, ripple-effect impacts of a trend or event.
- Identify unexpected connections and second- or third-order consequences that are not immediately obvious.
- Stimulate creative thinking by revealing unforeseen challenges that require innovative solutions.
- Facilitate a structured and comprehensive brainstorming session about the future implications of a change.
- Build a deeper and more systemic understanding of how a single trend can reshape an entire system.

Expert Tips

Look for Opportunities in the Consequences
The goal is not just to map problems. Every consequence, especially in the second and third rings, is a potential area for innovation. A consequence like "decline of rural farming communities" can be reframed as a **"How Might We"** question to spark new ideas.

Balance Positive and Negative Paths
A common pitfall is to focus only on dystopian or negative consequences. Intentionally push the team to explore positive ripple effects as well. A balanced view that considers both opportunities and threats will lead to more robust and realistic insights.

Use It to Test a Desired Future
Do not just use the wheel for external trends. Place a proposed solution or a **"Future Headline" (see page 104)** in the center. Exploring the full spectrum of its potential consequences is a powerful way to stress-test an idea and is a foundational practice for the **Ethical Consequences Scanner (see page 162).**

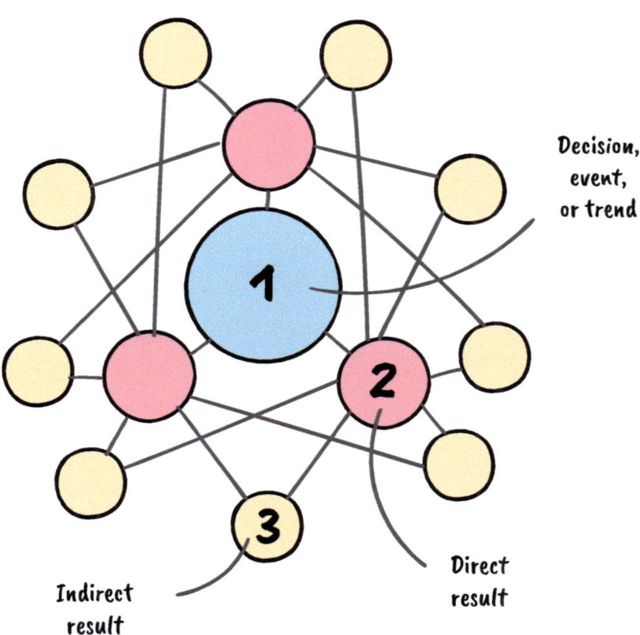

Example consequences:
Consequence Path 1: The Nature of Work

Consequence Path 2: Social Structure & Communication

Consequence Path 3: The Human Experience

DOWNLOAD TOOL
www.design-humanity.com/
en/futures-wheel

The futures wheel is a visual brainstorming tool that helps a team map the cascading consequences of a future event. It encourages a structured exploration of what might happen next.

Step 1: Define the Central Event
Place the specific future trend, event, or change you want to explore in the center of a large canvas. Be as precise as possible.

Example Step 1: "By 2040, Brain-Computer Interfaces (BCIs) are widely adopted, co-existing with the emergence of artificial general intelligence (AGI)."

Step 2: Brainstorm First-Order Consequences
As a team, brainstorm the direct, immediate consequences of the central event. These are the "if-then" results. Write each consequence on a sticky note and place it in a circle around the central idea, connecting them with lines.

Example first-order consequence: "If everyone has a BCI, **then** communication becomes instantaneous and telepathic."

Example first-order consequence: "If AGI and BCIs co-exist, **then** human intelligence is seamlessly augmented with machine intelligence."

Step 3: Explore Second- and Third-Order Consequences
For each first-order consequence, repeat the process. Ask, "If this happens, what happens next?" This will reveal the second-order consequences. Repeat the process again for the most significant second-order impacts to uncover the third-order consequences. This outward expansion reveals the full ripple effect of the initial change.

Example second-order consequence (from "telepathic communication"): "If communication is telepathic, **then** the concept of personal privacy is fundamentally redefined."

Example third-order consequence (from "redefined privacy"): "If privacy is redefined, **then** new social norms and legal frameworks must be created to govern 'thought crime' and mental autonomy."

Creative Mash-Up

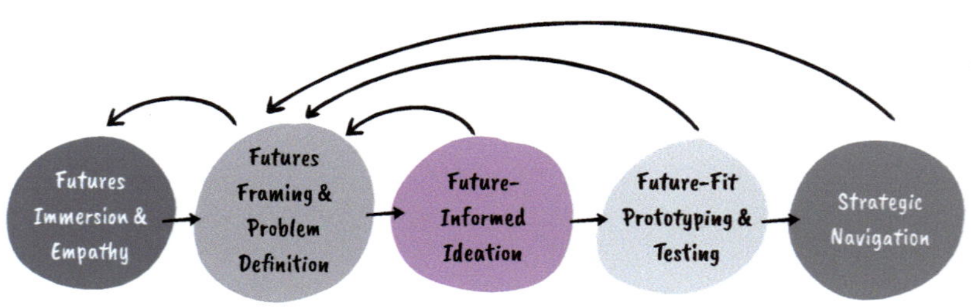

I would like to...

...spark novel ideas by forcing the combination of two or more unrelated concepts.

What you can do with the tool:

- Break free from conventional thinking and incremental improvements.
- Generate a high volume of unexpected and original ideas in a short amount of time.
- Systematically explore new possibilities at the intersection of different domains.
- Create a playful and energetic atmosphere that encourages creative risk-taking.
- Develop future-ready concepts by combining current needs with future trends.

Expert Tips

Embrace the Absurd
Not every mash-up will lead to a viable idea, which remains the point. Some of the most absurd combinations can unlock the most creative thinking. Do not discard a pairing because it seems strange. Lean into the absurdity and see what unexpected ideas it sparks.

Use Visuals for Your Lists
Instead of just using words for the two lists, use images. For "Core Human Needs," use evocative photos. For "Future Trends," use futuristic illustrations. This will make the mash-up process more creative and less analytical.

Reverse the Mash-Up
If a team gets stuck, reverse the prompt. Instead of asking what product combines "Safety" and "Ubiquitous AI," ask: "In a world with 'Ubiquitous AI,' how would the fundamental human need for 'Safety' be completely redefined?" This shift in perspective can lead to deeper, more systemic innovations.

The creative mash-up is a powerful ideation technique that operates on the principle that innovation often emerges from combining existing elements in new ways. In a futures context, it involves a structured collision of ideas to generate unique concepts.

Step 1: Create Two Distinct Lists

On a large canvas, create two columns.

- **Column A: Core Human & Planetary Needs.** List fundamental and timeless needs. These could be derived from empathy work or frameworks like the **Social Foundation (see page 204)** from the Doughnut Economics model (e.g., "Belonging," "Safety," "Clean Water," "Biodiversity").

- **Column B: Future Trends & Technologies.** List the speculative trends and technologies identified during **Horizon Scanning (see page 80)** or **Exponential Trends Scanning (see page 286)** (e.g., "Ubiquitous AI," "Circular Economies," "Synthetic Biology").

Step 2: Force Random Combinations

Systematically or randomly, draw a line connecting one item from Column A to one item from Column B. The goal is to create an unexpected pairing. For example, connect "Belonging" with "Synthetic Biology," or "Safety" with "Ubiquitous AI."

Step 3: Brainstorm the Mash-Up

For each pairing, use it as a creative prompt for a short, focused brainstorm. Ask the team: "What kind of product, service, or experience could exist at the intersection of these two concepts?" For "Belonging + Synthetic Biology," ideas might include bio-luminescent tattoos that change color when near a friend or a community garden that grows a unique, shared food source.

Future Headline

I would like to...

...use a compelling future vision as a direct prompt for generating innovative ideas.

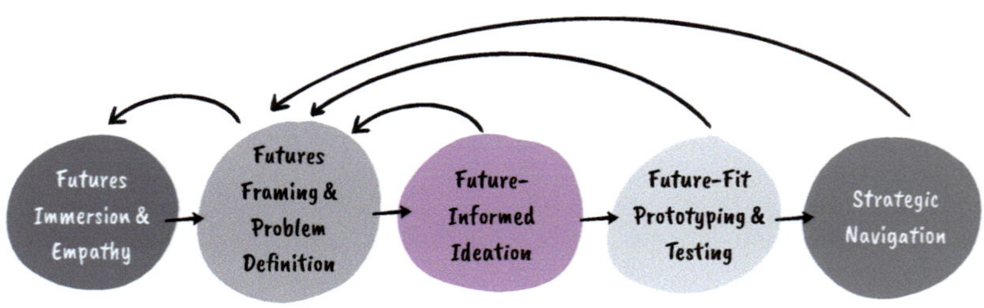

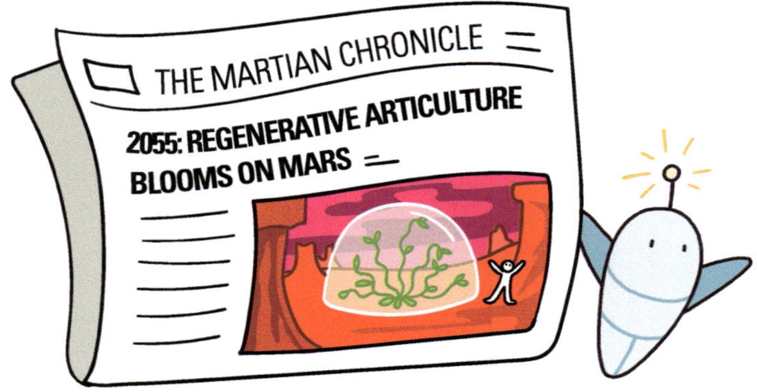

What you can do with the tool:

- Bridge the gap between abstract future scenarios and concrete ideation.
- Generate "breakthrough" ideas by starting with a successful outcome and working backward.
- Create a powerful and memorable vision that aligns and energizes a team.
- Encourage creative, narrative-based thinking rather than purely analytical brainstorming.
- Provide a clear and tangible focal point for an entire innovation project.

Expert Tips

Make It Tangible

Do not just write the headline on a sticky note. Design a realistic front page of a newspaper or a screenshot of a news website from the future. The more tangible and believable the artifact is, the more powerful it will be as a creative prompt.

Write from Different Perspectives

To generate a wider range of ideas, create multiple headlines about the same future event from different perspectives. What would the headline be in a mainstream newspaper versus a niche industry journal or a skeptical blog? Each perspective will uncover different aspects of the future being explored.

Combine with Other Tools

Use a powerful headline as the central event for a futures wheel (see page 100). This allows for the exploration of not only the positive innovations that led to the headline but also the potential second- and third-order consequences, both positive and negative, that might result from that success.

Step 1: Envision a preferable future

Ambitious success/preferable future
(align with Vision Cone)

Step 2: Write
the headline

Step 3: Brainstorm
the backstory

FUTURE-INFORMED IDEAS

Future Headlines is a creative technique that reverses the typical brainstorming process. Instead of starting with a problem and generating ideas, you start with a headline from a future where a major, positive outcome has already been achieved.

Step 1: Envision a Preferable Future

Based on the foresight work, envision a bold and ambitious success for the project, community, or for humanity. This should be a significant achievement that aligns with the "preferable future" identified in the **Vision Cone (see page 61).**

Step 2: Write the Headline

As a team, write a clear, compelling, and specific news headline that announces this future success. The headline should be dated 5, 10, or even 20+ years in the future.

For example: "Global Literacy Rate Reaches 99% as AI Tutors Become Freely Accessible to All" or "Amazon Rainforest Deforestation Reversed for the First Time in a Century" or "Regenerative Agriculture Blooms on Mars."

Step 3: Brainstorm the "Backstory"

With the headline as your endpoint, brainstorm the "story behind the story." Ask the team:

- What innovations, products, or services had to be created for this headline to be true?
- What social or behavioral shifts occurred?
- What new business models or policies were implemented? The answers to these questions are your future-informed ideas.

DOWNLOAD TOOL
www.design-humanity.com/en/future-headline

Object from the Future

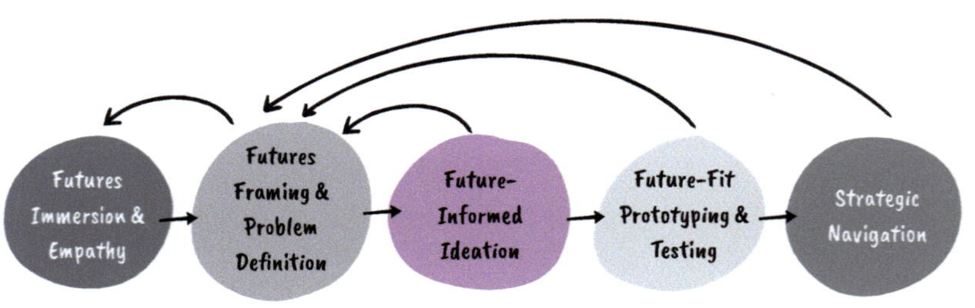

I would like to...

...make a future scenario tangible and explore its implications through a physical or digital artifact.

What you can do with the tool:

- Transform abstract future concepts into concrete, relatable objects.
- Spark deep, empathetic conversations about the human experience in a potential future.
- Test the implications of a future scenario in a hands-on, experiential way.
- Unlock novel ideas by focusing on the details of how an object would be designed and used in a different world.
- Create a powerful storytelling artifact that communicates a future vision more effectively than words alone.

Expert Tips

Focus on the Story, Not the Technology

Do not aim to accurately predict future technology. Find value in the story the object tells about the people and the culture of its time. An object that reveals a new social norm or a shift in human values is often more insightful than one that simply showcases futuristic tech.

Use the Object as an Interview Prompt

The artifact you create is a powerful research tool. Present your "object from the future" to stakeholders or users and ask them to interact with it. Ask questions like, "What do you think this is? Who would use it? What does it tell you about the world it came from?" Their reactions will provide rich insights into the desirability of your envisioned future.

Prototype the "Negative" Object

To explore potential dystopian futures or unintended consequences, try creating an object that represents a negative outcome. An artifact like a "personal carbon-rationing card" or a "social credit score statement" can provoke powerful conversations about the kind of future we want to avoid and, therefore, what we must do in the present to steer away from it.

What if this object, which offers perfect convenience, has an unintended consequence that erodes a fundamental human skill or freedom (e.g., the ability to navigate, to remember, or to be truly alone)?

What if this object solves our current planetary waste problem but, in doing so, creates a new and unforeseen ecological dependency that is even more fragile?

What if this object can only exist in an economic model that is not based on individual ownership or exponential growth but on shared access and regeneration?

What if this object, designed to connect humanity in a deeper way, accidentally creates a new and more profound kind of social divide between those who embrace it and those who refuse it?

What if this object is a symbol of a future that has successfully achieved resilience, and what difficult but necessary trade-offs about our present-day lives does its existence force us to confront?

Object from the Future is a creative prototyping method that challenges a team to design and create a tangible artifact that would exist in a specific future scenario. This moves ideation from the conceptual to the concrete.

Step 1: Choose a Future Scenario
Select one of the compelling future scenarios you developed during your **Scenario Planning (see page 92)** activity. Be clear about the key characteristics and rules of this future world.

Step 2: Brainstorm an Everyday Object
As a team, brainstorm a list of common, everyday objects that a **Future Persona (see page 144)** would interact with (e.g., a food package, a child's toy, a medical device). Select one object that would likely be significantly different in the chosen future.

Step 3: Design and Prototype the Future Object
Create a low-fidelity prototype of the chosen object as it would exist in the future scenario. Do not just focus on aesthetics; consider the entire user experience. What materials is it made from? What information does it display? What does its use imply about the values and economy of that future? For example, a food package from a "circular economy" future might be edible or made from self-composting materials.

Step 4: Ask "What if" Questions
Use the object as a prompt to ask deep, critical questions about the systemic implications of that future. The powerful "what if" questions explore the deeper consequences and the impact on the system-of-systems.

Experiential Futures

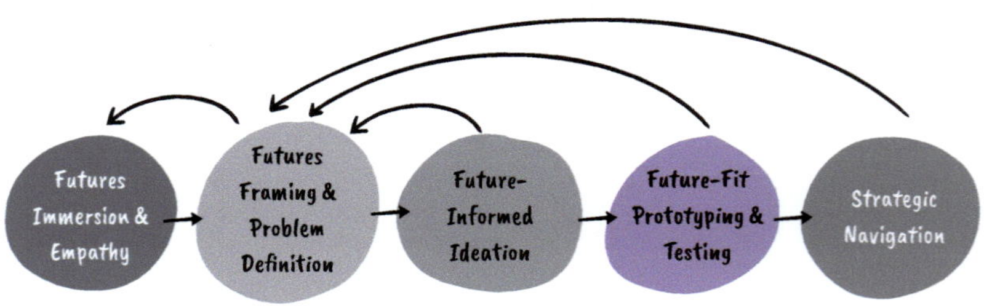

I would like to...

...move beyond just describing a future and create an immersive experience that allows people to "feel" what it might be like to live there.

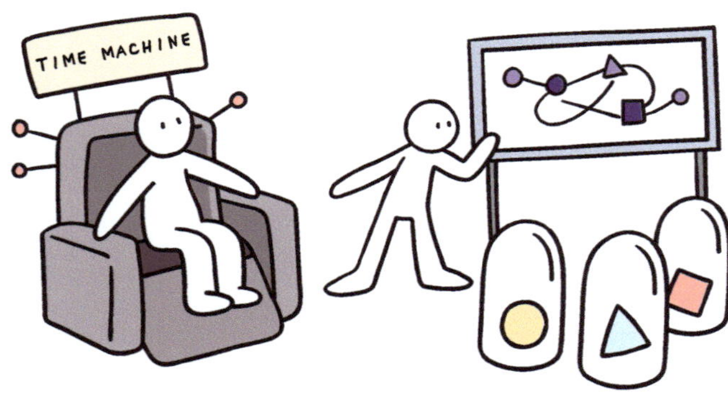

What you can do with the tool:

- Make abstract future scenarios tangible, emotional, and memorable for stakeholders.
- Generate deep, empathetic insights by observing how people react and behave within a simulated future environment.
- Test the human and social implications of a future concept, not just its technical feasibility.
- Facilitate more profound and meaningful conversations about the kind of future we want to create or avoid.
- Create powerful storytelling artifacts that communicate a future vision far more effectively than a report or presentation.

Expert Tips

Engage All the Senses
The most powerful experiential futures are multisensory. Do not just focus on what people will see. Consider the sounds, smells, and even the tastes of the future being prototyped. A simple audio track or a specific scent can make the experience dramatically more immersive.

Prototype the Mundane
While it is tempting to create spectacular, high-tech artifacts, some of the most profound insights come from prototyping the mundane objects of a future world. A receipt, a bus ticket, or a piece of junk mail from the future can reveal more about its underlying values and systems than a shiny gadget.

Use It for Co-creation
Do not just use the experience as a test. Use it as a platform for co-creation. After the initial immersion, invite participants to modify the artifacts or create new ones that would improve their experience. This turns the audience into active collaborators in the design of a preferable future.

Experiential Futures is a prototyping method that uses tangible artifacts and immersive scenarios to bring a potential future to life. It shifts the focus from talking about the future to experiencing a piece of it directly.

Step 1: Choose a Scenario and a Human Context
Select a specific future scenario developed during **Scenario Planning**. Then, define a relatable human context within that future, such as "a family grocery shopping trip in a world of personalized nutrition" or "a student's first day at a university without physical classrooms."

Step 2: Create the "Artifacts from the Future"
Brainstorm and create the tangible objects that would exist in this context, using the **Object from the Future (see page 106)** tool. These artifacts are the prototypes. They could be physical, like a "carbon ration card," or digital, like a simulated user interface for a future service.

Step 3: Stage the Immersive Experience
Set up an environment where participants can interact with the future artifacts in a simulated scenario. This can be as simple as a tabletop display or as complex as a fully staged room. Guide participants through the experience, encouraging them to think aloud and react naturally. The goal is to observe their authentic behaviors and emotional responses.

Example Prototypes for "Object from the Future"

1. Paper Prototypes of a "Digital Twin" Interface: A series of hand-drawn sketches showing the user interface for a city-management dashboard that allows citizens to see the real-time health of their local ecosystem (e.g., air quality, water levels, biodiversity) and vote on environmental policies.

2. A "Personal Carbon Currency" Wallet (Mock-Up): A physical, 3D-printed mock-up of a personal device, similar to a credit card or mobile phone, that displays a user's daily "carbon budget" and shows how different lifestyle choices create debits and credits.

3. An "Edible Food Packaging" Sample: A real, tangible prototype of a food wrapper made from a seaweed or plant-based polymer. The prototype is not just compostable but also safe and nutritious to eat, demonstrating a future without single-use plastic waste.

4. A "De-Extinction" Educational Toy (Storyboard): A visual storyboard, like a comic strip, that illustrates how a child would interact with a future toy. The story shows the child caring for a digital habitat to "bring back" an extinct species, teaching concepts of ecological stewardship.

5. A "Post-Growth" Corporate Annual Report (PDF): A professionally designed, multipage PDF of an annual report for a major corporation from the year 2050. The report's key success metrics are not profit and growth but "Regenerative Impact," "Employee Well-Being," and "Community Resilience."

6. A "Modular, Repairable Smartphone" (Physical Model): A physical, nonfunctional model made of simple, snap-together components (camera, battery, screen). This prototype demonstrates a future based on a circular economy, challenging the concept of disposable electronics.

7. A "BCI-Powered Empathy" Headset (Role-Playing Script): A short script for a role-playing scenario where one person acts as a conflict mediator using a mock-up headset. The script guides them to describe what it feels like to briefly experience the emotional perspective of the other person.

8. A "Democratic AI" Governance Interface (Interactive Mock-Up): A simple, clickable digital prototype of a voting interface. The mock-up allows users to simulate providing input on the ethical rules and priorities governing a public AI system, like an autonomous public transport network.

9. A "Cross-Generational Storytelling" Device (Audio Prototype): A short audio file that simulates the experience of using a simple, screen-less device. The audio prototype would feature a child's voice asking a question, a pause, and then the voice of an elderly relative telling a story in response.

10. A "Future of Work" Employment Contract (Document): A one-page employment contract from the year 2045. The document's terms would reflect a future of work dominated by AI and automation, with clauses not for a "job" but for "lifelong learning contributions," "creative output," and a "guaranteed basic income."

Wind Tunneling

I would like to...

...test the resilience of our current strategies, products, or ideas against a range of different future scenarios.

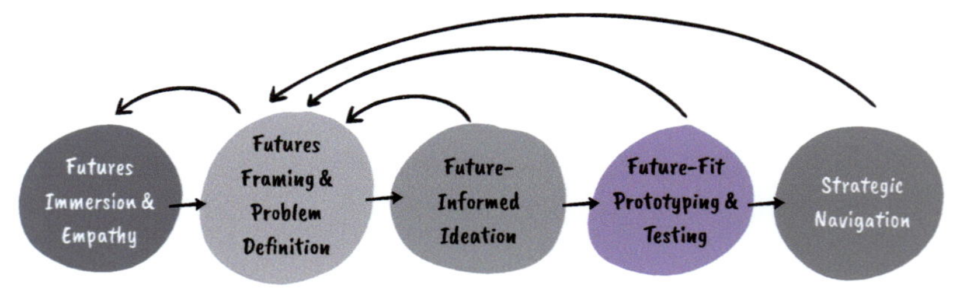

What you can do with the tool:

- Identify the strengths and weaknesses of a strategy when it is exposed to different future conditions.
- Uncover hidden vulnerabilities and assumptions in your current plans.
- Develop more robust and exponentializing strategies that can adapt and even thrive in the face of uncertainty.
- Facilitate a structured and objective conversation about the long-term viability of a project or idea.
- Make more confident decisions by understanding how a strategy performs across a spectrum of possibilities, not just a single predicted outcome.

Expert Tips

Look for Common Threads
After testing a strategy against all scenarios, look for common themes. Are there specific weaknesses that were exposed in multiple futures? Are there strengths that held up across all of them? These common threads are often the most critical areas for strategic adjustment.

Test for "Thrive-ability," Not Just Survival
Do not just check if a strategy "survives" in a different future. Ask what it would take for the idea to thrive. This shifts the focus from a defensive posture to a creative and opportunistic one.

Develop "If-Then" Action Triggers
The output of a Wind Tunneling exercise can be a set of "if-then" strategic triggers. For example: "We will continue with Strategy A, but **if** we see early signals that Scenario B is emerging (e.g., a specific new regulation is passed), **then** we will pivot to Strategy B.1." This creates a truly adaptive strategy.

Wind Tunneling is a strategic stress test. The process involves metaphorically placing your current strategy or idea into the "wind tunnel" of each future scenario you have developed to see how it holds up under pressure.

Step 1: Clearly Define the Strategy or Idea
Before a strategy can be tested, it must be articulated clearly. What is the core value proposition? What are the key assumptions the plan is based on? What are the critical success factors? Be as specific as possible.

DOWNLOAD TOOL
www.design-humanity.com/
en/wind-tunneling

Step 2: Revisit the Future Scenarios
Select the two to four distinct future scenarios created using the **Scenario Planning and the 2x2 Matrix (see page 111)** tool. Briefly review the key characteristics and "rules" of each of these future worlds to ensure the whole team has them fresh in their minds.

Step 3: Run the Wind Tunnel Test
For each scenario, the team should ask a series of critical questions: In this future, does our strategy succeed or fail? Why? Which core assumptions are challenged or invalidated in this scenario? What new opportunities or threats emerge for the idea in this world? How would the strategy need to adapt or pivot to thrive in this future?

STEPS 2 & 3: RUN THE WIND TUNNEL TEST (Revisit Scenarios & Critically Question)

OUTCOME: ADAPT, PIVOT, OR THRIVE? (Future-Informed Decisions)

Future Role-Playing

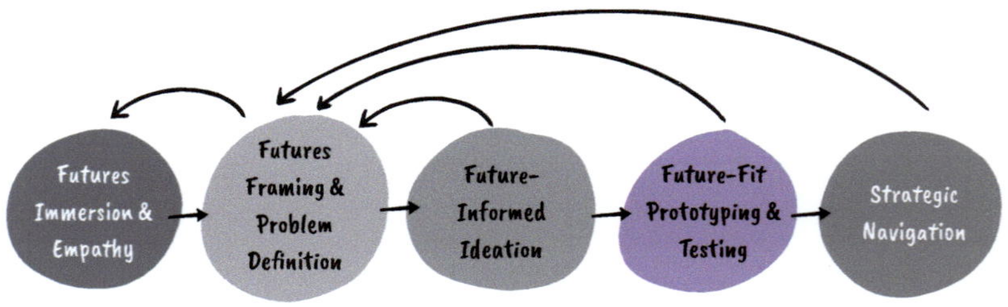

I would like to...

...explore the human, social, and emotional dynamics of a potential future in an immersive, interactive way.

What you can do with the tool:

- Move beyond technical testing to understand the real-world human experience of a future scenario.
- Uncover unforeseen social norms, conflicts, power dynamics, and ethical dilemmas.
- Build deep, embodied empathy for the people who will live in the future you are designing.
- Generate rich, qualitative insights that are often missed in purely analytical exercises.
- Test and refine the design of services, social systems, and human interactions, not just physical products.

Expert Tips

Use Simple Props and Artifacts
A high-tech stage is not needed. Use simple props and some of the Objects from the Future (see page 106) already created to make the scene more believable. A printed "AI Diagnostic Report" or a redesigned doctor's office layout can be enough to make the role-play much more immersive.

Focus on the Debriefing
The most valuable insights often come from the debriefing session immediately after the role-play ends. Ask participants: "What did you feel in your role? Where were the moments of tension or confusion? What surprised you about the interaction?" These reflections are where the deep learning occurs.

Introduce a "Wild Card" Event
To test the resilience of the social system, have the facilitator introduce an unexpected "wild card" event midway through the role-play. For example, "The AI system suddenly goes offline." Observing how the participants negotiate this disruption can be incredibly insightful.

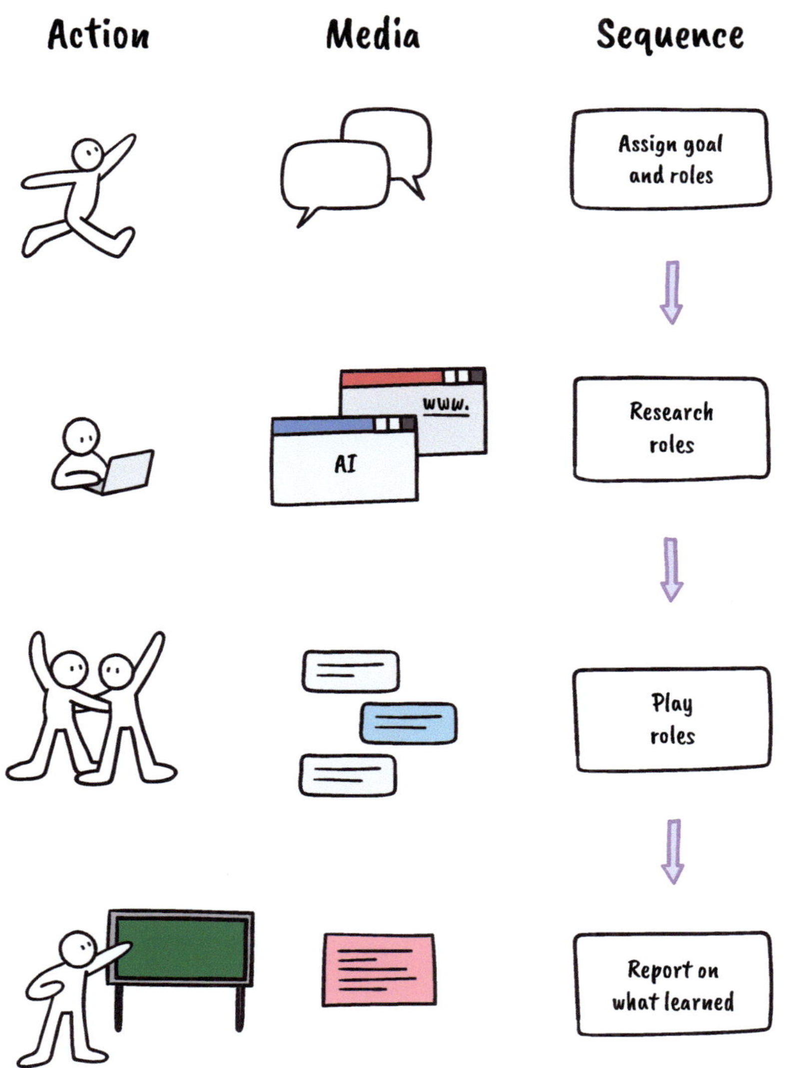

Future Role-Playing is an immersive method where participants act out a specific situation as if they were living in a future scenario. It is a powerful way to prototype and test the social systems that might emerge around a new technology or trend.

Step 1: Define the Scenario and Context

Choose a specific future scenario and a clear, relatable human context within it. For example: "A family doctor's consultation in a world where AI handles all primary diagnostics," or "A community meeting to resolve a resource dispute in a city powered entirely by a decentralized energy grid."

Step 2: Assign Roles and Personas

Assign clear roles to the participants. These should be specific **Future Personas (page 144)** with their own goals, values, and perspectives. For the medical scenario, roles could include the "AI-Assisted Patient," the "Human Doctor" (whose role is now more of a coach), and the "AI System" itself (perhaps represented by a facilitator reading from a script).

Step 3: Act Out the Scenario

Have the participants act out the defined situation for a set period of time, such as 10–15 minutes. Encourage them to improvise and react authentically based on their assigned role. Do not aim to perform perfectly. Focus on exploring the interactions and emotions that arise naturally. The rest of the team should observe carefully.

To capture the observations, well-known design thinking tools like the **AEIOU framework** can be used. It observes and documents the **A**ctivities, **E**nvironments, **I**nteractions, **O**bjects, and **U**sers.

Backcasting

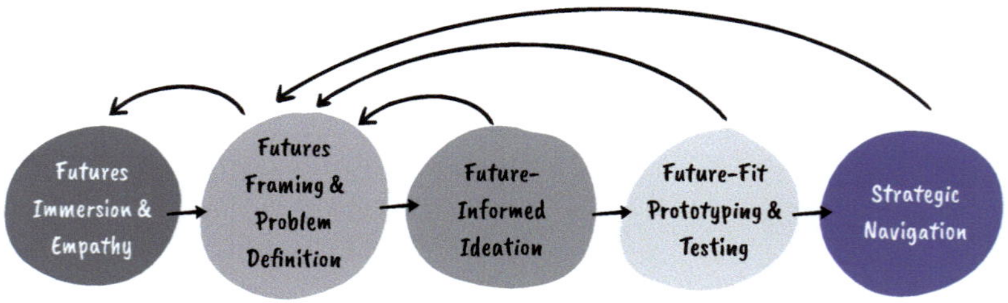

I would like to...

...create a clear and actionable path from a desired future back to the present day.

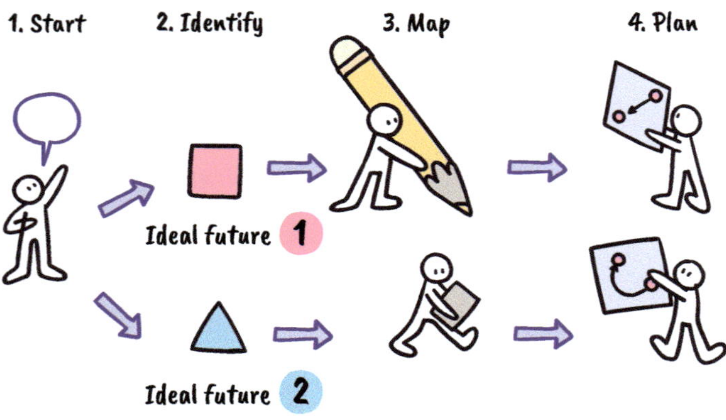

What you can do with the tool:

- Translate a long-term vision into a concrete sequence of achievable steps and milestones.
- Identify the critical policy changes, technological developments, and social shifts required to achieve a preferable future.
- Create a more strategic and proactive plan, as opposed to a reactive one that simply extends current trends.
- Build consensus and alignment within a team by creating a shared and logical map of the path forward.
- Identify potential roadblocks and critical decision points long before they are reached.

Expert Tips

Make It a Story

Do not just list milestones as bullet points. Weave them together into a compelling narrative. Telling the story of "how we got here" from the perspective of someone in a desired future is a powerful way to make the strategic path more engaging and memorable.

Identify Critical Dependencies

As milestones are mapped backward, pay close attention to dependencies. Does Milestone B require a technology that is only developed in Milestone C? Visualizing these dependencies is crucial for understanding the critical path and potential bottlenecks in a strategy.

Combine with Forecasting

Backcasting is most powerful when combined with traditional forecasting. Once a "backcast" path from the future has been created, compare it with a "prediction" path from the present. The gap between these two pathways is the strategic challenge; it highlights where innovation and action are needed to bend the curve of the present toward the preferred future.

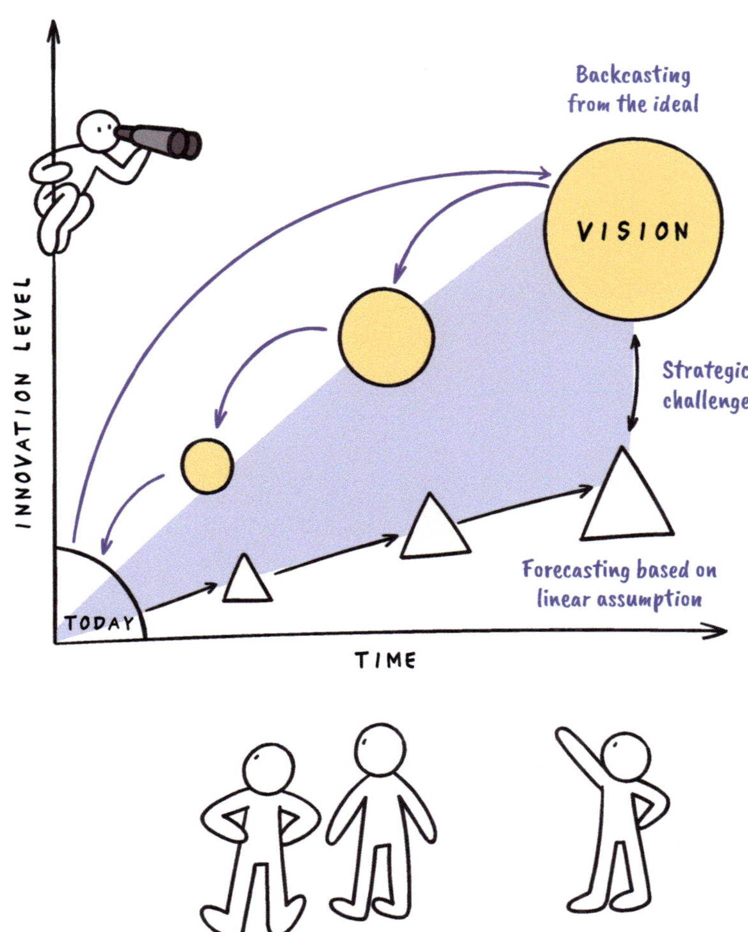

Backcasting is a strategic planning method that reverses the traditional forecasting process. Instead of starting from today and moving forward, you begin with a vividly imagined, preferable future and work backward to the present, identifying the necessary steps along the way.

Step 1: Define Your Desired Future

Start with a clear, compelling, and specific vision of a successful future, typically dated 10–30 years from now. This vision should be the "preferable future" identified through tools like the **Vision Cone (see page 60)** or the **Future Headlines (see page 104)** exercise. The more detailed and tangible this future vision is, the more effective the backcasting process will be.

Step 2: Map Major Milestones Backward in Time

Working backward from your future vision, identify the major milestones that would have needed to happen just before that future could be realized. Then, ask what would have needed to happen just before that milestone, and so on, until you arrive back at the present day.

Step 3: Detail the Necessary Actions and Policies

For each milestone on your timeline, detail the specific actions, policies, technological breakthroughs, or social shifts that would be required to achieve it. This step turns the high-level roadmap into a more granular action plan.

Future-Ready Roadmapping

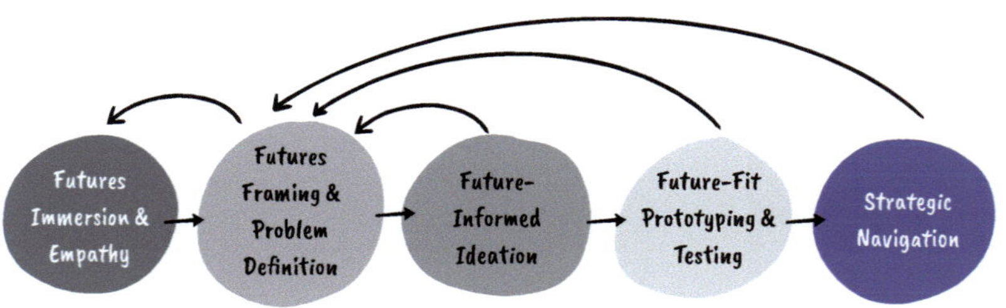

I would like to...

...create a dynamic and adaptive strategic roadmap that can navigate uncertainty and evolve as the future unfolds.

What you can do with the tool:

- Move beyond a rigid, linear plan to a more flexible and resilient strategic framework.
- Clearly communicate a strategic path forward while still accounting for future uncertainty.
- Proactively identify key decision points and "signpost indicators" to monitor over time.
- Empower a team to make adaptive decisions without having to constantly rewrite the entire strategy.
- Build a strategy that is not brittle but is designed to learn and evolve.

Expert Tips

Focus on "No-Regret" Moves
When analyzing a roadmap, identify the "no-regret" actions. These are the strategic moves that are valuable and make sense across all of the most plausible future scenarios. These should be the highest priority for immediate investment and action.

Distinguish Between an "Action" and a "Decision"
A powerful roadmap clearly distinguishes between actions to be taken now and decisions that must be made later. Do not aim to have every future decision made in advance. Instead, identify when a key choice must be made.

Make the Roadmap a Visual Artifact
Create a large, visual representation of the roadmap and display it in a shared team space. This turns the strategy into a living document that can be easily referenced, discussed, and updated. A visual map facilitates dynamic conversations far more effectively than a dense text document.

A Future-Ready Roadmap builds on the insights from **Backcasting (see page 114)** to create an actionable, adaptive plan. It acknowledges that while the long-term vision is clear, the specific path to get there may need to change as the future becomes clearer.

Step 1: Define the Core Path
Using the output from the **Backcasting** exercise, lay out the primary sequence of milestones and actions required to reach the desired future. This forms the central trunk of the roadmap.

Step 2: Identify Key Uncertainties and Alternative Paths
For each major phase of the roadmap, identify the most critical uncertainties that could alter the path. For each uncertainty, brainstorm an alternative pathway or a set of adaptive tactics. This builds flexibility directly into the plan.

Step 3: Define "Signposts" and "Triggers"
A strategy cannot adapt if it is not clear when to change course. For each uncertainty, define:

- **Signposts:** What early signals or data points will be monitored to see how the future is actually unfolding (e.g., a specific policy change, a new technology reaching a certain price point)?

- **Triggers:** At what specific threshold will a signpost "trigger" a decision (e.g., "If consumer adoption of X reaches 20%, the team will activate Pathway B")?

DOWNLOAD TOOL
www.design-humanity.com/
en/future-ready-roadmapping

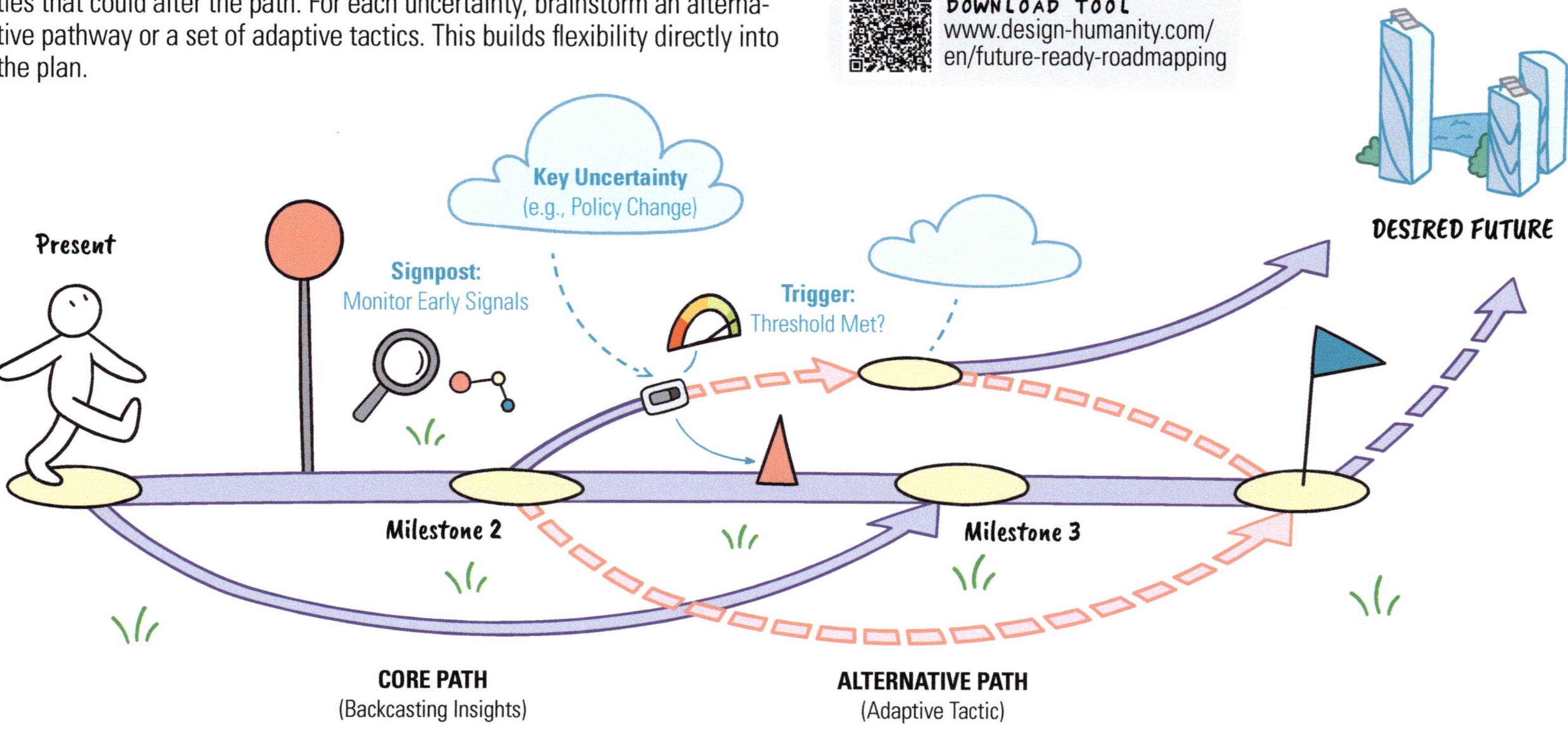

Extension: Operationalizing the Roadmap

To move from speculative foresight to tangible impact, we must operationalize our findings. The **Futures Thinking Strategic Grid** acts as a final filter, mapping our tools against specific strategic intents and levels of unpredictability. This framework ensures that every chosen method strengthens our roadmap, prepares us to transition seamlessly into the iterative prototyping of design thinking, and makes the preferable future a tangible, actionable reality today.

Transition to Design Thinking

Prototype Solutions, Policies, & Ecosystems

Referred Regeneration

North Star for Today's Action

Strategic Intent / **Perceived Unpredictability**

Predictive Planning (Targeted Agency)

- Backcasting
- Strategic Pathways
- Adaptive Tactics
- Plausible Scenarios

Transformative Agency (Futures Immersion)

- Speculative Artifacts
- Experiential Futures
- Creative Mash-Ups
- Future-Fit-Prototyping

Descriptive Exploration (Current Understanding)

- Horizon Scanning
- PESTLE Analysis
- Causal Layered Analysis (CLA)
- Assumptions Surfacing

Resilient Adaptation (Scenario Validation)

- Scenario-Based Validation
- Resilience Testing: Correct
- 2x2 Matrix: Correct
- Object from the Future

Expert Tips for Transitioning to Design Thinking

Avoid the Prediction Trap
Focus on building agency rather than aiming for a fixed forecast. This capacity allows an organization to invent its future instead of merely reacting to trends.

Prototype the System
Treat the strategic roadmap as a hypothesis. Use Experiential Scenarios to test governance structures, policies, and business models before full deployment.

Identify No-Regret Moves
Prioritize strategic actions that provide value regardless of which future scenario unfolds. Examples include investing in foundational soil health monitoring or developing farmer-centric platforms.

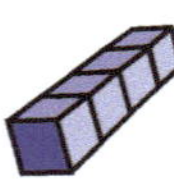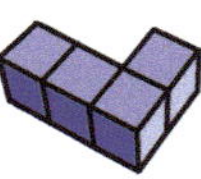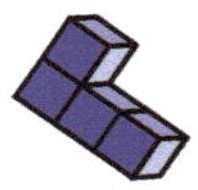

Futures thinking is a strategic discipline that moves beyond a single, predicted future to explore a full spectrum of possibilities, providing the essential long-term context for any meaningful design intervention.

The practice is not about predicting the future but about making more resilient decisions in the present by stress-testing strategies against multiple plausible scenarios and identifying a clear "preferable future" to guide action.

A core function of this work is to systematically challenge our own mental models, using tools like the Ladder of Inference and Causal Layered Analysis to uncover the hidden biases and deep-seated myths that shape our perception of what is possible.

The goal is to translate weak signals and emerging trends into powerful insights, informing a strategic direction that allows us to move beyond reacting to change and begin to proactively shape a more desirable, win-win-win world.

DESIGN THINKING

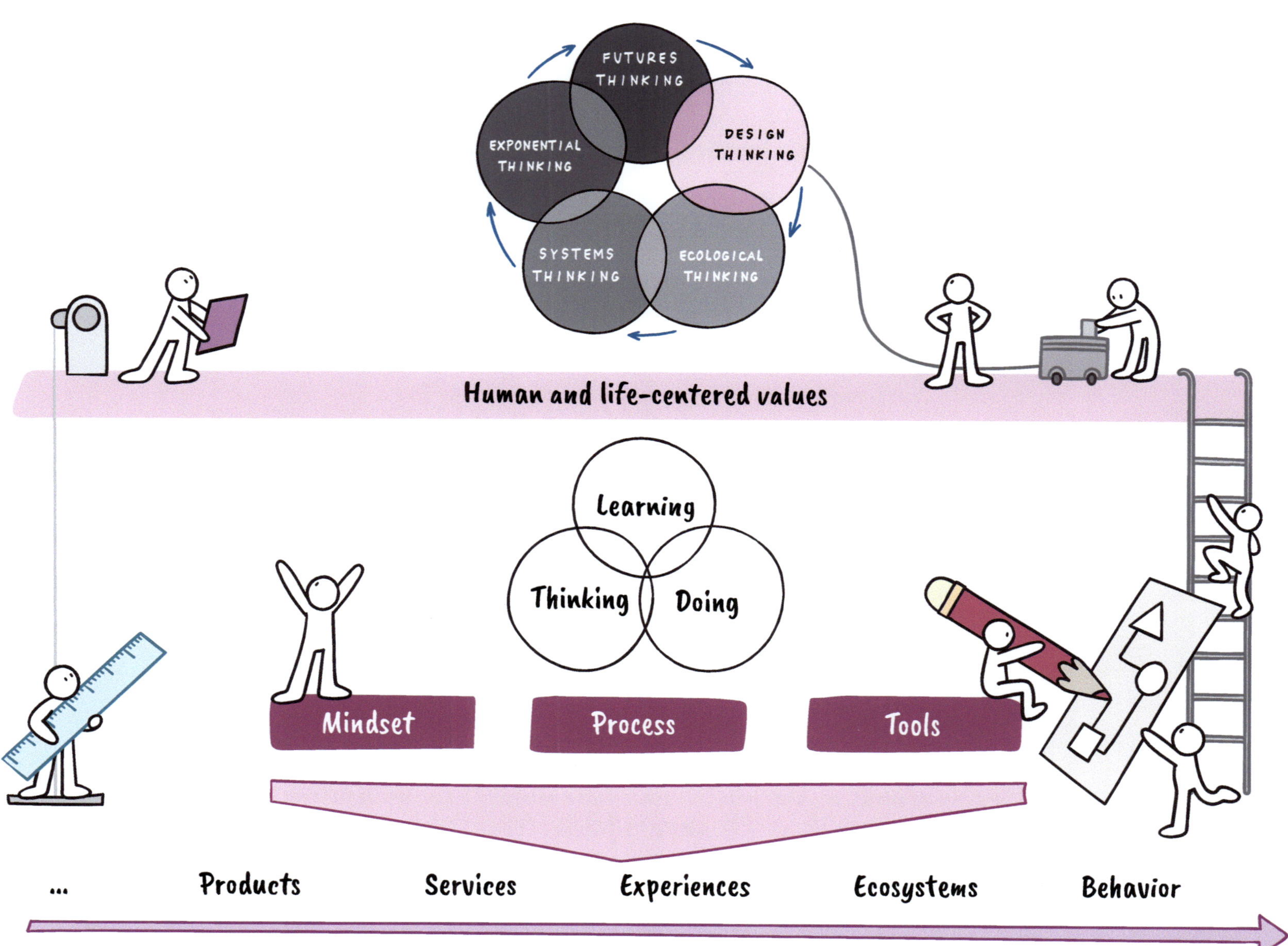

FUTURES THINKING
EXPONENTIAL THINKING
DESIGN THINKING
SYSTEMS THINKING
ECOLOGICAL THINKING
Human and life-centered values
Learning
Thinking
Doing
Mindset
Process
Tools
...
Products
Services
Experiences
Ecosystems
Behavior
THE SPECTRUM OF POSITIVE, RESILIENT CHANGE WE AIM TO CREATE

Deep Empathy & Problem Framing

Design Thinking for Humanity demands a return to the paradigm's foundational purpose: **creating real and meaningful impact**. We move beyond the narrow interpretation of business metrics and short-term profit, shifting the focus to life-centered considerations that encompass people and the planet. We do not replace this unique problem-solving approach; we amplify it to tackle wicked problems with the scale and impact they demand.

Creating a better world for all living things necessitates a broader perspective and a new set of life-centered considerations. This re-emphasis is not a rejection of progress. On the contrary, **embracing the opportunities presented by new exponential technologies** is essential for maximizing effectiveness. The essence of Design Thinking for Humanity lies in strategically integrating these powerful tools and the broader thinking lenses.

Design thinking stands as the most formidable mindset for navigating and transforming wicked problems. Its unparalleled strength lies in starting at the true beginning: cultivating a deep, human-centered empathy to uncover the authentic needs that drive breakthrough innovation across products, services, business models, and, ultimately, lasting behavioral change.

Even with advanced technology applied across the design cycle, certain core principles remain constant. A profound and disciplined exploration of the **problem space** is the single most important factor for success. This first phase requires building deep, systemic empathy, questioning every assumption, and uncovering the true, underlying root causes of a challenge. Without this rigorous up-front work, any team risks creating an elegant solution to the wrong problem.

The goal of Design Thinking for Humanity is to create lasting, positive impact. This necessitates spending the majority of time and effort understanding the full complexity of the problem before any solutions are considered. The most critical juncture occurs where the two diamonds of the process meet: the Define Point of View stage.

Here, the deep learning from the problem space is synthesized into a focused and powerful **"How Might We" question (see distinct trajectories, pages 31–32)**. A well-framed problem statement, born from this convergence, acts as a guiding star. It provides the clarity and direction needed to ensure the creative energy of the team focuses on a challenge that is both meaningful and solvable.

Only once the problem is well-defined has a team earned the right to enter the solution space. The second diamond is where ideation, prototyping, and testing take place. However, a brilliantly executed solution for a poorly understood problem is a failure. The **solution space** is not the main event; it is the logical conclusion to a journey that must always begin with a deep, humble, and relentless exploration of the problem itself.

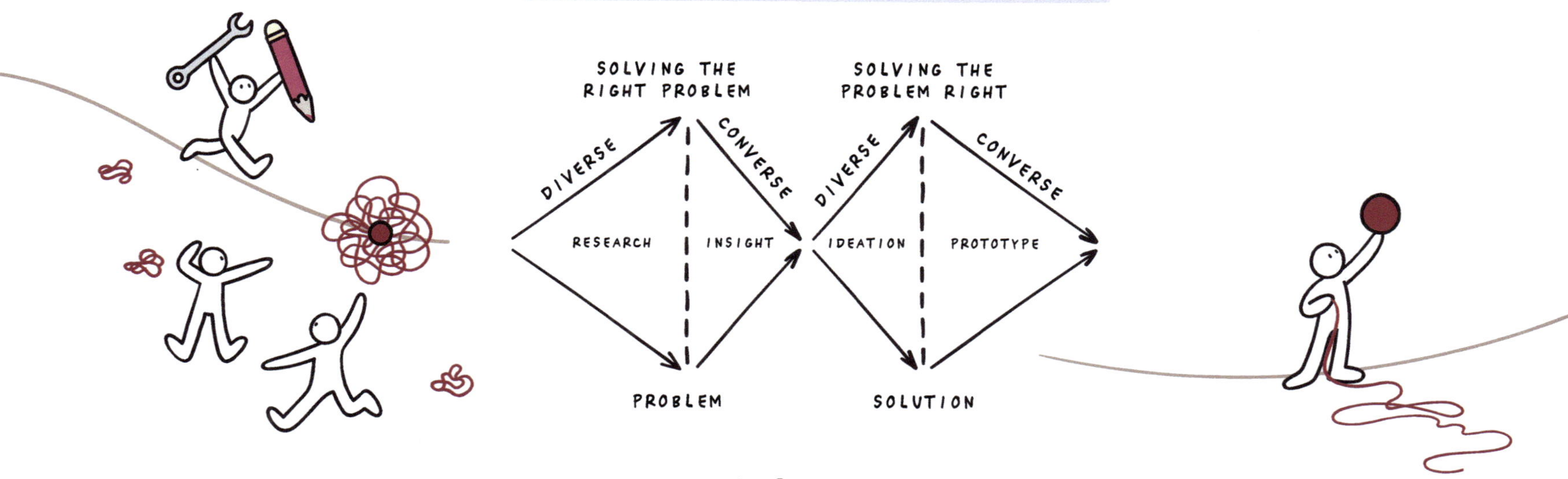

Human and Life-Centered Values

The Problem Framing Funnel

The journey into the Design Thinking for Humanity process does not begin with a blank slate. It starts from a foundation established by **Futures Thinking**. This provides a clear direction and ensures the problem is already embedded within a broader future context.

The "How Might We" (HMW) questions framed here are not aimed at solving a simple user need. They are designed for **intervening in a complex system**. This rigorous and expanded problem framing is the critical groundwork that enables all subsequent ideation and prototyping.

The first HMW questions are fundamentally influenced by the work done in the futures thinking lens. By first exploring potential future scenarios, the team frames a challenge that is not just about solving today's problems. It is a strategic intervention designed to guide us toward a more resilient and sustainable world.

Solutions developed from this approach are truly beneficial and resilient for humanity and the planet. The second HMW iteration applies the **System Empathy Map (see page 148)** to deepen the understanding of the systemic context.

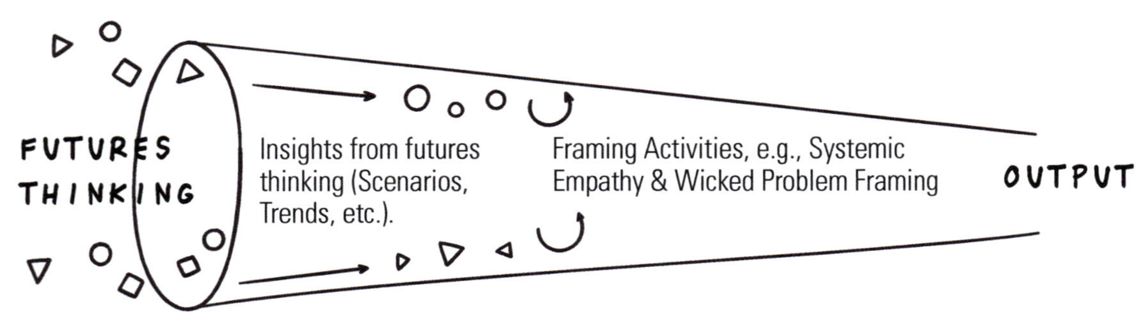

Example of First HMW Question and Structure:

HMW: "How might we..."
+ Action Verb: "...co-design..."
+ Intended Action: "...a network of modular, community-owned vertical farms..."
+ For (User(s)/Context): "...for residents in dense urban 'food deserts'..."
+ So That (Benefit): "...they can increase their access to affordable, nutritious food, build local economic resilience, and regenerate biodiversity in the neighborhood?"

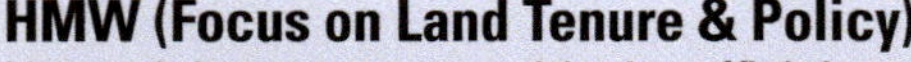

HMW (Focus on Land Tenure & Policy):
How might we partner with city officials and land trust organizations to establish permanent, policy-protected sites for community food production so that residents in urban "food deserts" can build long-term economic assets that resist gentrification?

HMW (Focus on Financial Viability & Distrust):
How might we design a self-sustaining micro-enterprise model for local food production that generates profit for residents and is collectively managed, thereby overcoming local distrust in outside interventions and securing financial independence from grants?

Wicked Problems

Many of the Design Thinking for Humanity challenges faced by a global society are not simple puzzles with clear solutions. They are **"wicked problems."** Issues like climate change, systemic poverty, and global public health are classic examples. They lack clarity both in their aims and in their solutions and are subject to real-world constraints that prevent easy, risk-free attempts at resolution.

In a hyperconnected world, these challenges are best understood as **complex socio-technical system**s. Problems related to sustainability are not isolated issues; they are deeply intertwined with existing manufacturing systems, economic models, and cultural norms. To address the issue of waste, for example, a focus on recycling alone is insufficient. The design of products built for obsolescence and the economic incentives that reward disposable consumption must also be examined. Any meaningful intervention must acknowledge this complexity.

The Design Solution

It is for these reasons that design thinking has become intrinsically linked to tackling wicked problems. Unlike rigid, analytical approaches that seek a single correct answer, Design Thinking for Humanity embraces ambiguity. Its focus first mentality for the problem space is perfectly suited for gaining **deep insights into the varied perspectives of stakeholders (see Systemic Empathy Map, page 148)**.

To be truly effective, design thinking must be augmented with a systems thinking lens. By visualizing information, collaborating with diverse stakeholders, and relentlessly testing ideas, it becomes possible to untangle the web of a complex socio-technical system and develop solutions that evolve with the problem itself.

Core Truths of Wicked Problems

- **The Symptom, Not the Disease:** Every wicked problem is a symptom of deeper issues; solving one part risks unforeseen consequences elsewhere.
- **No Stopping Rule:** Unlike simple puzzles, challenges like climate change have no definitive formula, endpoint, or stopping rule.
- **The Ambiguity Mandate:** Wicked problems require embracing ambiguity and navigating complexity with an iterative, human-centered approach.
- **Integrated Complexity:** Tackling these challenges requires integrating systems thinking to understand interconnected causes and effects.

Radical Collaboration

To tackle the interconnected challenges of our time, innovation must evolve beyond siloed efforts and embrace a new synergy between human imagination, diverse expertise, and intelligent technology. Wicked problems are too complex and interconnected to be solved by any one individual, organization, or discipline. **Collaboration is the core engine of Design Thinking for Humanity**; it is the mechanism that integrates the five thinking disciplines, from futures thinking to exponential scaling.

I Can Do: The Human Role

The shift to transdisciplinary teams. True collaboration moves beyond traditional, siloed ways of working. Success requires building rich, multilayered understanding by bringing together interdisciplinary teams with diverse backgrounds in science, policy, business, and design. The individual's primary contribution is to ensure the problem is seen from every angle, identifying the true root causes, not just surface-level symptoms.

AI Can Do: Integrating the Co-creator

The emergence of hybrid teams. This new paradigm has expanded to include non-human partners. We must treat powerful generative and specialized AI agents not merely as passive tools for executing commands but as active and integrated team members. AI's role is to leverage machine intelligence for deep context analysis, providing access to relevant project data and research that a human team might miss. This human-AI teaming represents the next evolutionary step in radical collaboration.

We Can Do: The Collaborative Outcome

Building trust and resilience. Effective collaboration is the foundation of trust. Working openly and transparently builds the social fabric necessary for collective action and for navigating the difficult trade-offs inherent in systemic change. This shared purpose extends to the relationship with the public, customers, and users. We must drive widespread behavioral change by engaging citizens as co-creators in the design process. This shared ownership is the only way to build a resilient, thriving, and equitable future for all.

Radical Collaboration Mandate

1. **Shift Mindset:** View AI as an active co-creator, not just a passive tool.

2. **Cultivate Trust:** Work openly and transparently to build the social fabric for collective action.

3. **Ensure Ownership:** Move from top-down directives to engaging citizens and users as co-creators.

4. **Embrace Fusion:** Integrate transdisciplinary expertise to achieve collective intelligence.

1. Frame the Problem in a Future Context!

The first act of collaboration is to agree on the problem. Within Design Thinking for Humanity, this means using futures thinking to frame the challenge not as it exists today but as it might evolve. The team must collaboratively build a shared understanding of the long-term context, ensuring that the problem being solved is one that truly matters for creating a resilient and preferable future.

6. Cultivate Hybrid Intelligence!

Collective intelligence is fueled by diversity, and the definition of a "diverse team" must now be expanded. It is essential to blend a wide range of human life experiences and thinking styles with the analytical and generative power of specialized AI agents. By treating AI as a collaborator (giving it context and a clear mission), teams can leverage exponential thinking to uncover novel patterns and co-create solutions at a scale previously unimaginable.

5. Foster Psychological Safety for Wicked Problems!

Tackling wicked problems requires teams to navigate ambiguity, challenge deeply held assumptions and confront ethical dilemmas. This is only possible in an environment of profound psychological safety. It is a leader's responsibility to create a culture where team members feel safe to be vulnerable, to respectfully challenge ideas (not people), and to learn from failure. This is the core of the design thinking mindset, applied to the most complex of challenges.

2. Build a Shared Systemic View!

Effective collaboration requires a shared understanding of the entire system in which a problem exists. This moves beyond a simple shared folder to a collectively built systems map where the needs of all stakeholders, including the planet, are visible. This practice, rooted in systems thinking and ecological thinking, ensures the team designs for the health of the whole ecosystem, not just for a single user.

3. Default to Deliberate Trust!

Trust is the cornerstone of any ambitious collaboration, especially one that spans disciplines and organizations. In the face of uncertainty, teams must make a conscious and deliberate choice to trust first. This means acting with the assumption that all partners, human and machine, are aligned with the project's Massive Transformative Purpose. This trust is the currency that enables the speed and agility required for meaningful impact.

4. Balance Deep Work with Collective Synthesis.

The complex, multilensed nature of this work requires two distinct modes of thinking. Radical collaboration depends on a rhythm that balances focused, individual deep work (where team members can grapple with complex information) and intense, collaborative collective synthesis (where those individual insights are integrated to build a richer, more holistic understanding). The process should intentionally protect time for both modes of thinking.

The Beginner's Mind

Embrace the power of Shoshin, the Japanese concept of a "beginner's mind." This powerful mindset encourages practitioners to **approach every situation with an open, accepting, and profoundly curious perspective**. It strips away preconceived notions and expert biases.

Cultivating a beginner's mind is a prerequisite for the radical collaboration needed to tackle systemic challenges. It enhances the capacity for improvisation and grounds teams firmly in the present moment. This cognitive openness is vital for decomposing wicked problems to their foundational elements. When the hierarchy of expertise is flattened, the team is empowered to see the problem with fresh eyes, question long-held assumptions, and uncover novel connections that an "expert" mind might overlook.

This collective state of curiosity unlocks a greater capacity for ground-breaking invention, **ensuring solutions are truly innovative** and not merely incremental. While powerfully transformative, cultivating the beginner's mind is challenging. It demands a commitment to active listening, a willingness to be wrong, and the humility to acknowledge that in the face of wicked problems, we are all beginners.

We apply the beginner's mind by deliberately setting aside assumptions and pre-existing knowledge, allowing us to:

Explore all possible futures: Rather than limiting ourselves to incremental changes, the beginner's mind enables unconstrained ideation for radically new scenarios and possibilities, crucial for effective futures thinking.

Uncover new concepts for regeneration: By suspending judgment and conventional thinking, we can identify novel pathways and design interventions that aim for regenerative outcomes, going beyond mere sustainability.

Break existing rules and behaviors: It fosters a willingness to challenge established norms, processes, and industry conventions, paving the way for truly disruptive innovations that deliver fundamentally different value to customers and stakeholders.

Leverage exponential technologies for true innovation: Instead of simply using new technologies to optimize existing processes for efficiency, the beginner's mind encourages us to reimagine what's possible, harnessing exponential advancements to create entirely new products, services, and systems that address complex challenges in unprecedented ways.

The Design Thinking Mandate

Design thinking is the discipline of empathetic intent. It empowers us to descend past surface-level symptoms to **understand the true root of the problem**. We synthesize this complexity into a single point of view. The discipline requires relentless iteration on narratives and stories that mobilize collective action to build a resilient and equitable future.

The application of **design thinking** in the context of humanity necessitates a fundamental evolution of our intent as designers and innovators. This mandate is not merely a technical update to existing methodologies; it represents a significant **shift in direction**. We are moving from the pursuit of individual convenience toward the cultivation of collective **resilience** and **regeneration**.

FEATURE	CLASSICAL DESIGN THINKING MANDATE	DESIGN THINKING FOR HUMANITY MANDATE
Primary Focus	Solving for the immediate needs and "pain points" of a specific user/customer	Prioritizing the vitality of the entire biological and social ecosystem
Core Objective	Achieving the "sweet spot" between user needs, market viability, and technical feasibility	Designing systems that actively restore environments and withstand future disruptions
Target Scale	Optimizing the interaction between a person and a product, service, or experience	Mapping the interdependencies within a global, interconnected system
Role of Narrative	Utilizing stories to map individual experiences and drive product adoption	Using narratives to mobilize communities and catalyze collective, systemic action
Time Horizon	Focusing on iterative improvements and near-term market success	Anticipating future scenarios and designing for the well-being of future generations
Definition of Success	Measured by individual satisfaction, efficiency, and commercial growth	Measured by the ability to solve "wicked problems" and promote planetary health

The Design Thinking Process

The challenges addressed by Design Thinking for Humanity are vast and systemic, yet the core process for navigating them remains rooted in the proven, human-centered sequence: Understand, Observe, Define Point of View, Ideate, Prototype, and Test. This structured yet flexible process provides the essential scaffolding for moving from the ambiguity of a wicked problem to a tangible, resilient solution. However, the scope and focus of each phase must now be **intentionally expanded** to meet our demands.

It is no longer enough to simply understand a single user or test a single product. Each phase must now be conducted through the **"life-centered" lens**, considering the broader ecosystem of stakeholders, the long-term future consequences, and the health of the planet itself. This section details how each phase of the classic design thinking process is **elevated** to meet the demands of designing for humanity.

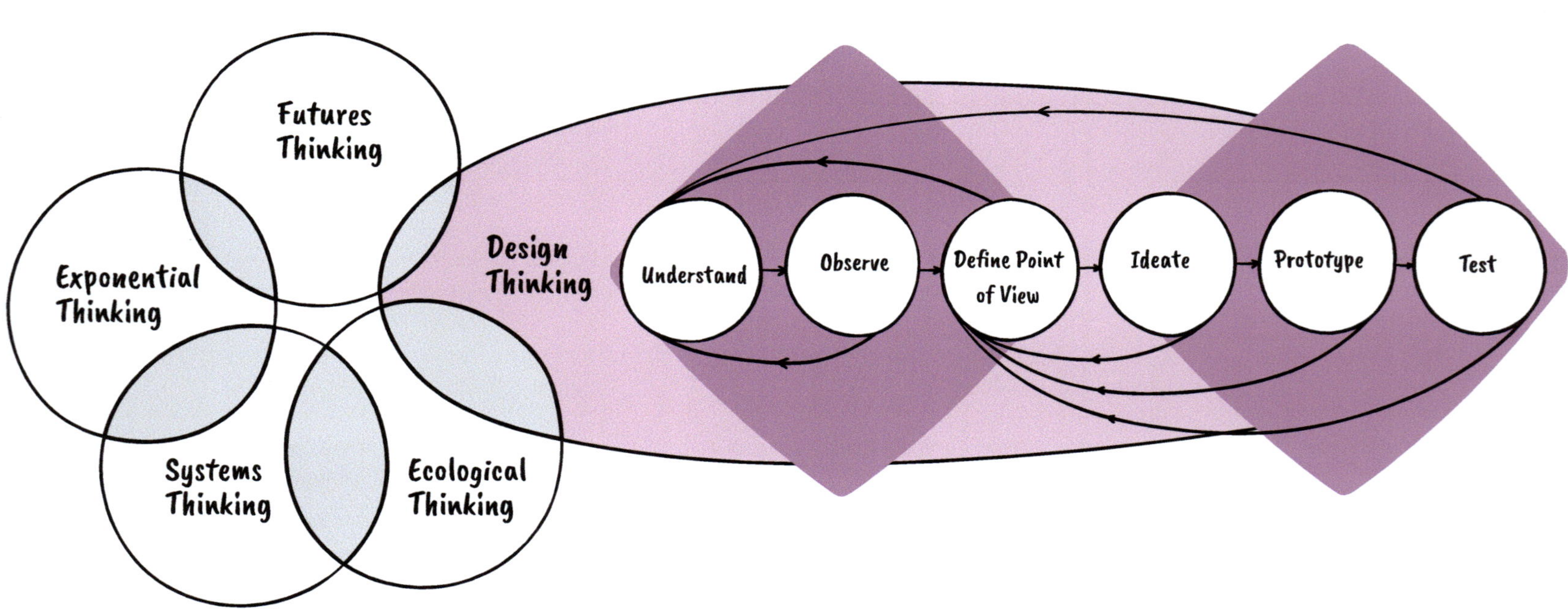

Understand & Observe

The journey from users to systems begins, as always, with empathy. However, the scope of that empathy is radically expanded. The goal is not just to understand the needs of an individual user but to gain a deep and holistic understanding of the entire system.

This expansion involves using tools like Systemic Empathy Mapping (see page 152) and Wicked Problem Framing (see page 148) to see the challenge through the eyes of diverse stakeholders, including communities, future generations, and the planet itself. Observation moves beyond user behavior to include the analysis of systemic patterns, resource flows, and ecological impacts.

Define Point of View

In this critical phase, broad insights from the problem space are synthesized into a focused, actionable challenge. A point of view becomes a well-framed "How Might We" question, identifying a key leverage point for a positive systemic intervention. This extends far beyond a user-centric problem statement. The result is a hypothesis on how a targeted action can create a ripple effect of positive change across an entire ecosystem.

Ideate

Ideation is expanded from features and experiences to "win-win-win" solutions. Teams move beyond brainstorming product features to generating concepts for new services, policies, business models, and behavioral shifts.

The primary tool for this expansion is the **Value Proposition for Humanity Canvas (see page 154)**. This tool forces ideation to be "win-win-win." Ideas are judged not just on their novelty but on their potential to create tangible value for users, society, and the planet simultaneously.

Prototype & Test

From products to narratives and interventions, prototyping and testing in this context must go beyond physical mock-ups. To test systemic and behavioral solutions, we use advanced methods.

These methods include **Future Storytelling & Narrative Prototyping (see page 292)** and **Future Role-Playing (see page 112)**. These tools allow teams to test the human experience and social dynamics of a potential future.

Furthermore, testing is not just for desirability. Tools like the **Exponential Ethics Compass (see page 294)** and **Wind Tunneling (see page 141)** are used to test for long-term resilience and responsible impact.

The best results are achieved when the design thinking process is skillfully facilitated, ensuring the fusion of complex thinking lenses and the creation of resilient solutions.

A Design Thinking Facilitator...

The role of the facilitator is elevated to that of a system steward, responsible for guiding the team through complexity and uncertainty.

- Champion the mindset by using empathy, iteration, and radical collaboration to overcome the cognitive biases that hinder foresight.
- Steward the process by guiding the team through the Double Diamond framework, creating the conditions for both broad exploration and focused decision-making, with a relentless emphasis on the problem space.
- Orchestrate the journey from a preferable future to a tangible reality, holding the team accountable to the vision and the principles of the work.
- Adapt tools to scale by selecting the appropriate methods to guide the team whether they are designing a single product or a complex ecosystem.

Storytelling: The Narrative Mandate

Storytelling is a crucial part of Design Thinking for Humanity. Humans are meaning-seeking creatures who connect most deeply with narratives that resonate with their values and understanding. The world's complexity is inherent; simplicity resides in the mind of the beholder. Crafting compelling, understandable storylines is therefore essential. **A narrative approach, connecting events and information through a compelling arc**, is far more effective than factually accurate but socially uncontextualized expository writing. This is especially true when communicating the outcomes of Design Thinking for Humanity initiatives, from climate science to behavioral change.

Defining the Emotional Journey

Personas and Future Personas are key tools in design thinking, providing a powerful foundation for building these resonant stories. Understanding different communication styles, perhaps informed by models of brain function, allows us to tailor the balance of facts, emotions, vision, and detail to best suit the specific needs and preferences of our target audience. We apply design thinking to narrative creation, deeply understanding the audience's existing mental models, aspirations, and pain points. This understanding informs the crafting of compelling stories that resonate on an emotional level, shifting perspectives and inspiring action.

The Process Shift

A classic narrative arc follows the pattern of **Situation -> Complication -> Resolution**. To put this into practice, the **Future Storytelling & Narrative Prototyping tool (page 292)** provides a step-by-step process for creating these narrative prototypes.

A powerful story illuminates a lesson learned, a transformation achieved, or a new possibility. It must contain five essential elements.

What Makes a Powerful Story?

Clear Context and Focus!
A good story immediately establishes the parameters of the problem or opportunity it addresses, preventing audience confusion and maintaining engagement. It sets the stage for understanding the human need or challenge at hand.

Authenticity and Empathy!
The narrative must be genuine and rooted in real human experiences. It avoids contrived scenarios, fostering trust and allowing the audience to connect emotionally with the characters and their struggles or triumphs. This mirrors the empathetic core of design thinking.

Meaningful Outcome and Call to Action!
A powerful story does not just entertain; it illuminates a lesson learned, a transformation achieved, or a new possibility. Outcomes from Design Thinking for Humanity often points toward a solution, a shift in behavior, or an invitation for the audience to participate in creating a better future.

Coherence and Clarity!
The story should be well-structured and consistently told, reflecting a deep understanding of the journey from problem to potential solution. This ensures the message is easily digestible and memorable, echoing the iterative refinement of a design process.

Emotional Resonance and Connection!
Effective storytelling evokes an emotional response, allowing the audience to feel invested in the narrative. By sharing the human impact of a problem or the positive effects of a design solution, it builds a bridge between the storyteller and the audience, fostering shared understanding and a sense of collective purpose.

Example: Telling Stories

BEFORE

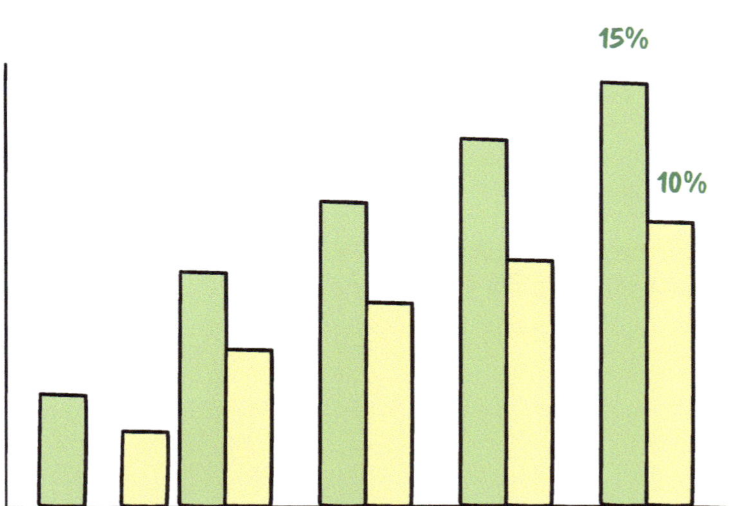

AFTER

Headline: The new community garden initiative resulted in a **15% increase in local vegetable consumption** and a **10% reported increase in neighborhood interaction over the last 12 months**.

Meet Maria. A single mother who worried about affording fresh vegetables. Today, she and her son harvest their own food at the community garden, a place where he now plays with neighbors Maria knows by name. **The garden did not just bring food; it brought the community together**.

Narratives as Powerful Tools of Changemaking

Designing effective narratives is paramount for driving change toward sustainable and regenerative business models. These narratives serve as powerful tools, shaping how individuals and organizations perceive themselves, their connection to broader society, and their role in the world.

Well-crafted narratives can shift mental models within a business context, **moving the focus from mere profit maximization to prioritizing environmental and social well-being**. Narratives can inspire collective action and foster a deeper understanding of the interconnectedness between economic prosperity and ecological health.

The current landscape features dominant narratives that hinder progress, such as the idea that overconsumption is an acceptable business practice or that economic growth is always superior to degrowth. The battle of narratives is a critical front in the fight for a sustainable future.

Genuinely embracing sustainable and regenerative models requires new narratives that challenge these ingrained beliefs. We must reorient business strategies, encouraging companies to evaluate every element through an ecological and social lens before considering economic value.

Levels of Objectives and Change

We must move beyond theory to practice. A structured approach is needed to craft these transformative stories. The **Narrative Design Canvas (see page 135)** provides a practical tool for teams to deconstruct the dominant, limiting narratives and build a new, compelling narrative that can inspire and mobilize a community toward a more resilient and regenerative future.

This is the journey of shifting objectives, moving from minimizing harm to actively creating abundance:

Compliance-Driven

Our primary goal is to meet the bare minimum requirements, ensuring we stay out of legal trouble and maintain our license to operate.

Reactive Changes

We implement changes only when external pressures demand it, focusing on efficiency and managing our public image to stay relevant.

Sustainable Design

We strategically embed sustainability into our core operations and offerings, believing it's essential for long-term competitive advantage and shared value creation.

Regenerative Design

Our ultimate purpose is to actively regenerate and enhance the health of natural and social systems, creating net-positive impact and fostering true abundance.

Design the Shifts Toward Potential New Narratives: The Narrative Design Canvas

<table>
<tr>
<td>

DECONSTRUCT THE PRESENT
(THE "AS-IS" STORY)

</td>
<td>

DESIGN THE FUTURE
(THE "TO-BE" STORY)

</td>
<td>

INSPIRE TO ACTION
(THE "CALL TO ADVENTURE")

</td>
</tr>
<tr>
<td>

OLD NARRATIVE
What is the dominant and limiting story that currently perpetuates the unsustainable status quo?

</td>
<td>

THE NEW NARATIVE
What is the compelling and regenerative new story that offers a tangible vision of a preferable future?

</td>
<td>

THE EMOTIONAL IMPACT
What is the precise emotional shift we want to create, transitioning the audience from a state of apathy to one of empowerment?

</td>
</tr>
<tr>
<td>

THE CORE AUDIENCE
Who believes this old story, and what are their underlying values, hopes, and fears?

</td>
<td>

THE CORE MESSAGE
If the audience could remember only one thing from our new story, what is the single, undeniable truth we want them to carry with them?

</td>
<td>

THE CALL FOR ACTION
What is the single, clear, and tangible first step we want our audience to take after hearing our story?

</td>
</tr>
<tr>
<td>

THE HIDDEN PAYOFF
What benefit or sense of security does the old narrative provide that makes it so difficult to change?

</td>
<td>

THE HUMAN CONNECTION
How does our new narrative connect with the deepest values of our audience and make the future feel not just possible but desirable?

</td>
<td>

THE FIRST REWARD
How do we make that first action feel both immediately achievable and meaningful, reinforcing their commitment to the new narrative?

</td>
</tr>
</table>

DOWNLOAD TOOL
www.design-humanity.com/en/narrative-design

Examples of Shifts in Narratives

Integrating Systemic Resilience

Classic innovation focuses on the "sweet spot" **intersection of desirability, viability, and feasibility**. Design Thinking for Humanity fundamentally reorders these priorities. We move beyond simply having ethical practices and integrate social, ecological, and political responsibility as foundational elements of innovation.

The Ethical Boundary

Any design innovation must first prove its positive or neutral impact on people and the planet before considering profit and production. The ecological boundary acts as a non-negotiable constraint, ensuring all design and business decisions are made within a framework of long-term sustainability and equity. This transformation creates one truth: innovation is only truly achieved when it is desirable, viable, feasible, and built without violating the mandates of social, ethical, and ecological well-being.

The Challenge of Validation

Traditional validation focuses on market and emotional success, but this is insufficient. We must rigorously validate the system against governance and political requirements. This move requires moving beyond simply confirming emotional or behavioral success to adopting a new mindset about verifying the robustness of the entire system that supports that behavior.

Before any successful prototype is implemented on a societal scale, the system must address these fundamental questions:

- Will the new mechanism be recognized and honored by governing bodies?
- Will existing financial institutions integrate and honor it?
- Is the foundational policy stable enough to avoid immediate political capture or reversal by opposing interests?

Core Design Thinking Lenses
(Desirability, Viability, and Feasibility)

Responsibility
(Ecological, Ethical, Social, Political)

+

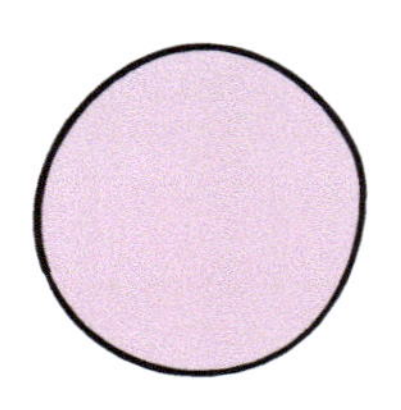

Including Policy in Core Design Process

We must integrate political and policy feasibility directly into the core design process. Design teams should not just run standard checks on desirability, viability, and feasibility. Failure to integrate early policy analysis creates the common failure points for social innovations: momentum is lost, regulations crush the solution, or public financial support is lacking. This early political and structural integration is essential for designing resilient solutions.

Part 2

A Speculative Case Study

Applying Design Thinking

Following the design challenge introduced on pages 68–69, we now delve into design thinking as one of the core intellectual disciplines. This section aims to provide a high-level overview of how to apply various mindsets and tools within a real-world context, illustrating their comprehensive integration into an actionable strategy.

The overarching goal for our case study is both ambitious and essential.

The Living Soil Mandate

Our objective within this challenge is to design a new global economic and agricultural model that makes the regeneration of the world's topsoil the primary measure of agricultural success, ensuring long-term food security, reversing climate change, and restoring biodiversity by 2050.

The journey through the futures thinking lens has provided the essential strategic context for our challenge. The exploration of four distinct future scenarios, from "Regenerative Abundance" to "The Great Dust Bowl," has given us a deep understanding of the potential landscapes we must navigate. This foresight work culminated in a clear, ambitious, and preferable future to aim for: a world where agriculture is a primary engine for planetary regeneration. The initial ideation, through methods like the "Creative Mash-Up," even yielded a provocative early concept: the "Carbon Harvest" platform, designed to create a direct financial incentive for regenerative practices.

With this future-oriented foundation in place, the process now moves into the core of design thinking. The task involves translating this high-level vision into a deeply human and tangible reality. This requires a profound dive into the problem space to build empathy for the stewards of the land, followed by a rigorous exploration of the solution space to design and test a concept that is innovative, resilient, equitable, and life-centered. To illustrate this process, key tools from the Design Thinking for Humanity Toolbox will now be applied.

Applying the Toolbox: From Vision to Value

Problem Definition: We start with Understand and Observe, building insights directly conducted from the preceding futures thinking phase.

Name: Javier Rodriguez

Demographics: 55, male, runs a multigenerational family farm in a region facing increasing water scarcity

Role: A respected, pragmatic farmer and community leader

Bio: Javier is a skilled farmer who has managed his family's land for more than 30 years. He is deeply committed to his community and to the long-term health of his land but is under immense financial pressure from volatile commodity prices and the rising costs of inputs like fertilizer and water. He is skeptical of complex new technologies but is open to practical solutions that offer clear, tangible benefits.

Pains (Fears & Frustrations): Javier feels trapped in a system that is both economically and ecologically unsustainable. He is under constant financial pressure from volatile markets and rising costs, leading to a loss of autonomy and a deep anxiety about the future health of his land. His greatest fear is that this downward spiral will make it impossible to pass a viable and healthy farm on to his children, breaking a multigenerational legacy.

Gains (Hopes & Desires): Javier desires a future of resilient prosperity, where he is rewarded for his stewardship of the land with a stable and diversified income. He hopes to practice a form of agriculture that is more in tune with nature, allowing him to leave a lasting legacy of a healthy and profitable farm. Ultimately, he wishes to be a respected leader in his community, pioneering a new way of farming that ensures a thriving future for all.

Jobs-to-Be-Done:

1. "Ensure the long-term viability and profitability of my family farm." Javier needs to find a way to make his business more resilient to both economic and environmental shocks.

2. "Pass on a healthy, productive farm to my children." His deepest motivation is to leave a legacy of healthy land, but his current economic reality often forces him into short-term, degenerative practices.

Wicked Problem Framing

Based on Javier's perspective, a specific, actionable challenge can now be framed.

HMW Question: "How might we (re)design a simple and trustworthy system for farmers like Javier to directly monetize the ecological value they create through regenerative practices so that they can increase their economic resilience and become the heroes of a regenerative future?"

Ideation

Following the definition of the wicked problem, the team moves into Ideation. To spark innovative solutions for our HMW question, we use again the **Creative Mash-Up** or (if appropriate) any other creative ideation tool. The Creative Mash-Up tool compels the team to generate radical ideas by fusing a **core human need identified** in the problem space with an **exponential future trend**.

The Mash-Up

- **Human Need:** Direct, fair compensation (a solution must reward farmers like Javier directly for their stewardship).

- **Future Trend:** Verifiable Earth observation data (the solution must leverage technology to make the invisible, visible, and therefore quantifiable).

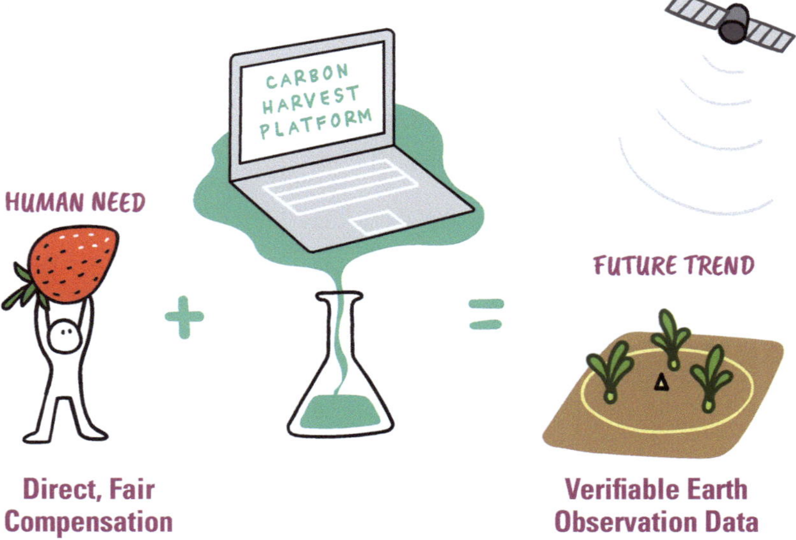

The Idea: The Carbon Harvest Platform

This fusion sparks the refined concept of the **"Carbon Harvest" platform**. This intuitive, farmer-centric digital platform uses verifiable, real-time data from soil sensors and satellites to issue **"regeneration credits."** These credits monetize the ecological value created by regenerative practices, including sequestered carbon, improved water retention, and increased biodiversity. This ensures economic reward is intrinsically linked to planetary health.

Connecting Need to Tech

The Creative Mash-Up forces the team to create solutions that are not dependent on regulation or grants. By using verifiable data to prove the ecological value of Javier's labor, the platform transforms him from a vulnerable commodity producer into a steward of planetary resources, creating a new, verifiable income stream based on verifiable facts.

The Ethical Consequences Scanner

Before developing the final concept, the team uses the Ethical Consequences Scanner for rigorous testing of potential negative consequences. The Carbon Harvest platform is placed at the center of the scanner.

- **First-Order Negative Consequence:** The platform could create a new "digital divide," benefiting large, tech-savvy agribusinesses while leaving smaller, less-connected farmers like Javier behind.
- **Second-Order Negative Consequence:** This could lead to further consolidation of farmland and the marginalization of the very communities the platform was intended to help.

New Design Constraint: This insight leads to a crucial design principle: "The platform must be co-designed with farmers like Javier and include a 'high-touch' support network to ensure it is accessible and equitable for farms of all sizes."

The support network should not just be a help desk but a team of on-the-ground agronomists and community leaders who co-design the platform, provide hands-on training, and ensure the technology is accessible and equitable for farms of all sizes.

Applying the Value Proposition for Humanity Canvas

With this refined and ethically grounded concept, its "win-win-win" value proposition is now mapped:

- **Value for People (Javier & Farmers):** Creates a new, diversified revenue stream based on stewardship. Provides data-driven insights to improve farm resilience and profitability. Builds a community of practice.

- **Value for the Planet (the Soil):** Creates a direct financial incentive to rapidly accelerate the adoption of regenerative practices, leading to healthier soil, sequestered carbon, and restored biodiversity.

- **Value for Society (Global Community):** Increases the resilience of the global food system. Provides a transparent and verifiable way for corporations and individuals to invest in genuine climate solutions.

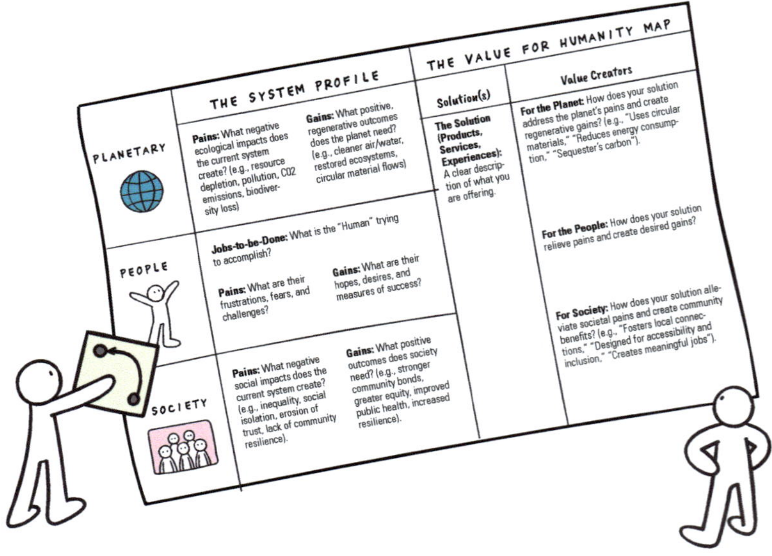

Future Storytelling & Narrative Prototyping

We create a short "day in the life" story to prototype the human experience of this solution.

The Story:
Javier starts his day by opening the Carbon Harvest app instead of checking commodity prices. The dashboard shows that the cover crops he planted increased his soil's water retention by 5%, automatically issuing new "water resilience credits."

Later, a video call with a young tech entrepreneur in a distant city connects him to a team whose company is buying his credits to meet their corporate climate goals. He finally sees a clear path to passing a thriving, healthy farm to his children, embracing his new role as a respected steward of a vital planetary resource.

Validating Systemic Robustness

Finally, we test the underlying accountability, governance, and financial policies. We move beyond merely confirming the emotional or behavioral success of a prototype (such as testing if an individual feels like a "steward" after hearing a specific narrative) to validating the robustness of the entire system that enables that behavior. Consequently, we must test the legal frameworks, financial mechanisms, and political durability of the credit system itself, not simply the personal appeal to Javier. The following questions must be addressed at this stage:

- Will governments recognize the credits?
- Will banks and financial bodies honor them?
- Is the foundational policy stable enough to avoid immediate political capture or reversal?

By putting political and policy validation first, our mission changes from merely proposing a solution to actively designing the conditions for its scalable success. **This method acknowledges a key truth: large-scale system change depends on institutional change, not just widespread user adoption**. The ultimate goal is to build interventions that are desirable for people, technologically feasible, and, crucially, politically resilient and structurally sound. This preemptive integration of policy design is essential to allow that the Carbon Harvest platform can transition from a compelling idea into a foundational pillar of the new global economic model, fulfilling the promise of the Living Soil Mandate.

Design Thinking Tools

Beyond the evolved mindset and process, a rich and diverse array of tools is required to empower practitioners of Design Thinking for Humanity. The primary purpose of the following section is to initiate and guide the complex dialogues, creative activities, and strategic conversations necessary to tackle systemic challenges. These methods are designed to facilitate effective systems-level, future-oriented, and planet-centric work.

This toolbox specifically curates and builds upon foundational methods detailed in the original **The Design Thinking Toolbox**. We do not discard foundational tools like Interview for Empathy or Brainstorming. Instead, this collection serves as an essential supplement, offering new and adapted tools that are necessary for applying design thinking to the wicked problems facing humanity and our planet.

Think of these new tools as specialized implements for mastering Design Thinking for Humanity. The tools and methods, ranging from Future Persona to the Ethical Consequences Scanner, are designed to equip all design and innovation teams with advanced capabilities. They help move teams from human-centered to a Design Thinking for Humanity perspective, ensuring the solutions created are not only innovative but also resilient, responsible, and ready for the future.

Design Thinking Toolbox

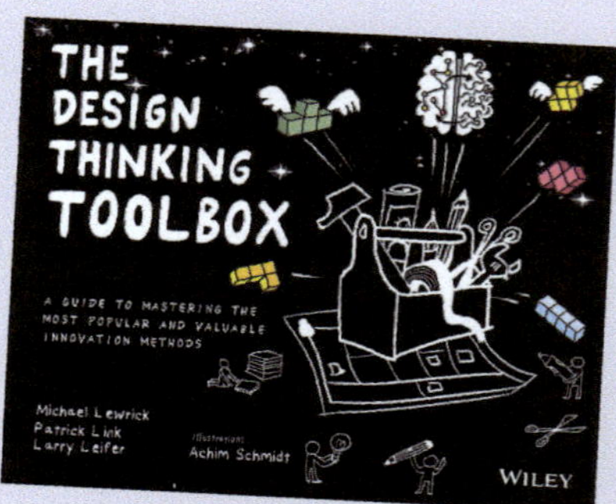

Tip: Find more than 50 powerful innovation methods in The Design Thinking Toolbox.

Advanced Tools for Systemic Interventions

Problem Space

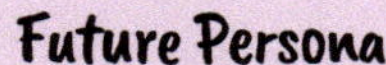

Future Persona

This tool adapts the classic "Persona" method by creating a detailed profile of a person living within a specific future scenario. It moves beyond understanding the needs of a user today to building deep, contextual empathy for the people who will inhabit the future worlds we are trying to shape.

Systemic Empathy Map

This tool evolves the standard empathy map by expanding the focus to an entire ecosystem of stakeholders. It is used to map the pains, gains, needs, and influences of multiple actors. These actors include communities, partners, and even the planet. This fosters a more holistic and relational understanding of a complex problem.

Wicked Problem Framing

This tool provides a structured canvas for deconstructing a complex "wicked problem" without oversimplifying it. It helps teams map the interconnected elements, identify conflicting values and stakeholders, and define a specific, actionable area of focus, ensuring that the problem is framed from a systemic perspective.

Solution Space

Value Proposition for Humanity Canvas

This tool directly evolves the classic Value Proposition Canvas by adding dimensions that force a win-win-win solution. It prompts teams to define not only the value to the user and the business but also the "value to society" and "value to the planet," ensuring a more holistic and responsible approach to innovation.

Future Storytelling & Narrative Prototyping

This tool adapts prototyping to test systemic solutions like services, policies, or behavioral changes. Instead of a product mock-up, the team creates a compelling narrative such as a "day in the life" story, a comic strip, or a short video. This narrative shows how their solution has positively impacted individuals, society, and the planet in a preferable future.

Ethical Consequences Scanner

This tool makes ethical reflection a formal part of the design process. Using a structured method similar to a Futures Wheel, it prompts a team to brainstorm the potential unintended negative consequences of their innovation across different social groups, communities, and time, building a more responsible and resilient solution.

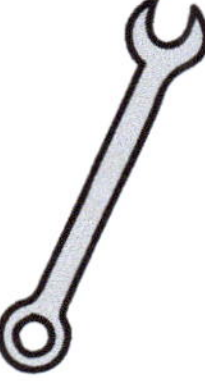

Future Persona

I would like to...

...build deep, contextual empathy for the people who will live in the future worlds we are trying to shape.

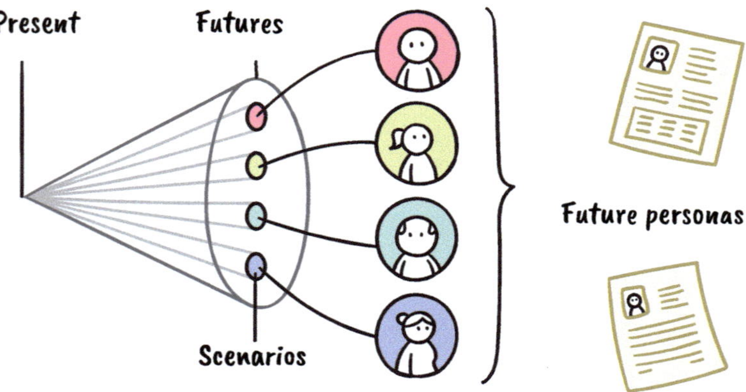

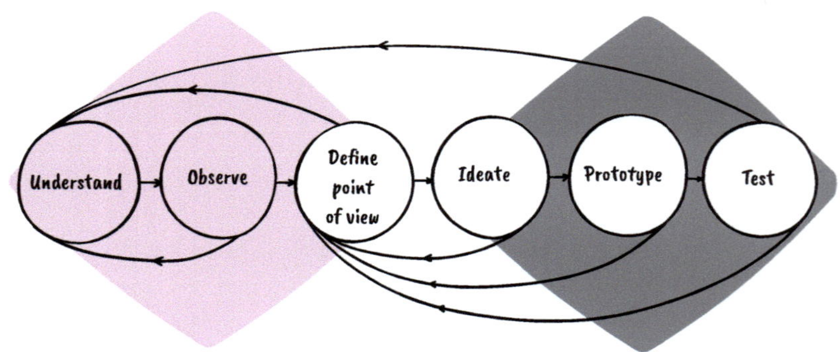

What you can do with the tool:

- Move beyond understanding the needs of a user today to exploring the motivations, values, and challenges of a person in a specific future.
- Ground abstract future scenarios in a relatable, human story.
- Make the potential human impact of a future trend or disruption tangible and emotional.
- Provide a clear and empathetic focal point for future-informed ideation and prototyping.
- Test the human desirability of a potential future before investing heavily in it.

Expert Tips

Focus on Tensions and Contradictions
A compelling Future Persona is not one-dimensional. The most insightful personas are those who experience a tension or conflict with their future world. Exploring these contradictions will lead to richer, more nuanced design opportunities.

Use a Real Person as a Seed
To make a persona feel more authentic, base their core personality on a real person interviewed or observed during empathy work. Then, ask the question: "How would this person adapt, struggle, or thrive if they were living in this specific future scenario?"

Bring the Persona to Life Visually
Do not just write about the persona. Create a visual mood board or a simple sketch. Use AI image generation tools to create a "portrait" of what they might look like. Giving a Future Persona a face makes them far more memorable and powerful as a tool for building team empathy.

Future Persona Canvas

Future Scenario:
Persona Name:
Quote:

Profile

Who is this person?

Demographics: How old is the person? What is their occupation and social role in this future society?

Bio: What is their backstory? What significant life events led them to where they are today?

Their World:

Key Technologies: What technologies do they use daily? What new skills have they had to learn?

Societal Norms: What are the new social rules or expectations in this future world? How do people interact with each other and with technology?

Values & Motivations

Pains: What are their biggest frustrations, fears, and challenges? What is the core conflict they experience in their daily life?

Gains: What are their hopes, desires, and measures of success? What is the ideal outcome they are striving for?

Jobs-to-Be-Done: What is the fundamental task or goal this person is trying to accomplish? What problem are they trying to solve in their life?

Day in the Life

A Narrative Description: Write a short, compelling story of a typical day for this persona. How do they navigate their routines? How do they interact with the new systems and social structures? What are the subtle human implications of this future world?

Tensions and Contradictions: Where does their personal experience conflict with the promises of the future world? Where do they feel a push-and-pull between their values and the new reality?

How this tool is applied:

A Future Persona adapts the classic persona method by creating a detailed, fictional profile of an individual living within a specific future scenario. This goes beyond demographics to explore a person's life in a world that does not yet exist.

Step 1: Select a Future Scenario
Choose one of the distinct future scenarios created using the **Scenario Planning & the 2x2 Matrix (see page 92)** tool. Immerse the team in the rules, characteristics, and key technologies of this specific future world.

Step 2: Create the Persona's Profile
Give the persona a name, an age, and a role relevant to that future society. Go deeper by describing their daily routines, primary goals, and biggest frustrations. What new skills do they have? What values might they hold that are different from today's values? What do they hope for, and what do they fear in their world?

Step 3: Define Their "Day in the Life"
Write a short, narrative description of a "day in the life" of the Future Persona. Describe how they interact with the technology, systems, and social norms of their time. This story is the most critical part, as it makes the future tangible and reveals the subtle, human-scale implications of the systemic changes envisioned. This narrative can serve as a powerful input for **Future Storytelling & Narrative Prototyping (see page 160)**.

Variation: Future Persona Stereotypes in Combination with the Future Wheel

This method uses familiar persona stereotypes as a creative shortcut and combines them with the rigor of the **Futures Wheel (see page 100)** to generate provocative, future-focused character sketches. These characters are designed not as finished profiles but as catalysts to ignite dialogue about the human implications of a potential future.

Step 1: Define the Future Context
Choose one of the distinct future scenarios you created using the **Scenario Planning & the 2x2 Matrix** tool. For this example, we will use the scenario from our **Futures Wheel** exercise: "By 2040, brain-computer interfaces (BCIs) are widely adopted, co-existing with the emergence of artificial general intelligence (AGI)."

Step 2: Select a Persona Stereotype
From the list of common archetypes, select one stereotype that would create an interesting tension or dynamic within your chosen future scenario. The goal is to use the stereotypes (see list of 12 common stereotypes) as a familiar starting point for exploring the unfamiliar.

Step 3: Give the Stereotype a Future Identity
Flesh out the chosen stereotype with a name and a specific role within the future scenario. What is their primary goal or motivation? For example, in a world of seamless BCI/AGI integration, we might choose "The Sage," naming him Kaelen, an elderly man whose goal is to curate and preserve authentic, unaugmented human memories.

The Joker: Challenges conventions, injects levity into serious situations, and reveals absurdities in the system

The Lover: Pursues deep connection, intimacy, and shared meaning, focusing on the emotional and relational aspects of a future experience

The Hero: Strives to overcome great challenges for the greater good, often acting as the protagonist who drives a story of change

The Nurturer: Provides support, care, and compassion, focusing on the well-being and security of others within a future scenario

The Rebel: Actively challenges the status quo, questions authority, and seeks to disrupt established norms and systems

The Explorer: Ventures into the unknown, driven by curiosity to discover new possibilities, experiences, and ways of living

The Visionary: Envisions a radically different future, challenges current assumptions, and inspires others with innovative ideas

The Innocent: Approaches the future with a optimistic, and idealistic outlook, often highlighting the gap between a desired future and a complex reality

The Loyalist: Seeks to preserve core values, traditions, and relationships, acting as an anchor of stability in the face of radical change

The Ruler: Focuses on establishing order, governance, and stable systems, exploring how power and control might operate in a future world

The Sage: Seeks wisdom and truth through introspection and analysis, often acting as a mentor or guide who offers a deeper understanding of the future

The Everyman: Embodies the common values and experiences of the general population, providing a relatable perspective on how the future will shape and impact society

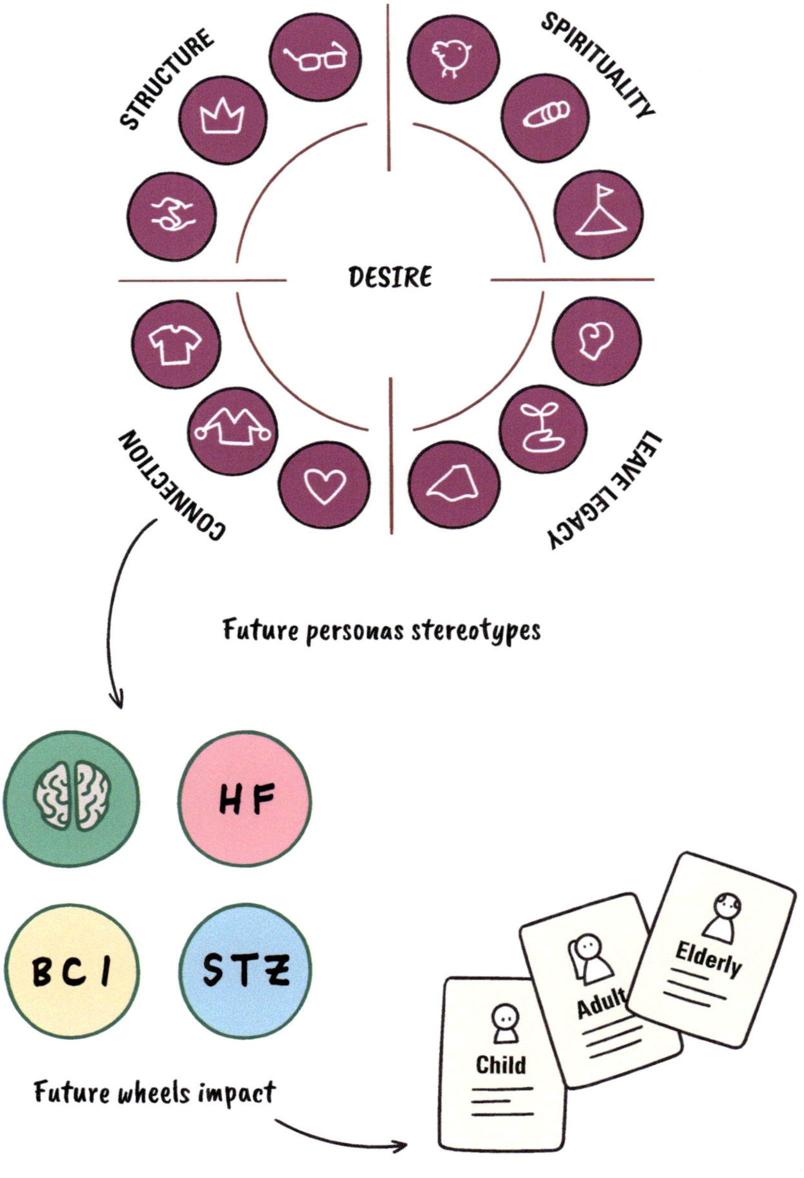

Step 4: Place a Core Decision at the Center of a Futures Wheel
This is the crucial step where the persona and the Futures Wheel merge. Define a core decision or provocative action that your Future Persona stereotype would take. Place this decision in the center of a **Futures Wheel**.

Example: For Kaelen, the Sage, the central event could be: "Kaelen creates a 'memory sanctuary,' a disconnected, offline community where people can experience life without their BCIs."

Step 5: Explore the Consequences with the Futures Wheel
Use the Futures Wheel to map the cascading consequences of your persona's action.

First Order: What are the immediate results? (e.g., "A small but dedicated following emerges," "The community is labeled as 'luddite' or 'regressive' by mainstream society.")

Second Order: What happens next? (e.g., "The Sanctuary becomes a refuge for those suffering from 'network anxiety'," "Governments debate whether to regulate or shut down such 'offline' zones.")

Third Order: What are the long-term societal shifts? (e.g., "A new philosophy emerges celebrating 'digital minimalism' and the value of disconnected thought," "The concept of 'human heritage' is expanded to include specific cognitive states and experiences.")

Step 6: Synthesize the Character Narrative
Weave the insights from the Futures Wheel into a rich narrative. This story is the provocative character sketch. It should describe not just who the person is, but the systemic effects of their actions. This narrative becomes a powerful tool to challenge assumptions about the human experience in an envisioned future.

Systemic Empathy Map

I would like to...

...move beyond understanding a single user/customer to build empathy for an entire ecosystem of stakeholders.

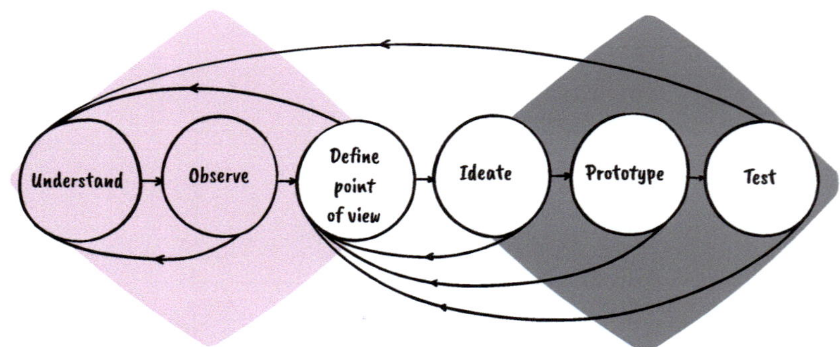

What you can do with the tool:

- Visualize the complex network of relationships and perspectives within a wicked problem.
- Identify the often-conflicting needs, pains, and gains of different actors in a system.
- Foster a more holistic and "life-centered" understanding of a challenge by including non-human stakeholders.
- Uncover opportunities for systemic solutions that create value for multiple stakeholders simultaneously.
- Build a shared "big picture" understanding within a team before diving into ideation.

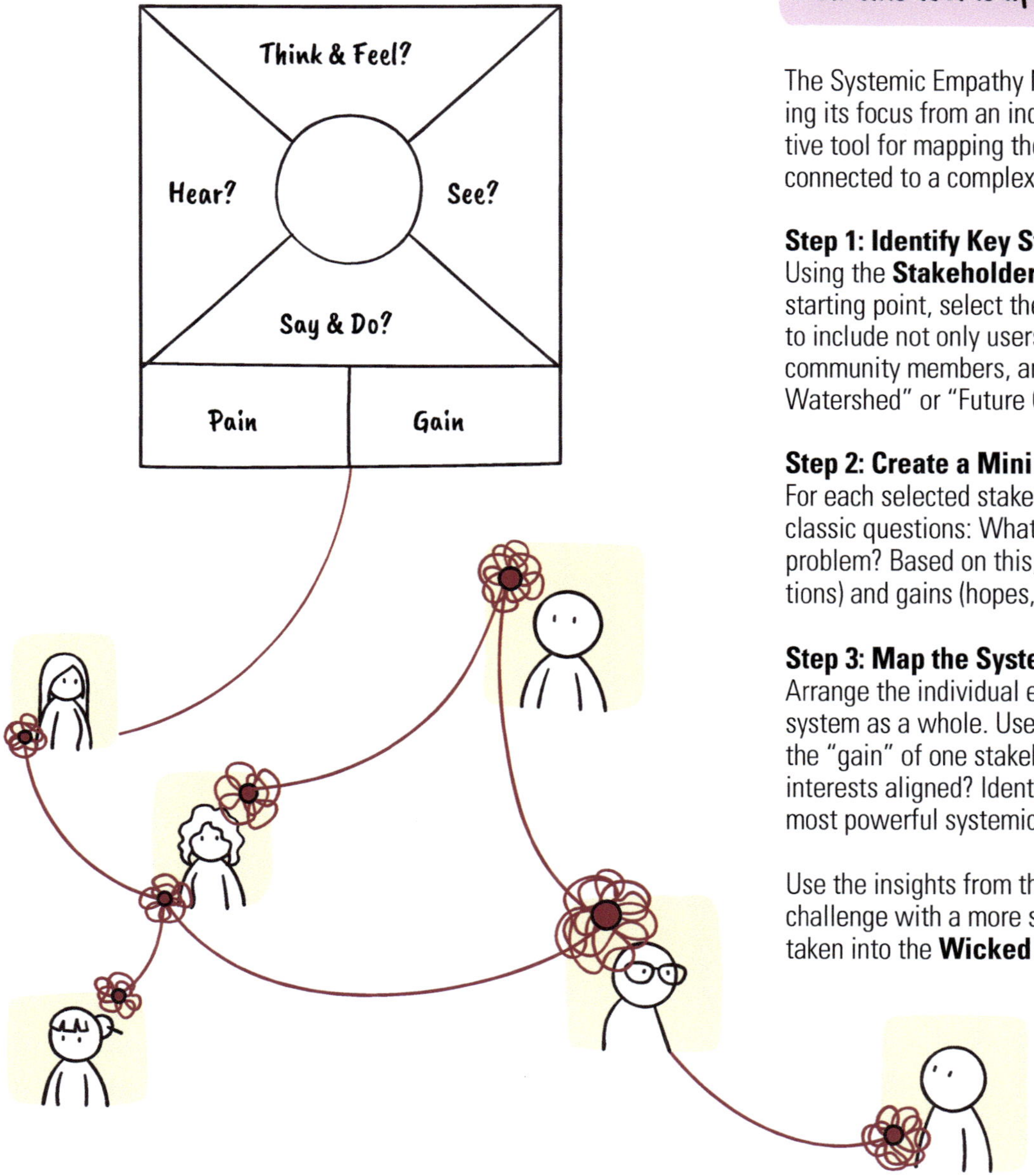

The Systemic Empathy Map evolves the classic empathy map by expanding its focus from an individual user to a whole system. It is a collaborative tool for mapping the diverse experiences and motivations of all actors connected to a complex problem.

Step 1: Identify Key Stakeholders

Using the **Stakeholder Analysis & Mapping (see page 82)** as a starting point, select the most critical actors in the ecosystem. Be sure to include not only users and customers but also partners, employees, community members, and crucial non-human stakeholders like "The Local Watershed" or "Future Generations."

Step 2: Create a Mini Empathy Map for Each Stakeholder

For each selected stakeholder, create a dedicated empathy map. Ask the classic questions: What do they see, say, do, and hear in relation to the problem? Based on this, what are their underlying pains (fears, frustrations) and gains (hopes, desires)?

Step 3: Map the Systemic Connections and Tensions

Arrange the individual empathy maps on a large canvas. Now, analyze the system as a whole. Use lines and notes to connect the maps. Where does the "gain" of one stakeholder create a "pain" for another? Where are their interests aligned? Identifying these tensions and synergies is where the most powerful systemic insights are found.

Use the insights from the interconnected pains and gains to reframe the challenge with a more systemic "How Might We" question that can be taken into the **Wicked Problem Framing tool (see page 152)**.

Extension: The System Empathy Map Canvas

I would like to...

…bridge from single actors toward the ecosystem by synthesizing the previous elaborated insights to understand the system itself.

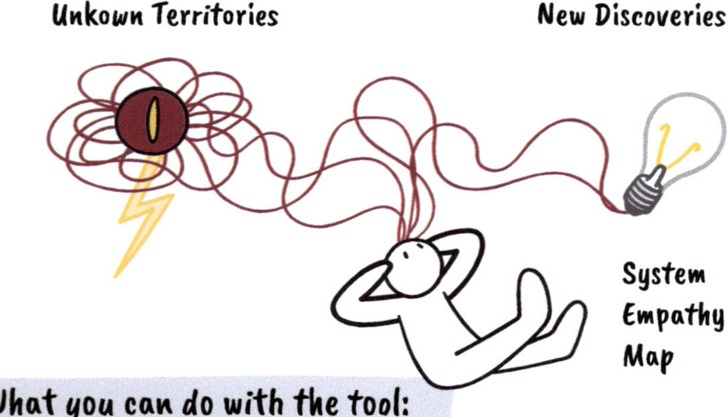

What you can do with the tool:

- Shift the focus from the individual user (micro-level) to the entire ecosystem (macro level), allowing the team to build systemic empathy.
- Conceptualize the entire system (such as a financial market or a local community) as a single entity with its own distinct thoughts, narratives, and behaviors related to the challenge.
- Articulate clearly what the "System" thinks, says, and and does, to reveal the deeply held cultural beliefs and institutional inertia that sustain complex problems.
- Synthesis the systemic insights to understand what is blocking meaningful change and effectively prepare to reframe the wicked problem at its root.

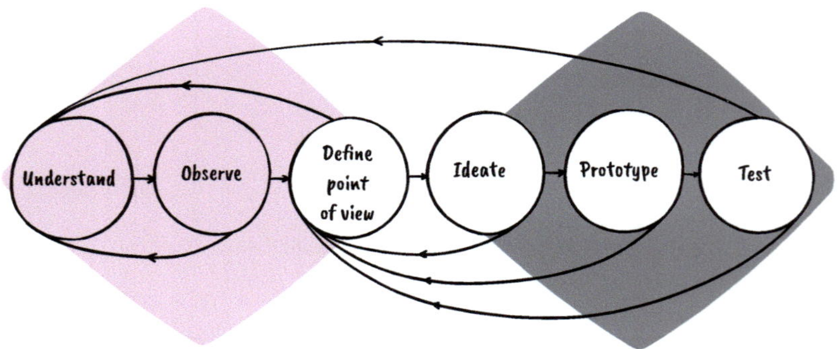

Expert Tips

Reframe for Humanity-Centricity
Identify the critical systemic insights that allow to reframe the challenge. Use the synthesized "System Think & Feel" and "System Says & Does" to craft a more powerful HMW question. The best HMW questions target the root systemic beliefs and policy barriers, ensuring that the next ideation phase moves from human-centered to humanity-centric solutions.

Give the System a Voice
Treat the entire system (the market, the community, the policy landscape) as a single, complex entity. By consolidating the diverse experiences of all actors, it provides the basis to give a voice to the collective. Ask: What deep-seated cultural norms or political narratives is the system saying? What emotional inertia is the system feeling?

Ideate from Systemic Needs
Take the opportunity to address the system's needs. Focus the ideation on solutions that challenge the core assumptions listed in the "System Thinks & Feels" section or those that disrupt the status quo behaviors described in the "System Says & Does." Solutions that successfully resolve a systemic tension will naturally create value for multiple stakeholders simultaneously.

System Empathy Map Canvas

Challenge Focus:
Describe the scope of the challenge

Who Is Impacted?	System Thinks & Feels	System Says & Does
Beyond the direct "user," list all stakeholders, environments, and future generations affected by this challenge.	What are the underlying assumptions, cultural norms, or deeply held beliefs within the system that contribute to or are impacted by the challenge? What are the emotional, social, or environmental impacts and sentiments associated with the challenge across various stakeholders and the system as a whole?	What are the prevailing narratives, policies, data, or media messages related to the challenge at a societal or systemic level? What are the current behaviors, processes, actions, or policies within the system that are relevant to the challenge?

How this tool is applied:

The System Empathy Map Canvas allows you to aggregate the collective insights from individual Empathy Maps into a cohesive systemic view.

Step 1: Define the Impacted Ecosystem

Review the complete list of stakeholders generated in the Systemic Empathy Map exercise. Go beyond the direct "user" to consolidate the list of all entities affected by the challenge, including partners, environments, and especially future generations. The goal is to clearly establish the boundary of the system currently analyzed.

Step 2: Synthesize Systemic Beliefs and Sentiments

Based on the combined "Think & Feel" sections of all the empathy maps, identify the core underlying assumptions and cultural norms that hold the current system in place. Ask powerful questions: What are the deeply held beliefs within the system that contribute to the challenge?

Additionally, capture the aggregated emotional, social, or environmental impacts and sentiments associated with the challenge across all stakeholders. This synthesizes the collective pains and gains into a single "System Think & Feel."

Step 3: Articulate Systemic Narratives and Actions

Review the "Say & Do" sections of the individual maps to identify patterns in collective behavior. Articulate the prevailing narratives, policies, data, or media messages related to the challenge at a societal level. Then, list the current behaviors, processes, actions, or policies within the system (e.g., subsidies, regulations, investment trends) that are relevant to the challenge. This step translates fragmented stakeholder actions into a cohesive description of what the system currently communicates and executes.

Wicked Problem Framing

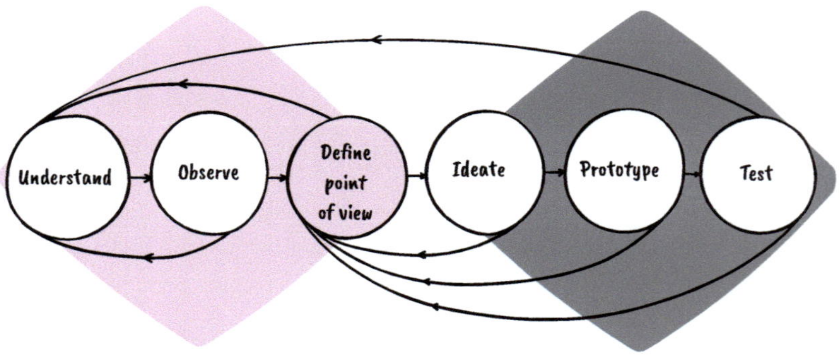

I would like to...

...deconstruct a complex "wicked problem" to define a clear and action-able area of focus without oversimplifying the challenge.

What you can do with the tool:

- Move beyond linear problem-solving to embrace the complexity and interconnectedness of major challenges.
- Map the diverse stakeholders, conflicting values, and systemic forces that keep a wicked problem in place.
- Avoid the trap of solving the wrong problem by ensuring a deep and shared understanding of the challenge.
- Align a team around a specific, well-framed intervention point within a larger system.
- Provide a solid foundation for generating systemic solutions that build long-term resilience.

Expert Tips

Embrace the "Mess"
The goal of this exercise is to embrace the mess. A good wicked problem map should look complex, reflecting the challenge's nature. The value lies in the shared conversation and the process of grappling with the complexity as a team.

Frame for Intervention, Not a "Solution"
Wicked problems are never truly solved. Frame the challenge with the goal of making a positive intervention that shifts the system in a more desirable, resilient direction, rather than trying to find a definitive, final solution.

Involve Diverse Voices
It is impossible to frame a wicked problem from a single per-spective. Ensure the framing session includes a diverse group of people who represent the different stakeholders mapped. A city planner, a community activist, and a farmer will all see the problem of urban food resilience differently.

A wicked problem is a complex societal or cultural problem that is difficult to solve because of incomplete, contradictory, and changing requirements. Wicked Problem Framing is a structured method for deconstructing these challenges to find a meaningful starting point for action.

Step 1: State the Wicked Problem
Start by stating the wicked problem in broad, open-ended terms.

Example: "How might we build resilient food systems for urban populations in the face of climate change?"

Step 2: Map the Systemic Context
Using the insights from the **Systemic Empathy Map (see page 148)**, identify and map the key elements of the problem on a large canvas:

Stakeholders: Who is affected or has influence (e.g., farmers, city dwellers, governments, corporations, ecosystems)?

Conflicting Values: What core values are in tension (e.g., food affordability versus ecological health; economic efficiency versus community resilience)?

Systemic Drivers: What larger forces are at play (e.g., global supply chains, consumer habits, agricultural policies)?

Step 3: Reframe the Problem with a "How Might We" Question
Based on the map, identify a specific leverage point or relationship where an intervention could create a positive ripple effect. Reframe the initial broad problem into a focused HMW question using the following structure: **"How might we"** + [action verb] + [intended action] + **"for"** [specific user/context] + **"so that"** [desired benefit].

Reframed Example: "How might we **create** a network of shared urban community gardens **for** low-income neighborhoods **so that** they can increase their access to nutritious food and build stronger community bonds?"

WICKED PROBLEM FRAMING

1

The Broad Wicked Problem Statement:
What is the overarching, multilayered, and contradictory problem we are trying to solve?

Stakeholders:
Which people, institutions, and non-human entities are key actors in this system?

2

Conflicting Values
What trade-offs are the key actors being forced to make? (e.g., short-term profit versus long-term health)

Systemic Drivers
What are the key economic, political, and environmental mechanisms locking the current system in place?

3

Leverage Point Identification
Where can a small intervention create the greatest positive ripple effect that solves a pain for the persona?

The Focused HMW Question
How do we make the intervention (leverage point) directly benefit our core persona to achieve their deepest desires (gains)?

DOWNLOAD TOOL
www.design-humanity.com/en/wicked-problem

Value Proposition for Humanity Canvas

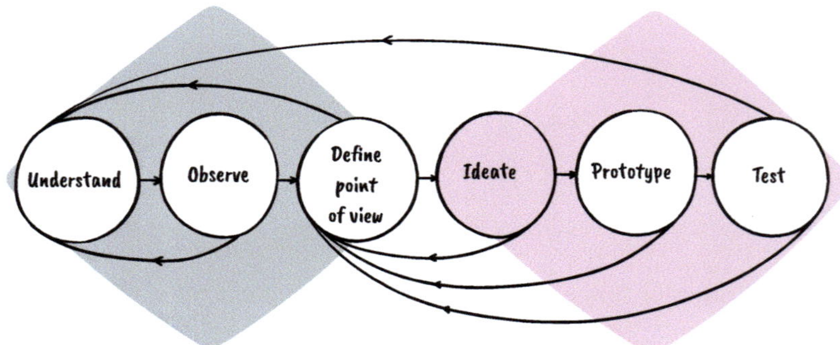

...design and test a value proposition that creates a "win-win-win" by benefiting humans, the planet, and the broader system.

What you can do with the tool:

- Evolve the classic value proposition canvas to meet the demands of systemic, 21st-century challenges.
- Ensure your solution is not only desirable for users but also beneficial for society and the environment.
- Systematically think through the positive and negative impacts of your idea on a wider scale.
- Align your team around a more holistic and responsible definition of "value."
- Create more resilient and sustainable solutions that are built to last and contribute positively to the world.

Expert Tips

Define Specific Metrics
Do not leave the new value dimensions vague. For "Value to Planet," define specific metrics that could be tracked, such as "reduced Co2 emissions." For "Value to Society," use metrics like "improved access for marginalized communities."

Look for Synergies, Not Trade-Offs
The goal of this canvas is not to create a zero-sum game. The most powerful innovations are those where the different value propositions reinforce each other. Ask: "How can improving the ecological value of our solution also create a more meaningful experience for our user?"

Use It to Test Your "Why"
This canvas is a powerful tool for testing the purpose behind a project. If a team is struggling to articulate the value to the planet and society, it may be a sign that the solution is not systemic enough. Use the canvas to challenge the team to think bigger and to re-align the project with a more holistic and resilient vision.

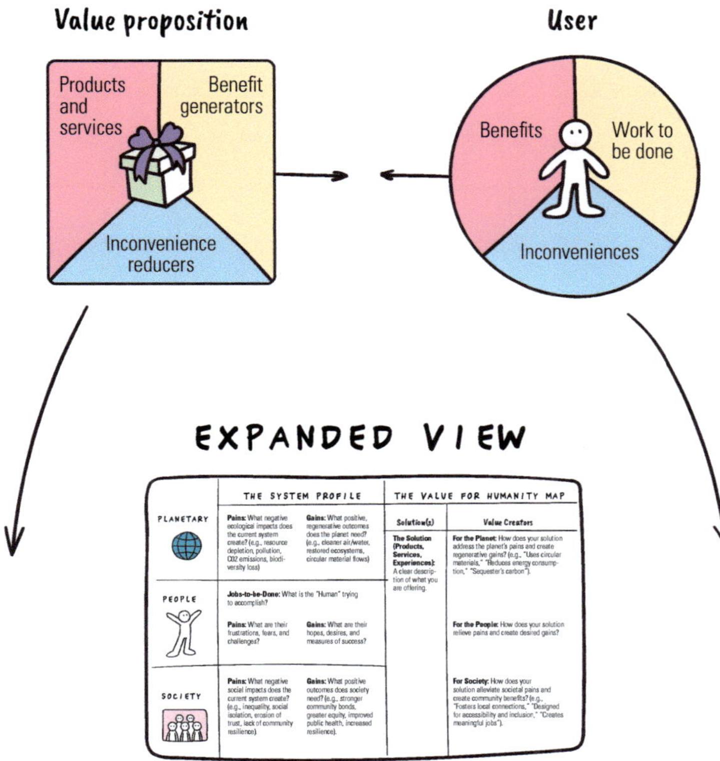

See canvas and example on pages 156–159

How this tool is applied:

The Value Proposition for Humanity Canvas expands on the classic canvas by adding dimensions that force a systemic view. The tool challenges a team to define value beyond the immediate customer and business, ensuring a more holistic and responsible approach to innovation.

Step 1: Define the System Profile

Start with the insights from the problem space. Detail the profile of the **Future Persona (see page 144)**. Then, expand this view to include the "pains" and "gains" of both the planet and society, as identified in the **Systemic Empathy Map (see page 148)**.

Step 2: Map the Solution's Value

On the other side, describe the proposed solution that addresses the **Wicked Problem Framing**. How does it relieve the persona's pains and create their desired gains? This establishes the core user-centric value proposition.

Step 3: Expand to a "Win-Win-Win" Proposition

This is the critical new step. Add two new sections to the value map:

- **Value to Planet:** How does the solution positively impact ecological systems? Does it use regenerative materials, reduce waste, or improve biodiversity?

- **Value to Society:** How does the solution improve community resilience, social equity, or public well-being? Does it create new forms of connection or strengthen social fabric?

Value Proposition for Humanity Canvas

	THE SYSTEM PROFILE		THE VALUE FOR HUMANITY MAP	
			Solution(s)	Value Creators
PLANETARY	**Pains:** What negative ecological impacts does the current system create (e.g., resource depletion, pollution, CO2 emissions, biodiversity loss)?	**Gains:** What positive, regenerative outcomes does the planet need (e.g., cleaner air/water, restored ecosystems, circular material flows)?	**The Solution (Products, Services, Experiences):** A clear description of what you are offering.	**For the Planet:** How does your solution address the planet's pains and create regenerative gains (e.g., "Uses circular materials," "Reduces energy consumption," "Sequester's carbon")?
PEOPLE	**Jobs-to-Be-Done:** What is the "human" trying to accomplish? **Pains:** What are their frustrations, fears, and challenges?	**Gains:** What are their hopes, desires, and measures of success?		**For the People:** How does your solution relieve pains and create desired gains?
SOCIETY	**Pains:** What negative social impacts does the current system create (e.g., inequality, social isolation, erosion of trust, lack of community resilience)?	**Gains:** What positive outcomes does society need (e.g., stronger community bonds, greater equity, improved public health, increased resilience)?		**For Society:** How does your solution alleviate societal pains and create community benefits (e.g., "Fosters local connections," "Designed for accessibility and inclusion," "Creates meaningful jobs")?

Example Application: From Theory to Systemic Value

The following two pages provide a powerful example of applying the Value Proposition for Humanity Canvas methodology within the framework of Design Thinking for Humanity. This example shows how the insights gathered from the system profile directly inform the development of the Value for Humanity Map, which guides the subsequent Ideate and Prototype stages. The solution proposed is "The Community Harvest Network," a subscription-based service.

The resulting value creators for the planet, people, and society demonstrate how this single solution is intentionally designed to alleviate previously identified pains and deliver desired gains across all three dimensions simultaneously. For the planet, the network acts as a "carbon sink" and promotes a closed-loop system for organic waste. For people, it provides ultra-local, affordable access to fresh food and offers community workshops.

This structure ensures that the final value proposition is holistic, regenerative, and truly human-centered, optimizing for collective and ecological flourishing rather than just economic return. This shift ensures the design process delivers a "regenerative outcome": a solution that improves the social, ecological, and communal capital of the system. This should be the ultimate goal of applying Design Thinking for Humanity to complex, real-world problems.

The core innovation mandate has changed. We no longer ask, "Does this make profit?" We ask, "Does this create profit only by simultaneously increasing the health of the planet, the resilience of society, and the well-being of the user?" The new sweet spot is the "win-win-win" where purpose drives prosperity.

Two Critical Shifts in Value Proposition Thinking

The example of applying the canvas demonstrates two important shifts in applying value proposition thinking:

1. How to Expand the "Customer" Profile Beyond Revenue: To overcome traditional business thinking, explicitly mandate the inclusion of nonpaying beneficiaries, community entities, and the environment as separate, defined segments within the canvas. This means creating profiles for **the planet** and **society**, detailing their pains and gains. This immediate shift forces a **triple-bottom-line perspective**, ensuring the resulting value proposition optimizes for collective, systemic well-being rather than just individual user profit.

2. How to Prioritize Systemic Impact over Immediate Profit: Instead of ranking pain relievers and gain creators based on revenue potential, change the criteria to focus on **ethical and systemic impact**. Prioritize features that address the most urgent planetary pains (e.g., carbon reduction) and deliver the most equitable social gains (e.g., access for vulnerable populations). This deliberate re-ranking ensures the final solution is **fundamentally responsible and sustainable**, integrating social and ecological benefit as a core design principle.

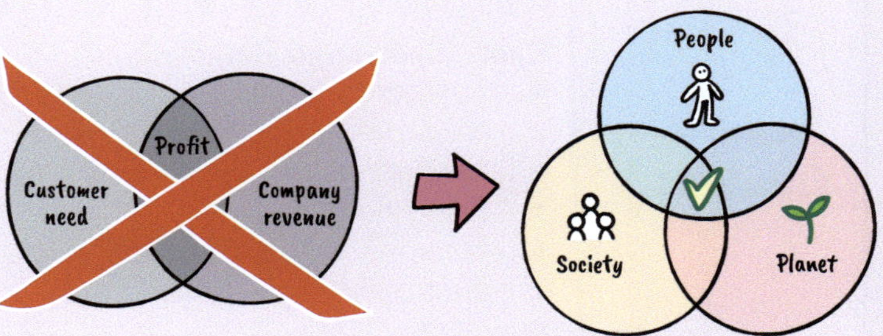

Idea: A service that provides access to shared community garden plots, tools, and education for urban residents.

Example

THE SYSTEM PROFILE

<table>
<tr>
<td rowspan="1">PLANETARY

The Urban Ecosystem</td>
<td>Pains (Systemic Harms):
• High carbon footprint from food transported long distances
• Loss of biodiversity due to concrete and lack of green space
• Stormwater runoff overwhelming sewer systems
• Organic food waste going to landfills</td>
<td>Gains (Regenerative Outcomes):
• Increased local biodiversity (pollinators, soil microbes)
• Reduced "food miles" and associated carbon emissions
• Improved soil health and water absorption
• Creation of local, closed-loop composting systems</td>
</tr>
<tr>
<td rowspan="2">PEOPLE

Urban Families in Low-Income Neighborhoods</td>
<td>Jobs-to-Be-Done:
• Access affordable, fresh, and healthy food
• Find safe, positive activities for their children
• Connect with neighbors and feel part of a community</td>
<td></td>
</tr>
<tr>
<td>Pains:
• High cost of fresh produce at supermarkets ("food deserts")
• Anxiety about food security and where food comes from
• Lack of green space and connection to nature
• Feeling of social isolation in a dense urban environment</td>
<td>Gains:
• Desire for their children to eat healthier
• Desire to learn new, practical skills (gardening, preserving)
• Hope for a stronger, safer, and more collaborative neighborhood</td>
</tr>
<tr>
<td>SOCIETY

The Urban Community</td>
<td>Gains (Community Benefits):
• Stronger social ties and increased trust between neighbors
• Intergenerational knowledge sharing
• Greater local food sovereignty and resilience
• Increased sense of collective ownership and pride in the neighborhood</td>
<td>Gains:
• Erosion of community trust and "third places" for interaction
• Generational disconnect; loss of traditional knowledge (e.g., growing food)
• Lack of neighborhood resilience to economic shocks or supply chain disruptions</td>
</tr>
</table>

THE VALUE FOR HUMANITY MAP

Solution(s)	Value Creators
The Solution: **The "Community Harvest" Network** A subscription-based service providing garden plots, tools, seeds, and educational workshops, managed through a simple mobile app that also facilitates community interaction.	**For the Planet:** • The gardens act as "carbon sinks" and biodiversity hubs in urban areas • We provide on-site composting bins for all organic waste, creating a closed-loop system • Our seed kits prioritize native and pollinator-friendly plants
	**For the People (Urban Family):** • Provides ultra-local, affordable access to fresh, organic produce • Offers workshops on gardening and cooking, building skills and confidence • The app features a community forum and event scheduler to foster connection
	For Society: • The gardens are designed as safe, accessible community hubs, hosting events like harvest festivals and potlucks • We partner with local schools and senior centers to create inter-generational gardening programs • By localizing a portion of the food supply, we build tangible neighborhood resilience

Future Storytelling & Narrative Prototyping

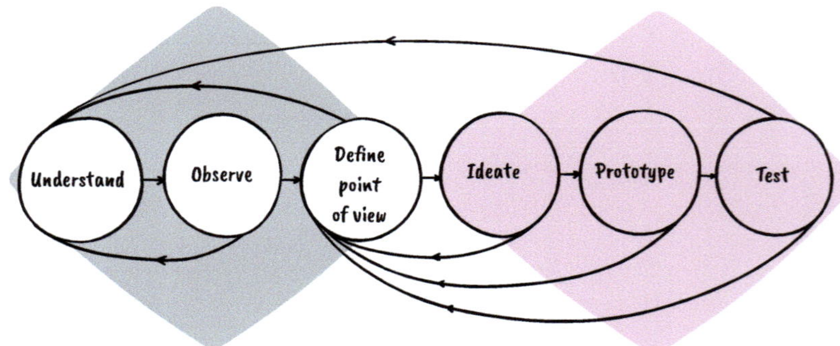

I would like to...

...prototype a complex solution by creating a compelling story about a "day in the life" of a preferable future.

What you can do with the tool:

- Test and communicate systemic solutions like services, policies, or behavioral changes that are difficult to prototype physically.
- Create a rich, human-centered vision of the future that stakeholders can connect with emotionally.
- Uncover the subtle, human-scale implications and consequences of a large-scale systemic shift.
- Generate powerful artifacts (stories, comics, videos) that can be used to align teams and persuade decision-makers.
- Build empathy and understanding for your solution by showing it through the eyes of the people who will experience it.

Expert Tips

Show, Do Not Tell

The core principle of effective storytelling is to show the future in action rather than just explaining it. Instead of saying a solution "improves community resilience," write a short scene where neighbors use the solution to help each other during a crisis. This makes the benefit tangible and emotional.

Focus on a "Moment of Truth"

A powerful narrative prototype does not need to show a person's entire life. Focus on a single, critical "moment of truth" where the solution makes a real difference. This focus will make the story more impactful and easier to produce.

Use It as a Research Tool

A narrative prototype is not just a presentation tool; it is a research tool. Share the story with stakeholders and users and treat it like a prototype test. Ask them: "Does this future feel believable? Is this a world you would want to live in? What would you change about this story?" Their feedback is invaluable for refining the solution.

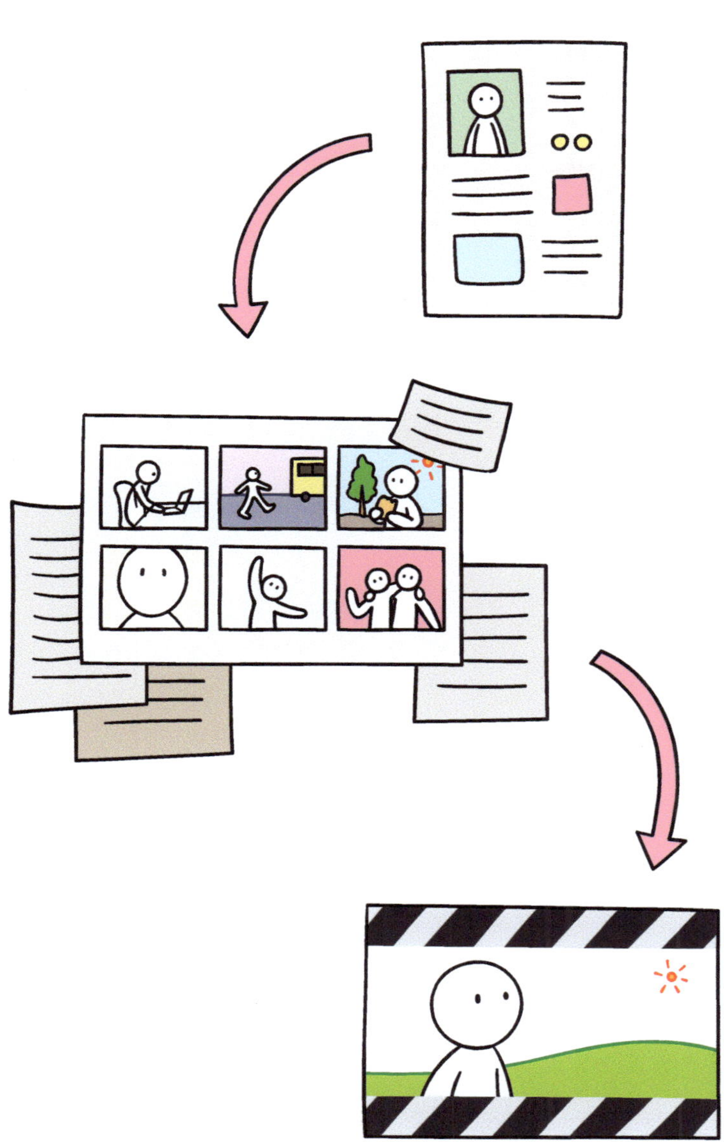

How this tool is applied:

Future Storytelling is a prototyping method that focuses on building a narrative to test and communicate a systemic solution. Instead of building a mock-up of a product, you build a story that shows your solution in action within a specific future world.

Step 1: Choose the Persona and Value Proposition
Select the **Future Persona (see page 144)** created previously, and the core **"win-win-win" value proposition (see page 154)**. The goal is to tell a story that brings this specific value proposition to life from the persona's perspective.

Step 2: Define the Narrative Arc
Create a simple story arc for the persona that showcases the proposed solution. A simple arc includes:
- **The Situation:** Briefly describe the persona's context and the challenge they face.
- **The Intervention:** Show how they interact with the new solution, service, or system.
- **The Resolution:** Describe the new reality and the positive outcomes for the persona, society, and the planet.

Step 3: Create the Narrative Prototype
Bring the story to life in a tangible format. This can take many forms depending on the resources and audience, such as a written story, a storyboard or comic strip, an audio prototype, or a video prototype.

Ethical Consequences Scanner

I would like to...

...proactively identify and mitigate the potential unintended negative consequences of my innovation.

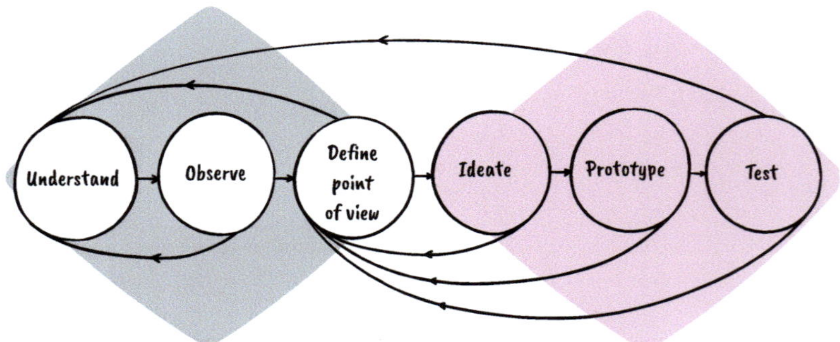

What you can do with the tool:

- Move beyond testing just for desirability, feasibility, viability to include ethical and societal impacts.
- Systematically map the potential negative ripple effects of a solution before it is launched.
- Identify which stakeholder groups might be unintentionally harmed by your innovation.
- Facilitate a structured and honest conversation about the ethical responsibilities of your team.
- Build more resilient, responsible, and "future-proofed" solutions by addressing ethical risks early in the process.

Expert Tips

Use an Ethical Framework

To structure the brainstorming, use an ethical framework to prompt thinking. For example, consequences could be organized into categories like: Harm to Individuals, Harm to Society, Environmental Harm, and Harm to Democratic Values. This ensures a more comprehensive scan.

Assign a Red Team

To ensure a truly critical and honest assessment, assign a red team. This is a subgroup whose only job is to think pessimistically and identify all the possible ways a solution could fail or be misused. This formalizes the critical perspective and removes the social pressure to be optimistic.

Turn Risks into Design Constraints

The goal of this tool is not to stop innovation but to make it better. For every significant negative consequence identified, turn it into a positive design constraint. For example, if the solution could "increase social isolation," create a new design constraint: "How might we design our solution to actively foster community connection?"

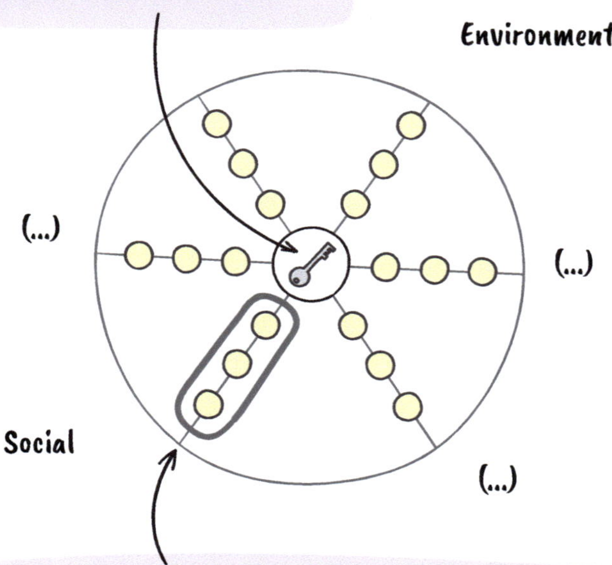

Consequence Path 1: The "Gentrification" Effect
First-Order Negative Consequence: The community gardens are successful and make the neighborhood more desirable and aesthetically pleasing.

Second-Order Negative Consequence: This success attracts wealthier residents and developers, causing local property values and rents to rise.

Third-Order Negative Consequence: The original low-income residents for whom the project was intended are eventually priced out and forced to leave their own neighborhood. The solution inadvertently displaces the very people it was meant to help.

How this tool is applied:

The Ethical Consequences Scanner is a structured brainstorming method, similar to the **Futures Wheel (see page 100)** but focused specifically on mapping potential negative outcomes. The tool challenges teams to think like a critic and rigorously explore what could go wrong.

Step 1: Place the Solution at the Center
Start with a clear and concise description of the proposed solution (from the **Value Proposition for Humanity Canvas, see page 154**). Place this at the center of a large canvas.

Step 2: Brainstorm First-Order Negative Consequences
As a team, brainstorm the direct, first-order negative consequences that the solution might create.
Ask critical questions:
- Who could be harmed by this?
- What is the worst-case-scenario use of our product?
- What existing jobs or systems might this disrupt in a negative way?

Step 3: Map Second- and Third-Order Consequences
For each first-order negative consequence, explore the ripple effects. Ask, "If that negative thing happens, what happens next?" This will reveal the deeper, systemic, and often unforeseen ethical challenges that could emerge over time. Continue mapping outward to see the full picture of potential risks.

After completing the Ethical Consequences Scanner, use these questions as a final filter to ensure your solution is fundamentally responsible and aligns with the mandate of systemic resilience.

1. The Question of Equity (Social Impact)

- **Who is unintentionally harmed, and who benefits most?** Does the solution create a new social or digital divide, benefiting the privileged while leaving vulnerable communities behind?
- **Is power centralized or decentralized?** Does the innovation consolidate power within a single organization or technology (like an AI agent), or does it democratize access and empower decentralized decision-making?
- **Have we designed for a "Just Transition"?** Does our plan explicitly mitigate the short-term negative impact on the communities or industries that may be displaced by the new regenerative system?

2. The Question of Integrity (Ecological Impact)

- **Does our solution violate the non-negotiable ecological boundary?** Does achieving short-term success put unsustainable pressure on Earth's critical systems, such as contributing to biodiversity loss or freshwater depletion?
- **Is our solution truly regenerative, or just "less bad"?** Does it actively contribute to ecological flourishing (e.g., sequestering carbon, restoring soil health), or does it merely slow the rate of damage?
- **Are we shifting the burden?** Does solving one environmental problem (e.g., carbon emissions) inadvertently create a worse problem elsewhere (e.g., relying on materials that generate toxic waste)?

3. The Question of Legacy (Temporal Impact)

- **What is the long-term, intergenerational consequence?** How will this solution affect the well-being and autonomy of the generation 50 years from now?
- **Are we accelerating learning or dependence?** Does the innovation strengthen fundamental human capabilities (critical thinking, creativity), or does it automate them away, leading to a profound dependence on technology?
- **What is the myth we are replacing?** Does the solution challenge the old, limiting myth (e.g., "endless growth") and build a new, regenerative narrative that can inspire long-term cultural change?

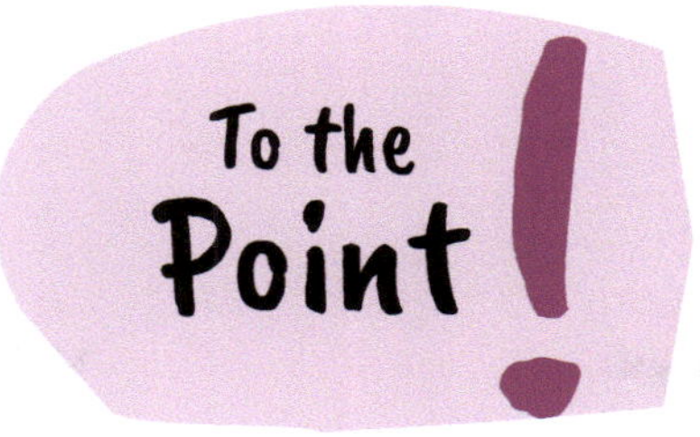

Design thinking is uniquely suited to address wicked problems because it embraces ambiguity, using an iterative and deeply empathetic approach to navigate complexity and uncover the true root causes of a challenge.

Design Thinking for Humanity represents a return to the practice's foundational purpose: to create real and meaningful impact that extends beyond immediate user needs to the well-being of society and the planet.

The "How Might We" questions that drive the creative process are not arbitrary; they are strategic interventions derived from the rigorous foresight and future-oriented context established in the Futures Thinking phase.

Within this new paradigm, the classic Double Diamond process is embedded in a broader context of human and life-centered values, ensuring that every stage of design is guided by a commitment to creating resilient, equitable, and regenerative outcomes.

ECOLOGICAL THINKING

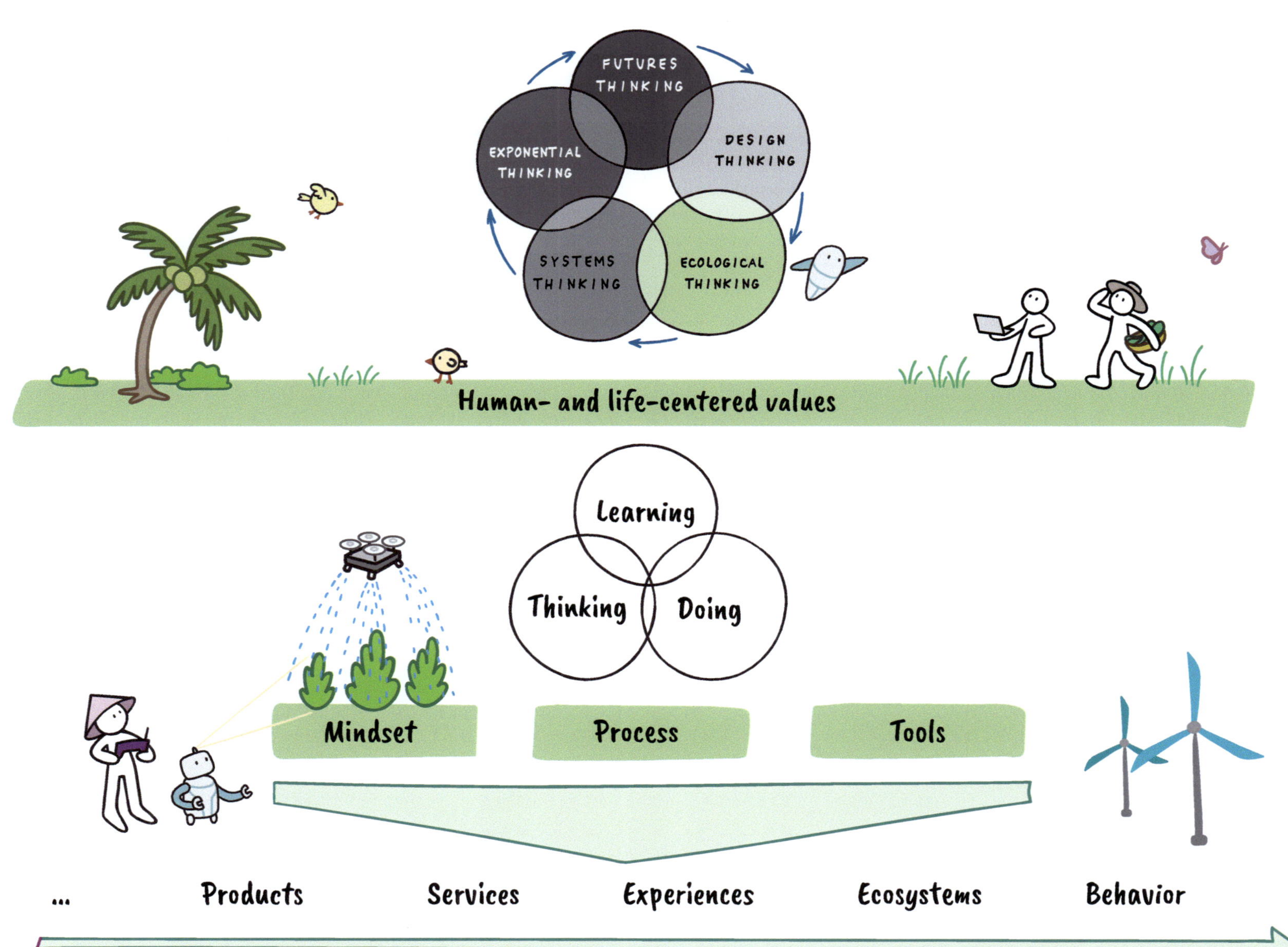

FUTURES THINKING
EXPONENTIAL THINKING
DESIGN THINKING
SYSTEMS THINKING
ECOLOGICAL THINKING
Human- and life-centered values
Learning
Thinking
Doing
Mindset
Process
Tools
...
Products
Services
Experiences
Ecosystems
Behavior
THE SPECTRUM OF POSITIVE, RESILIENT CHANGE WE AIM TO CREATE

Cultivating an Ecological Self

The global sustainability movement has been frustratingly slow, not due to a lack of innovative solutions, technological capabilities, or scientific data. The most significant barrier to creating a thriving, regenerative future is our failure to challenge the mental models and worldviews that drive unsustainable behavior. **To design a better world, it is first necessary to evolve the way the world is perceived**.

Ecological thinking is the vital evolution of design thinking, shifting focus from a narrow human-centric lens to a holistic, life-centered perspective. This evolution acknowledges that **human flourishing** is inextricably linked to the **health of the planet**. It demands that every stage of design actively integrates an awareness of natural processes, resource flows, and the long-term well-being of the entire web of life.

This requires the **cultivation of an "ecological self,"** a profound shift in identity where individuals and organizations see themselves not as separate from nature, but as integral participants within it. This is the practical application of the **"widening identity" concept**. As this shift takes hold, the purpose of design evolves from merely solving human problems to designing with the planet, actively producing solutions that replenish, restore, and foster mutual thriving.

By fostering this mindset, practitioners are liberated from unsustainable pasts and empowered to invent anew, creating the regenerative systems that are the foundation of a truly resilient future. This life-centered view is then used to fundamentally re-design business models, transitioning them from linear, extractive systems to circular, regenerative engines of value. This crucial strategic re-framing ensures the design process delivers solutions that optimize for collective, systemic well-being.

[Ecological thinking is essential for addressing the interconnected crises of the modern era, representing a necessary intellectual shift from reductionist methodologies to a holistic understanding of complex living systems. This foundational paradigm governs the development of regenerative business models and effective behavioral interventions.]

Broadening Identity and Holistic Systems

Embracing ecological thinking necessitates a profound broadening of identity, redefining how individuals perceive themselves in relation to the world. This translates to an expansion of focus beyond individual user needs to a deep consideration of how creations actively engage with broader communities and the living world.

It requires a conscious effort to see humanity as part of, rather than superior to, the natural world, engaging with the human aspects of a context in direct relationship with the biophysical environment. Ecology itself is underpinned by **core principles such as wholeness, interdependence, diversity, and sustainability**.

This point of view presents a universe defined by dynamic relationships and ongoing processes, emphasizing a globally integrated perspective that acknowledges diversity and focuses on the long-term well-being of the entire world system.

Widening of identity is a transition from "me" (egocentric) to "my group" (ethnocentric) to "my country" (sociocentric) to "all of us" (worldcentric) to "all beings" (planetcentric).

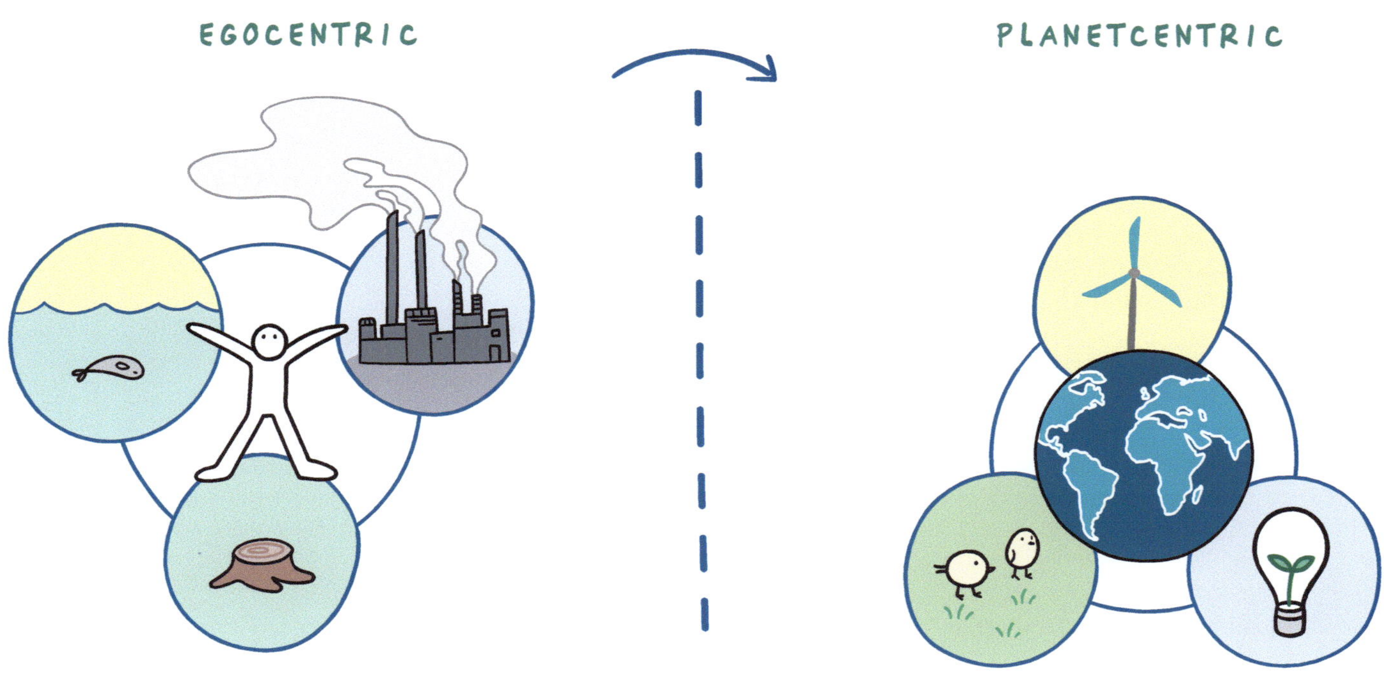

Applying Design Boundaries

While the philosophical shift toward a "planet-centric" view is the mindset required for ecological thinking, this mindset must be immediately constrained by non-negotiable scientific reality. **The Doughnut Economics model (see page 172)** provides the canvas for our ambition, the "safe and just space for humanity." However, the perimeter of this safe space is defined by the **nine planetary boundaries**.

Developed by the scientific community, these boundaries identify the critical Earth systems that regulate our planet's stable state, making human life possible. They act as the ultimate ecological ceiling, defining the upper limit of impact within which all societal, economic, and design activity must occur. To transgress these boundaries is to "overshoot" the ecological ceiling, pushing Earth into a less predictable and potentially catastrophic new state.

Therefore, the practitioner of design thinking for Humanity understands that these nine boundaries are not abstract environmental concerns; they are the absolute constraints on feasibility and viability. A design solution that might be desirable and technically feasible, yet further destabilizes an already stressed boundary, is fundamentally a flawed product, service, or policy. The mandate for innovation thus becomes profoundly clear: **every new solution must be regenerative by design, actively aiming to pull us back from the edge of the boundaries we have already breached, rather than merely slowing the rate of damage.**

This framework immediately reframes the starting point for every design thinking project. Before asking, "How might we design a product to meet a market need?" we must first ask: **"How might we design this entire system to operate within the integrity of the planetary boundaries?"**

This intellectual rigor prevents the fatal flaw of simply shifting the burden from one boundary to another (e.g., solving the carbon problem with a material that relies on excessive freshwater withdrawal). The ultimate measure of a truly intelligent solution is its simultaneous respect for all nine environmental constraints.

This foundation transforms the traditional focus on efficiency, which merely optimizes processes, into a drive toward **systemic resilience**, ensuring that the innovations we pursue inherently support Earth's capacity for self-regulation.

Pushing Our Solutions Toward Being Regenerative by Design

We must push our solutions toward being regenerative by design (ecological ceiling) and distributive by design (social foundation) by asking key questions:

Ecological Stewardship (Respecting the Planet)

- **Local Generosity:** Can our system be as generous as the wildlands next door? Does it naturally store carbon, cycle water, and protect local soil?

- **Global Health:** Have we fully examined the impact of our energy use, imports, and waste streams on the global ecological ceiling?

Social Resilience (Respecting People)

- **Industry Thrive:** How does our organization actively ensure the well-being of all connected people: employees, suppliers, consumers, and local communities?

- **Equitable Design:** Does our design, including supply chain relationships and intellectual property strategy, benefit all people, not just our organization?

The Embedded Ecological Thinking Cycle

Embedding life-centered constraints into the design process means we must operate within the Doughnut Economics model (first circle). This dual mandate dictates that the entire product lifecycle must actively move from a linear, extractive model to a regenerative and circular system. This systemic approach ensures that innovation not only serves human needs but actively contributes to the health and resilience of the planet.

This critical shift in value is applied across the following stages of the product lifecycle:
- **Raw Materials:** Focus on restore/renew.
- **Production:** Focus on design out waste/pollution.
- **Business Model:** Focus on being contributive/systemic/exponential.
- **End-of-Life (Make It Last):** Focus on repair/reuse/recycle.

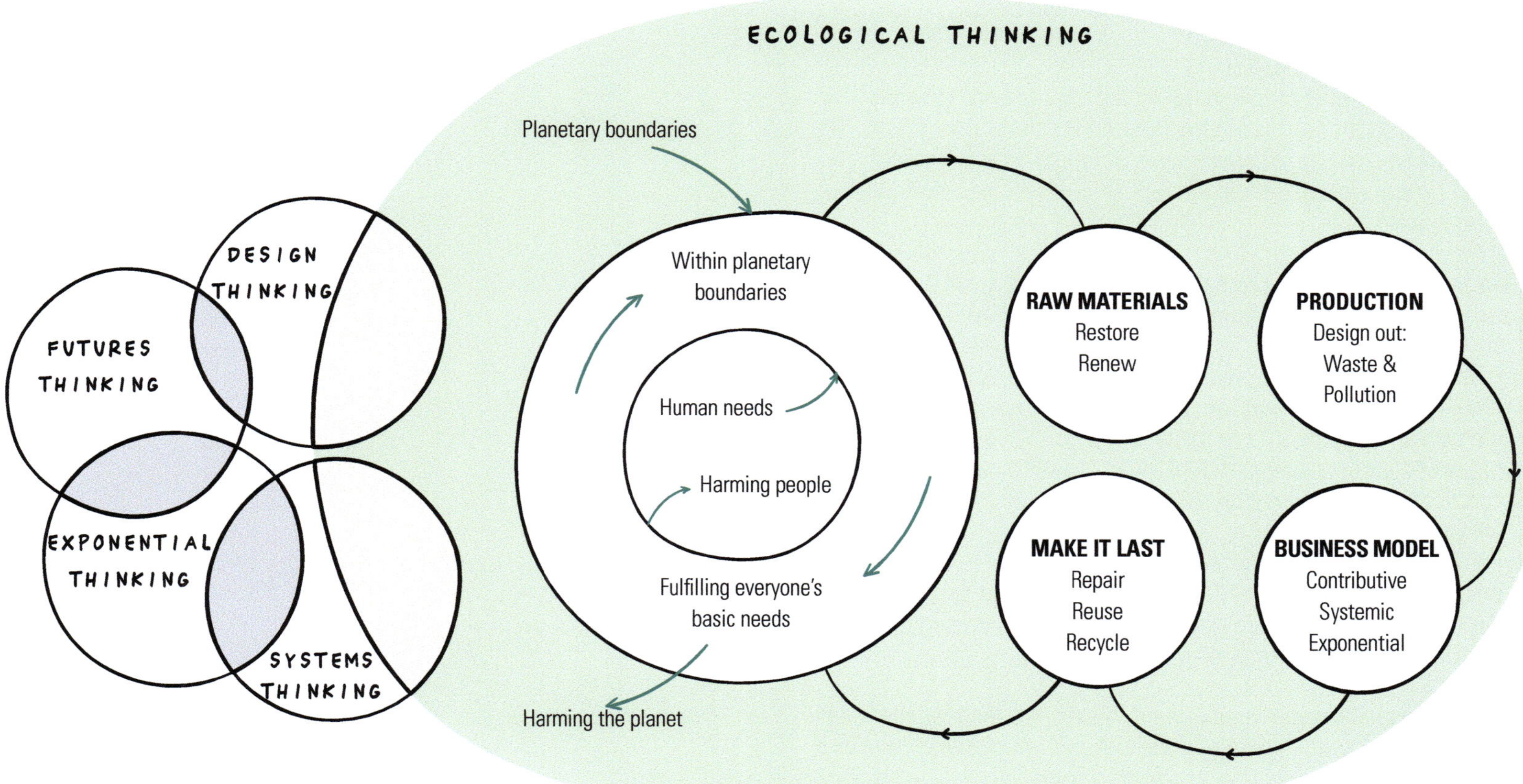

In the context of ecological thinking, sustainability takes on a profound, even urgent, meaning. While the traditional definition of sustainability often implies merely maintaining the current status indefinitely, applying it to our planet and humanity demands a far more nuanced understanding. **True sustainability means maintaining life in a stable, thriving state.** This can be achieved only if all stakeholders collectively cease activities that cause harm and, ideally, actively work to reverse the damage already inflicted.

Three Fields of Application

Redesigning our status quo is indeed challenging, necessitating a new approach that prioritizes a resilient and regenerative future. The design thinking mindset empowers practitioners to break existing rules and behaviors, challenging established norms to create disruptive innovations.

Within this chapter, three critical application fields will be explored where ecological thinking can profoundly impact humanity's future:

- **Circularity:** Describing the concept of circularity, including the eight "R" strategies and the underlying principle of widening identity from egocentric to planet-centric. The focus will shift to how to apply ecological thinking in creating new materials, products, and services that fulfill societal needs without harming our planet.

- **Regenerative Business Models:** Exploring the design of sustainable and regenerative business models, moving beyond traditional paradigms.

- **Behavioral Change:** Investigating one of the biggest challenges: fostering behavioral change in the context of ecological thinking.

We must recognize that it is impossible to sustain the unsustainable. Simply preserving the current trajectory, with its inherent environmental degradation, resource depletion, and social inequities, is not a path to sustainability; it is a path to further decline. Design Thinking for Humanity, therefore, calls for a radical reimagining of our systems and practices. The goal is to move beyond simply minimizing harm to actively creating a regenerative and flourishing future where human and natural systems coexist in harmony.

The Principles of Circularity

A fundamental shift away from the linear **"take-make-dispose" model** is needed to build this regenerative future. Circular design is not just about reducing waste; it is about creating a closed-loop system where resources are continuously cycled and natural systems are replenished. This involves three core shifts: eliminating waste and pollution, circulating products and materials for as long as possible, and actively regenerating natural systems. To put this into practice, a set of circular strategies, often referred to as the **"Rs,"** provides a clear roadmap (see page 174). These are not isolated actions but interconnected elements that collectively contribute to a truly comprehensive circular economy. These strategies provide the practical building blocks for a circular future, a concept now profoundly transformed by technological advancements.

This involves three core shifts:

1. **Eliminating Waste and Pollution:** Rethinking materials and manufacturing processes to minimize waste and pollution from the outset.

2. **Circulating Products and Materials:** Keeping products and materials in use for as long as possible requires designing for durability, repairability, and adaptability.

3. **Regenerating Natural Systems:** Actively contributing to the health and resilience of the environment by designing in ways that replenish, restore, and foster mutual thriving.

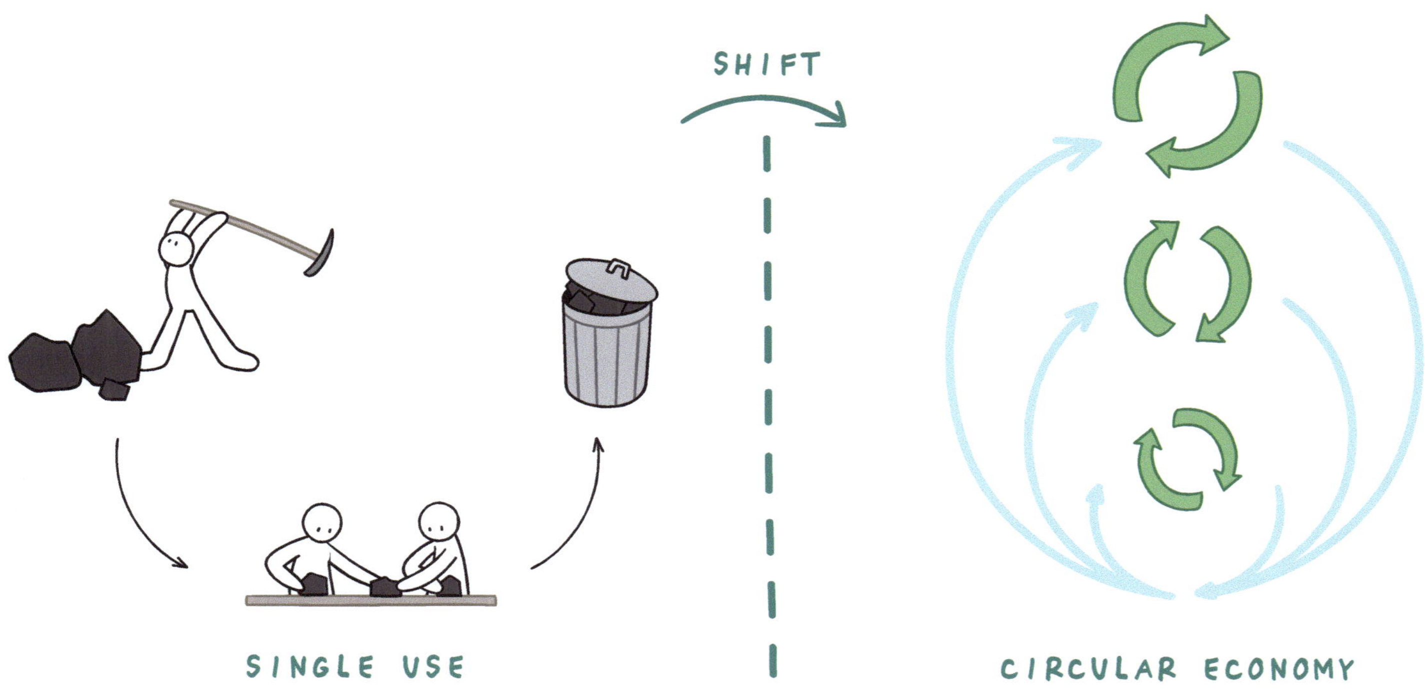

The 9 Rs of Circular Strategies

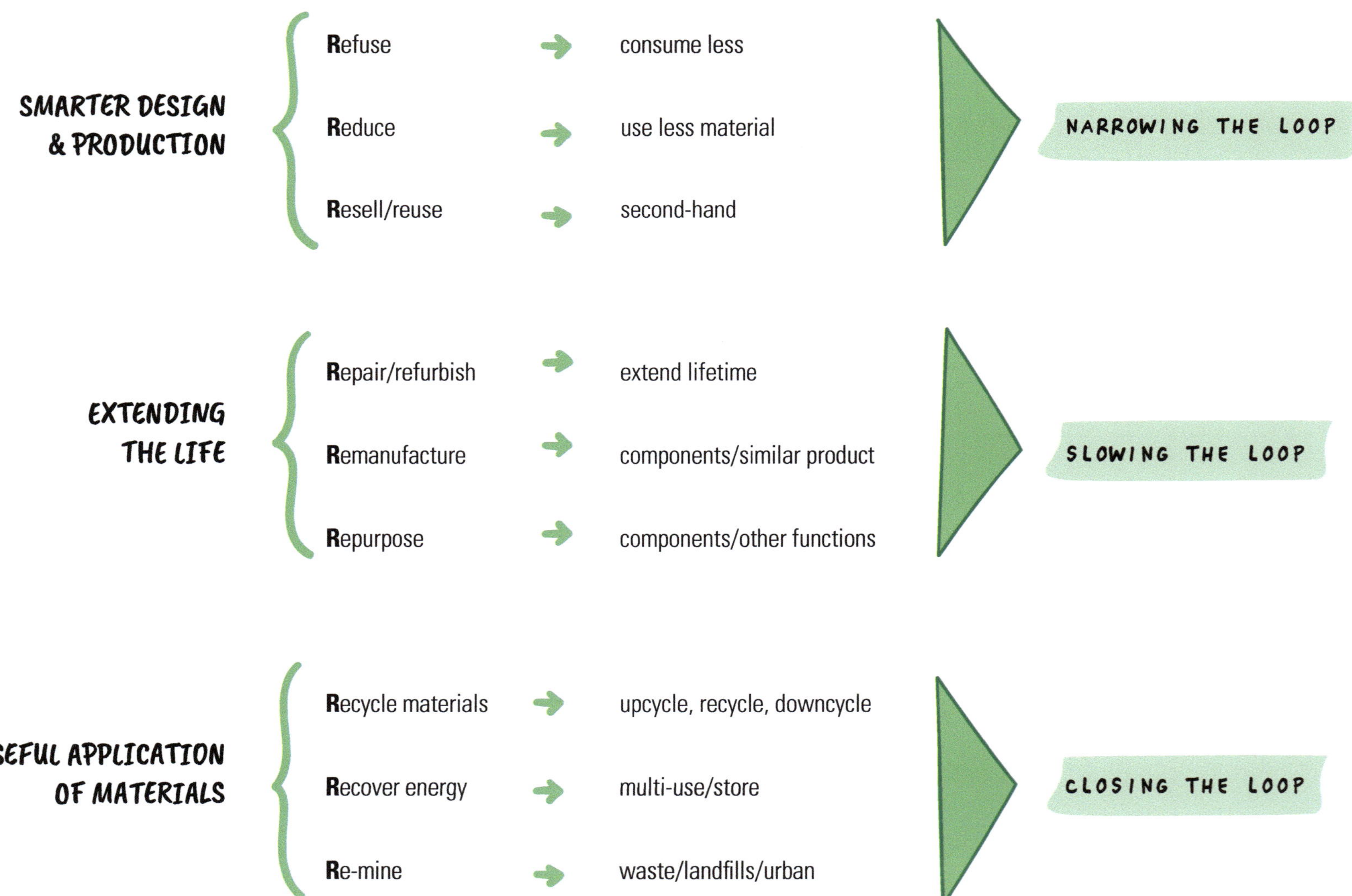

Technology and The Circular Bioeconomy

The traditional "Rs" of circularity are no longer static principles but have become dynamic opportunities, profoundly transformed by technological advancements. Decades of digitization and Industry 4.0 have fundamentally reshaped the approach to each "R." Beyond optimizing existing processes, these technologies empower the creation of entirely new, inherently circular products, making the goal of closing material loops relevant to renewable, biological resources. This technology-supercharged approach also enables a crucial expansion of these principles into the biological realm, giving rise to the **circular bioeconomy**.

Exponential technologies are unlocking entirely new possibilities for closed-loop systems:

- **Data and Transparency:** Distributed ledgers provide material traceability, and AI/machine learning optimize resource allocation, predictive maintenance, and complex recycling.
- **Virtual Prototyping:** Digital twins and virtual replicas enable proactive design for circularity by simulating product performance and end-of-life scenarios.
- **On-Demand Production:** Additive manufacturing (3D printing) facilitates spare parts for repair, while robotics streamline disassembly for effective remanufacturing.
- **Bioeconomy Focus:** Innovations in new materials science empower the creation of inherently circular, biological products.

Examples: Sectors like food and agriculture

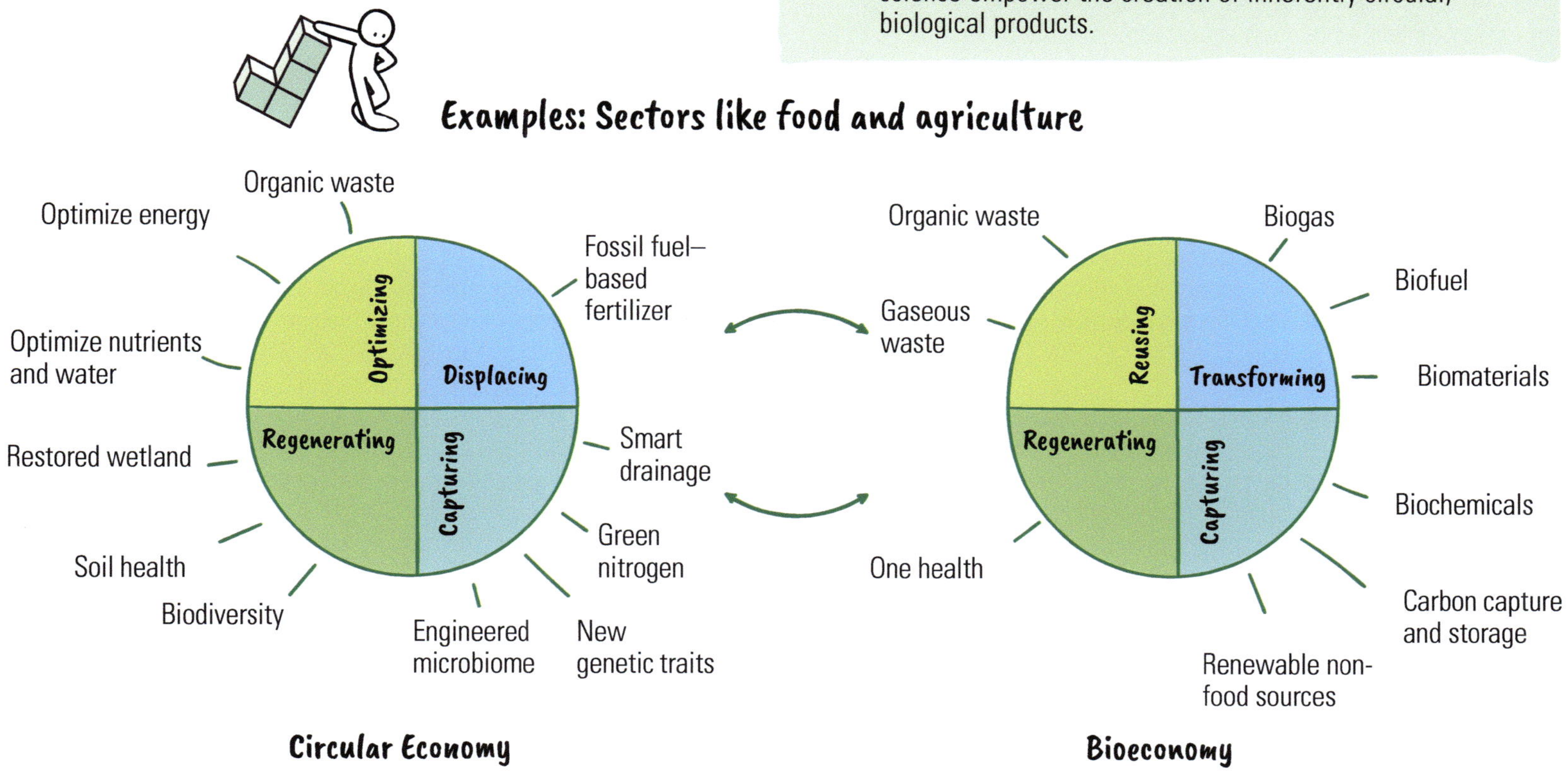

Circular Economy

Bioeconomy

Exponential Technologies Drive Regenerative Shift

The journey from managing environmental decline (sustainability) to actively creating renewal (regeneration) demands tools with commensurate power and reach. This transformative leap stems from the critical intersection of ecological thinking and exponential thinking. Traditional, linear approaches struggle to match the speed and scale of global ecological crises. The rapidly decreasing cost and increasing capability of exponential technologies fundamentally change this operational challenge. This convergence moves us beyond incremental, isolated improvements, enabling the orchestration of regenerative interventions that scale nonlinearly for a truly systemic reversal of damage across vast ecosystems.

Exponential technologies enable a regenerative shift by fulfilling three powerful roles:

Scanners: Mapping the Real-Time Health of "Living Capitals"
Remote-sensing satellites and AI-driven data analytics map the real-time health of the planet's "Living Capitals" (e.g., monitoring soil organic matter, water purity, and biodiversity). This immediate, granular feedback creates a crucial feedback loop for regeneration, providing the necessary data for systemic intervention.

Scientists: Accelerating the Discovery of Nature's Genius
AI and high-throughput computing accelerate the discovery of biomimicry principles and natural solutions. This helps designers and engineers rapidly create new regenerative materials, nontoxic chemical formulas, and resilient biological systems in days, rather than decades.

Orchestrators: Scaling New Behaviors
AI-powered social platforms efficiently identify and amplify regenerative narratives. This fosters the collective belief and social tipping points necessary to scale new behaviors, ensuring solutions are not just ecologically sound but also digitally smart and economically viable at a global scale.

New Materials, Products, Services, and Experiences

Creating products for a circular economy necessitates expertise beyond traditional linear models. It requires designing not just the offering itself, but also the supporting processes and ecosystem collaborations needed for circularity to function effectively. This expanded scope of design in Design Thinking for Humanity inevitably drives a demand for new skills and a **deeper understanding of value chains, material lifecycles, and the principles of serviceability and repairability**.

The unique properties of recycled raw materials and a product's inherent recyclability are not mere afterthoughts; they are critical considerations woven into the initial design and subsequent technology development phases. Everything related to resources, from responsible extraction to how operations and lifecycles are managed, must emphasize the commitment to **realize closed-loop systems**. This demands a specialized competence in managing material properties, extending directly into the production stage.

This holistic integration, from the fundamental problem definition through to the core operations of a business, necessitates a profound shift in both mindset and skillset. The design of supply chains and operations must **integrate circular principles throughout the entire product journey**, advocating for a continuous cycle rather than a linear progression. This begins with circular inputs in the preproduction phase and extends to product life extension and resource recovery at the product's end, ensuring that designs are not only desirable and feasible but genuinely regenerative for humanity and the planet.

Designing for a Circular Future: 80% of Sustainability Starts with Design Thinking

The statistic is clear: more than **80% of a product's environmental impact is determined at the design stage**. This emphasizes that managing environmental impact is not a production or disposal problem, but fundamentally a **design problem**.

This approach allows to move from smarter production and extending the life of products to ensuring the useful application of all materials at their end-of-life. These are not isolated actions but interconnected elements that collectively contribute to a truly comprehensive circular economy.

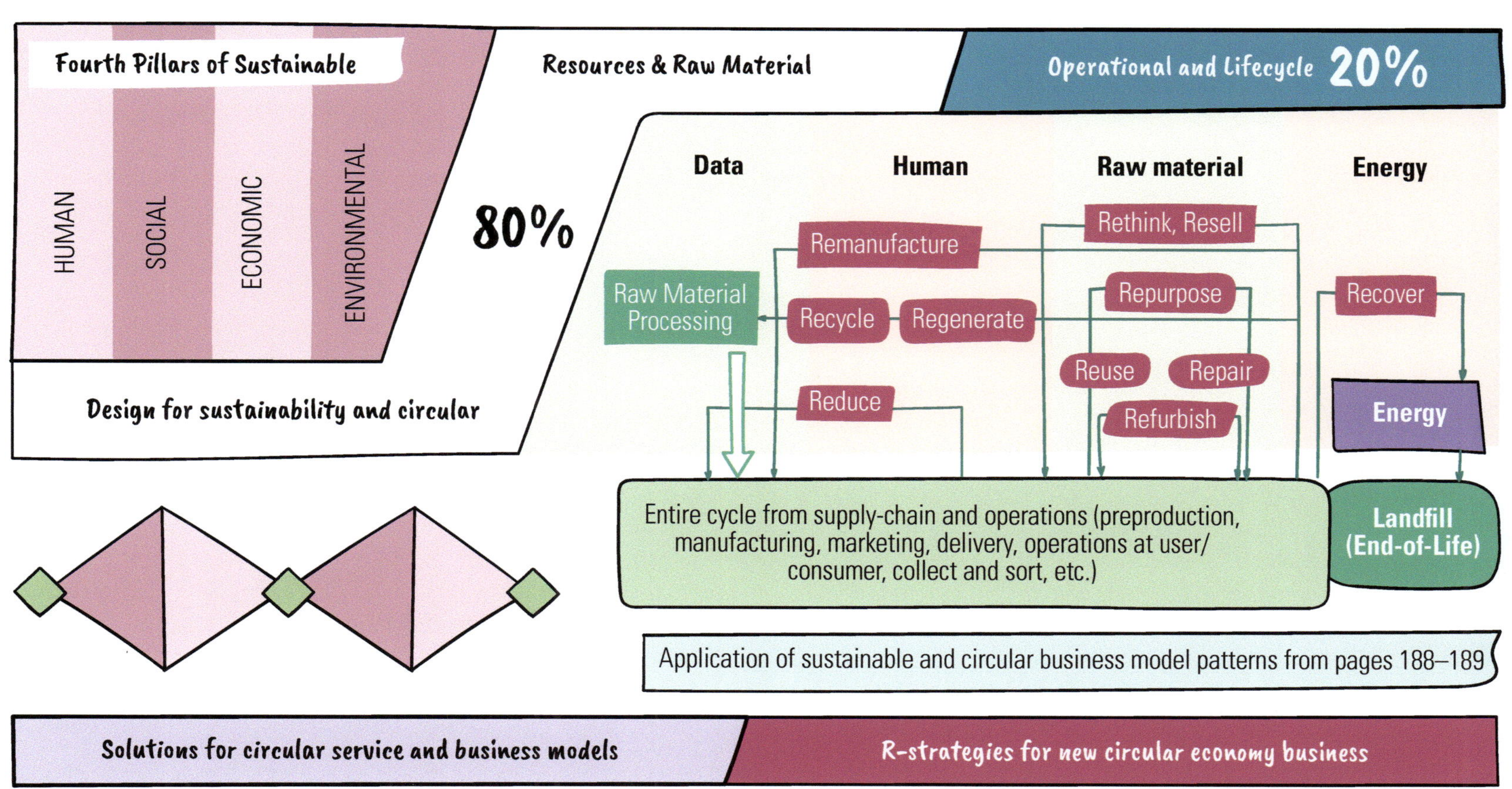

Shifts in Business Model Design

The progression from how business models are designed today to a future aiming to enhance social and ecological systems is central for innovators. The status quo, often driven by profit maximization at the expense of people and planet, is inherently misaligned with humanity's long-term well-being. **Moving to sustainable models is a necessary step, but regenerative business models embrace a truly holistic and forward-thinking approach, actively designing for positive social and environmental outcomes**. This proactive and restorative mindset is critical for addressing global challenges like climate change, resource depletion, and social inequality.

Designing regenerative business models is a critical endeavor that necessitates the comprehensive application of all lenses within the Design Thinking for Humanity framework. This approach calls for a fundamental reimagining of how businesses create value, not just for shareholders, but for the planet as a whole, emphasizing a shift from merely reducing harm to actively contributing to the health and vitality of interconnected social, economic, and ecological systems. The **Regenerative Business Design Canvas (see page 210)** offers a structured pathway for this transformation, guiding teams to ensure their operations not only achieve sustainability but actively contribute to the well-being of the ecosystems in which they operate.

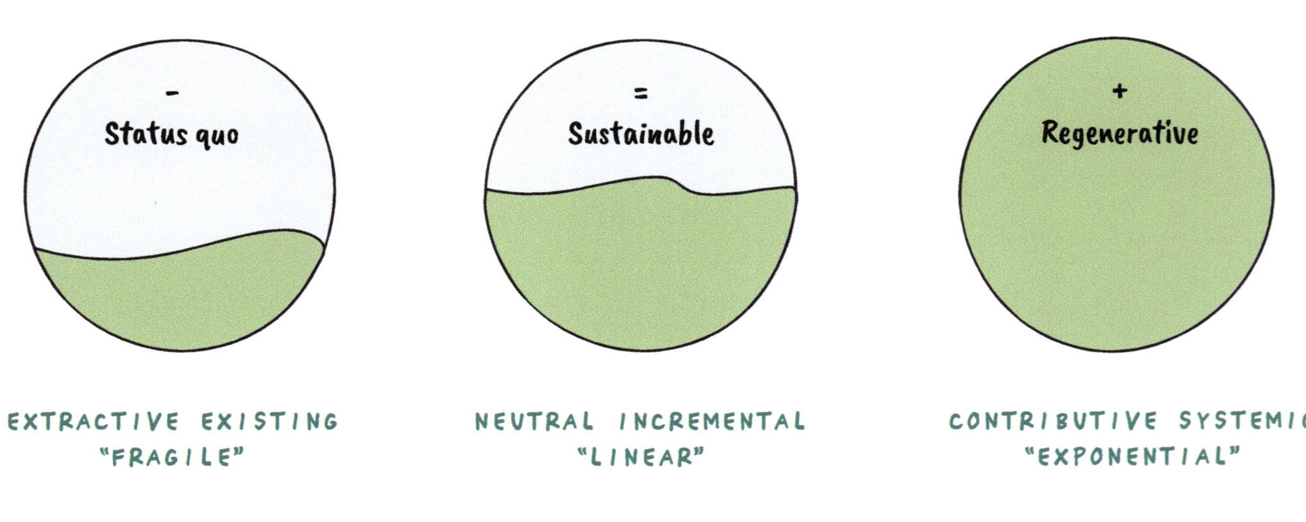

Maturity Levels in Business Model (Re)design

Feature/ Category	Level 1: Compliance-Driven	Level 2: Reactive Changes	Level 3: Sustainable Design	Level 4: Regenerative Design
Primary Driver	Avoiding penalties, meeting minimum legal requirements	Responding to external pressures (market, investors, NGOs, public opinion)	Proactive pursuit of competitive advantage through integrated sustainability	Actively restoring and enhancing natural and social systems; net-positive impact
Sustainability Approach	"Do no harm" (minimal interpretation), often superficial or symbolic	Risk mitigation, efficiency gains, reputation management	Systemic integration of environmental and social considerations into core value creation	Active restoration, regeneration, and co-evolution with living systems
Value Proposition	Standard product/service, with compliance as a cost	Standard product/service, with "green" features or reduced negative impact	Products/services offer superior environmental/social performance alongside economic value	Products/services directly contribute to ecological and social flourishing; intrinsic value beyond profit
Innovation Focus	Process improvements for compliance; minor adjustments	Incremental changes to existing products/processes; "bolt-on" solutions	Redesigning products, processes, and entire business models for sustainability from the ground up	Biomimicry, closed-loop biogeochemical cycles, ecosystem restoration technologies, social innovation for systemic health
Relationship with Nature	Resource extraction, waste disposal (externalized costs)	Reducing negative footprint, minimizing pollution, more efficient resource use	Decoupling growth from resource depletion and pollution; striving for circularity	Active restoration of ecosystems, enhancing biodiversity, rebuilding natural capital
Relationship with Society	Meeting labor laws, basic CSR (philanthropy, PR)	Addressing stakeholder concerns, some social initiatives	Fair labor, community engagement, addressing societal needs through core business	Fostering thriving, equitable communities; distributed ownership, co-creation, social capital building
Decision Making	Centralized, top-down, focused on legal/financial risk avoidance	Centralized, reactive to external signals, often short-term	Strategic, integrated, often involving cross-functional teams; long-term perspective	Empowered, decentralized, collaborative, adaptive; guided by systems thinking and long-term ecological/social health
Impact	Limited results on competitiveness or societal benefits at scale	Single-point innovations, often reactive, may not scale	Co-optimizing for business and societal benefits; expanding influence through integrated value	Net-positive impact, expanding influence through systemic change, fostering resilience and abundance
Key Activities	Basic environmental controls, legal checks, minimal reporting	Waste reduction, energy efficiency, some ethical sourcing, basic CSR reporting	Life Cycle Assessment, eco-design, circular economy principles, stakeholder engagement, transparent reporting	Ecosystem restoration, regenerative agriculture, closed-loop systems, community co-governance, biomimicry research, adaptive management
Time Horizon	Short-term (compliance cycles)	Short to medium-term (responding to immediate pressures)	Medium to long-term (strategic advantage, systemic change)	Long-term, multigenerational (planetary and societal health)

From Sustainability to Regenerative Impact

To advance our ecological perspective, the following pages examine how to create value through two distinct lenses of organizational evolution. We first explore **Sustainable Business Models (see pages 180–183)** to establish common patterns such as the circular economy or product as a service. These frameworks prioritize reversing harm and ensuring that operations remain within planetary boundaries.

We then move toward **Designing Regenerative Business Models (see pages 184–192)**, which requires a significant mindset shift to actively heal and enrich the world. By separating these steps, we distinguish between the immediate necessity of refusing to sustain the unsustainable and the long-term goal of contributing restorative vitality to interconnected social and ecological systems.

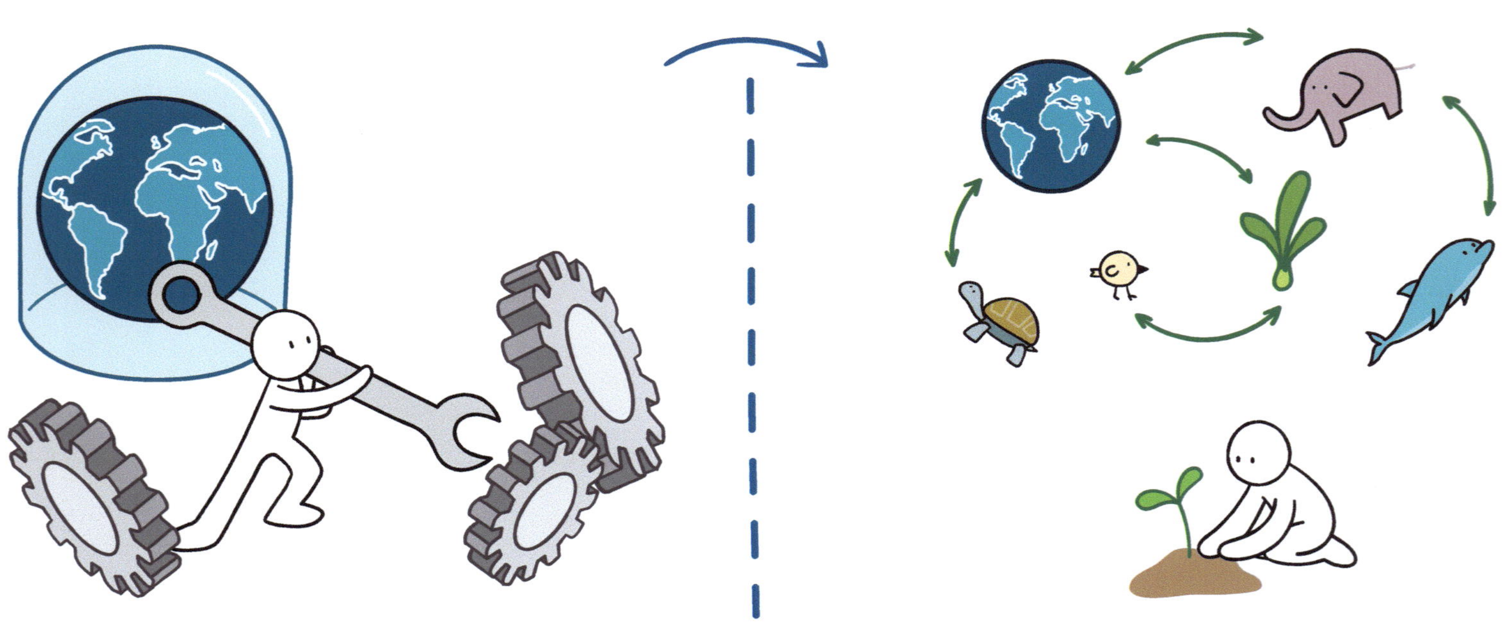

Sustainable Business Models

Sustainable business model patterns serve as established "recipes" for creating value while actively benefiting the planet and people. While economic viability and resilience remain key elements, these patterns compel us to prioritize our impact on the environment and society.

For example, implementing the Circular Economy paradigm (introduced on page 173) means **designing products to be reused, repaired**, or recycled. This forms a closed loop where materials keep flowing instead of being thrown away. Another vital pattern is Product-as-a-Service (PaaS), where the product is leased rather than sold. This inherently incentivizes manufacturers to create more durable, long-lasting products and maintain them, significantly reducing the need for constant new production.

These patterns are crucial because they offer proven ways to build resilient businesses. They require **changing our core operations**, moving beyond making products merely "a little greener" toward integrating strategies like utilizing renewable energy, sourcing materials ethically, or creating social enterprises that explicitly aim to solve a societal problem. By adopting these patterns, we become **more resilient**, attract customers who value sustainability, and actively **contribute to a healthier future**.

Resiliency > Efficiency

Relationships > Transactions

Most common business model patterns aim to improve sustainability or apply circular business models principles.

Most **sustainable business models** observed in the market today aim to reduce negative environmental and social impacts while remaining economically viable.

Sustainable Sourcing & Supply Chain:
Focuses on procuring raw materials and components from ethical, environmentally responsible, and socially just sources. This includes fair trade, certified sustainable materials, and local sourcing to reduce transportation impacts.

Resource Efficiency & Waste Reduction:
Minimizes the consumption of energy, water, and materials throughout operations, and actively works to reduce waste generation through process optimization and smart design.

Green Product/Service Innovation:
Develops and offers products or services that inherently have a lower environmental footprint or provide environmental benefits. This includes eco-friendly materials, nontoxic formulations, and energy-saving designs.

Social Enterprise/Impact-Driven:
Prioritizes social or environmental mission alongside financial viability. A significant portion of profits is often reinvested into the mission or community.

Shared Value Creation:
Identifies and addresses societal needs and challenges with a business model that simultaneously creates economic value for the company and value for society.

Ethical Labor Practices:
Ensures fair wages and safe working conditions, promotes diversity and inclusion, and respects labor rights across its operations and supply chain.

Digitalization for Sustainability:
Leverages digital technologies (e.g., IoT, AI, data analytics) to optimize resource use, track environmental performance, or enable sustainable services.

Local & Community Focus:
Prioritizes local economic development, community engagement, and supporting local suppliers and customers.

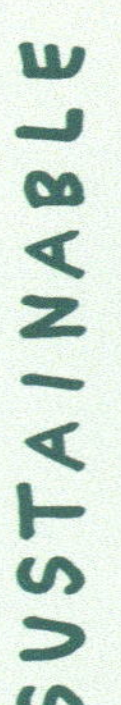

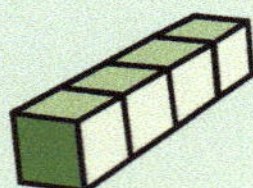

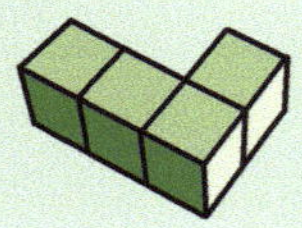

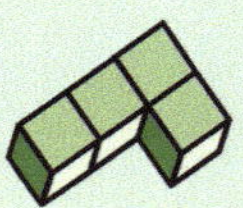

Circular business models are a subset of sustainable models that focus specifically on keeping products, components, and materials in use at their highest value for as long as possible.

Product-as-a-Service (PaaS):
Focuses on access over ownership by selling the function or performance of the product. This incentivizes the manufacturer to design for durability, repair, and upgradeability, as they retain ownership and responsibility for the product's lifespan.

Product Life Extension:
Focuses on designing durable products, offering repair services, spare parts, refurbishment, and upgrades to extend the lifespan of products and components.

Resource Recovery & Recycling:
Aims to recover valuable materials and energy from products at the end of their useful life, turning waste into new inputs for production.

Circular Inputs:
Utilizes renewable, bio-based, or high-recycled content materials as primary inputs for production, reducing reliance on virgin, finite resources.

Sharing Platforms:
Enables multiple users to share access to products or assets, increasing utilization rates and reducing the need for individual ownership.

Remanufacturing/Refurbishment:
Focuses on rebuilding to last by taking used products or components, disassembling them, inspecting, cleaning, repairing, and reassembling them to a "like new" condition, often with a new warranty.

Take-Back and Buy-Back Programs:
Aims to create systems to take back their own products from customers at the end of their life, ensuring proper disposal, recycling, or re-entry into the circular economy.

Industrial Symbiosis Ecosystems:
Utilizes waste or by-product to become a valuable input for another company, creating a collaborative ecosystem of resource exchange.

Design for Circularity:
Designs products consciously from the outset to be durable, repairable, modular, easily disassembled, and made from safe, recyclable materials.

Digital Product Passports/Tracking:
Utilizes digital technology (e.g., blockchain, QR codes, AI) to track materials and products throughout their lifecycle, enabling better recovery, sorting, and reuse.

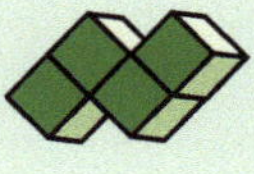

Designing Regenerative Business Models

The challenge of the 21st century is not merely to build a business that endures but one that actively contributes to the endurance of the planet. Designing a truly regenerative business model requires more than marginal improvement; it demands a radical, systemic shift from linear, extractive logic to a circular, restorative one.

However, the pursuit of regeneration is confronted by significant barriers. The biggest hurdles in regenerative business model design center on three core challenges:

- Achieving a **fundamental mindset shift** away from extractive, profit-first thinking toward a systems view that prioritizes net-positive social and ecological impact.

- Overcoming **economic and investment obstacles** due to high up-front transition costs, long-term payback periods, and the difficulty of measuring nonfinancial value creation.

- Navigating the **lack of regulatory and institutional support**, which includes uncertain policy environments, a dependence on complex value chain collaboration to scale, and a lack of widespread expertise and standardized metrics for regenerative success.

This approach calls for a fundamental reimagining of how organizations create value, emphasizing a move from merely reducing harm to actively contributing to the health and vitality of interconnected social, economic, and ecological systems.

A regenerative business doesn't just reduce harm; it actively heals and enriches our world.

To meet this challenge, the **Regenerative Business Design Canvas (see pages 186–187)** evolves traditional business design by embedding the full mandate of Design Thinking for Humanity at its core.

The Foundational Shift

Traditional business models prioritize financial profit, treating ecological and social consequences as externalized costs. The Regenerative Canvas mandates a strategic reversal of this logic:

The Focus: It compels the team to design a venture that actively contributes to the restoration and health of social, ecological, and economic systems. The goal is net-positive impact, moving beyond the neutral goal of sustainability.

The Assets: Success is measured not just by financial returns but by prioritizing the growth of Living Capitals (e.g., soil health, water purity, community trust) as primary business assets.

The Mandate: The model must function as an integral part of living systems, with financial viability explicitly contingent upon the verifiable achievement of positive ecological and social outcomes.

This canvas serves as the structured pathway, guiding innovators through a comprehensive re-imagining of how value is created, delivered, and measured.

Core Principles in Regenerative Business Model Design

- **Net Positive Impact!**
  We aim to give back more than we take, creating positive outcomes on the "triple bottom line" (people, planet, and profit) with a restorative focus.

- **(Business) Ecosystems Thinking!**
  Understand your business as an interconnected part of larger social, environmental, and economic systems. Recognize feedback loops and interdependencies.

- **Co-evolution and Co-creation!**
  Foster mutualistic relationships with nature and all stakeholders, recognizing that systems evolve together.

- **Circularity!**
  Embrace circular economy principles (eliminate waste and pollution, circulate products and materials, regenerate nature) as a fundamental design element.

- **Purpose-Driven!**
  Anchor any business in a clear, regenerative vision and mission that goes beyond profit maximization.

- **Adaptability and Resilience!**
  Design for continuous learning, evolution, and the ability to thrive in a dynamic environment, mimicking natural systems.

REGENERATIVE BUSINESS DESIGN CANVAS

Living Capitals & Ecosystem

The fundamental assets the business relies on, prioritizing living and social capital

- **Key Assets:** Healthy ecosystems, strong trust-based relationships with communities, and decentralized systems for production are prioritized as primary living capital.

Key Partners & Stakeholders

The groups the business partners with to foster collaboration and co-create resilient, regenerative business ecosystems.

- **Ecosystem Partners:** Collaborators are selected to build resilient, circular, and regenerative supply chains, fostering a regenerative economy.

Impact Value Proposition

How the solution addresses pains/gains for the Planet, People, and Society

The Solution (Products, Services, Experiences): Products/services directly contribute to restoring ecosystems (e.g., reforestation, soil regeneration, water purification, biodiversity enhancement).

Regenerative Value Streams

The various ways value is generated, including ecological and social gains.

- **Revenue Streams:** Revenue reflects the true cost of production, including ecological and social restoration, with the potential for revenue from providing ecosystem services.

Key Activities & Resource Inputs

The actions required to deliver the value proposition

- **Key Activities:** Actions must include actively participating in regenerating degraded ecosystems and investing in natural capital via shared decision-making models.

DOWNLOAD TOOL

www.design-humanity.com/en/regenerative-bmc

- **Value for the Planet:** Design is for 100% renewable energy, nutrient cycling, water stewardship, and the enhancement of natural systems when materials return to the environment.

- **Value for the People:** Solutions foster thriving communities, promote equity and well-being, and distribute value equitably across individuals and organizations.

- **Value for Society:** The business integrates the inherent value of nature and human well-being beyond monetary metrics, engaging citizens on regenerative principles and empowering them to make collective choices.

Regenerative Purpose and Vision

The overarching goal and vision for the business

- **Vision:** Business as an integral part of living systems, actively restoring and enhancing ecological and social well-being. A net-positive impact on the planet and society, generating abundance and resilience.

Customer Segments & Participants

Who the business serves and who participates in the regenerative process

- **Participants:** Reaching conscious, ethically driven consumers who are actively engaged and participate in the regenerative activities.

Channels & Relationships

How the business interacts with customers and moves product/service

- **Key Link:** Distribution is localized, partnerships are with other regenerative businesses, and customer relationships foster a sense of belonging and collective responsibility for positive impact.

Cost and Reinvestment Structure

Where costs occur, prioritizing reinvestment in capital regeneration

- **Cost Structure:** Significant cost allocation prioritizes ecosystem restoration, community development, fair wages, and reinvestment in nature-inspired design and restorative processes.

Regenerative Business Model Pattern

The regenerative business model aims to actively restore and enhance social and ecological well-being, generating net-positive impact by mimicking and strengthening living systems.

Multi-Capital Value Creation:
Prioritizes and measures success not only by financial returns but by actively building Natural (soil, water), Social (trust, relationships), and Human (health, knowledge) Capital, recognizing them as core assets.

Place-Based & Context-Specific Design:
Tailors the business design and its solutions to the unique ecological, social, and cultural context of its operating location, ensuring the activity contributes to the health of the specific place (e.g., a local watershed or community).

Regenerative/Nature-Positive Sourcing:
Procures raw materials using methods (like regenerative agriculture) that actively increase the health of ecosystems, improve soil organic matter, and boost biodiversity, resulting in a net-positive ecological "handprint."

Co-evolutionary Partnership & Governance:
Implements shared ownership, stewardship models (e.g., steward ownership), and governance structures that distribute power and decision-making to align long-term goals with ecological and social outcomes.

Systemic Leapfrog/Innovation:
Develops entirely new business models or technologies that bypass existing extractive, linear systems, fundamentally changing how value is created, distributed, and used (e.g., decentralized local production).

Restoration-as-a-Service (RaaS):
The core offering is the delivery of a measurable ecological or social outcome (e.g., carbon sequestration, clean water, or skill development), with revenue tied directly to the positive impact achieved.

Adaptive Learning & Feedback Loop Model:
Establishes real-time monitoring and feedback loops across ecological and social performance indicators, allowing the organization to rapidly adapt its operations to optimize the system's overall health and resilience.

Regenerative Leadership & Culture:
Fosters an organizational culture and leadership that encourages systems thinking, self-organization, diversity, and collective stewardship, mirroring the principles of health and adaptation found in natural systems.

Future business model patterns leverage exponential technologies and advanced systemic design to create solutions that optimize human well-being, social equity, and planetary health by applying the Design Thinking for Humanity paradigm.

System Orchestration-as-a-Service:
The primary function is to design and govern a multistakeholder ecosystem required to solve a complex "wicked problem," acting as a system steward to coordinate value flow.

Resilience/Anti-Fragility-as-a-Metric:
The value proposition sells measurable increases in systemic resilience, with revenue tied to the ability of the system to adapt and thrive by leveraging shocks (exponentializing).

Regenerative Outcomes Financing:
The financial model generates profits directly and exclusively from achieving verifiable, net-positive ecological or social regeneration outcomes.

Pluriversal/Contextual Adaptation:
Provides an open-source solution framework where revenue comes from hyper-local, co-created adaptation to ensure equitable, place-based relevance for specific communities.

Policy-Embedded Solution Design:
The solution is purpose-built for scalable adoption by explicitly designing, validating, and integrating the necessary policy, governance, and legal frameworks.

Hybrid Intelligence Co-creation Model:
The model leverages a collaboration between human creativity and specialized AI agents to rapidly discover novel solutions optimized for systemic impact and future resilience.

Narrative-Driven Behavioral Transformation:
The core offering is the design and dissemination of compelling narratives that successfully shift collective mindset and inspire resilient, sustainable, and equitable behaviors.

Long-Term Value Alignment Fund:
Uses a financing structure to incentivize strategic actions today that secure long-term human and planetary well-being over immediate short-term financial gains.

Applying Principles of Biomimicry

To design truly regenerative business models, it is necessary to move beyond simply optimizing current industrial processes. The most profound source of inspiration for a thriving, resilient, and sustainable world already exists in the living systems all around us. This is the core principle of **biomimicry**: the conscious emulation of nature's genius to solve complex human problems.

After 3.8 billion years of evolution, life has already solved the challenges now being grappled with, from energy production and waste management to resilient community building. Biomimicry is the most rigorous methodological framework for the convergence of ecological and design thinking.

This approach is fundamentally aligned with the core tenets of Design Thinking for Humanity:

- It is an act of profound **empathy**, requiring a deep and humble observation of the living world.
- It is inherently **systemic**, as nature's solutions are always interconnected and context-aware.
- It is the ultimate source of **regenerative design**, as the principle of life is to create conditions conducive to more life.

Integrating biomimicry into the design process begins by asking a different question; instead of asking, "What can be designed?" a biomimetic approach asks, **"How does nature solve this?"**

This shift can be applied at three distinct levels:
1. **Form Emulation:** Mimicking a specific physical shape found in nature (e.g., the design of a fan blade inspired by a whale's flipper).
2. **Process Emulation:** Mimicking a natural manufacturing or chemical process (e.g., a non-toxic manufacturing technique inspired by the way a spider spins its web).
3. **Ecosystem Emulation:** Mimicking entire ecological systems, designing cities, industries, and economies to function like a mature forest where waste is food and the entire system builds resilience and abundance over time. **This is the most powerful and systemic level.**

This systemic level of biomimicry is now profoundly amplified by **exponential technologies**. AI, for example, can analyze the immense complexity of a natural system, like a coral reef, and extract the underlying rules of collaboration and resource flow. These principles can then be used to design more robust supply chains or collaborative business ecosystems. Integrating biomimicry is an act of radical optimism and practical wisdom.

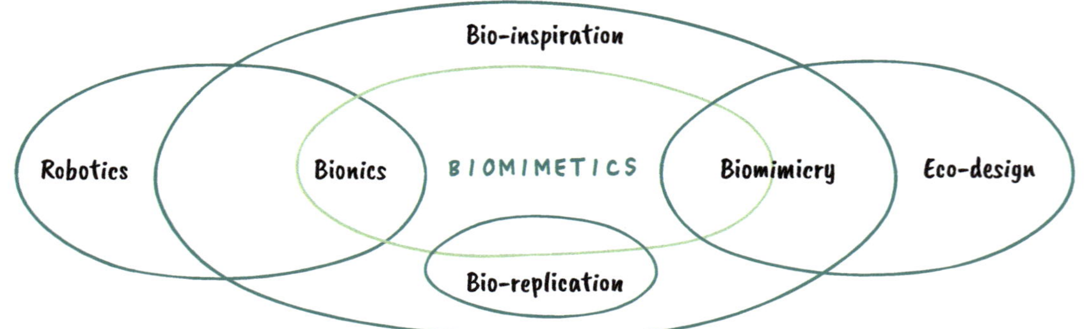

The Biomimicry Life's Principles

Why does a natural system, like a healthy pond, self-regulate and resist shocks? It is because its inputs and outputs are perfectly balanced, creating reinforcing positive feedback loops that promote health and adaptation. Therefore, applying ecosystem-level biomimicry is a prerequisite for successful systems thinking: the former provides the ideal regenerative model, and the latter provides the analytical tools to map the complexity, find the leverage points, and engineer the collaborative relationships needed to achieve that resilient, regenerative state.

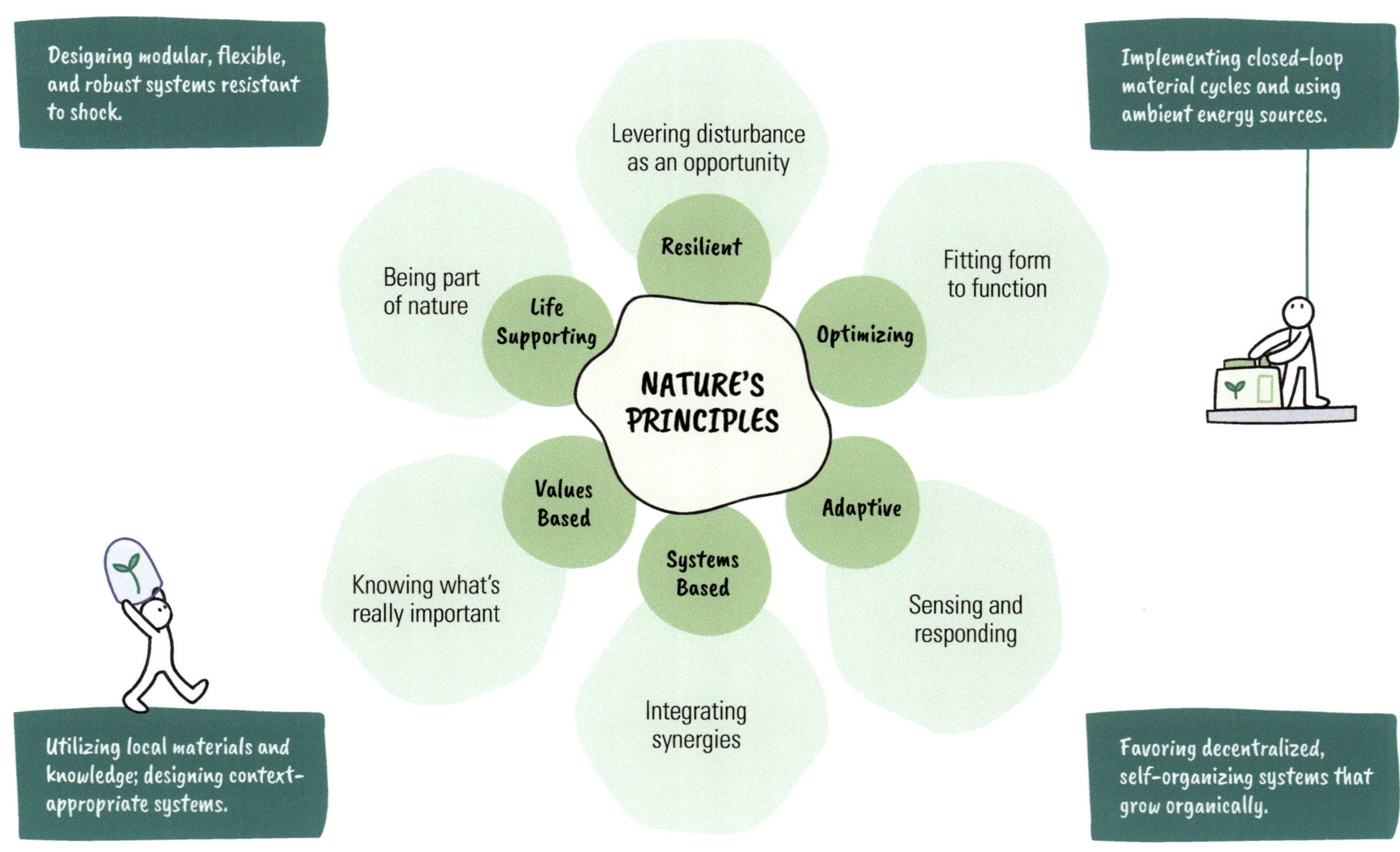

Defining Regenerative Ecological Metrics

The goal of regenerative metrics is to quantify the net positive change a business creates on the essential "living capitals" (soil, water, air, and biodiversity) upon which it depends. This moves the measurement focus from mitigating negative externalities (the focus of traditional compliance or ESG) to increasing positive internalities.

The adoption of these specific nature-based metrics is driven by two main groups: pioneering multinational corporations integrating these targets into their supply chains and specialized standard-setting organizations that provide the necessary frameworks and verification protocols.

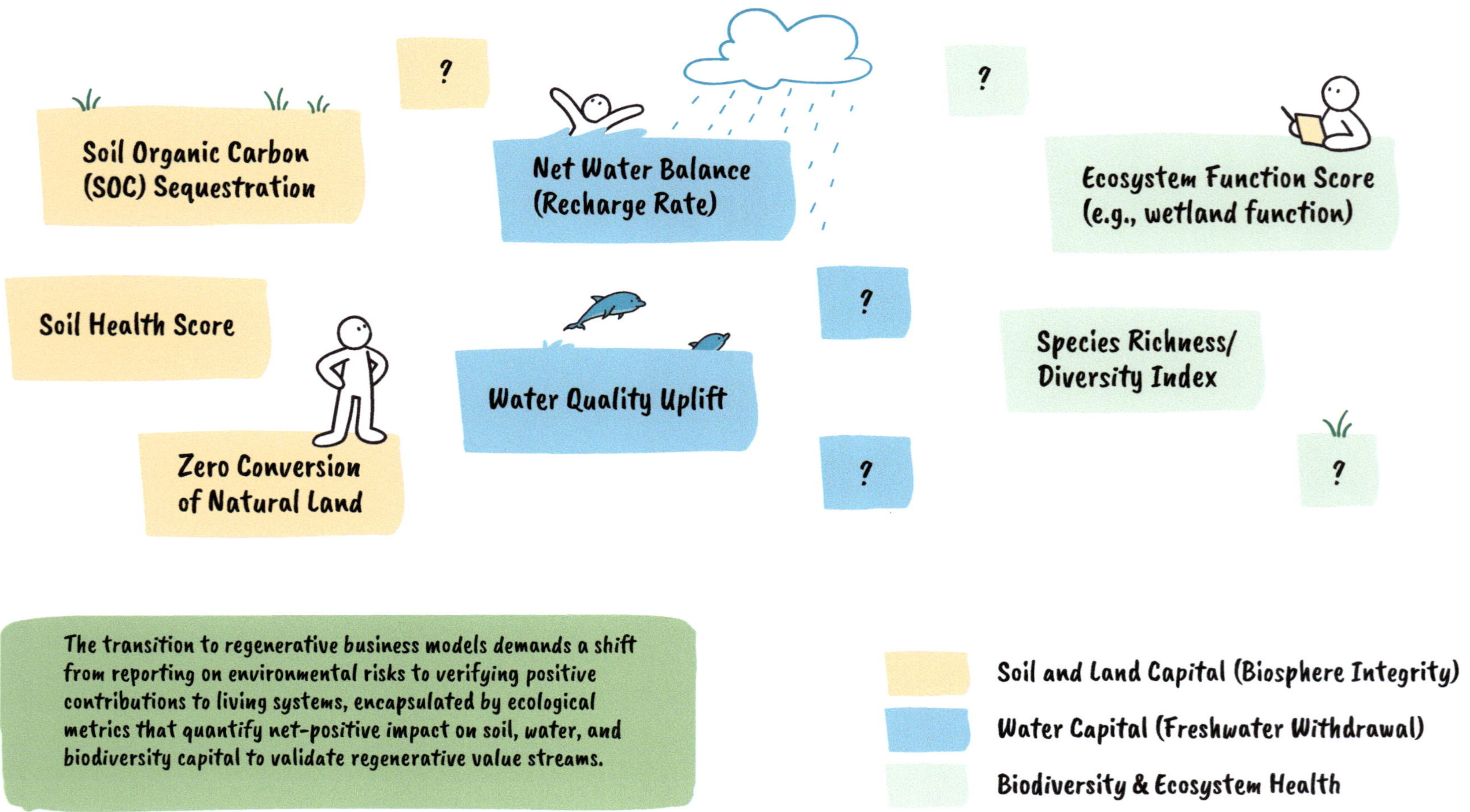

The transition to regenerative business models demands a shift from reporting on environmental risks to verifying positive contributions to living systems, encapsulated by ecological metrics that quantify net-positive impact on soil, water, and biodiversity capital to validate regenerative value streams.

To effectively foster positive behavioral shifts within the framework of Design Thinking for Humanity, a diverse set of tools and methods comes into play. Traditional tools like nudges, choice architecture, social norms, and gamification can guide individuals toward more sustainable decisions.

However, a truly regenerative future requires a deeper and more lasting transformation. The ultimate goal is not just to design sustainable behaviors, but to foster a **regenerative identity**.

This goal is achieved through a multilevel shift:

- **Identity Shift:** Moving beyond changing a single behavior to cultivating a new sense of self in relation to the planet.

- **Widening Identity:** A transition that moves from a narrow, egocentric "me" to a more inclusive "all of us" and ultimately to a planet-centric "all beings" perspective.

- **Core Foundation:** As this sense of self expands, so too does the understanding of the interconnectedness of all things, triggering a corresponding shift in values and behaviors. This is the deep, psychological foundation upon which a truly regenerative culture is built.

[Ecological thinking is essential for addressing the interconnected crises of the modern era, representing a necessary intellectual shift from reductionist methodologies to a holistic understanding of complex living systems. This foundational paradigm governs the development of regenerative business models and effective behavioral interventions.]

Engineering the Regenerative Identity

A regenerative identity does not emerge in a vacuum; it is a social phenomenon. The most powerful mechanism for cultivating it at scale is the intentional design for **social tipping points**. A social tipping point is the moment when a small minority of a population adopts a new belief or behavior, and that new norm is then rapidly and nonlinearly adopted by the majority.

The goal of design is to create a cascade of adoption that can transform an entire community or society. This involves a design-led transformation:

- **Narrative Shift:** Creating a compelling **new narrative** that replaces the old, limiting story (e.g., short-term maximization). Effective stories frame the regenerative transition as an inspiring journey toward a more connected, healthy, and meaningful way of life.

- **Contagion by Design:** The intervention must design a solution that is not just a substitute but is desirable and visible in its own right. As high-quality regenerative practices become visible and are adopted by respected members of a community, a rapid social tipping point is reached.

- **The Multiscalar Process:** This cascade of adoption operates across three interconnected scales (see page 195):
    Micro Level: Individual choices, social networks, and local community norms
    Meso Level: Infrastructures, policies, and market conditions within a city or region
    Macro Level: Global trends, international agreements, and large-scale cultural narratives

A successful intervention creates alignment across all three of these scales, ensuring that the new, regenerative behavior becomes the accepted default.

A powerful example is the Carbon Harvest platform (from the case study): the regenerative identity of the farmer (planetary steward) is reinforced not just by personal profit but by highly visible, measurable outputs like the Soil Health Score (micro), which automatically qualifies them for lower-interest loans through financial institutions (meso), ultimately making the regenerative choice the financially and socially prudent default.

Factors Influencing Sustainable Adaption

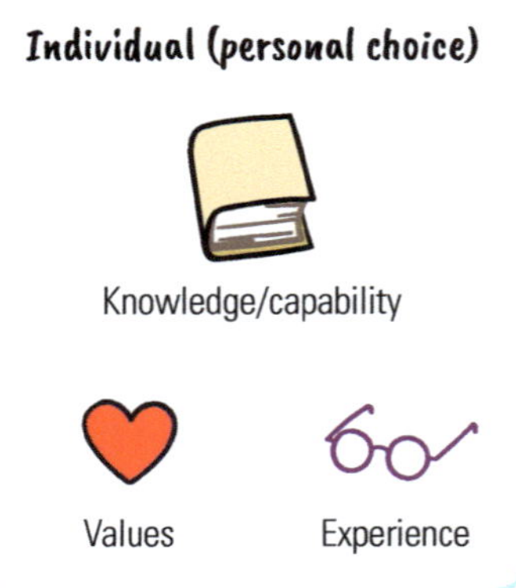

Design Thinking for Humanity as a Cohesive Change Model

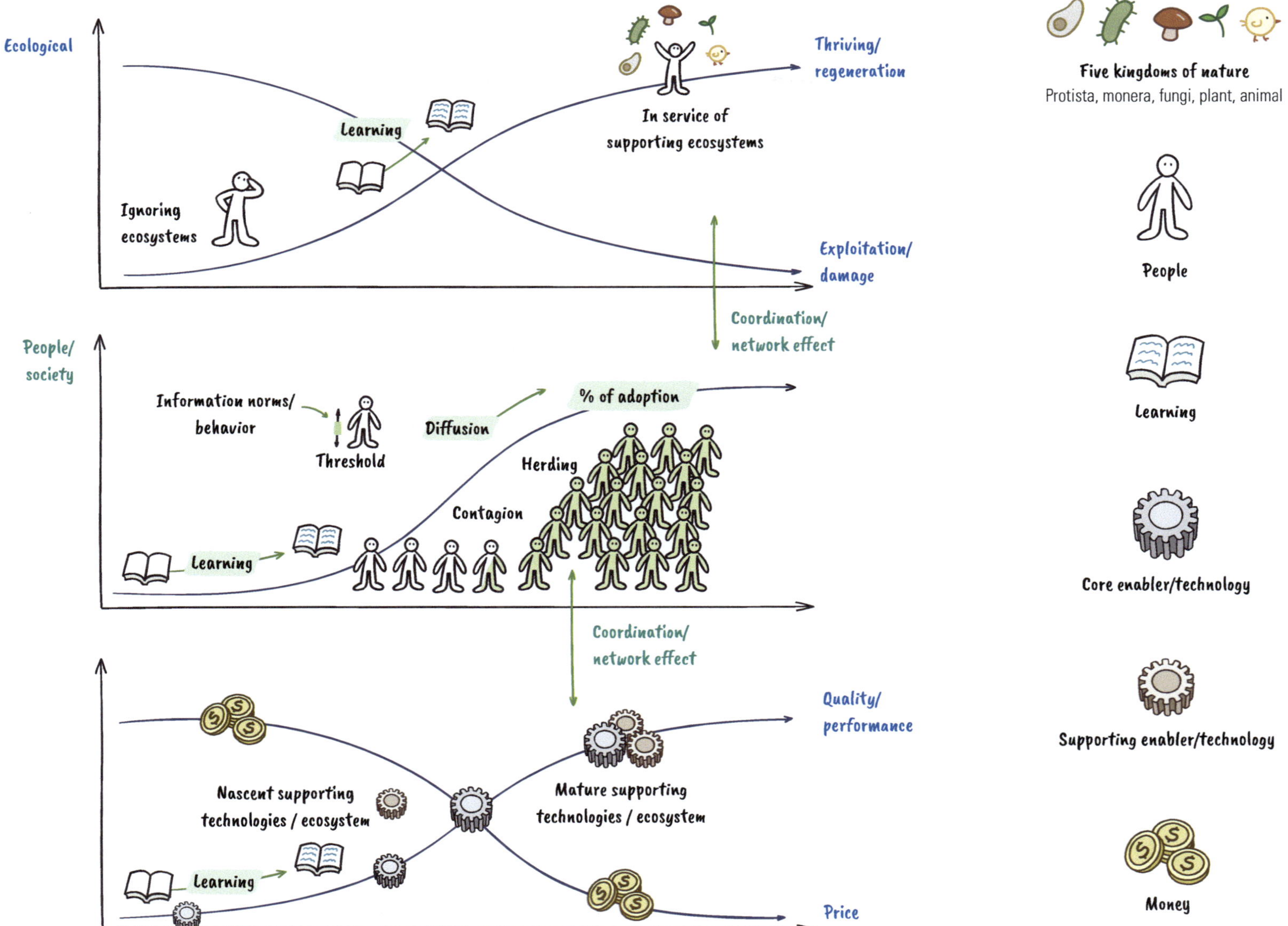

The engine for creating a social tipping point is the intentional cultivation of **individual agency** and **collective efficacy**, which is the shared belief that a community can achieve its goals. This requires moving beyond simply presenting information and instead designing the very conditions in which people feel empowered to act.

1. Design for Visible Contribution
The first step is to design systems that make positive contributions visible. By using digital platforms, public installations, or gamified feedback loops, the collective impact of individual regenerative actions can be shown in real time. This creates a powerful reinforcing loop: when people see that their actions matter and that others are participating, it builds the momentum needed to shift a social norm.

2. Create Community Incubation Hubs
The second critical component is the creation of physical and digital spaces where a new regenerative culture can be practiced and strengthened. These community hubs are incubators for the new social norm, fostering connection, collaboration, and building the trust that is the foundation of collective action. These hubs must empower a new generation of active, capable Resilience Builders, moving beyond passively nudging consumers.

3. Empower Systemic Resilience
Long-term change is only possible when individuals are empowered with the skills and confidence to participate and thrive in the new system. This involves providing accessible education and practical tools that lower the barrier to entry for regenerative activities (e.g., tool-lending libraries or simplified soil-testing kits). The ultimate goal is to embed the regenerative identity into the everyday capabilities of the community.

The Role of Narrative and Systems Design
The entire process of building agency and creating social tipping points is fueled by the power of storytelling. A community's capacity to change is not ultimately driven by data or logic, but by a shared and compelling story about the future.

Value-Based Storytelling: Effective stories frame the regenerative transition as an inspiring journey toward a more connected, healthy, and meaningful way of life, focusing on what everyone stands to gain.

Systems Design Mandate: Success requires transitioning from solely targeting the individual through information to targeting the context through systems design.

Contextual Intervention: Interventions must target the system (defaults, incentives, context) rather than solely the person (education), structurally supporting the desired change.

The Narrative Design Canvas (see page 135) provides a practical tool for intentionally crafting these value-based stories. It guides practitioners to deconstruct the old, limiting narratives and to build new ones that resonate with an audience's deepest values.

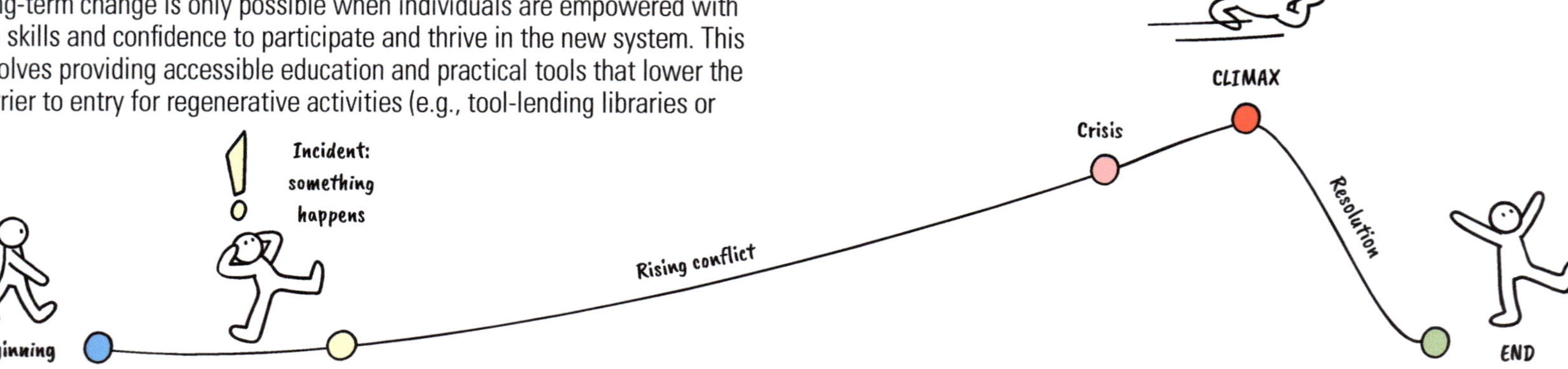

Transitioning from Information Deficit to Systems Design

An essential strategic shift in Design Thinking for Humanity is the move from addressing an information deficit (assuming people just need more data) to leveraging exponential technology for systems design. These new approaches harness data, AI, and network effects to move beyond mere information delivery, strategically empowering individuals as active co-creators of a regenerative world.

Key Technological Levers

The most important aspects of this transition are the application of personalized, forward-looking feedback mechanisms and the creation of decentralized, regenerative incentives:

Environmental Digital Twins: This concept creates a personalized, real-time digital twin of an individual's or a family's ecological footprint. Crucially, it uses predictive analytics to simulate the future impact of different choices (e.g., visualizing a product's full lifecycle before purchase). This moves beyond abstract data to create a tangible, forward-looking feedback loop.

Tokenization and Regeneration Credits: Regenerative actions (like restoring an ecosystem or choosing regenerative products) can be verified and rewarded with regeneration credits using secure, transparent digital ledgers. This transforms pro-environmental behavior from a private act into a visible, rewarding, and engaging public good that can be utilized within local or global economies.

Narrative Amplification: AI-powered community building can scale the stories that shape our culture. Gen AI can craft and personalize compelling narratives, making the regenerative future feel more achievable and relatable, fostering collective belief and shared purpose.

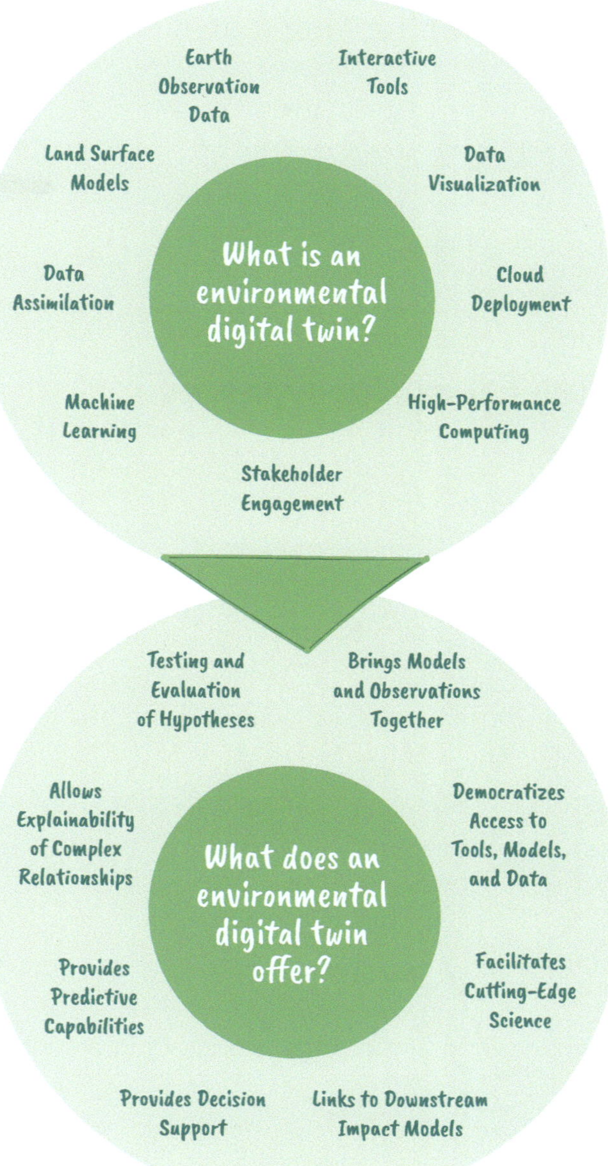

Part 3

A Speculative Case Study

Applying Ecological Thinking

Following the design challenge introduced on pages 68–69, we now delve into ecological thinking, the critical lens that ensures our human-centered solutions are inherently regenerative and operate within the planet's finite boundaries. This part moves beyond mere problem-solving to embedding a life-centered mandate at every stage. It is no longer sufficient for our designs to simply avoid harm; they must actively contribute to the replenishment, restoration, and flourishing of natural systems.

The overarching goal for our case study is both ambitious and essential.

The Living Soil Mandate

Our objective within this challenge is to design a new global economic and agricultural model that makes the regeneration of the world's topsoil the primary measure of agricultural success, ensuring long-term food security, reversing climate change, and restoring biodiversity by 2050.

The previous journey through the design thinking lens provided a crucial human-centered anchor for our ambitious goal. Starting with the Future Persona of Javier Rodriguez, a pragmatic family farmer, we framed a tangible wicked problem: the need for a new model that rewards farmers for their stewardship of the land. Our ideation and ethical scanning led to a refined concept, the "Carbon Harvest" platform, which is grounded in a powerful Value Proposition for Humanity Canvas that is not only innovative but also equitable and ethically considered.

With this human and plant-centric solution designed, we now apply the ecological thinking lens to ensure its very foundation is regenerative. It is not enough for the outcome of the platform to be positive; its operations and the behaviors it encourages must also be in harmony with the natural systems it is designed to protect. To achieve this, key tools from the Ecological Thinking Toolbox will now be applied.

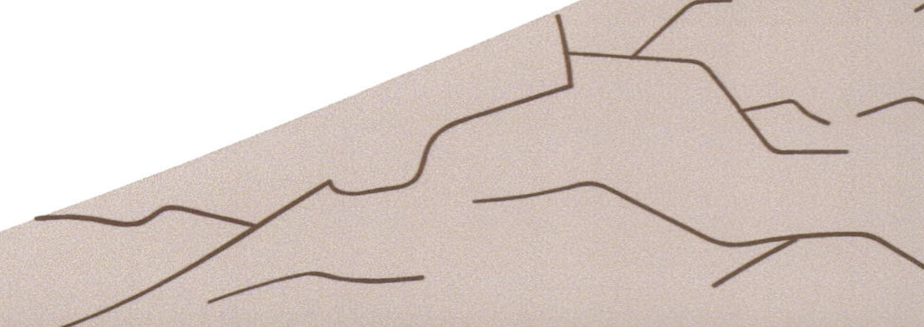

Applying the Toolbox: From a Good Idea to a Regenerative System

1. The Doughnut Economics Model (Strategic Framing)

First, the Doughnut Economics model is used to frame the entire "Carbon Harvest" concept within a "safe and just space for humanity." This tool helps define the non-negotiable boundaries for the solution.

- **Ecological Ceiling:** The platform's own operations (e.g., the energy consumption of its AI and data centers, the manufacturing of its soil sensors) must not transgress any planetary boundaries. For example, all data centers must run on 100% renewable energy to avoid impacting the climate change boundary.

- **Social Foundation:** The platform's governance must ensure it contributes to the social foundation. For example, its data ownership rules must be equitable, empowering farmers like Javier rather than extracting their valuable data, thus strengthening the "voice" and "income" foundations.

2. Life Cycle Assessment (LCA) Simplified (Material & Production Analysis)

Next, a simplified LCA is applied to the physical components of the system, such as the thousands of soil sensors that would be deployed on farms.

- **Lifecycle Map:** The entire lifecycle is mapped and includes raw material extraction for the sensors, the energy used in their manufacturing, the logistics of their deployment, their operational energy use, and their end-of-life.

- **Hotspot Identification:** The analysis reveals that the biggest potential negative impact is not the operational energy (which will be solar-powered) but the creation of electronic waste at the end of the sensors' 10-year lifespan. This becomes a critical "hotspot" for redesign.

- **Design Intervention:** This insight leads to a new design constraint, applying the principles of Design for Durability, Repair & Disassembly. The sensors must be designed using modular components and fully circular, nontoxic materials.

3. Sustainable Behavior Design Canvas (Behavioral Change)

This is perhaps the hardest and most important challenge: how to encourage pragmatic farmers like Javier to adopt a new practice. The canvas is used to design the necessary behavioral interventions.

Target Behavior: Encourage farmers to install and trust the Carbon Harvest sensor network.

Barriers: Javier's skepticism of new technology, fear of data misuse, and the up-front cost/effort of installation.

Drivers: His desire for a new, stable income stream and his deep-seated wish to leave healthy land for his children.

Potential Interventions:

Nudge: Make the onboarding process incredibly simple, with a "white glove" installation service.

Social Proof: Create a community platform where Javier can see testimonials and real-time success stories from other respected farmers in his region.

Feedback Loop: The app provides immediate, clear, and tangible feedback, showing him exactly how his regenerative practices are improving his soil health and increasing his "regeneration credits."

By focusing on these behavioral aspects, the platform moves from being just a technology to a trusted partner in a farmer's journey toward a more resilient and profitable future.

"Out-of-the-Box" Thinking for Behavioral Change

Transforming the abstract concept of soil health into a tangible and joyful experience.

A powerful and often-overlooked vector for change is the next generation. To accelerate the adoption of new practices, the focus must also be on creating "joyful sustainable products and services" that engage children directly. A child's genuine excitement can be the most powerful "nudge" of all, influencing the behavior of an entire family. For the Carbon Harvest platform, this could **manifest as a gamified educational module designed for farmers' children**. Imagine a simple, playful app where a child helps a digital avatar of a tree grow taller or a worm enrich the soil, with the game's progress directly linked to the real-time data from the farm's soil sensors. This transforms the abstract concept of soil health into an engaging and joyful experience, creating a new generation of "soil stewards" who, in turn, become the most passionate and effective advocates for their parents' transition to regenerative practices. This approach uses the **emotional hook of intergenerational love and responsibility** as a powerful catalyst for change.

4. Transforming Identity and Purpose

The most profound shift in farmer behavior is not coming from external incentives alone, but from cultivating a **regenerative identity**. For Javier, the narrative needs to shift from identifying primarily as a **Commodity Producer** (driven by output volume and survival) to a **Planetary Steward** (valued for ecological outcomes and intergenerational legacy).

The Carbon Harvest platform's visual and feedback elements should be deliberately designed to reinforce this identity. For example, instead of displaying a single "profit" number, the main dashboard should prominently showcase the **Soil Health Score** (the regenerative metric) of his farm and the collective **Net Water Balance** improvement for his entire watershed, making his contribution to the Living Capitals visible and a source of community status. This moves the psychological goal from anxiety-reduction to a sense of profound purpose and collective efficacy.

5. Engineering the New Social Norm via Narrative

To scale adoption beyond early adopters, the solution must actively engineer a social tipping point to establish regenerative farming as the new cultural default. This is achieved by **creating a compelling new narrative** that deliberately replaces the limiting old narrative of inevitable decline and short-term maximization.

The intervention should fund Future Storytelling & Narrative Prototyping designed for the farming community, framing the transition not as a costly risk, but as a path to a more connected, healthy, and meaningful way of life. This involves amplifying the success stories of influential farmers in Javier's region (social proof) and leveraging the emotional hook of intergenerational responsibility by showing Javier's children thriving in the new system to **create the necessary social contagion that accelerates mass adoption**.

Ecological Design Tools

To move from the principles of ecological thinking to its practical application, a dedicated set of tools is required. The methods in the following section are designed to empower practitioners with the core capabilities of a life-centered design approach. They provide the frameworks needed to understand the full lifecycle impact of a solution, to design for circularity and regeneration, and to foster the behavioral changes necessary for a sustainable future.

This toolbox provides the essential methods for moving beyond simply "doing less harm" to actively creating solutions that restore and revitalize the social and ecological systems they are a part of. The tools that follow will guide practitioners through the process of analyzing a product's environmental footprint, framing challenges within planetary boundaries, and applying nature's own principles to inspire innovative, regenerative designs.

The following collection of tools provides the practical methods needed to apply the most important frameworks for ecological design. It covers the core aspects of understanding a solution's material and production impact, provides a strategic framework for designing within a "safe and just space for humanity," and offers canvases for creating regenerative business models and sustainable behaviors.

By mastering these methods, innovators and leaders can move beyond a narrow focus on user needs and instead begin to architect solutions that are not only desirable for people but are also resilient and beneficial for the entire web of life. It is through the practical application of these tools that the vision of a truly regenerative future can be made a reality.

Ecological Design Toolbox

The Doughnut Economics Model

This is the essential strategic framework for this chapter, providing a clear visual model for the core challenge: meeting the needs of all people (the "social foundation") while operating within the means of the living planet (the "ecological ceiling"). It serves as a powerful canvas for framing problems and defining the "safe and just space" for any solution.

Biomimicry & Permaculture Principles

This tool serves as a powerful source of creative inspiration, introducing the core principles of learning from nature's genius (biomimicry) and designing human systems that mimic the resilience of natural ecosystems (permaculture). It provides a wellspring of proven strategies for creating truly regenerative designs.

Life Cycle Assessment (LCA) Simplified

This tool provides a practical framework to map the complete environmental footprint of a product, service, or system. It guides teams to analyze every stage, from raw material extraction and production to use and end-of-life, in order to identify the most significant "hotspots" for ecological impact and prioritize areas for redesign.

Regenerative Business Model Canvas

This tool evolves the traditional business model canvas by embedding regenerative principles at its core. It prompts teams to design ventures that are not just sustainable but actively contribute to the health of social and ecological systems by focusing on "net-positive impact" and the enhancement of "living capitals."

Design for Durability, Repair, & Disassembly

This is a practical, hands-on tool that provides a set of design principles for creating products built for longevity. It challenges teams to move beyond planned obsolescence by focusing on modular design, the availability of spare parts, and the ease of disassembly, ensuring that materials can be kept in use at their highest value for as long as possible.

Sustainable Behavior Design Canvas

This tool provides a structured canvas for intentionally designing interventions that foster sustainable behaviors. It integrates key principles from behavioral science, such as Nudges, Social Norms, and Feedback Loops, to help teams understand the drivers of current behaviors and design solutions that make sustainable choices easy, attractive, and socially rewarding.

The Doughnut Economics Model

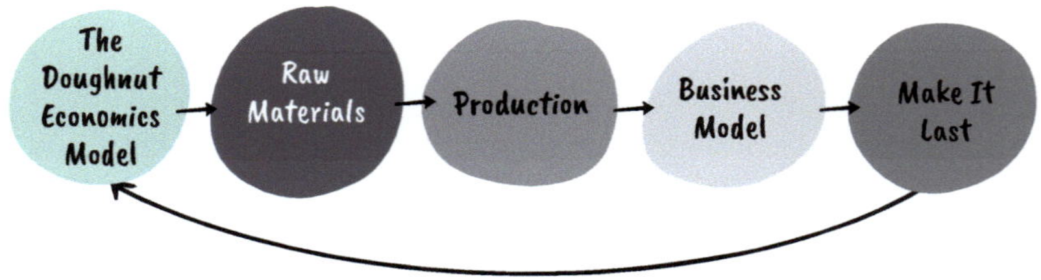

I would like to...

...use a clear and compelling framework to define a "safe and just space" for humanity, balancing social needs with planetary boundaries.

What you can do with the tool:

- Provide a powerful visual model for the core challenge of Design Thinking for Humanity.
- Frame "wicked problems" in the context of both social shortfalls and ecological overshoots.
- Establish a clear, holistic set of criteria for evaluating the true sustainability and equity of a solution.
- Shift the goal of innovation from limitless growth to thriving in balance.
- Align diverse stakeholders around a shared, science-based understanding of a sustainable and just future.

Expert Tips

Use It as a Diagnostic Tool
Before designing a new solution, use the Doughnut to diagnose the current system. For a specific city, region, or industry, map its performance. Where are the most significant social shortfalls? Where are the most critical ecological overshoots? This diagnostic provides a clear and powerful starting point for any design challenge.

From "Less Bad" to "More Good"
The Doughnut challenges teams to move beyond simply making degenerative systems "less bad" (e.g., slightly more efficient). The goal is to design solutions that are regenerative by design, actively contributing to the health of both the social foundation and the ecological ceiling.

Downscale the Doughnut
While the Doughnut is a global model, its real power is in its application at a local level. Facilitate a workshop where a team or a community creates its own "City Doughnut" or "Business Doughnut." This process of contextualizing the social and ecological priorities for a specific place makes the model a powerful tool for local action and innovation.

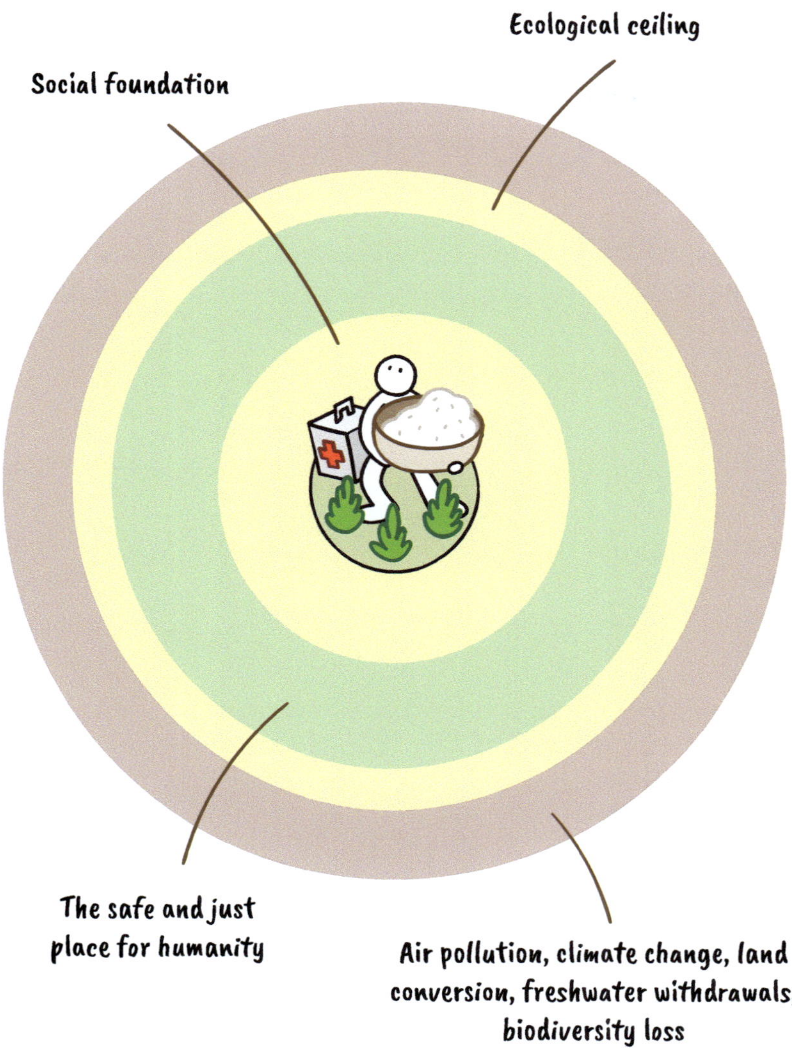

The Doughnut Economics model, developed by economist Kate Raworth, is a strategic framework that re-envisions the goal of economic activity. It replaces the endless pursuit of GDP growth with the goal of operating within a "doughnut" that represents a safe and just space for humanity.

Step 1: Understand the Social Foundation

The inner ring of the doughnut represents the **social foundation**. This is a set of critical social outcomes, derived from the UN's Sustainable Development Goals, that are essential for human well-being (e.g., food security, housing, education, health, social equity). The first goal is to design solutions that ensure no one is left in the "hole" in the middle, falling short of these essential needs.

Step 2: Understand the Ecological Ceiling

The outer ring of the doughnut represents the **ecological ceiling**. This is defined by nine planetary boundaries (e.g., climate change, biodiversity loss, freshwater use) that scientists have identified as critical for maintaining a stable planet. The second goal is to design solutions that do not "overshoot" this ceiling, putting unsustainable pressure on Earth's life-support systems.

Step 3: Design for the "Doughnut"

The space between the social foundation and the ecological ceiling is the doughnut itself: the "safe and just space for humanity." The core task of Design Thinking for Humanity is to use this model as a canvas to design solutions, business models, and systems that operate entirely within this space, simultaneously addressing social needs while respecting planetary boundaries.

Biomimicry & Permaculture Principles

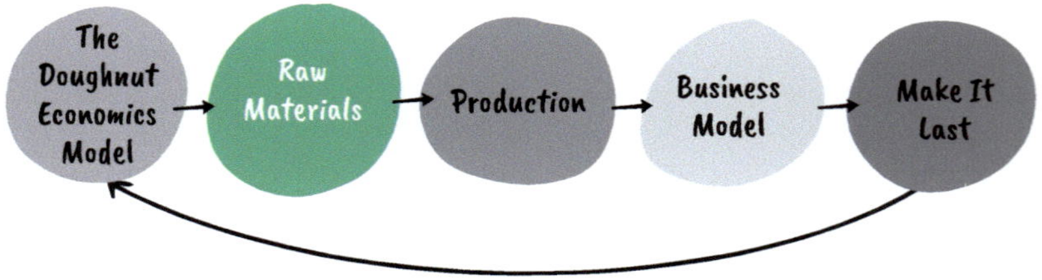

I would like to...

...learn from nature's genius to create innovative solutions that are inherently sustainable, resilient, and regenerative.

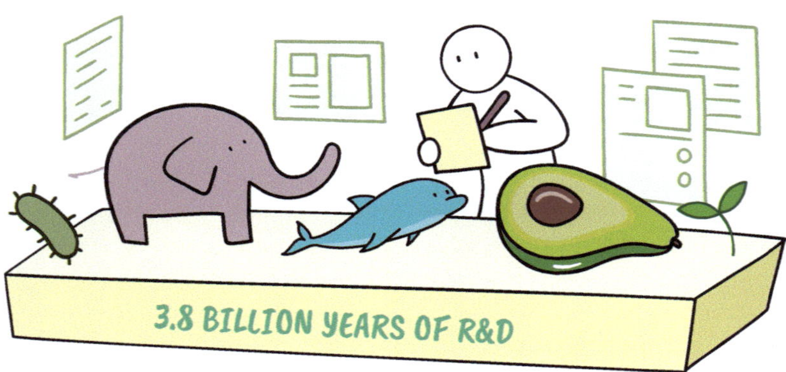

What you can do with the tool:

- Go beyond simply reducing harm to creating designs that actively co-evolve with nature.
- Unlock a vast library of 3.8 billion years of proven, time-tested strategies for resilience and efficiency.
- Foster a deeper, more respectful relationship with the natural world, viewing it as a mentor.
- Generate breakthrough innovations by applying biological principles to technical or social challenges.
- Provide a powerful source of inspiration for creating truly regenerative products, services, and systems.

Expert Tips

Nature as Mentor, Not Supermarket
The core mindset shift required for this tool is to view nature not as a warehouse of resources to be extracted, but as a library of brilliant strategies to be learned from. This is a move from a relationship of exploitation to one of respectful mentorship.

Start with a Function, Not an Organism
A common mistake is to pick a "cool" animal and then try to invent a product based on it. The more effective approach is to start with a human design problem or a desired function and then ask the question, "How does nature solve this function?" This leads to much more meaningful and applicable innovations.

Observe Your Local Ecosystem
Inspiration is not limited to exotic documentaries. Some of the most powerful lessons in resilient design can be learned by observing a local park, forest, or even a vacant lot. The most resilient solutions are often those that are deeply attuned to their specific local context, climate, and ecology.

This tool combines two complementary disciplines. Biomimicry is the practice of learning from and emulating the strategies found in nature to solve human design challenges. Permaculture is a design philosophy that uses principles from natural ecosystems to create sustainable and self-sufficient human systems.

Step 1: Define the Design Challenge as a Function

Start by clearly stating the core function or problem to be solved. Be specific.

Example: "How can we create a building facade that passively cools itself in a hot climate?"

Step 2: Identify Nature's Champions (Biomimicry)

Research how nature and different organisms have already solved a similar challenge. This involves "biologizing" the problem by asking: "How do desert animals or plants stay cool without air conditioning?" This research might lead to studying the incredible self-regulating ventilation systems of termite mounds or the heat-reflecting properties of certain plant leaves. The goal is to identify the underlying principle, not just to copy the form.

Step 3: Apply Ecosystem Principles (Permaculture)

Once a core idea is inspired by a natural model, apply principles from permaculture to ensure the solution works as part of a larger, beneficial system. Ask key questions:

- **Stacking Functions:** How can this solution perform multiple functions (e.g., the facade not only cools but also harvests rainwater)?
- **Creating No Waste:** How can the outputs of this system become inputs for another (e.g., the harvested water irrigates a green roof)?
- **Integration, Not Segregation:** How does the solution integrate with and benefit its surrounding environment (e.g., the green roof provides a habitat for local pollinators)?

Life Cycle Assessment (LCA) Simplified

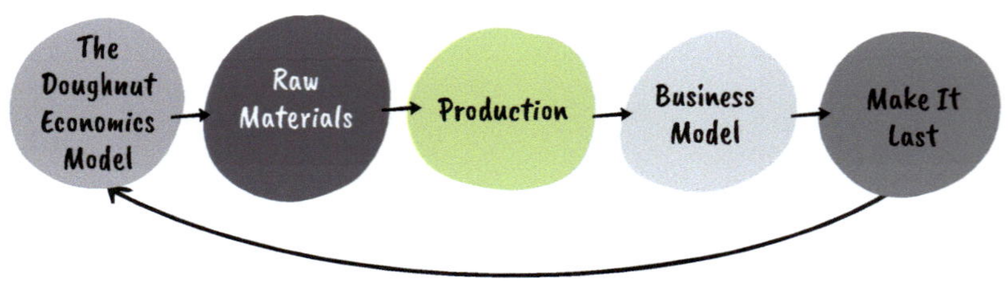

I would like to...

...understand the complete environmental footprint of a product, service, or system to identify the most significant areas of ecological impact.

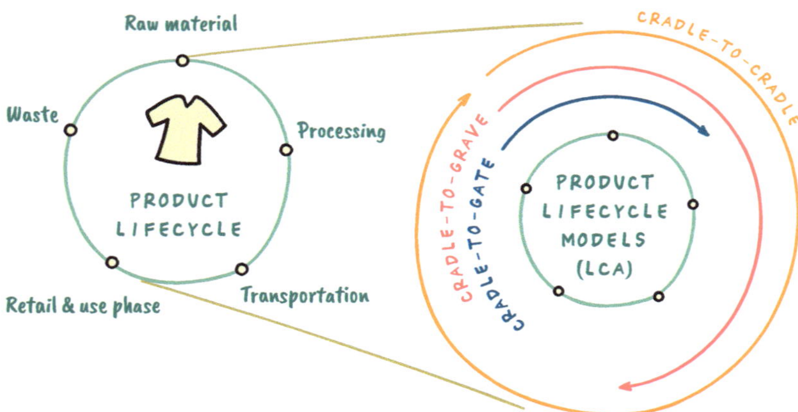

What you can do with the tool:

- Map the full lifecycle of an offering, from raw material extraction ("cradle") to end-of-life disposal ("grave").
- Identify hidden "hotspots" of environmental impact that are not immediately obvious.
- Make more informed, evidence-based decisions about material selection, manufacturing processes, and supply chain design.
- Avoid "burden shifting," where solving a problem in one area (e.g., reducing manufacturing energy) creates a new problem elsewhere (e.g., using a material that is impossible to recycle).
- Provide a credible, data-informed foundation for making sustainability claims and building trust with stakeholders.

Expert Tips

Think Beyond Carbon
While carbon emissions are a critical metric, do not let them be the only one. A comprehensive LCA also considers other crucial impacts like water depletion, biodiversity loss, and land-use change. A holistic view is essential for true ecological design.

The "Use Phase" Is Often Overlooked
For many products, especially electronics or appliances, the most significant environmental impact occurs during the "use phase" due to energy consumption. Do not just focus on making the product out of sustainable materials; also focus on making it radically more efficient to use.

Use It as a Comparative Tool
LCA is most powerful when used to compare two or more alternative design choices. For example, you can create a simplified LCA for a product made with plastic versus one made with a new biomaterial. This allows you to make a more informed, data-driven decision about which path is genuinely more sustainable.

THE LCA CANVAS

1. Map Lifecycle Stages

Use the table below to sketch or list the inputs, processes, and outputs for each of the five stages of the product's life. Include a simple icon or image to represent the flow.

1.1 Raw Material	1.2 Processing	1.3 Distribution	1.4 Use Phase	1.5 End-of-Life

2. Identify 2-4 Key Impacts at Each Stage

For each stage identified in step 1, brainstorm and list the primary environmental impacts. Map these onto the table below.

1. 2. 3. 4.	1. 2. 3. 4.	1. 2. 3. 4.	1. 2. 3. 4.	1. 2. 3. 4.

3. Identify the "Hotspot" and Focus

Analyze the completed tables above to identify the one or two stages that, based on your team's qualitative assessment, have the most significant negative ecological impact.

A. Hotspot Selection

Based on the evidence gathered, which stage(s) pose the most critical environmental challenge?

- **Hotspot 1:** ___________________ (e.g., Manufacturing & Processing)
- **Reasoning/Evidence:** ___________________ (Why did we choose this stage? Mention the specific high-level impacts like high energy use, toxic waste, etc.)
- **Hotspot 2 (Optional):** ___________________ (e.g., End-of-Life)
- **Reasoning/Evidence:** ___________________

B. Hotspot Focus

What is the primary objective for redesigning the product based only on the identified hotspot(s)?

Focus Objective: Reduce the environmental impact associated with the _________ stage.

Next Actionable Step:

A Life Cycle Assessment (LCA) is a systematic analysis of the environmental impacts of a product throughout its entire life. This simplified version focuses on a qualitative mapping of the key stages to identify major areas for intervention.

Step 1: Map the Lifecycle Stages

On a large canvas, map the five key stages of your product or service's life:

1.1 Raw Material Extraction: How are the raw materials acquired?
1.2 Manufacturing & Processing: What energy and resources are used to produce the final product?
1.3 Distribution: How is the product transported to the user?
1.4 Use Phase: What is the environmental impact during the product's active use (e.g., energy consumption, emissions)?
1.5 End-of-Life: What happens to the product when the user is finished with it? Is it landfilled, recycled, or composted?

Step 2: Identify Key Impacts at Each Stage

For each stage, brainstorm the primary environmental impacts. Consider key areas like energy consumption, water use, carbon emissions, pollution, and waste generation. Use sticky notes to map these impacts onto your lifecycle diagram.

Step 3: Identify the "Hotspots"

As a team, analyze the completed map to identify the hotspots, which are the one or two stages that have the most significant negative ecological impact. This is the most critical step, as it provides a clear and evidence-based focus for your redesign efforts.

Regenerative Business Model Canvas

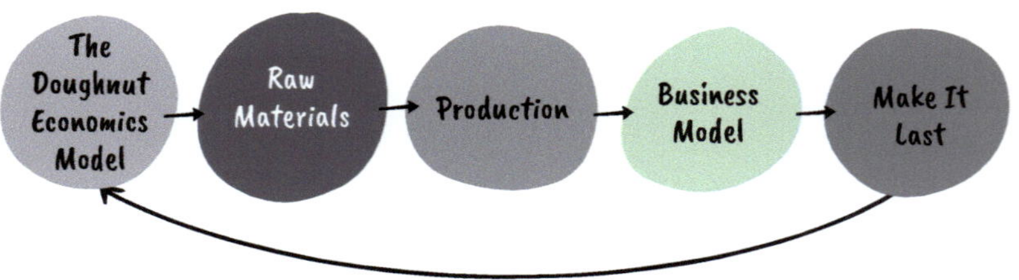

I would like to...

...design a business model that is not just sustainable but actively contributes to the restoration and revitalization of social and ecological systems.

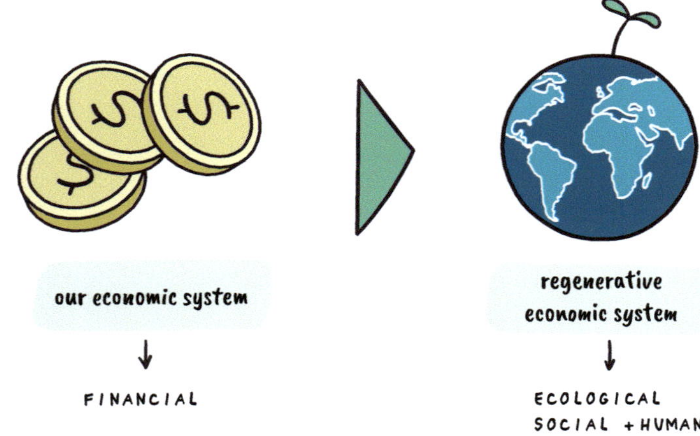

What you can do with the tool:

- Move beyond simply "doing less harm" to designing a business that has a net-positive impact.
- Systematically integrate regenerative principles into the core logic of how your organization creates, delivers, and captures value.
- Foster a deeper understanding of your business as an interconnected part of larger living systems.
- Align your entire team around a shared vision of the business as a force for regeneration.
- Create a truly resilient and future-fit business model that thrives by enhancing the well-being of people and the planet.

Expert Tips

Think in Systems, Not Silos
A regenerative business model understands the profound interconnectedness of all its parts. Use this canvas to map the feedback loops between your activities, your impact on living capitals, and your financial success. The goal is to design a business where positive ecological and social outcomes are a direct driver of profitability.

Co-evolve with Your Community
Regenerative design is not a top-down process; it requires co-evolution with all stakeholders. Use this canvas as a tool for collaboration. Engage your customers, partners, and local communities in the design of your business model to foster mutualistic relationships and a sense of shared ownership.

Embrace an Adaptive Mindset
Natural systems are not static; they are constantly learning and adapting. Your business model should be the same. Treat this canvas as a living document. Continuously monitor your ecological and social impacts, learn from the feedback the system gives you, and be prepared to adapt your strategy to thrive in a dynamic world.

The Regenerative Business Model Canvas

Living Capitals & Ecosystem	Key Activities & Resource Inputs	Impact Value Proposition			Channels & Relationships	Regenerative Purpose and Vision
		Solution(s)		**Value Creators**		
Key Partners & Stakeholders		**The solution (Products, Services, Experiences):** A clear description of what you are offering		**For the planet:** How does your solution address the planet's pains and create regenerative gains (e.g., "Uses circular materials," "Reduces energy consumption," "Sequester carbon")?		**Customer Segments & Participants**
Cost and Reinvestment Structure				**For the people:** How does your solution relieve pains and create desired gains?		
				For Society: How does your solution alleviate societal pains and create community benefits (e.g., "Fosters local connections," "Designed for accessibility and inclusion," "Creates meaningful jobs")?	**Regenerative Value Streams**	

DOWNLOAD TOOL
www.design-humanity.com/en/regenerative-bmc

The Regenerative Business Model Canvas is an advanced tool that moves beyond the traditional focus on profitability to design a business that actively creates net-positive impact across social, ecological, and economic systems. Note: The steps to fill the canvas might vary on previous tools applied.

Step 1: Define Purpose
Set the audacious "win-win-win" mission. State the net-positive impact the business aims to create for the planet, people, and society, anchoring all design choices in regeneration.

Step 2: Map the System
Identify "living capitals" (e.g., soil health, trust) as core assets. Map all key partners, stakeholders, and customer segments you depend on and have a responsibility to enhance.

Step 3: Design Regenerative Flows
(Re)Design the core value proposition and key activities to deliver simultaneous ecological, social, and financial value. Define channels and relationships that foster mutualistic, continuous engagement.

Step 4: Design Regenerative Value Streams
Detail costs, prioritizing reinvestment back into the living capitals. Define regenerative value streams where financial returns are explicitly linked to, and inseparable from, positive ecological and social outcomes.

Design for Durability, Repair, & Disassembly

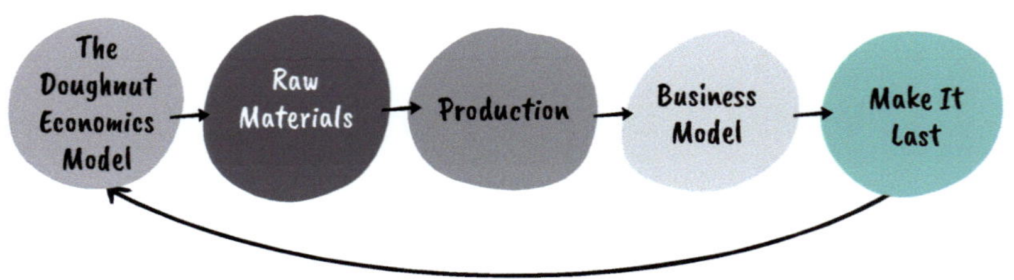

I would like to...

...design products that last longer, are easy to repair, and can be gracefully disassembled to keep materials in a circular flow.

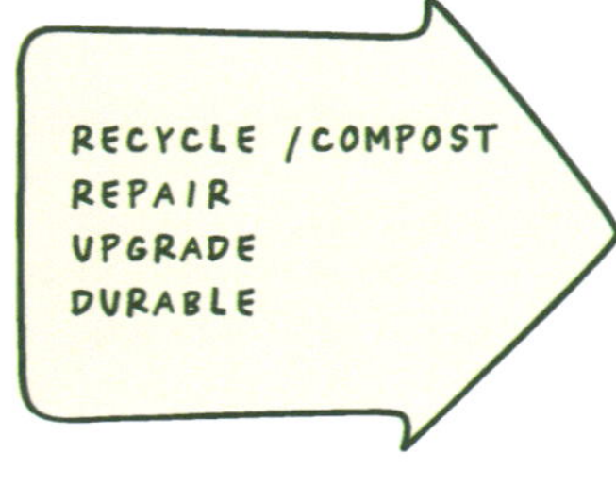

What you can do with the tool:

- Move beyond the linear "take-make-dispose" model by designing out waste from the very beginning.
- Significantly reduce a product's environmental footprint by extending its useful life.
- Create new business opportunities in repair, refurbishment, and remanufacturing.
- Build stronger customer loyalty by offering products that are a long-term investment, not a disposable convenience.
- Provide a practical framework for applying circular economy principles at the product design level.

Expert Tips

Create a "Repairability Score"
To make this a formal part of your process, develop a simple, internal "repairability score" for your products. Create a checklist: Can it be opened with standard tools? Are spare parts available? Is the battery replaceable? Scoring your designs against these criteria makes repairability a tangible and measurable innovation goal.

Partner with the Repair Community
Collaborate with the global community of independent repair cafes and activists. They are the experts on why products fail and what makes them difficult to fix. Providing them with early prototypes for feedback is an invaluable way to identify and eliminate design flaws that hinder repair.

Make Repair a Beautiful Experience
Frame the act of repair not as a chore but as an empowering and positive experience. Design elegant toolkits that are a pleasure to use. Celebrate beautifully mended, long-lasting items. Repair manuals can celebrate the stories of well-loved, well-maintained products to build a culture that values longevity over novelty.

Durability, Repair, & Disassembly Checklist

1. Durability
- Have we selected the most robust and long-lasting materials available for this product's intended use?
- Is the design timeless, or is it based on a short-term trend that will quickly look dated?

2. Repair
- Can the product be opened and reassembled using standard, common tools?
- Are key components modular and easily replaceable if they fail?

3. Disassembly
- Have we avoided using permanent glues or welds, favoring screws or clips instead?
- Is the product made from a few, clearly marked mono-materials to make recycling simple and effective?

This tool provides a set of core principles for challenging the culture of disposability and planned obsolescence. It guides a team to make intentional design choices that extend the life of products and the value of the materials they contain.

Step 1: Design for Durability

The first principle is to create high-quality products that are built to last. This involves selecting robust, long-lasting materials and designing with a timeless aesthetic that will not quickly go out of fashion. The goal is to create objects that users form a lasting emotional connection with, encouraging them to keep and care for them over many years.

Step 2: Design for Repair

The second principle is to make products easy to fix. This means using modular components that can be easily replaced by the user or a technician. It requires the use of standard fasteners instead of proprietary screws or glues, and it necessitates providing clear, accessible instructions and a reliable supply of spare parts.

Step 3: Design for Disassembly

The final principle is to plan for the product's end-of-life from the very beginning. Products should be designed for easy and efficient disassembly. This involves using a limited number of pure, unblended materials (mono-materials) and avoiding permanent adhesives. This ensures that when a product can no longer be used, its components and materials can be easily separated and channeled into high-quality recycling or remanufacturing streams.

Sustainable Behavior Design Canvas

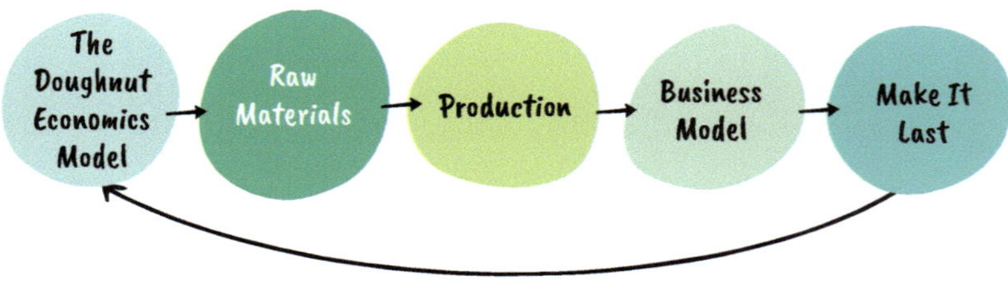

I would like to...

...intentionally design interventions that make sustainable choices easy, attractive, and socially rewarding.

What you can do with the tool:

- Move beyond simply raising awareness to actively designing for behavioral change.
- Apply proven principles from behavioral science to increase the adoption of sustainable practices.
- Create a structured canvas for understanding the drivers of current behaviors and identifying leverage points for change.
- Design products, services, and systems that make sustainability the default, not the alternative.
- Foster a more holistic approach to innovation that considers the human element of the ecological transition.

Expert Tips

Make It Easy
The single most important principle of behavior change is to make the desired action as easy as possible. Before designing a complex incentive program, first focus on removing every point of friction that makes the sustainable choice even slightly more difficult than the unsustainable one.

Focus on a Single Behavior at a Time
Avoid trying to change too many things at once. A successful intervention targets one specific, measurable behavior. By focusing your efforts, you can design a more effective and targeted solution, and the success from changing one behavior can often create a positive spillover effect, making subsequent changes easier.

Test, Learn, and Iterate
Behavioral design is not an exact science; it is an experimental one. Always treat your interventions as prototypes. Test them with a small group, measure the results, learn what works and what doesn't, and iterate on your design. A continuous cycle of testing and learning is essential for creating interventions that are truly effective in the real world.

Current Behavior — WHAT? — Target Behavior

Current Behavior

What is the current, undesirable default behavior we need to disrupt?

Target Behavior

What is the smallest, single action that would create the largest positive impact if adopted at scale?

Barriers — WHY? — Drivers

Barriers

What immediate and structural friction prevents the target audience from doing this already?

Drivers

What deep human motivation or purpose does the target behavior fulfill, and what emotional benefit can we amplify?

Nudges — HOW? — Social Norm

Nudges

How can we make the desired action instant, effortless, and friction-free?

Social Norm

How can we visibly celebrate the behavior of early adopters to make the new norm compelling and widely desirable?

FEEDBACK LOOPS

How can we immediately show the user the value of their action (e.g., carbon sequestered, water saved, community strengthened)?

DOWNLOAD TOOL
www.design-humanity.com/
en/sustainable-behavior

The Sustainable Behavior Design Canvas provides a structured framework for designing interventions that foster sustainable behaviors. It integrates key principles from behavioral science to guide the creation of effective and empathetic solutions.

Step 1: Define the Target Behavior
Start by defining a single, specific, and observable sustainable behavior that is the target for change. Be as precise as possible.

Example: "Increase the percentage of residents in a building who correctly sort their organic waste for composting."

Step 2: Analyze Barriers and Drivers
For the target behavior, analyze the forces at play:
- **Barriers:** What makes the desired behavior difficult (e.g., inconvenient bin location, confusion about what to compost, lack of perceived benefit)?
- **Drivers:** What motivates the desired behavior (e.g., a desire to help the environment, seeing neighbors do it, financial incentives)?

Step 3: Design the Interventions
Based on the analysis, design a set of interventions using key principles from behavioral science:
- **Nudges & Choice Architecture:** How can the environment be designed to make the behavior easier (e.g., place a visually attractive compost bin right next to the main trash can)?
- **Social Norms & Proof:** How can the behavior be made more socially visible and desirable (e.g., share statistics on the building's collective positive impact)?
- **Feedback Loops:** How can people be provided with clear and immediate feedback on their actions (e.g., a smart bin that shows the weight of composted material and its environmental benefit)?

For lasting change, all micro-level behavioral interventions must be structurally supported by policy or system design to make the regenerative choice the inevitable default (see page 216).

Tool Extension: Elevating to Systemic Context (Scale)

The goal of the extension is to move beyond product-level optimization to architecting a systemic transition. A regenerative solution is only truly successful when it has achieved the necessary critical mass to become the new societal default.

Three high-leverage questions help us to transform a good design into a self-sustaining regenerative system:

1. The Identity Mandate

Focus: Transforming the user's perception of self and purpose.

The Question
How do we make the intervention a catalyst for a lasting identity shift rooted in purpose and legacy?

The Design Mandate
Design all dashboards, feedback loops, and communication to reinforce the desired regenerative identity (e.g., planetary steward instead of commodity producer).

Leverage Point
Cultivate identity by shifting the psychological goal from anxiety reduction to a sense of profound purpose and collective efficacy.

2. The Policy Lever

Focus: Identifying the structural incentive that accelerates adoption.

The Question
What single policy change would structurally mandate or incentivize this behavior at a community or state level?

The Design Mandate
Design the solution to integrate with a single, high-leverage policy (e.g., a carbon tax, a subsidy for ecosystem services, or new procurement rules).

Leverage Point
Ensure the regenerative choice is the easiest, most advantageous, and inevitable default by integrating policy directly into the system's architecture.

3. The Tipping Point

Focus: Engineering the nonlinear cascade of mass adoption.

The Question
What is the critical mass (threshold) we need to reach to trigger a nonlinear cascade of adoption across the entire system?

The Design Mandate
Amplify the success stories of influential early adopters (social proof) and leverage intergenerational vectors (e.g., children's engagement) to create powerful social contagion.

Leverage Point
Apply narrative engineering by funding future storytelling that frames the transition not as a costly risk but as a path to a more connected, healthy, and meaningful way of life.

Ecological thinking expands the design lens from being purely human-centered to being life-centered, recognizing that human flourishing is inextricably linked to the health of the planet.

The goal of this lens is not just sustainability, which is doing "less harm," but active regeneration, which is creating solutions that restore and revitalize the social and ecological systems they are a part of.

This is put into practice by applying the principles of the circular economy and bio-mimicry to design products, services, and business models that eliminate waste and emulate nature's genius.

A core function of this work is to address the profound challenge of behavioral change, using design to foster a regenerative mindset and make sustainable living a joyful and desirable pursuit.

SYSTEMS THINKING

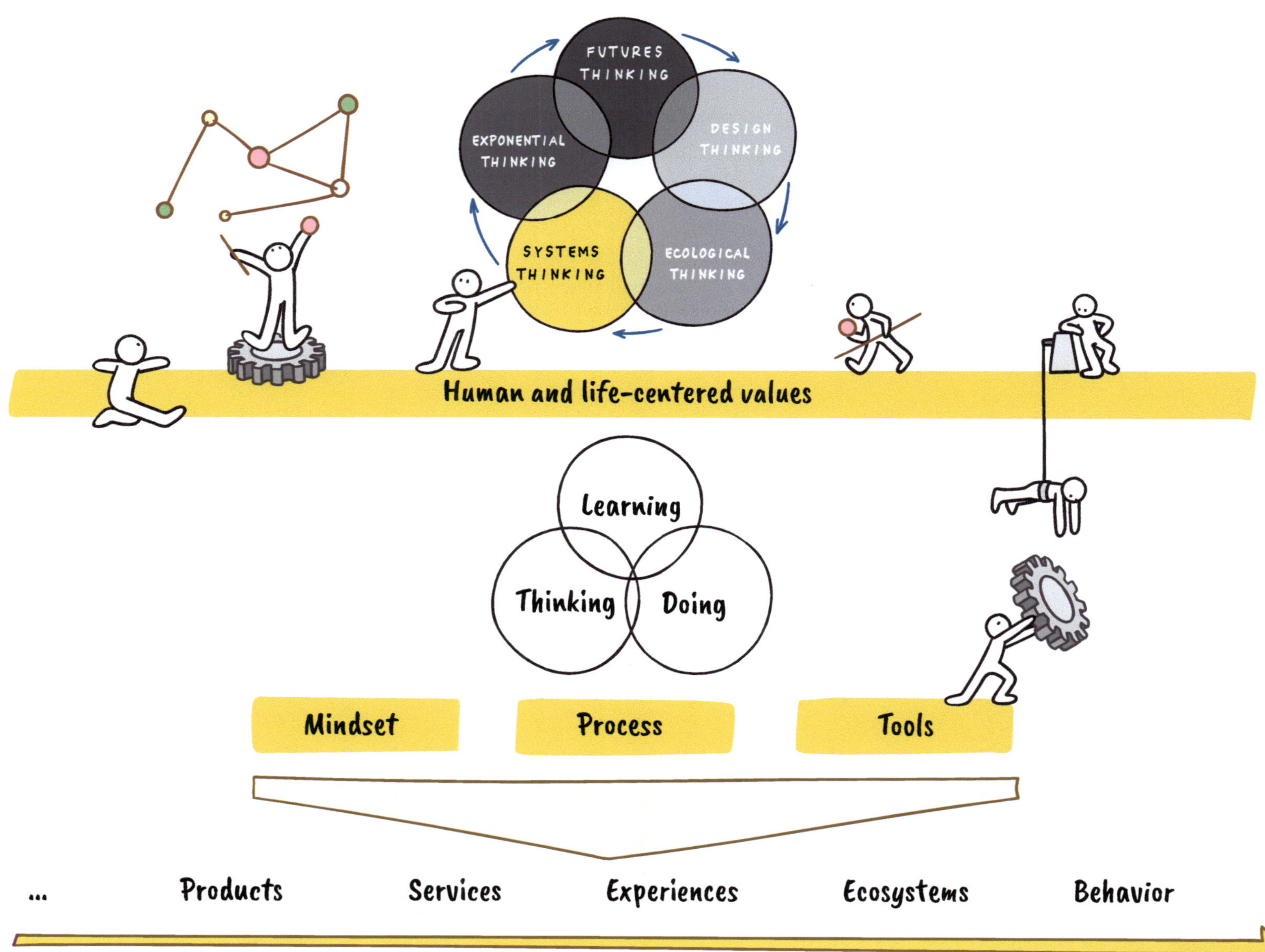
FUTURES THINKING
EXPONENTIAL THINKING
DESIGN THINKING
SYSTEMS THINKING
ECOLOGICAL THINKING
Human and life-centered values
Learning
Thinking
Doing
Mindset
Process
Tools
...
Products
Services
Experiences
Ecosystems
Behavior
THE SPECTRUM OF POSITIVE, RESILIENT CHANGE WE AIM TO CREATE

Understanding Complexity

The world is a complex, interconnected system where nearly everything is related. This complexity arises from a confluence of factors, from the physical forces that shaped our planet to the intricate web of life that connects all species. Yet, humans tend to think linearly, often perceiving causality as a simple action-reaction pattern. This natural inclination frequently leads innovation teams to oversimplify the world, overlooking the complex interdependencies that shape reality. To navigate these systems requires a different way of thinking: **systems thinking**. A systems thinking approach moves beyond viewing problems as isolated events. It translates ecological principles into an analytical map.

Instead, **it encourages a "zoom out"** to gain a holistic understanding of how different problems interrelate and influence one another. Taking this broader perspective is crucial for identifying seemingly effective "fixes" that ultimately fail within the larger system. Without this holistic view, there is a risk of encountering the same problems repeatedly or discovering that addressing one issue only exacerbates another. This is where the practice of **designing entire business ecosystems** becomes critical, as it provides a framework to connect the dots and orchestrate change at a truly systemic level, building the resilience and adaptability required for long-term well-being.

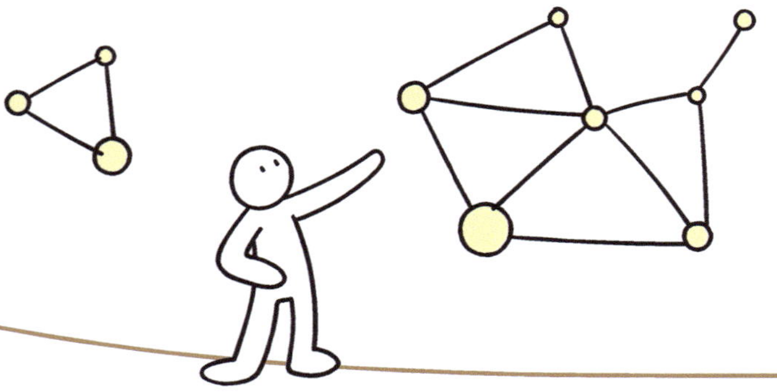

[Systems thinking is the indispensable lens that compels us to transcend linear problem-solving, enabling us to holistically understand the intricate, interconnected web of physical, biological, and human-made forces, thereby designing interventions that avoid unforeseen consequences and foster truly sustainable, regenerative solutions for the entire planetary system.]

The Mandate for Systems Thinking

It is important to recognize that designing within complex systems can be akin to playing an **infinite game**. We are unlikely to ever "fully" solve a complex problem, as these systems, much like a living organism, are dynamic and constantly evolving. Challenges like climate change, waste management, and the exploitation of migrant workers are never truly "solved"; they persist in various forms. Therefore, rather than striving for a final solution, our focus should **shift toward making the system healthier**, enabling it to generate positive and sustainable outcomes. This involves building resilience, fostering adaptability, and creating conditions that promote long-term well-being for both people and the planet. By applying systems thinking, we aim to create conditions that enable a system to generate positive change on its own, sustainably, rather than attempting to fix a single, isolated element, as outlined previously as ideal conditions in ecological thinking. Systemic design is never simply about improving or eliminating one "bad part" of a system. True systemic change requires a confluence of factors working together. The key lies in **identifying leverage points**, which are strategic interventions that have the potential to unlock broader positive change within the system. Leverage points are the short-term actions designed to serve the long-term infinite goal (see page 248). We must accept that designing within complex systems is an ongoing process, **a never-ending game**. As the system dynamically shifts, we must remain observant, sensing these changes and adapting our approach accordingly. Just as a city's transportation network requires constant monitoring and adjustments to traffic flow, public transit schedules, and infrastructure to adapt to changing commuter patterns and urban growth, so too must **our approach to systemic design be iterative, continuously sensing and adapting to the evolving landscape**.

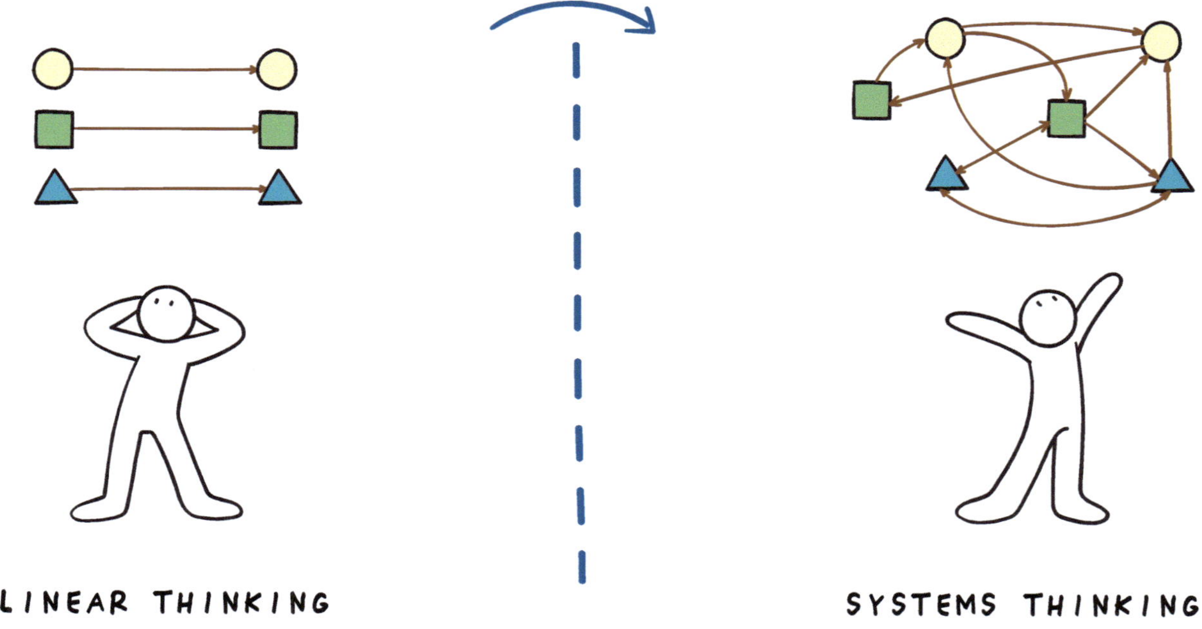

CATEGORY	LINEAR THINKING	SYSTEMS THINKING
Causality	There is a direct connection between problem symptoms and their underlying causes.	System performance is largely determined by interdependencies among system elements that are indirect, circular, and non-obvious. The goal is to analyze feedback loops (e.g., social contagion, resource depletion cycles).
Time	A policy that achieves short-term success ensures long-term success.	The unintended and delayed consequences of most quick fixes neutralize or reverse immediate gains over time, making long-term consequence modeling essential.
Responsibility	Most problems are caused by external factors beyond our control.	Because actions taken by one group have delayed negative consequences on its own performance, each group tends to unwittingly contribute to the very problems it tries to solve. Responsibility is framed as an integrated relationship with the planet (ecological ceiling).
Strategy	To improve the performance of the whole, we must improve the performance of its parts. Tackle many independent initiatives simultaneously to improve all the parts.	To improve the performance of the whole, improve relationships and governance structures among the parts. Identify a few key interdependencies that have the greatest leverage on system-wide performance (leverage points) and shift them in a sustained, coordinated way over time.
Goal/ Constraint	Solutions are optimized primarily for desirability (user) and viability (profit).	Solutions must be designed to operate within the dual constraint of the ecological ceiling and the social foundation to achieve true regenerative viability (net-positive impact).
Analytical Prerequisite	No explicit analytical toolset beyond basic business metrics.	Ecological thinking provides the necessary regenerative ideal (e.g., biomimicry), while systems thinking provides the analytical tools (CLDs, Leverage Points Analysis) to engineer the system toward that ideal.

The Infinite Game of Resilience

A profound and necessary second shift in perspective is required to effectively design within complex systems. This is the shift from a finite to an infinite mindset. **A finite game is played for the purpose of winning**, with known players, fixed rules, and a clear endpoint. An infinite game, however, is played for the purpose of continuing the play. The players, rules, and boundaries are dynamic, and there is no such thing as "winning." The traditional mindset of business, with its focus on quarterly earnings and beating the competition, is a finite game.

The challenges addressed by **Design Thinking for Humanity**, however, are inherently **infinite games**. One does not "win" at climate change, "solve" social equity, or "complete" the task of building a resilient society. These are ongoing, ever-evolving challenges that require a completely different approach. An infinite-minded practitioner does not seek to defeat a competitor or to find a final, permanent solution. Instead, the primary objective is to **strengthen the system**, to perpetuate the play, and to ensure that the game can continue for future generations.

This mindset is the essential foundation for **true resilience**. It frees teams from the pressure of finding a single, perfect answer and instead encourages the creation of adaptive, evolving solutions. It reframes "failure" not as a loss but as a crucial source of learning that makes the system stronger. For an infinite-minded leader, the goal is not to be the best in the system but **to be the best for the system**, fostering the conditions that allow all players to thrive.

As a result, embracing the infinite game is a profound act of long-term responsibility. It requires the application of tools like **Massive Transformative Purpose (see page 284)** to ensure it is worthy of endless striving, such as the creation of a truly regenerative society. This cause becomes the guiding principle, providing the stability and direction needed to navigate the constant flux of a complex world. By adopting this mindset, we can move **beyond short-term fixes** and begin the real work of building a future that is not just successful but enduring.

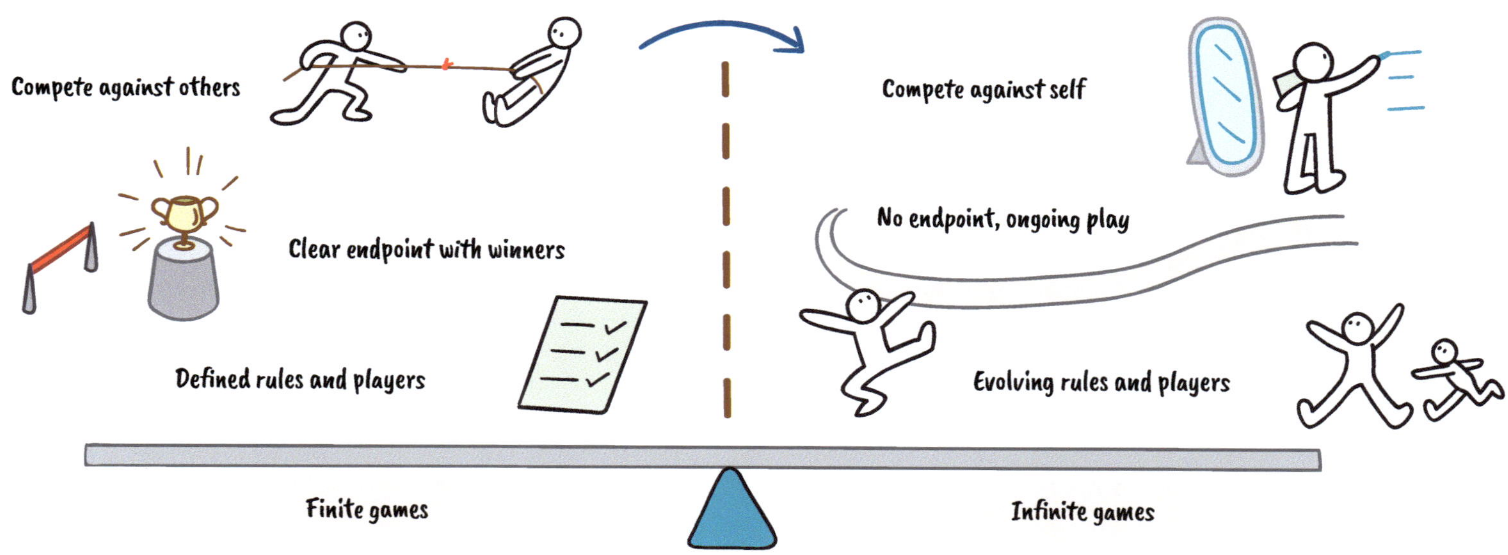

The Integrated Systems Thinking Flywheel

The systems thinking process moves beyond linear analysis to create fundamental, sustained systemic change. It is an iterative, four-phase flywheel that rigorously harmonizes problem analysis with collaborative ecosystem design to achieve **resilient and regenerative outcomes**. The goal is to shift the structure of a system to make positive, regenerative outcomes the new, self-sustaining default. This cyclical approach ensures that solutions are continuously learning and adapting, addressing complexity rather than avoiding it.

The flywheel touches four key areas over the cycle:

- **System Immersion & Analysis:** Map the system, boundaries, and feedback loops.
- **Defining Intervention & Vision:** Pinpoint high-leverage points and regenerative value flows.
- **Ecosystem Blueprint & Design:** Architect the multi-stakeholder network and governance model.
- **Transition & Adaptive Action:** Plan for real-world scaling and continuous system evolution.

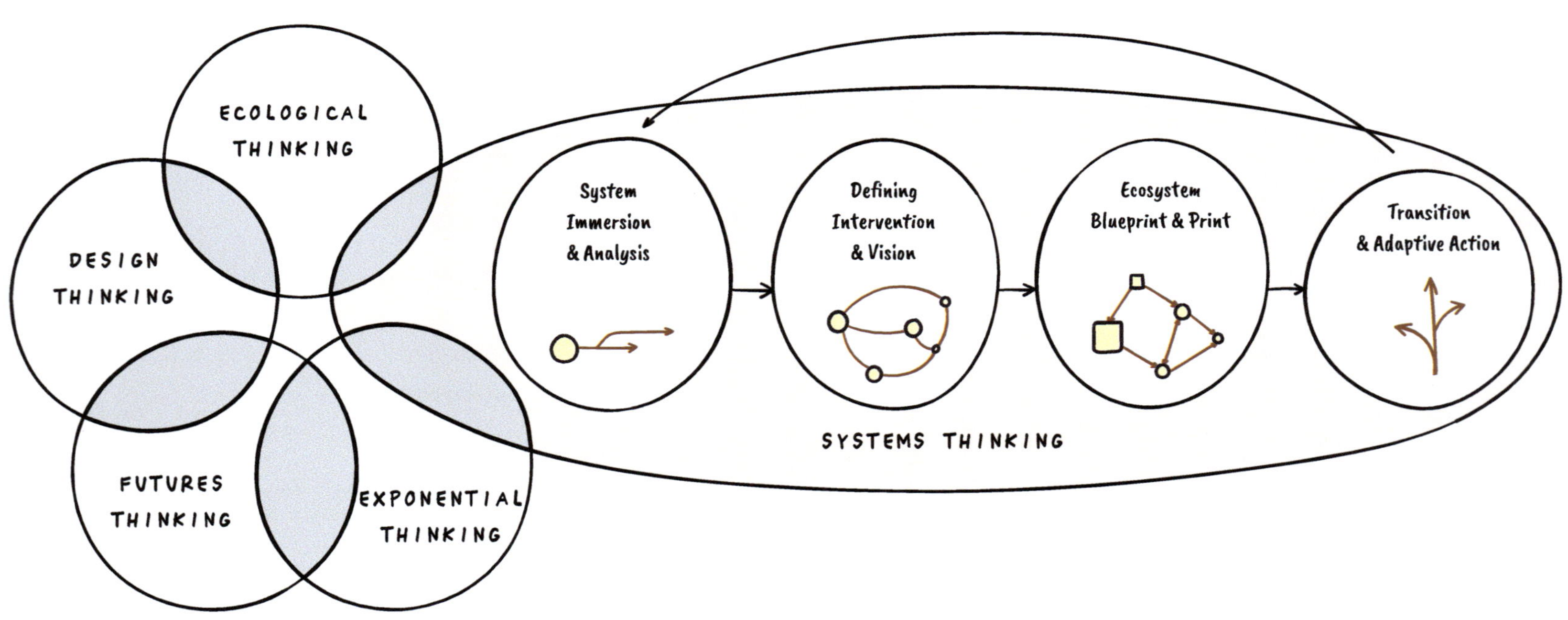

How to Apply Systems Thinking

To move from simply acknowledging complexity to actively designing within it, we must grasp a set of core principles. These are the foundational concepts of systems thinking. They provide the mental tools required to define the boundaries of a challenge, to understand the forces that govern a system's behavior, and to identify the most effective points of intervention. Mastering these principles is the first step toward moving beyond linear, cause-and-effect thinking to a more holistic and dynamic understanding of the world.

Core Principles of Systemic Design

The following principles transform simple analysis into strategic action by expanding the scope of empathy, causality, and resilience:

1. Defining Boundaries and Stakeholders

The first principle is the importance of defining system boundaries. To work on a problem, a team must define a boundary that is broad enough to include the critical interconnected components yet focused enough to be actionable. For Design Thinking for Humanity, this means intentionally drawing a wider boundary, one that explicitly includes marginalized communities, future generations, and the planet itself as key stakeholders.

2. Understanding Feedback Loops

Within these boundaries, a system's behavior is governed by feedback loops. These are the engines of a system, creating cycles of cause and effect that can be either reinforcing (amplifying change) or balancing (maintaining stability). Analyzing these loops is critical for understanding why a system behaves the way it does and how an intervention might amplify desired effects or dampen unintended ones.

3. Identifying Leverage Points

The goal of this deeper analysis is to identify leverage points. These are strategic places in a system where a small, well-focused intervention can produce a significant and lasting positive ripple effect. The most powerful leverage points are often not the most obvious ones; they are typically found in the system's rules, its information flows, or the mindset from which it arises.

4. Embracing Multivalue Perspectives

A truly systemic view also demands a consideration of diverse perspectives and value flows. The design of a resilient solution must consider the potential impacts on all actors across the entire system. This is why tools like Multi-stakeholder Value Network Mapping are so critical, as they force a multifaceted view of how not just financial but also social and ecological value is created and exchanged.

5. Designing for Emergence and Adaptation

We must understand and adapt to the emergent properties of a system. A complex system is always more than the sum of its parts; its behavior is dynamic and can change in unpredictable ways. A solution, therefore, cannot be based on a static, rigid plan. It must be designed for adaptation.

Activating the System

The principles provide the essence of designing for resilience in a constantly changing world. By mapping causal structures, identifying powerful leverage points, and designing adaptive, multi-stakeholder networks, we are equipped to move beyond addressing symptoms and put the principles of systemic resilience into immediate action against the world's most wicked problems.

The Language of Systems
Beyond the principles, systems thinking applies concepts like a foundational language to describe how complex entities operate, accumulate change, and sustain themselves over time.

Understanding this language of **stocks, flows, and feedback loops** is essential for transforming philosophical insight into effective design interventions that ensure resilience and planetary well-being.

1. Stocks: The Memory of the System
Every system, whether natural (like a forest) or human-made (like a city's economy), can be modeled using stocks and flows.

- A **stock** is the accumulated variable, representing the memory of the system that changes slowly over time.

- Stocks change slowly and represent the current state of a system, making them the crucial elements that drive momentum and long-term consequences.

Examples of Stocks: The Carbon in the Atmosphere, the Soil Organic Carbon (SOC) in a field, the Level of Trust in a Community, or a company's Inventory.

2. Flows: The Drivers of Change
- **Flows**, conversely, are the actions, decisions, or forces that increase (inflows) or decrease (outflows) a stock.

- Flows are the primary area where interventions are applied to shift the level of a stock.

Example (Soil Organic Carbon Stock): Regenerative Practices and Composting are **inflows** to the Soil Organic Carbon stock, while Erosion and Conventional Tilling act as **outflows**.

3. Feedback Loops: The Engine of Dynamics
The dynamic behavior of any system is entirely determined by its **feedback loops**.

- A feedback loop is a circular structure where a change in a stock feeds back through the system to influence the flows that created the change in the first place.
- These loops govern how a system responds to intervention, often determining why problems resist simple fixes.
- Systems thinking requires us to accurately identify these loops within our problem space, as they are the primary drivers of growth, collapse, and stability.

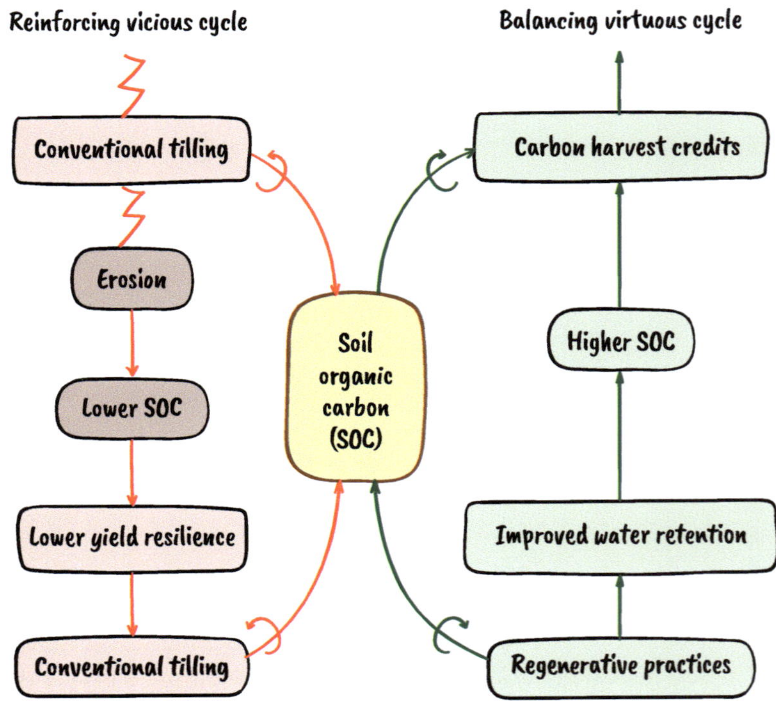

Fundamental Loop Types

The dynamic behavior of any system is determined by its feedback loops:

- **Reinforcing Loops (R):** A reinforcing loop accelerates change in the direction it is already headed. This is commonly known as a **vicious cycle** (creating exponential decline) or a virtuous cycle (creating exponential growth). If leveraged correctly, these loops can be harnessed to drive positive outcomes, such as accelerating the adoption of a new social norm once a social tipping point has been reached.

- **Balancing Loops (B):** A balancing loop seeks stability and drives the system toward a specific goal or state of equilibrium. These loops resist deviation and maintain a target condition. Designing a truly resilient system requires modeling new balancing loops that stabilize the system around the new, desirable, regenerative goal.

System Archetypes and Unintended Consequences

Beyond individual concepts, systems thinking offers **system archetypes** to recognize and categorize common, recurring problematic structures.

- **Value:** Recognizing an archetype allows practitioners to avoid reinventing the diagnostic wheel and immediately focus on the high-leverage intervention points already proven to work within that specific structure.

- **Example:** One classic archetype is the "**Tragedy of the Commons**," where individual rational actions collectively deplete a shared resource (see following example about water). Another is "**Shifting the Burden**," where a quick, symptomatic fix distracts from the deeper, systemic cause, worsening the problem over time (e.g., using chemical inputs for a soil problem).

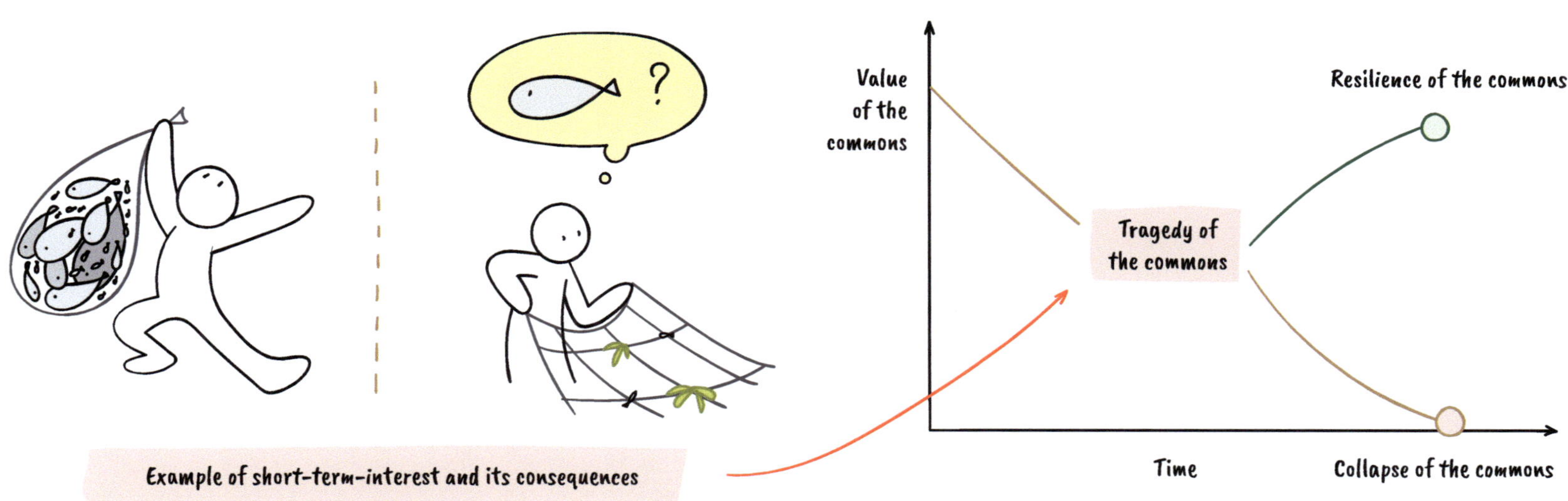

Example of short-term-interest and its consequences

Summary of the
SYSTEMS THINKING PRINCIPLES

1. Dual Mindset Shift:

3. Feedback Loops:

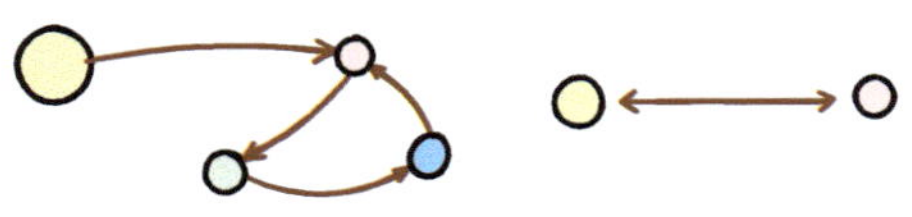

5. Causality:

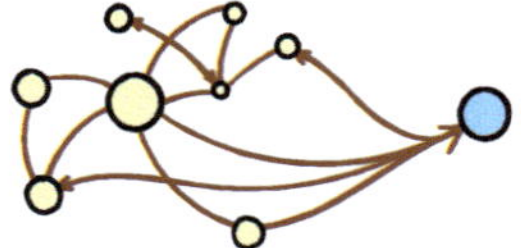

2. Understand the Whole:

4. Emergence:

6. Systems Mapping:

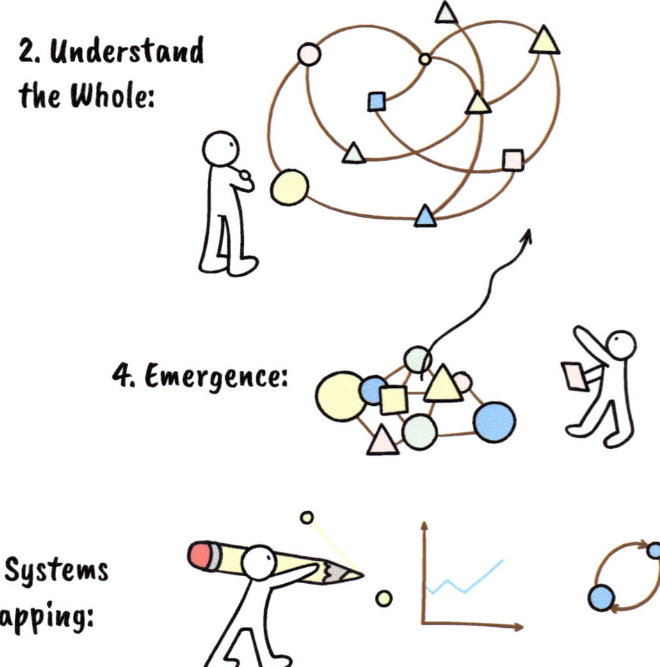

1. Dual Mindset Shift: Move from linear to circular thinking, recognizing everything is interconnected. And move from the finite game mindset to an infinite game mindset.

2. Understand the Whole: Focus on synthesis, not just analysis, seeing how parts create emergent behavior.

3. Feedback Loops: Identify Reinforcing (R) and Balancing (B) loops that drive system dynamics.

4. Emergence: Appreciate how complex, unpredictable behaviors arise from simple interactions within the system.

5. Causality: Understand that causality is circular and multidirectional, not just linear.

6. Systems Mapping: Utilize visual tools to map and understand system structures, enabling effective intervention.

Moving from the theoretical understanding of a system to designing effective change requires a transition into strategic action. This involves addressing three core challenges inherent in systemic design: selecting the right point of intervention, embedding governance for long-term resilience, and achieving the scale necessary for impact.

1. Selecting the Right Intervention

The most powerful leverage points in a system are often the least obvious. Systemic designers must resist the temptation to focus on low-leverage interventions, such as adjusting material flows or adding simple regulations, which typically provide only temporary relief. We must instead target high-leverage points that shift the fundamental behavior of the system. The highest leverage points reside in the most abstract elements of a system: its **rules, goals, and the mindset** from which it arises. True systemic change means designing a new governance structure (the rules) that is mandated to pursue regenerative goals (the goals) and is based on a deep-seated belief in mutual well-being (the mindset).

2. Embedding Governance for Resilience

In the context of the infinite game, resilience is not just about weathering external shocks. Resilience is about having the structural capacity to adapt and learn perpetually. This capacity is entirely dependent on the system's governance structure.

Governance defines the rules of collaboration, accountability, and resource sharing among partners in the new ecosystem. For regenerative solutions, governance must embed the triple-win mandate (financial, social, ecological) into its legal and operational fabric. This ensures that the system is structurally designed to prioritize the health of the entire ecosystem over the short-term profits of any single member. Effective governance is the mechanism that ensures the solution remains a perpetual force for regeneration.

3. Achieving Systemic Scale

A linear business model can be launched and scaled by a single entity; a systemic solution cannot. Achieving the scale necessary to shift an entire wicked problem (e.g., waste management, food insecurity) requires collaboration across an entire value network.

This challenge is addressed by designing a **minimum viable ecosystem (MVE)**. The MVE is the smallest viable network of partners, resources, and governance structures required to deliver the core regenerative value proposition. This approach shifts the design focus from a single product or service to the **architecture of a collaborative network**, ensuring that the solution has the necessary scale and influence to make a lasting, systemic impact.

Strategic Reminders for Systemic Design

- **Focus on High Leverage:** Target the system's rules, goals, and mindset, rather than just material flows, to create profound, nonlinear change.

- **Governance Is Resilience:** Embed the triple-win mandate into your governance structure. This ensures the system prioritizes the health of the entire ecosystem permanently.

- **Scale Requires Architecture:** Design an MVE. This is the smallest collaborative network required to achieve your regenerative goal.

Designing Business Ecosystems

The ultimate goal of systems thinking is to translate high-leverage interventions into real-world structures that can sustain regeneration perpetually. This requires moving beyond the traditional notion of a single company and designing an entire **regenerative business ecosystem.**

A regenerative business ecosystem differs fundamentally from a standard supply chain or competitive market. It is a network of independent organizations, users, regulators, and communities that collaborate to deliver collective value (the triple-win) while adhering to a shared, systemic mandate. The focus shifts from **value extraction**, where a single firm captures the maximum profit, to **value creation and sharing**, where the financial health of the core business is structurally dependent on the social and ecological health of the entire ecosystem.

Designing such an ecosystem is the practical application of the infinite game mindset. It ensures that the system is not only resilient to external shocks but is also capable of continuously learning, adapting, and regenerating its social and natural capital over time. This approach recognizes that in the face of wicked problems, no single entity can create the required level of systemic change alone. Success becomes a function of the network's integrity, not the individual firm's performance.

The Regenerative Ecosystem Design Flow

Designing the MVE involves a structured four-stage process that systematically integrates the triple-win mandate into the operational architecture. This flow serves as the strategic roadmap for applying the **Win-Win-Win Business Ecosystem Canvas** (page 232) and starts with the deeper purpose to reach. The tools outlined in the toolbox (pages 242–252) support the activities.

Stage 1: Ecosystem Scan

Analyze the current system, establishing boundaries, constraints, and opportunities.

Key Question: What are the system's current feedback loops, rules, and mindsets that govern behavior? What is the current exchange of financial, social, and ecological value?

Stage 2: Ecosystem Vision

Define the desired future state, establishing the non-negotiable regenerative mandate and collective purpose.

Key Question: What specific, measurable triple-win outcomes (financial, social, ecological) must the system achieve? What is the compelling, shared **massive transformative purpose (MTP) (see page 284)** that unites all partners?

Stage 3: Ecosystem Blueprint

Design the MVE and its operating model.

Key Question: What is the smallest, most impactful network of partners, resources, and shared activities required to achieve the triple-win mandate? How must value flow to incentivize every partner to participate and stay aligned?

Stage 4: Implementation and Scaling

Formalize governance, embed resilience, and test the system's ability to withstand shocks and adapt perpetually.

Key Question: What governance structures, agreements, and measurable KPIs (for all three wins) are necessary to ensure the ecosystem remains accountable? Can the MVE survive plausible future disruptions and adapt to remain an infinite game?

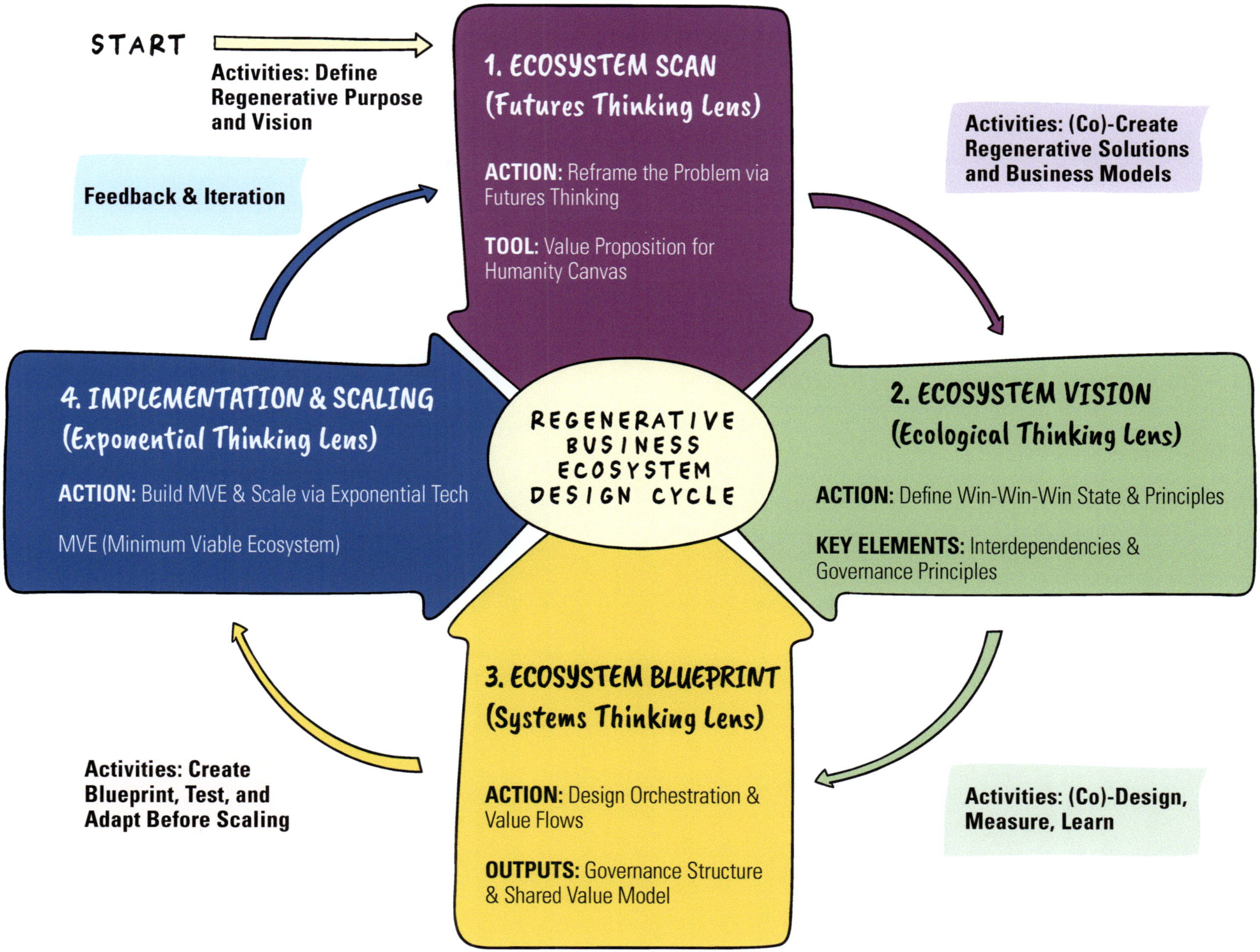

START
Activities: Define Regenerative Purpose and Vision
Feedback & Iteration
Activities: (Co)-Create Regenerative Solutions and Business Models
REGENERATIVE BUSINESS ECOSYSTEM DESIGN CYCLE
1. ECOSYSTEM SCAN (Futures Thinking Lens)
ACTION: Reframe the Problem via Futures Thinking
TOOL: Value Proposition for Humanity Canvas
2. ECOSYSTEM VISION (Ecological Thinking Lens)
ACTION: Define Win-Win-Win State & Principles
KEY ELEMENTS: Interdependencies & Governance Principles
3. ECOSYSTEM BLUEPRINT (Systems Thinking Lens)
ACTION: Design Orchestration & Value Flows
OUTPUTS: Governance Structure & Shared Value Model
4. IMPLEMENTATION & SCALING (Exponential Thinking Lens)
ACTION: Build MVE & Scale via Exponential Tech
MVE (Minimum Viable Ecosystem)
Activities: Create Blueprint, Test, and Adapt Before Scaling
Activities: (Co)-Design, Measure, Learn

Applying the Win-Win-Win Business Ecosystems Canvas

Following the definition of your **Ecosystem Vision** (stage 2) and the identification of leverage points, the next critical step is to develop the **Ecosystem Blueprint** (stage 3). The **Win-Win-Win Business Ecosystem Canvas** is the practical tool for this purpose.

This canvas serves as the architecture for the **Minimum Viable Ecosystem (MVE)**. It integrates the triple-win mandate directly into the core business model by forcing teams to define how financial viability is structurally dependent on delivering measurable social benefit and ecological restoration. It is the definitive visualization that replaces the linear model with a collaborative, net-positive network structure.

Building Blocks

The Win-Win-Win Business Ecosystem Canvas is structured to guide the design process from a shared vision to a fully governed operating model (see page 233). A stress test and how to apply the ecosystems canvas is outlined in the toolbox of this chapter (see page 253). The entire framework of ecosystems design in the context of humanity has evolved and adjusted from the Business Ecosystems Design paradigm outlined in the book *Design Thinking for Business Growth*.

A selection of possible ecosystems patterns are outlined on pages 234–235.

Core Principles in Regenerative Business Ecosystems Design

Life-Centered Stakeholder Integration!
Redefine the "Actors" block by intentionally mapping non-human systems (e.g., local ecosystems, water, soil) as primary, non-negotiable stakeholders with measurable restorative needs.

Integrated Value Synchronization!
Validate the multivalue flows by making financial value explicitly contingent upon the successful generation of ecological value and social value.

MVE as a Systemic Closed-Loop Test!
Design the MVE to test the governance, partners, and logistics required to successfully close resource loops and deliver net-positive impact at a defined scale.

Adaptive, Distributed Governance!
Establish a decentralized governance structure where transparent data sharing facilitates radical collaboration and adaptation based on real-time ecological and social performance metrics.

Responsible Scaling via Replication!
Define responsible scaling by planning the MVE for replication across diverse contexts, measuring success by the exponential growth of systemic impact (e.g., restored hectares, wealth distributed).

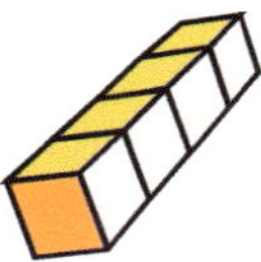

The "Win-Win-Win" Business Ecosystem Canvas

Purpose: Massive Transformative Purpose (MTP):

What is the single, audacious, and inspiring purpose that unites all partners in this ecosystem?
Why is this purpose so important that it will attract a passionate community and drive a movement?

Vision: Preferable Future:

If this ecosystem is profoundly successful, what does the world look like in 20 years?
What is the specific, tangible, "win-win-win" future we are building toward?

1

Actors

Who are the actors in the system? Who is the central steward? (Orchestrator?) Who is participating? Who are the primary non-human and human beneficiaries (users, communities) of the value created? Who are the external actors (e.g., policy-makers, investors, research institutions) whose support is critical for success?

2

Multivalue Flows

Financial Value:
How does money flow through the system in a way that is fair, transparent, and regenerative?
What are the new, circular, and regenerative revenue streams we are creating?

Social Value:
How is trust, knowledge, and community resilience intentionally created and exchanged between partners?
How does the ecosystem empower marginalized communities and increase social equity?

Ecological Value:
How does the ecosystem actively regenerate the living capitals it depends on?
What are the verifiable, net-positive ecological outcomes of our system (e.g., carbon sequestered, biodiversity increased)?

3

Governance & Adaption

What are the rules of the game? How are critical decisions made in a way that is both fair and effective? What are the key feedback loops that will allow the system to adapt and evolve in a changing world?

4

MVE

What is the "Minimum Viable Ecosystem"—the smallest possible configuration of partners that can start delivering the core value?
How will we test and validate our core assumptions with this MVE before scaling?

5

Responsible Scaling

What are the potential unintended negative consequences of our ecosystem at scale?
What are the non-negotiable ethical principles that will guide our growth and ensure we are a force for good?

DOWNLOAD TOOL
www.design-humanity.com/
en/ecosystems

Regenerative, Circular, and Sustainable Ecosystem Patterns

The ecosystems design aims to reconfigure the financial, material, and governance flows of the value chain to directly incentivize and monetize resource restoration and consumption reduction.

Regenerative Outcome Contracts:
Financial models where partnership agreements are tied to verifiable, net-positive ecological performance goals (e.g., a payment contingent on measured liters of water cleaned).

Material Passport and Smart Re-entry:
Digital tracking of all product components, automating disassembly and optimal re-entry into high-value circular loops across diverse partner industries.

Inverse Consumption Rewards:
A shared loyalty system that financially rewards customers and ecosystem partners specifically for reducing consumption, extending product life, or participating in repair and take-back services.

Bio-Intelligent Infrastructure Co-location:
Pattern where industrial facilities (e.g., manufacturing, energy generation) are intentionally co-located with biological systems (e.g., vertical farms, constructed wetlands) for resource symbiosis.

Place-Based Collective Ownership Trust:
A legal mechanism that holds critical ecosystem assets (such as land, shared infrastructure, or core intellectual property) in trust for a specific bioregion or community.

Decommissioning-as-a-Service (DaaS) Network:
A specialized network of partners whose core business is the efficient, regenerative deconstruction and safe processing of end-of-life products and industrial assets.

Sovereign Identity for Resource Users:
A digital identity system that grants users and communities explicit, auditable rights and controls over their share of local resources (e.g., water or energy allocation) within the ecosystem.

Anticipatory Policy Co-design Hubs!
Collaborative forums where ecosystem actors, regulators, and designers simulate future environmental scenarios to proactively design adaptive policy and governance frameworks.

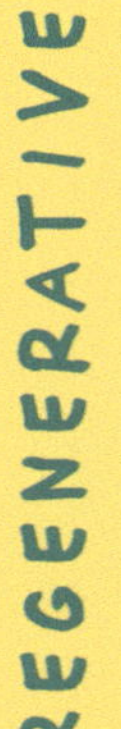

"""

Advanced Regenerative Ecosystem Design Patterns

These design patterns aim to utilize decentralized and exponential technologies to create systemic and auditable positive ecological and social change.

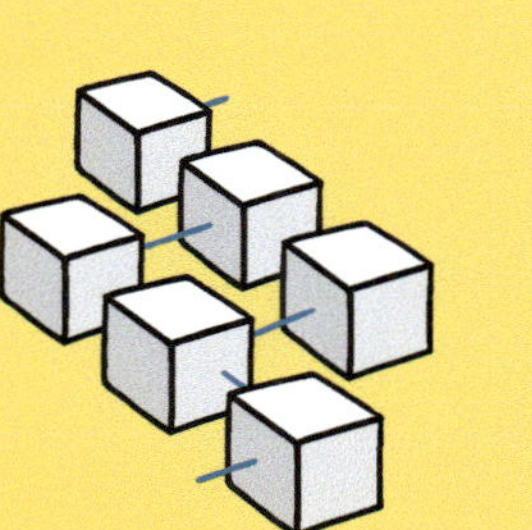

Distributed Autonomous Regeneration Organizations:
A decentralized, blockchain-governed network where local nodes (e.g., community farms, repair hubs) automatically coordinate regenerative actions and equitably distribute value.

Digital Twin for Ecological Integrity:
Use real-time data and AI to create a continuously updated digital model of the ecosystem (e.g., a watershed) that dictates partner activities to optimize systemic ecological health.

Mutualized Risk & Resilience Pool:
A shared, transparent financial mechanism across ecosystem partners to collectively ensure against climate shocks, incentivizing shared responsibility for systemic anti-fragility.

Open-Source Regeneration Protocol:
A public, modular framework (including APIs, data standards, and legal contracts) that allows any entity to plug in and measurably contribute to the ecosystem's regenerative mission.

Multispecies Design Integration:
A design constraint that includes non-human needs (e.g., pollinator pathways, soil microbial health) as essential inputs for product and service development, informed by biomimicry.

Hyper-Local Production & Consumption Pods:
The design of small, highly localized manufacturing and consumption loops (e.g., micro-factories) to drastically shorten supply chains and maximize local resource circulation.

Ethical Data Stewardships for Trust:
Governance protocols that ensure all ecosystem-generated data (performance, impact) is collectively owned, transparently shared, and used ethically to increase network intelligence and trust.

Time-Based Reciprocity Currencies:
Nonmonetary exchange systems used internally to incentivize high-effort, low-profit activities (like maintenance or education) essential for long-term ecosystem health.

How to Design the Transition

While the design of a regenerative business ecosystem provides a clear vision of the desired "end state," a critical question remains of the temporal journey:

How is the transition from the current, unsustainable system to this new, regenerative one navigated?

Transition design is a discipline focused on orchestrating long-term, systemic change. It provides the crucial "missing middle" between understanding a problem (via design thinking and systems thinking) and achieving a preferable future (via futures thinking), offering a framework for the practical and often political art of making a vision a reality.

Transition design acknowledges that wicked problems are deeply entrenched and cannot be solved with a single solution or product. Instead, it requires a **portfolio of interconnected interventions**, deployed over a multigenerational timeframe, that can guide a system's evolution. This involves fostering new cultural narratives, designing for policy change, and creating a series of "transition pathways" that can move an entire community, city, or industry toward a more sustainable and equitable state.

The greatest challenge in this process is confronting the inertia of the existing system. Entrenched economic incentives, established political power structures, and deeply ingrained cultural norms all work to maintain the status quo. A brilliant regenerative solution that is politically unviable or economically threatening to powerful incumbents will inevitably fail. Transition design, therefore, demands a pragmatic and astute understanding of these real-world barriers.

The Transition Strategy Canvas

A core practice of this discipline is the intentional design of new narratives. To shift a system, we must first shift the story it tells about itself. This involves crafting compelling, value-based narratives that can build a broad and diverse coalition for change. The goal is to create a shared vision that is so desirable and a story so resonant that it can overcome the natural resistance to fundamental change, aligning stakeholders who might otherwise have conflicting interests.

To make this complex work actionable, a new tool is required: The **Transition Strategy Canvas (see page 258, the final tool in the Systems Thinking Toolbox)** provides the practical framework for this task. It guides a team to move beyond the design of the solution itself and to begin architecting the strategy for its implementation. The canvas provides a structured space to map the political landscape, analyze economic incentives, design the persuasive narrative, and chart a tangible pathway for the solution to gain legitimacy.

Transition design is a profound act of long-term stewardship. It is a recognition that **the most brilliant regenerative vision is only as powerful as the strategy to make it real**. By embracing this discipline, we are equipped not just with the tools to design a better world but with a pragmatic and politically aware framework for actually building it in the face of profound and complex resistance.

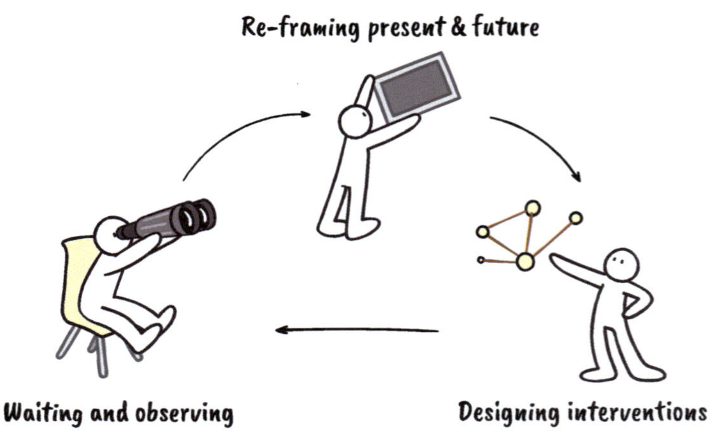

Part 4

A Speculative Case Study

Applying Systems Thinking

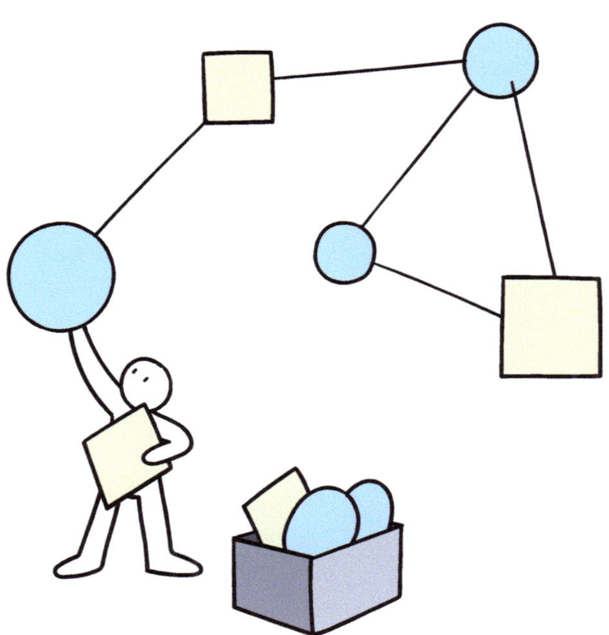

Having established the necessity for regenerative solutions in ecological thinking, we now delve into systems thinking, the critical lens that reveals the intricate web of interdependencies defining our complex world. This part moves beyond isolated interventions to understanding the dynamic whole, recognizing that no element exists in a vacuum. It is no longer sufficient to treat symptoms linearly; we must identify root causes and navigate the feedback loops that dictate how our designs will ripple through the broader socio-ecological fabric.

The overarching goal for our case study is both ambitious and essential.

The Living Soil Mandate

Our objective within this challenge is to design a new global economic and agricultural model that makes the regeneration of the world's topsoil the primary measure of agricultural success, ensuring long-term food security, reversing climate change, and restoring biodiversity by 2050.

The journey through ecological thinking has provided our Carbon Harvest platform with a strong regenerative foundation. By applying a Life Cycle Assessment to its physical components and using the Doughnut Economics model to frame its goals, we have ensured the solution is ecologically sound. Furthermore, by focusing on sustainable behavior design, we have considered how to make this new model attractive and accessible for farmers like Javier, even creating joyful, intergenerational hooks for adoption.

With this life-centered solution designed, we now apply the systems thinking lens to answer a critical question: how do we design the entire ecosystem of partners, policies, and value flows required for this solution to thrive? It is not enough to have a good idea; we must design the interconnected system that can bring it to life and sustain it over time. The ultimate goal is to achieve the Living Soil Mandate by 2050, and to do this, key tools from our Systems Thinking Toolbox will now be applied.

1. Causal Loop Diagramming (CLD): Mapping the Engine of Change

First, Causal Loop Diagramming is used to map the core feedback loops that will make the Carbon Harvest platform successful.

Reinforcing Loop (R1): The more regenerative practices a farmer adopts, the healthier the soil becomes. The healthier the soil, the more "regeneration credits" the platform can verify and issue. The more credits issued, the more revenue the farmer earns. The more revenue earned, the more the farmer can invest in regenerative practices. This is the core engine of growth.

Balancing Loop (B1): If a farmer's practices are not genuinely improving soil health, the AI and sensor data will detect this. Consequently, the platform will not issue new credits. This creates a balancing pressure, ensuring that only authentic, verifiable regeneration is rewarded and preventing the system from being "gamed."

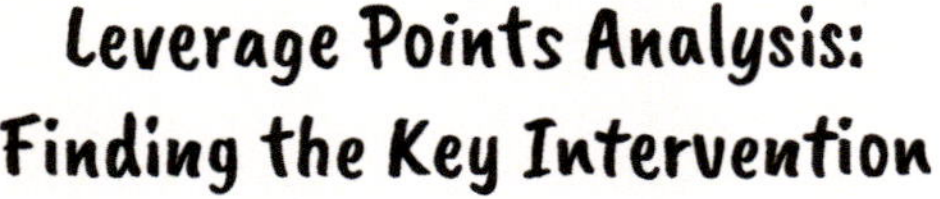

Leverage Points Analysis: Finding the Key Intervention

The CLD reveals that the most powerful leverage point is not the technology itself but the trust in the data of the platform produces.

The Leverage Point: To make the entire system work, the "regeneration credits" must be seen as a legitimate and incorruptible asset by the market (corporations, governments, individuals).

The Intervention: The key intervention is to create a radically transparent and decentralized governance model for the platform, using technologies like blockchain to make all data and financial transactions public and auditable. This builds the trust needed for the core reinforcing loop to function.

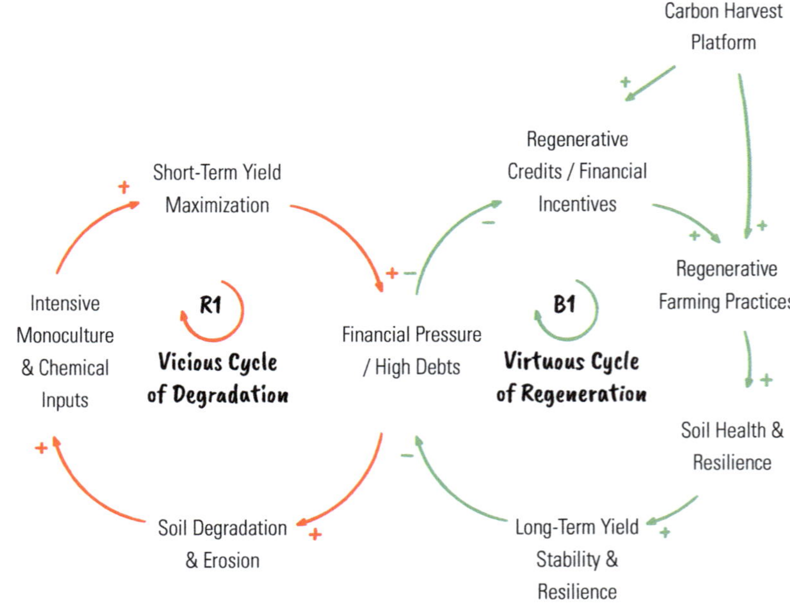

2. "Win-Win-Win" Business Ecosystem Canvas: Designing the Network

We now use the canvas to design the collaborative network required for the Carbon Harvest platform to succeed.

Who is initiating and orchestrating the platform?

The platform would be initiated by a founding multi-stakeholder consortium acting as "system stewards." This would include a neutral nonprofit foundation, a leading technology partner, and a global agricultural association. Their primary role as orchestrator is not to command and control but to facilitate a decentralized and transparent governance model, with the long-term vision of transitioning the platform's ownership to its participants.

Key Actors:

Orchestrator: The Carbon Harvest platform, the central entity that facilitates and governs the ecosystem, providing the digital infrastructure for verification, transaction, and communication.

Value Creators: Farmers (like Javier), soil scientists, agronomists, and the AI/data companies providing the monitoring technology.

Beneficiaries: The global community (through a more stable climate), future generations (through healthier soil), and the farmers themselves (through a new revenue stream).

Enablers: Governments (that officially recognize "regeneration credits" in their climate policies), corporations (that purchase the credits to meet their sustainability goals), and financial institutions (that may offer lower-interest loans to farmers with high "regeneration scores").

Examples of Multivalue Flows:

- Corporations provide financial value to farmers in exchange for ecological value (verified carbon sequestration and biodiversity).

- The platform provides knowledge value (data-driven insights) back to the farmers to help them improve their practices.

- The farmers provide social value (greater food security and community resilience) to society as a whole.

> This ecosystem design connects all the dots. It creates a self-sustaining, multi-stakeholder system where the AI models, the data infrastructure, and the human collaboration are perfectly aligned to scale the solution, helping us to achieve The Living Soil Mandate by 2050.

Note the **System Map (see page 240)** can be detailed with more concrete value streams, **related to the financial, ecological, social, knowledge, and data flows shown here**.

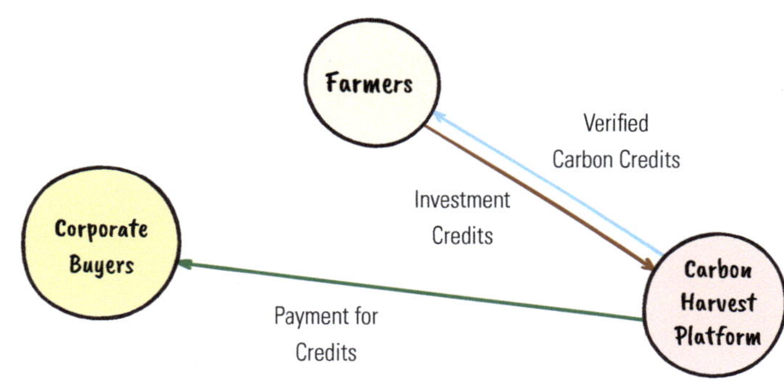

High-Level Systems Map of the Carbon Harvest Platform

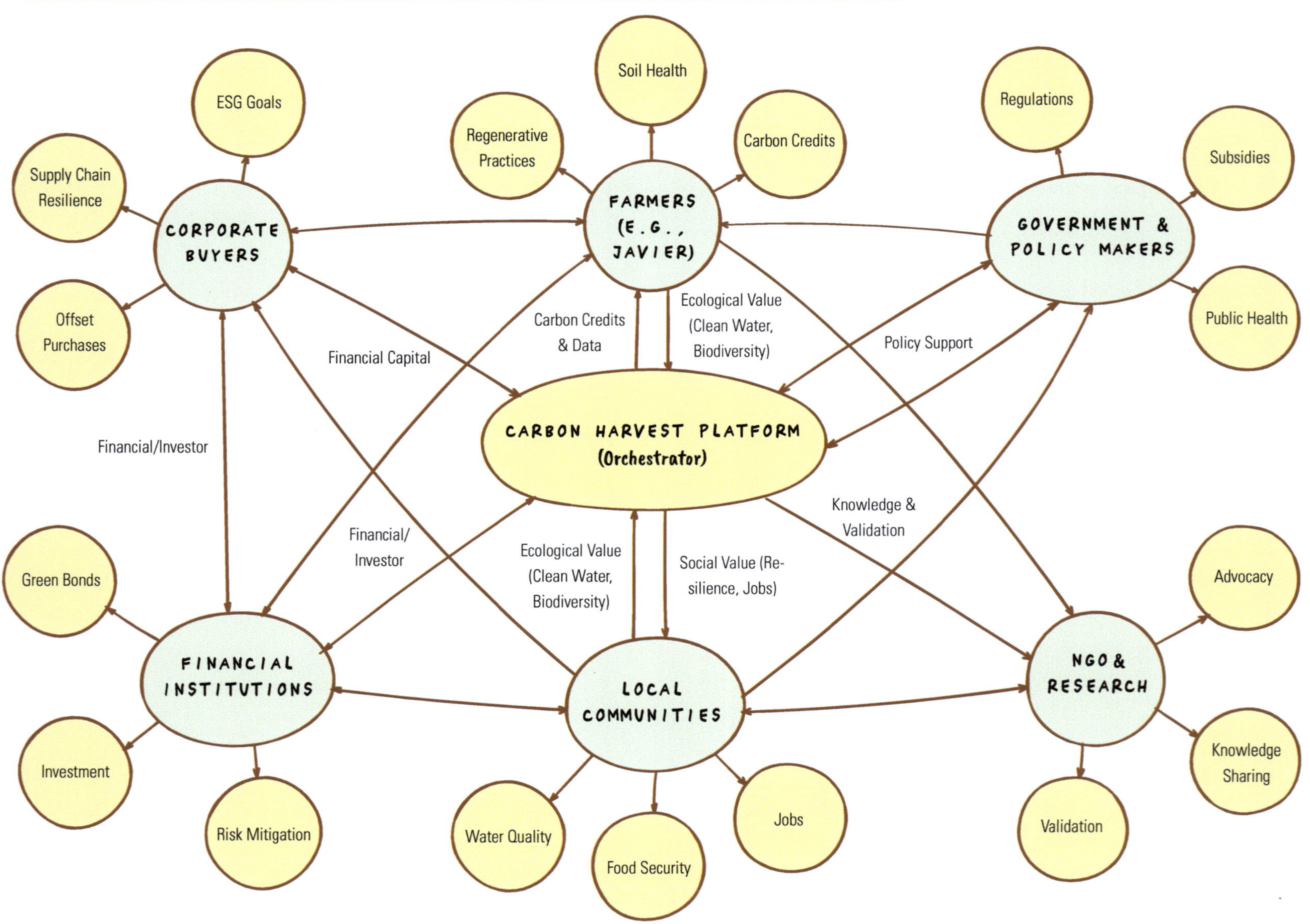

3. Transition Strategy Canvas: Architecting the Shift

With the speculative case study, we have designed the ideal "Carbon Harvest" ecosystem. Now we face the **final and most difficult challenge**. This is the reality gap. The current agricultural system operates on a rigid cycle of chemical dependency and debt. This is often called the "yield maximization complex." Farmers like Javier cannot simply switch to regenerative practices. They face a three-year transition period where yields often drop before soil health recovers. This creates a financial "valley of death" that current bank loans do not support. To navigate this resistance, we apply the Transition Strategy Canvas. We view the transition as a strategic two-step process. It is **orchestrated by the platform stewards**, a coalition of a global ag-co and the Carbon Harvest foundation.

Addressing Power, Politics, & Economics

Step 1: Disarming Resistance via the "Safe Harbor" Contract

The first strategic move neutralizes the economic fear blocking change. The incumbent system holds power because farmers bear all the risk. The chemical fertilizer lobbies and traditional lenders reinforce this structure. To break this cycle, the Orchestrator uses its market power to introduce a **"Safe Harbor" transition contract**:

The Pivot: The Orchestrator stops selling bulk fertilizer. Instead, they pivot to selling "yield insurance." Farmers subscribe to a "regenerative prescription," which includes bio-inputs and data services.

The Guarantee: The Orchestrator guarantees a floor price for the transition crops in exchange for adopting new practices. This effectively subsidizes the risk of the "valley of death."

The Political Win: This move aligns the Orchestrator with downstream food giants like Nestlé or PepsiCo. These companies need Scope 3 emission reductions. This creates a powerful "demand alliance" to counter the resistance of the old chemical lobby.

Addressing Narrative & Pathways

Step 2: Building Legitimacy via the "OneGreen" Standard

The second step institutionalizes the change. We shift the narrative from volume to value. We must move the industry standard from "bushels per acre" to "profit & resilience per acre."

The Narrative Shift: We reframe the story for policymakers. We are not asking for subsidies. We are providing the data to secure national food resilience. The platform creates a new metric called the **"regenerative score"** to measure soil health and carbon sequestration.

The Tipping Point: The strategy focuses on a single high-leverage policy win. We aim to get government crop insurance programs to recognize this "regenerative score." Once a farmer with a high score qualifies for lower insurance premiums, the Carbon Harvest model becomes the financially prudent industry standard.

The Result: We explicitly design this transition to build an economic bridge for the farmer. We then establish a new political standard for the industry. This ensures the Carbon Harvest ecosystem becomes a viable and inevitable reality rather than just a design concept.

Systems Thinking Tools

To move from acknowledging complexity to actively designing within it, a dedicated set of tools is required. The methods in the following section are designed to empower practitioners with the core capabilities of systems thinking. They provide the frameworks needed to see the world not as a collection of isolated parts but as a web of interconnected relationships. These tools are specifically curated to facilitate the analysis of complex interdependencies, the identification of high-leverage intervention points, and the design of entire business ecosystems that are resilient and regenerative by design.

This toolbox provides the essential methods for taking a "long view" and understanding the underlying structures that drive the behavior of wicked problems. The tools that follow will guide us through the process of defining system boundaries, mapping causal feedback loops, and identifying the most potent leverage points for creating lasting, systemic change. By mastering these methods, innovators and leaders can move beyond addressing symptoms to creating the conditions for a healthier, more resilient system to emerge.

This collection of tools provides the practical methods needed to apply the most important frameworks for systemic change. It covers the core aspects of systemic design by providing tools to map and understand complexity. All frameworks are essential to guide us toward the creation of the regenerative and resilient networks that are essential for bringing the vision of Design Thinking for Humanity to life.

Systems Thinking Toolbox

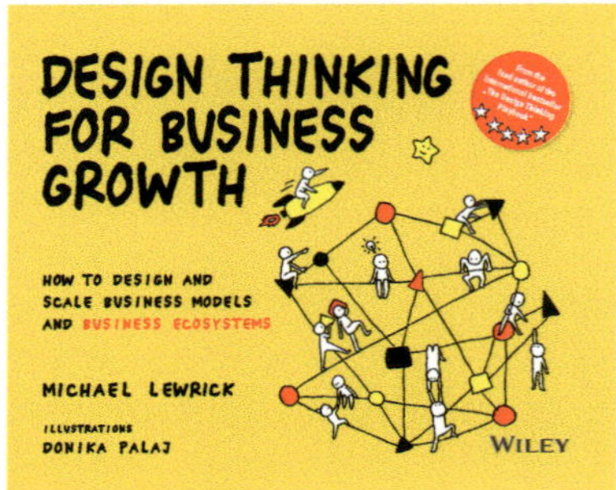

Tip: Find more powerful tools for business ecosystems design in *Design Thinking for Business Growth*.

Tool	Page Number
System Boundaries & Stakeholder Mapping	244
Causal Loop Diagramming (CLD)	246
Leverage Points Analysis	248
Multi-stakeholder Value Network Mapping	250
The "Win-Win-Win" Business Ecosystem Canvas	252
Collective Impact Canvas	254
Adaptive Strategy & the Infinite Game Mindset	256
Transition Strategy Canvas	258

1. System Boundaries & Stakeholder Mapping

This tool provides a framework for defining the scope of a wicked problem and identifying all the relevant interconnected components and actors. It is an essential first step to ensure a holistic approach, creating a foundational map of the problem space that includes often-overlooked non-human and future stakeholders.

2. Causal Loop Diagramming (CLD)

This is the classic tool for visualizing the underlying feedback loops that drive a system's behavior over time. By mapping the reinforcing (amplifying) and balancing (stabilizing) loops, it helps to uncover the root causes of a problem and anticipate potential unintended consequences of an intervention.

3. Leverage Points Analysis

This tool provides a powerful framework for identifying the most effective places to intervene in a system. It guides teams to move beyond obvious, low-impact fixes and focus on the deeper, more transformative changes such as shifting a system's rules, information flows, or goals. These transformative changes are what can create significant and lasting change.

4. Multi-stakeholder Value Network Mapping

This tool evolves the traditional value chain map to visualize the exchange of not just financial value, but also social and ecological value between all stakeholders in an ecosystem. It is used to analyze the overall health of the network and to identify opportunities for creating new "win-win-win" value streams.

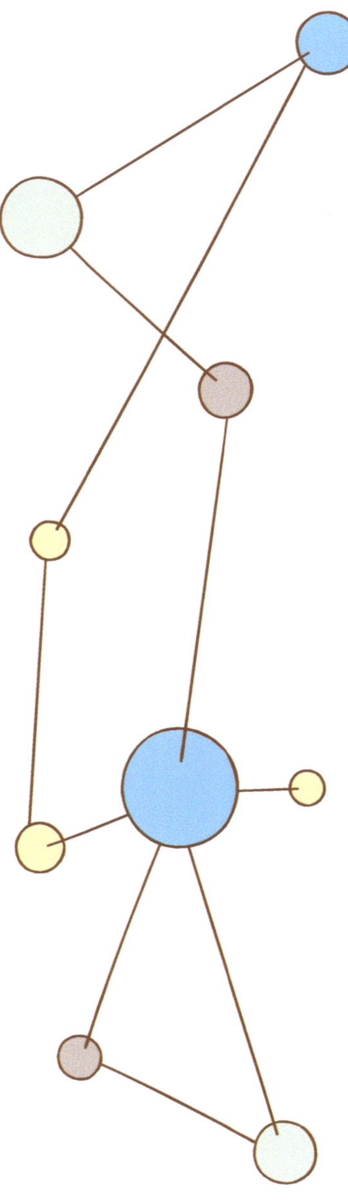

5. The "Win-Win-Win" Business Ecosystem Canvas

This is the core synthesis tool for this chapter, providing a comprehensive canvas for designing a multi-stakeholder ecosystem that is regenerative and resilient. It adapts the business ecosystem design model to the "for Humanity" context, orchestrating a collaborative network to solve a wicked problem.

6. Collective Impact Canvas

This tool provides a structured framework to operationalize a multi-stakeholder collaboration. It is used to align diverse partners around a common agenda, establish shared metrics, map mutually reinforcing activities, and define the communication and governance plan. This creates a clear, actionable plan for managing the complex human dynamics of a systemic initiative.

7. Adaptive Strategy & the Infinite Game Mindset

This tool provides a framework for designing strategies that can adapt and evolve within a dynamic system. It shifts the goal from "winning" or "solving" a problem to building a system that is resilient and capable of continuous, adaptive learning, preparing it for the "infinite game" of systemic change.

8. Transition Strategy Canvas

This tool is used to design a politically and economically viable strategy for transitioning from a current, unsustainable system to a desired regenerative model. It moves beyond designing the ideal solution to architecting the real-world implementation plan, focusing on mapping power dynamics, overcoming entrenched incentives, and building a persuasive narrative to create a broad coalition for change.

System Boundaries & Stakeholder Mapping

I would like to...

...define the scope of a wicked problem and identify all the relevant inter-connected components and actors within it.

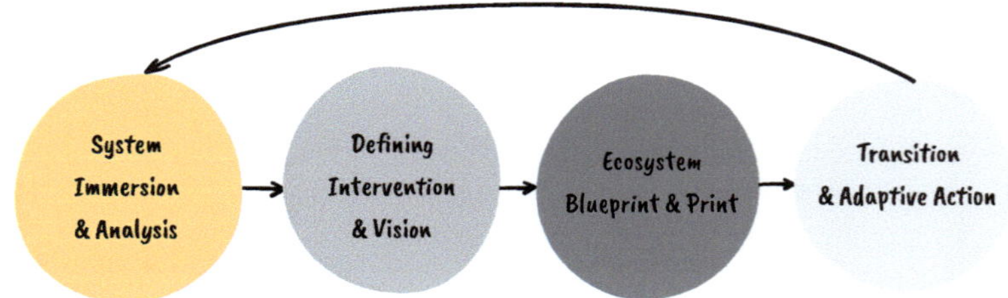

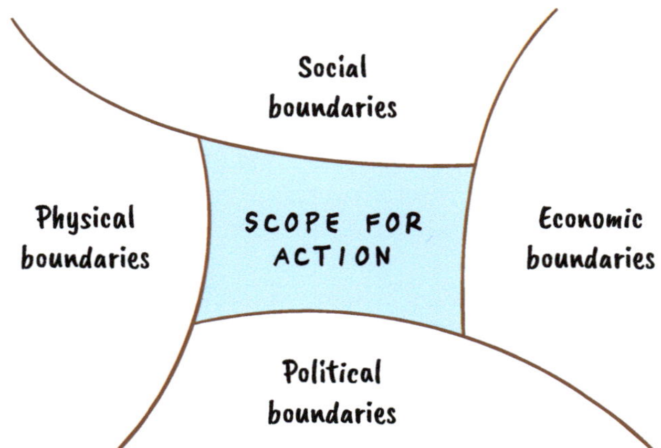

What you can do with the tool:

- Create a clear and shared understanding of the boundaries of the system being addressed.
- Identify all relevant stakeholders, including often-overlooked non-human or future stakeholders.
- Visualize the high-level relationships and interdependencies between the core components of a system.
- Provide a foundational "map" of the problem space, which is essential for all subsequent systems thinking activities.
- Avoid the common trap of defining a problem too narrowly, ensuring a more holistic and systemic approach from the start.

Expert Tips

Make the Boundary a Conscious Choice

There is no single "correct" boundary for a system. The boundary is a mental model that the team creates to make the problem workable. The key is to make this a conscious and deliberate choice. Have the team explicitly debate and agree upon the boundary, and be prepared to revisit and expand it as a deeper understanding of the problem emerges.

Identify the "Voice of the System"

For every non-human stakeholder you map, assign a "steward" from the team whose job it is to represent the "voice" of that part of the system. For example, one person could be the designated advocate for "future generations." This practice ensures these crucial but often-overlooked perspectives are consistently included in the conversation.

Map What's Missing

A powerful way to understand a system is to identify what is missing or broken. As the system is mapped, use a different color to note the missing connections, the broken feedback loops, or the marginalized stakeholders who are currently excluded. This often reveals the most potent areas for a design intervention.

Define Scope—Wicked Problem Framing

What is the history of the problem?

What are the cultural narratives?

What is in?

What is out?

PESTLE—Boundaries

List constraints…

Social & Cultural Boundaries

System Map Elements

Technological & Environmental Boundaries

Economic Boundaries

Key human stakeholders

Farmers, consumers, workers

Non-human stakeholders

Soil health, watersheds, biodiversity

Futures & abstract stakeholders

Future generations, community trust

Institutional actors

Government, NGOs, Corporations

Political & Legal Boundaries

Boundary check

- Is it broad enough to capture root cause?
- Is it narrow enough to be actionable?

System Map

Visualize who and what is in the system

This tool is the essential first step in any systemic analysis. It provides a framework for defining the scope of the challenge and mapping the key actors and elements that make up the system.

Step 1: Define the Wicked Problem and Initial Scope

Start with the **Wicked Problem Framing (see page 152)** to articulate the core challenge. Based on this, hold a collaborative session to define the initial boundaries of the system. Ask the team: "What is in our system, and what is outside of it for the purpose of this challenge?" This is a crucial framing decision that will guide the entire process.

Step 2: Brainstorm All Stakeholders and Components

Within the defined boundary, brainstorm all the actors, components, and forces that are part of the system. Use the **PESTLE framework (see page 84)** as a prompt to ensure a comprehensive scan. Crucially, in the context of Design Thinking for Humanity, this must include non-human stakeholders (e.g., "the local watershed," "soil health") and abstract stakeholders (e.g., "future generations," "community trust").

Step 3: Create the System Map

Visually arrange the stakeholders and components on a large canvas. Use simple connectors to show the primary relationships and interdependencies between them. This initial map is not meant to be a detailed causal loop diagram but a high-level visual inventory of "who and what is in our system." It serves as the foundational artifact for deeper analysis.

Causal Loop Diagramming (CLD)

I would like to...

...visualize the underlying feedback loops that drive a system's behavior over time.

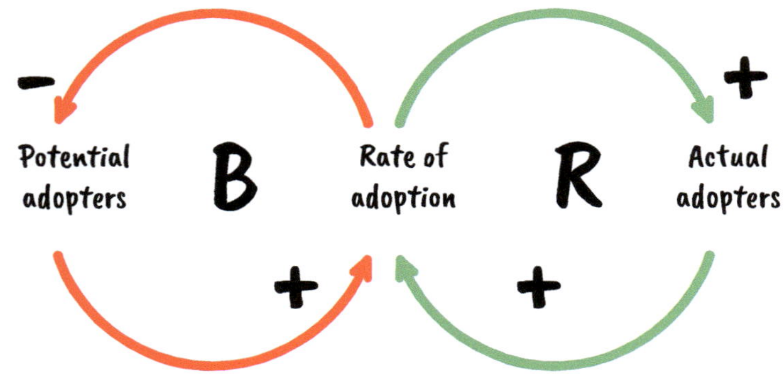

What you can do with the tool:

- Move beyond a simple list of parts to map the dynamic, cause-and-effect relationships within a system.
- Identify the reinforcing loops that create exponential growth or collapse, and the balancing loops that create stability.
- Uncover the root causes of a problem by understanding the underlying structures that perpetuate it.
- Anticipate potential unintended consequences by visualizing how an intervention might ripple through the system.
- Create a shared, dynamic model of a complex problem that the entire team can analyze and discuss.

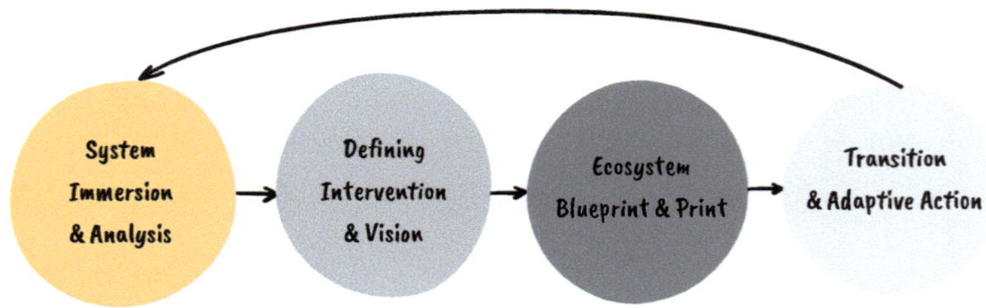

Expert Tips

Tell the Story of the Loop

A CLD is not just a technical diagram; it is a story. For each loop you identify, practice telling the story of how it works. For example: "The more the community gardens thrive (R), the more neighborhood pride increases, which leads to more volunteers, which helps the gardens thrive even more." This narrative approach makes the complex dynamics of the system much easier to understand and communicate.

Incorporate Delays

The most insightful CLDs often include delays. A cause does not always create an immediate effect. Use a symbol (like two hash marks // on a link) to represent a significant delay between a cause and its effect. Identifying these delays is often key to understanding why a system's behavior is so difficult to predict.

Find the "Fixes That Fail" Archetype

A common pattern in systems is the "Fixes That Fail" archetype. This occurs when a short-term solution to a problem creates a long-term, often worse, unintended consequence. Use your CLD to look for this pattern. Mapping out how a quick fix might create a negative reinforcing loop in the long run is a powerful way to avoid creating new problems.

VARIABLE INVENTORY

Brainstorm variables
1. Name of value
2._______________
3._______________

THE SYSTEM MAP

MAPPING KEY

+	Same direction (S)
-	Opposite (O)
R	Reinforcing loop
B	Balancing loop
||	Delay

LOOP NARRATIVES

REINFORCING (R)
Name the loop
(e.g., Viral growth)
Tell the story: as X goes up,
Y goes up...

LOOP TYPE?

BALANCING (B)
Name the loop
(e.g., Market Saturation)
Tell the story: as X grows, it
hits a limit...

LOOP TYPE?

Analysis Tip: Identify the engine (reinforcing) versus the brakes (balancing). Which loop is dominant right now?

Causal Loop Diagramming (CLD) is the classic tool for visualizing the feedback structures of a complex system. It is a map that shows how different variables influence one another, creating cycles of reinforcement or stability.

Step 1: Identify Key Variables
Start by brainstorming the key variables or factors that are part of your system. These should be things that can increase or decrease over time, such as "Urban Population," "Level of Pollution," "Community Trust," or "Number of Community Gardens."

Step 2: Map the Causal Links
Draw arrows between the variables to show the causal relationships. For each link, label it with either a "+" (same direction) or a "-" (opposite direction).
- A "+" link means that if the first variable increases, the second variable increases (e.g., more **Births** + leads to a higher **Population**).
- A "-" link means that if the first variable increases, the second variable decreases (e.g., a higher **Death Rate** - leads to a lower **Population**).

Step 3: Identify the Feedback Loops
Analyze the completed diagram to identify the closed loops of cause and effect. Determine whether each loop is:

Reinforcing (R): A loop that amplifies change. It has an even number of "-" links (or zero). These loops create exponential growth or collapse.

Balancing (B): A loop that seeks stability or a goal. It has an odd number of "-" links. These loops resist change and push a system toward equilibrium.

DOWNLOAD TOOL
www.design-humanity.com/
en/cld

Leverage Points Analysis

I would like to...

...identify the most effective places within a complex system to intervene to create significant and lasting change.

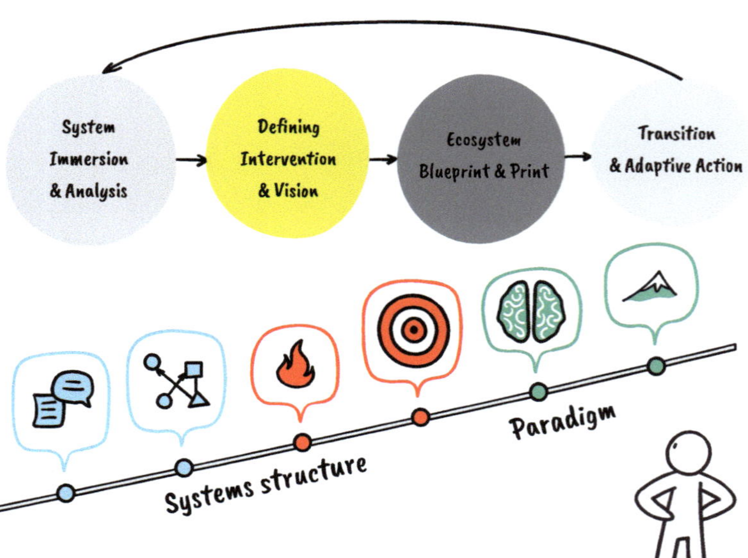

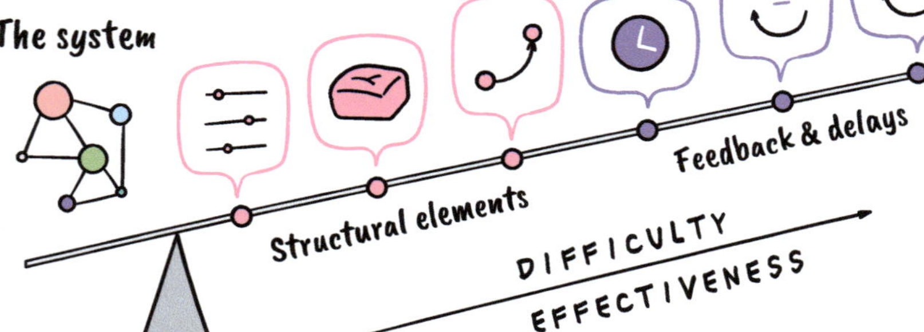

What you can do with the tool:

- Move beyond obvious, low-impact "fixes" to focus on interventions with the potential for transformation.
- Identify the often hidden or counter-intuitive places where a small, well-focused action can create a large ripple effect.
- Provide a structured framework for prioritizing potential interventions based on their systemic power.
- Foster a more strategic and long-term perspective, focusing on changing the underlying structure of a system, not just its surface-level events.
- Avoid wasting resources on actions that are unlikely to create meaningful, lasting change.

Expert tips

Close the Feedback Loop
Many systems fail because key actors are insulated from the consequences of their actions. A powerful leverage point involves "closing the loop" by delivering impact data directly back to the source. Making invisible metrics like soil health or labor conditions visible to consumers and investors can drive behavioral change often more effectively than regulation.

Change the Goal, Not Just the Parameters
It is tempting to focus on low-leverage parameters like subsidies or quotas, but systems often resist these tweaks. True transformation requires shifting the system's goal. If a system aims to "maximize yield," it will resist sustainability. By rewriting the goal to "maximize soil health," the entire system, including incentives, behaviors, and flows, will naturally self-organize around this new North Star.

Causal Loop Diagram (see page 246)

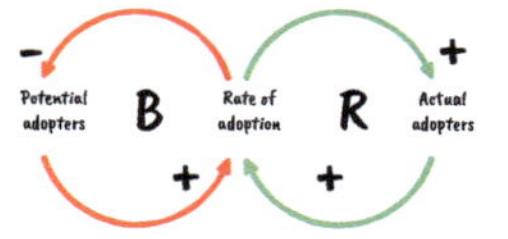

Identify Intervention Points
Brainstorm a wide range of potential fixes. Don't judge them yet.

Prioritization of Interventions

Shallow levels Parameters, numbers, stocks	Deep levels Delays, feedback loops	Transformational levels Design, rules, goals, mindset
		4. Information flows 3. Rules of the system 2. Goal of the system 1. Paradigm/mindset
10. Constants/standards 9. Buffer sizes 8. Stock structures	7. Delays 6. Balancing loops (strength) 5. Reinforcing loops (gain)	
Intervention idea: e.g., Increase fertilizer subsidy...	Intervention idea: e.g., Shorten data collection time...	Intervention idea: e.g., Make soil health data public...
Intervention idea: e.g., Change tax rate...	Intervention idea: e.g., Close the loop on pollution...	Intervention idea: e.g., Change goal to "Regeneration"...

Leverage Points Analysis is a method for identifying the most effective places to intervene in a system. Based on the work of systems thinker Donella Meadows, it provides a hierarchy of intervention points, from the least to the most powerful.

Step 1: Map the System's Structure

The first step is to have a clear, shared understanding of the system's structure. This requires a well-developed causal loop diagram that shows the key variables, relationships, and feedback loops that are driving the system's behavior. This map is the foundation for the analysis.

Step 2: Identify Potential Intervention Points

Using the CLD, the team brainstorms a wide range of potential interventions. The goal is to look beyond just the obvious physical elements (the "stocks" and "flows"). The analysis should include interventions that target the less visible, but more powerful, aspects of the system, such as its rules, information flows, and goals.

Step 3: Prioritize Interventions Using the Leverage Hierarchy

Evaluate the brainstormed interventions against the hierarchy of leverage points. According to Meadows, interventions that target the deeper structures of a system are far more powerful than those that target its surface elements. The hierarchy includes (from least to most powerful):

- **Numbers** (e.g., subsidies, taxes)
- **Buffers & Stocks** (e.g., inventory sizes)
- **Material Flows & Delays** (e.g., supply chain speed)
- **Balancing & Reinforcing Loops** (e.g., slowing a reinforcing loop)
- **Information Flows** (e.g., creating new feedback)
- **The Rules of the System** (e.g., policies, regulations)
- **The Goals of the System** (e.g., changing the definition of success)
- **The Mindset or Paradigm** (e.g., shifting the underlying worldview)

Multi-stakeholder Value Network Mapping

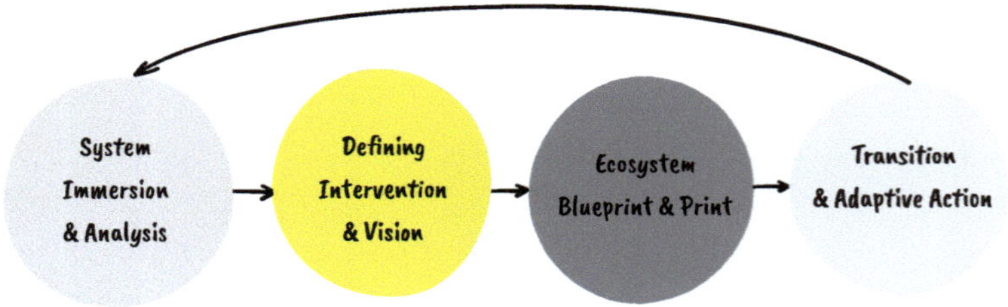

I would like to...

...visualize how not just money but also social and ecological value flows between all stakeholders in an ecosystem.

What you can do with the tool:

- Move beyond a linear value chain to map the complex, multi-directional exchange of value in a system.
- Make the often-invisible flows of social and ecological value tangible and explicit.
- Identify opportunities to create new forms of "win-win-win" value for multiple stakeholders.
- Analyze the overall health and resilience of an ecosystem by understanding how value is created, distributed, and exchanged.
- Provide a clear and compelling visual for communicating a more holistic, systemic business model.

Expert Tips

Define What "Value" Means
Before starting the mapping, facilitate a conversation with the team to define what each type of value means in the context of the specific project. For example, what does "social value" look like for this community? This ensures that the team is working with a shared and explicit understanding of these often-abstract concepts.

Look for Asymmetrical Relationships
The most powerful insights often come from identifying asymmetrical relationships where one stakeholder provides significant value but receives little in return. These imbalances are often sources of systemic instability and represent potent leverage points for designing more equitable and resilient interventions.

Design for "Value Circulation"
A healthy ecosystem is one where value circulates. The goal is to design a system where the output of one stakeholder becomes a valuable input for another, creating positive feedback loops of mutual benefit. Use this map to intentionally design these circular value flows, moving beyond simple, linear transactions.

A Multi-stakeholder Value Network Map is a visual tool that goes beyond a traditional value chain to map the diverse ways that value is exchanged in an entire ecosystem. It makes the intangible flows of social and ecological capital visible.

Step 1: Identify Stakeholders and Core Transactions

Starting with the **System Boundaries & Stakeholder Map (see page 244)**, place the key actors of the ecosystem on a large canvas. Identify the core transactions and exchanges that currently exist between them. At this stage, focus primarily on the tangible exchanges of goods, services, and money.

Step 2: Map the Intangible Value Flows

This is the crucial step. For each relationship, analyze and map the less obvious, intangible exchanges of value. Use different colors or line styles to represent different types of value.

Social Value: Is there an exchange of trust, reputation, community connection, or a sense of belonging?

Ecological Value: Is there an exchange of ecological benefits, such as clean air/water, improved biodiversity, or carbon sequestration?

Knowledge Value: Is there an exchange of data, insights, skills, or learning?

Step 3: Analyze the Network for Opportunities

Analyze the completed map to understand the health of the ecosystem. Ask key questions: Where is value being created? Where is it being extracted or destroyed? Are there any stakeholders who are consistently providing value but not receiving it in return? Based on this analysis, identify opportunities to design new interactions or connections that create more holistic value and strengthen the resilience of the entire network.

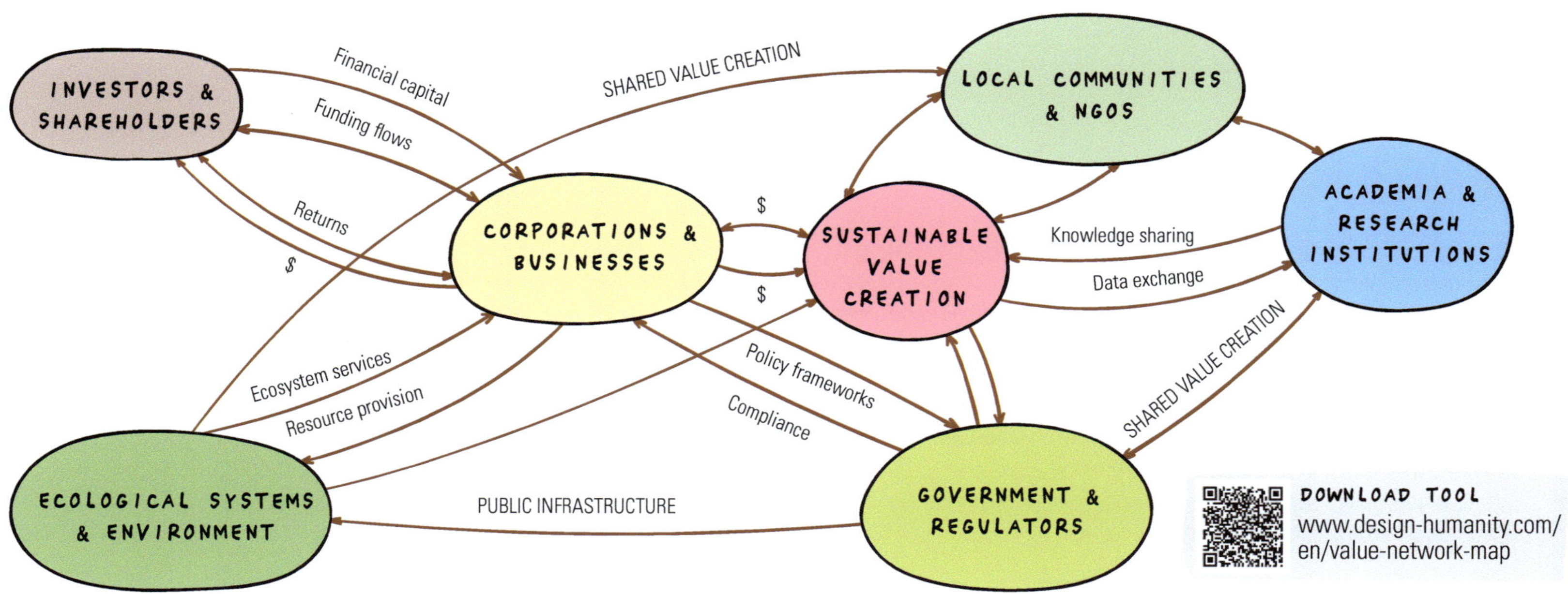

The "Win-Win-Win" Business Ecosystems Canvas

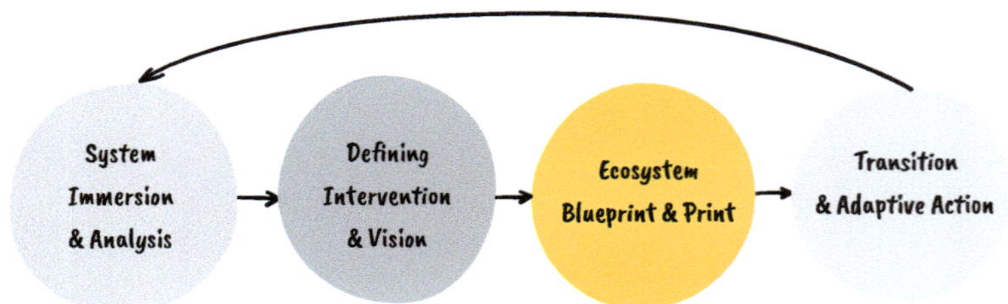

I would like to...

...design a multi-stakeholder ecosystem that is regenerative, equitable, and resilient by design.

What you can do with the tool:

- Move beyond designing a single business model to orchestrating a collaborative network of value creation.
- Provide a comprehensive, one-page canvas for designing a systemic solution to a wicked problem.
- Intentionally design for "win-win-win" outcomes that create value for users, society, and the planet.
- Align multiple, diverse stakeholders around a shared vision and a co-created value proposition.
- Create a blueprint for a resilient business ecosystem that can thrive in the face of future uncertainty.

Expert Tips

Design the Governance Model Explicitly
A common failure point for ecosystems is a lack of clear governance. As you design the canvas, explicitly define the "rules of the game." How are decisions made? How is value distributed fairly? How are conflicts resolved? A well-designed governance model is the invisible architecture that allows an ecosystem to thrive.

Start with a Minimum Viable Product (MVP)
Just as you would launch an MVP, start by designing an MVE Identify the smallest possible configuration of partners that can create and deliver a core piece of the "win-win-win" value proposition. This allows you to test and learn with a smaller, more agile network before scaling.

The Orchestrator as a "System Steward"
The role of the ecosystem orchestrator is not to command and control but to act as a "system steward." Their primary function is to maintain the health of the entire ecosystem, to foster trust and collaboration between the partners, and to ensure that the ecosystem remains true to its massive transformative purpose. This is a profound shift from a traditional, firm-centric view of leadership.

FOUR STRESS TEST QUESTIONS

1. The "Decoupling" Test
"Is the financial success of this ecosystem explicitly contingent upon the delivery of ecological value?"

2. The "Silent Stakeholder" Test
"If the soil (or the watershed or the forest) had a seat on the board, would they vote to approve this business model?"

3. The "Orchestrator's Ego" Test
"If the central Orchestrator disappears tomorrow, does the ecosystem collapse, or does the governance structure allow it to self-organize and survive?"

4. The "Success as a Threat" Test
"If this solution scales 100x next year, what new systemic problem does it accidentally create?"

DOWNLOAD TOOL
www.design-humanity.com/
en/ecosystems

This is the core synthesis tool for this chapter. It adapts the business ecosystem design model to the "for Humanity" context as detailed on pages 230–233. It is a comprehensive canvas for designing a multi-stakeholder network that works together to solve a wicked problem.

Step 1: Define the Ecosystem's Purpose
Start by placing the MTP (see page 284) at the top of the canvas. This is the North Star that will guide the entire ecosystem. Below this, summarize the core insights from the Value Proposition for Humanity Canvas (see page 48). This defines the central "win-win-win" value the ecosystem aims to create.

Step 2: Map the Core Stakeholder Roles
Identify the key stakeholder groups that must be part of the ecosystem to succeed. Group them into core roles, such as:

- **The Orchestrator:** The central entity that facilitates and governs the ecosystem.
- **Value Creators:** The partners who co-create the core products and services.
- **Beneficiaries:** The users, communities, and non-human stakeholders (e.g., ecosystems) who receive the value.
- **Enablers:** The actors who provide essential support (e.g., policymakers, investors, research institutions).

Step 3: Design the Multivalue Flows
Use the insights from the Multi-stakeholder Value Network Mapping (see page 250) to map the key exchanges between the stakeholders. For each critical relationship, define the flows of:

- **Financial Value:** Revenue, investment, cost-sharing
- **Social Value:** Trust, data, community resilience, knowledge
- **Ecological Value:** Regenerative materials, reduced waste, improved biodiversity

Collective Impact Canvas

I would like to...

...create a clear and structured agreement for a multi-stakeholder collaboration to ensure alignment and operational effectiveness.

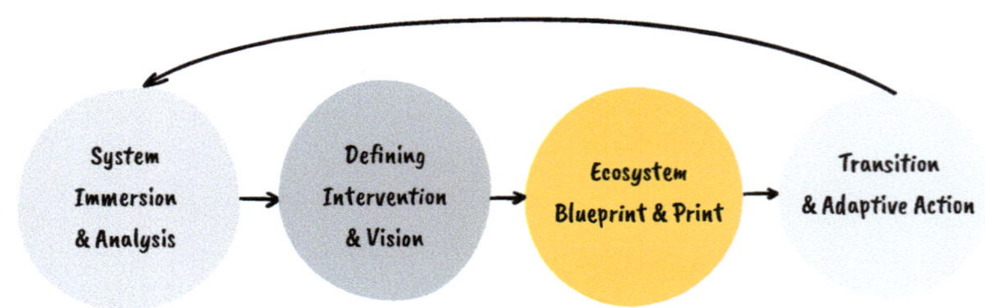

What you can do with the tool:

- Move beyond an informal agreement to a structured framework for collective action.
- Clearly define the roles, responsibilities, and activities of each partner in the ecosystem.
- Establish a shared system for measuring progress and holding all stakeholders accountable.
- Design the communication and governance structures needed to manage a complex, multi-stakeholder alliance.
- Provide a practical, one-page summary of the operational plan for a collaborative project.

Expert Tips

Co-create the Canvas with All Partners
This canvas should not be filled out by the orchestrator alone. To ensure genuine buy-in and a sense of shared ownership, the canvas should be co-created in a workshop that includes representatives from all key partner organizations.

Focus on a Few, High-Leverage Metrics
When defining the shared measurement system, resist the urge to track everything. A successful collective impact initiative focuses on a small number of high-leverage metrics that are directly tied to the common agenda. These shared metrics are the most powerful tool for keeping a diverse group of stakeholders aligned.

The Backbone Is a Facilitator, Not a Commander
The role of the backbone organization is one of facilitation, not command and control. Their primary function is to serve the entire network, build trust, and guide the process of collective learning and adaptation. A successful backbone leader operates with a mindset of stewardship and humility.

THE COLLECTIVE IMPACT CANVAS

Common agenda (MTP)

e.g., Regenerate 10M acres by 2035
Goal 1:   Goal 2:

Shared Metrics

Metric 1 (e.g., Soil organic carbon %)
Metric 2 (e.g., Farmer net income)
Metric 3 (e.g., Biodiversity index)

Reinforcement activities

How does Partner A's work amplify Partner B's work?

Communication

What is the rhythm? How do we build trust?

Support

Who facilitates? What are the key functions (e.g., data management, logistics)?

The Collective Impact Canvas is a tool for structuring the operational side of a collaborative ecosystem. It translates the high-level vision of a business ecosystem into a practical plan for working together, guiding a team to define the five core elements of a successful collaboration.

Step 1: Define the Common Agenda
At the top of the canvas, clearly state the **MTP (see page 254)** that unites all partners. Below this, define the specific, shared goals that the collaboration aims to achieve. This ensures that all stakeholders are aligned around a common vision of success.

Step 2: Establish Shared Measurement
Agree with your team on a small set of key metrics that will be used to measure progress toward the common agenda. These metrics must be consistent for all participants and should reflect the "win-win-win" value being created (e.g., tracking user, societal, and planetary outcomes).

Step 3: Map Mutually Reinforcing Activities
For each key partner in the ecosystem, list their unique activities and contributions. The goal is to identify and design a set of "mutually reinforcing" activities, where the work of each partner naturally supports and amplifies the work of the others, creating a powerful synergy.

Step 4: Design for Continuous Communication and Backbone Support
Define the rhythm and channels for communication that will keep all partners aligned. It is essential to also define the role of the orchestrator. This is the central entity responsible for facilitating the collaboration, managing the shared measurement systems, and guiding the overall strategy of the ecosystem.

Adaptive Strategy & The Infinite Game Mindset

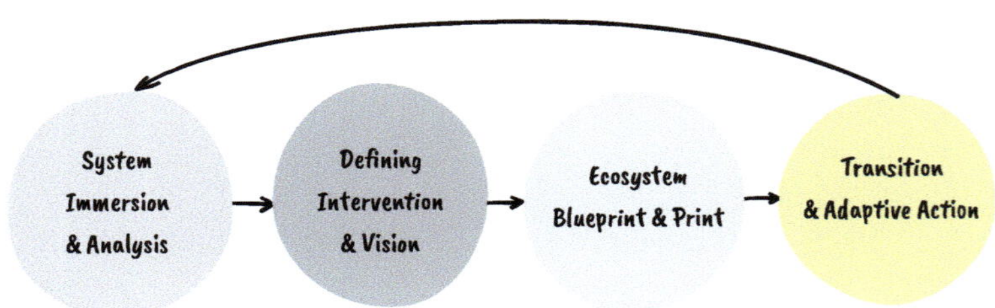

I would like to...

...design a strategy that can adapt and evolve with a complex system, rather than a rigid plan that breaks when conditions change.

What you can do with the tool:

- Shift the goal from "winning" or "solving" a problem to building a system that is resilient and capable of continuous learning.
- Create strategies that are designed to thrive in dynamic and unpredictable environments.
- Foster a long-term perspective, focusing on the health and longevity of the system rather than on short-term victories.
- Provide a framework for making decisions under conditions of high uncertainty.
- Build a more resilient and adaptable organization or movement that is prepared to navigate the "infinite game" of systemic change.

Expert Tips

Identify Your "Worthy Rival"
In an infinite game, the goal is not to vanquish competitors but to be pushed by them to become better. Identify "worthy rivals," which are other organizations or actors who are also working on the same wicked problem, perhaps with a different approach. The goal is to learn from them and to be inspired by them to improve, not to defeat them.

Build a Trusting Team
An organization cannot be truly adaptive if its internal culture is driven by fear or internal politics. An infinite game requires a high degree of trust, where people feel safe to admit mistakes, share bad news, and pivot when a strategy is not working. Fostering psychological safety is a non-negotiable prerequisite for adaptive strategy.

Flex on Strategy, Be Resolute on Purpose
The core paradox of an adaptive strategy is to be simultaneously flexible and resolute. The specific strategy, the "how," should always be open to change based on new information. However, the MTP, the "why," must remain stable. This unwavering commitment to the long-term purpose provides the anchor of stability that allows for constant tactical flexibility.

DESIGN FOR ADAPTABILITY CANVAS

Infinite Goal:

What is the cause so just we would sacrifice short-term gain to advance it?

Sensing (The Radar):

What feedback loops detect systematic shifts early? List signals: Customer behaviors, ecological data, policy shifts

Blind Spots: What are we ignoring?

Adapting (The Pivot):

If our current offering become obsolete, how do we pivot to stay true to the cause?

Resilience Assets:
What assets (trust, community) survive a "shock"?

Worth Rivals

Who is better than us at something that matters?

Reflection: What does it say about our weaknesses?

This tool combines a strategic framework with a core mindset shift. It acknowledges that wicked problems are not finite games that can be won but "infinite games" that are played for the purpose of continuing the play. The goal is not to win but to build a system healthy enough to keep playing.

Step 1: Adopt an Infinite Game Mindset
The first step is a mental one. The team must shift its perspective from a finite mindset (focused on beating competitors and achieving fixed goals) to an infinite mindset. This involves defining the purpose so profound that it can never be fully achieved but is worthy of endless striving (similar to the intention of the MTP). This cause, not a specific metric, becomes the ultimate guide for all strategic decisions.

Step 2: Design for Adaptability, Not Just Efficiency (See Canvas)
With an infinite mindset, the focus of strategy shifts. Instead of designing a single, "optimal" plan, the goal is to design a system with the built-in capacity to adapt. This involves creating flexible structures, fostering diverse approaches, and intentionally building in some redundancy. The key is to prioritize long-term resilience over short-term efficiency. Ask: What short-term metric are we willing to sacrifice this year to build resilience for the next decade?

Step 3: Implement Feedback Loops for Continuous Learning
An adaptive strategy is a learning strategy. This final step involves creating robust feedback loops that allow the organization or system to sense changes in the environment and adapt accordingly. This requires a commitment to radical transparency, a culture that learns from failure, and the use of tools like Future-Ready Roadmapping to translate real-time learning into an evolving strategic plan.

Transition Strategy Canvas

I would like to...

...design a politically and economically viable strategy for transitioning from the current, unsustainable system to our desired regenerative model.

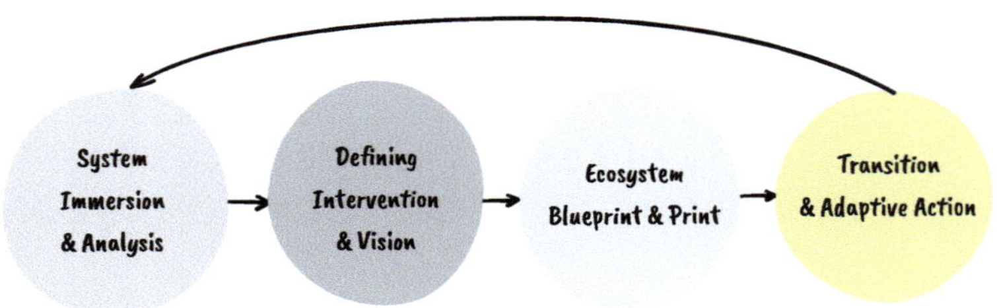

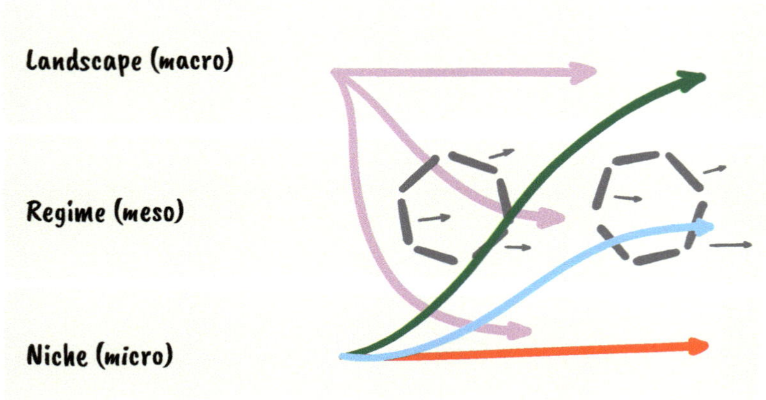

What you can do with the tool:

- Move beyond designing an ideal solution to designing an actionable implementation and transition plan.
- Systematically identify the key actors who have the power to block or enable systemic change.
- Map the entrenched economic incentives and political barriers that must be overcome.
- Design a compelling narrative and a persuasive strategy to build a broad coalition for change.
- Create a more realistic, politically astute, and ultimately more effective plan for real-world impact.

Expert Tips

Identify the "Unlikely Allies"
The most powerful coalitions are often formed with "unlikely allies." Look for stakeholders who, on the surface, might seem opposed to the change but who have a hidden, long-term interest in a more resilient future. Building a bridge to these groups can fundamentally shift the political calculus of a transition.

Design for a "Just Transition"
A transition strategy will inevitably create winners and losers in the short term. A key to building a broad and resilient coalition is to explicitly design for a "just transition." This means creating clear and tangible plans to support the individuals and communities who may be negatively impacted by the shift, ensuring that the move to a regenerative future is also an equitable one.

Start with a Minimum Viable Transition (MVT)
Just as an ecosystem is launched with a minimum viable ecosystem (MVE), a transition strategy should start with a "minimum viable transition." Identify a single, high-leverage policy change or a small-scale pilot project that can be achieved in the short term. A tangible, early win, no matter how small, is the most powerful way to build momentum and prove to a skeptical world that a new, regenerative future is not just possible but is already beginning.

THE TRANSITION STRATEGY CANVAS

1. POWER & POLITICS

Who blocks change?
Who enables it?

Blockers (Incumbents):
Who benefits from the
status quo?

Unlikely Allies:
Who has a hidden interest
in change?

2. ECONOMICS & INCENTIVES

How do we bridge the "valley
of death"?

The Cost of Change:
Why is transition expensive?

New Incentives/Safe Harbor:
How do we subsidize the
risk (e.g., premium pricing,
insurance)?

3. NARRATIVE & PERSUASION

What story wins the coalition?

Reframing the Problem:
e.g., From "environmentalism"
to "national security"

The "Just Transition" Promise:
How do we ensure no one is
left behind?

4. PATHWAYS TO LEGITIMACY

From fringe to mainstream

**Plot/MVT (Min Viable
Transition):**
What is the first small win?

Policy Window/Tipping Point:
What regulation or standard
locks it in?

The Transition Strategy Canvas is a tool for the pragmatist. It is used after a "win-win-win" solution has been designed, and it focuses on the messy, real-world work of making that solution a reality.

Step 1: Map the Power & Politics

In this first quadrant, the team identifies all the key actors who hold power in the current system. Ask the critical questions: Who benefits most from the status quo? Who has the formal and informal power to block this change? Who are our potential allies? What are the key political obstacles and opportunities?

Step 2: Analyze the Economics & Incentives

Next, the team maps the economic landscape. Ask: What are the dominant economic incentives that reinforce the current system? How does our proposed solution threaten those incentives? How can we design new, regenerative incentives that are compelling enough to shift behavior? Can we create a business case for transition for key incumbents?

Step 3: Design the Narrative & Persuasion Strategy

In this quadrant, the team designs the story of the change itself. Using the **Narrative Design Canvas (see page 235)**, craft a compelling and persuasive narrative for each key stakeholder group. The story for a policymaker will be different from the story for a community member or a corporate CEO. This is the art of political communication.

Step 4: Chart the Pathways to Legitimacy

Finally, the team charts a realistic, step-by-step pathway to making the new system legitimate. This is not a product roadmap, but a political one. It involves identifying key policy windows, building a coalition of allies, launching pilot projects to build evidence, and creating a tangible, phased plan for moving the solution from a fringe idea to the new, commonsense status quo.

Tool Extension for Dynamic Adaptation

The Transition Strategy Canvas (see page 258) provides a robust plan for political and economic change, but a system in transition is constantly shifting. The final crucial step in a transition strategy is establishing a framework for continuous learning and adaptation. To manage the uncertainty inherent in systemic change, we must integrate a rapid feedback and adaptation cycle.

The **Observe-Orient-Decide-Act (OODA)** loop provides this framework and adds a fifth step.

Step 5: Implement the Transition OODA Loop
This step ensures the strategy remains adaptive and resilient in the face of change.

How this tool is applied:

The OODA loop is a continuous, iterative cycle that transforms static plans into dynamic, resilient action. It is the framework for managing the uncertainty of systemic change:

Step 1: Observe (the Radar)
Gather raw data and signals from the political and economic environment. The focus is on tracking changes in the **consensus** and detecting the early warning signs of **rival responses**.

Step 2: Orient (the System Check)
This is the most critical phase for systemic change. Process and analyze new data against the existing **causal loop diagrams (see page 246)** to identify **Unintended Consequences (see page 246)** or shifts in **High Leverage Points (see page 248)**.

Step 3: Decide (the Pivot)
Formulate rapid, high-leverage courses of action based on the orientation. Weigh options for their impact on the system's **Resilience Assets (see page 256)** and select the action that best advances the **minimum viable transition (MVT)**.

Step 4: Act (the Experiment)
Execute the chosen policy change or pilot project as a high-impact experiment (see page 259). The outcome then feeds back into the **Observe** stage, starting the loop anew.

Systems thinking moves beyond viewing problems as isolated events, providing the essential lens to understand the interconnected feedback loops and root causes that drive wicked problems.

The core practice of this discipline is to identify and act upon high-leverage points, shifting focus from addressing visible symptoms to transforming the underlying structures of a system.

Its primary application is the design of regenerative business ecosystems, architecting multi-stakeholder collaborations that create "win-win-win" value for people, the planet, and the economy.

This approach requires adopting an infinite game mindset, where the goal is not to solve a problem but to build resilient and adaptive systems that can learn and thrive in a constantly changing world.

EXPONENTIAL THINKING

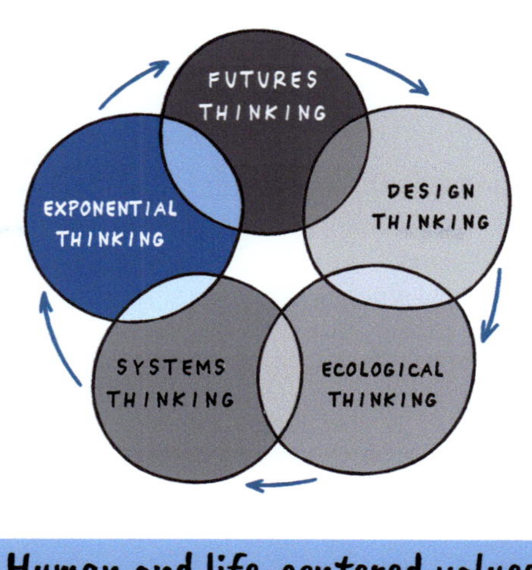

FUTURES THINKING
EXPONENTIAL THINKING
DESIGN THINKING
SYSTEMS THINKING
ECOLOGICAL THINKING

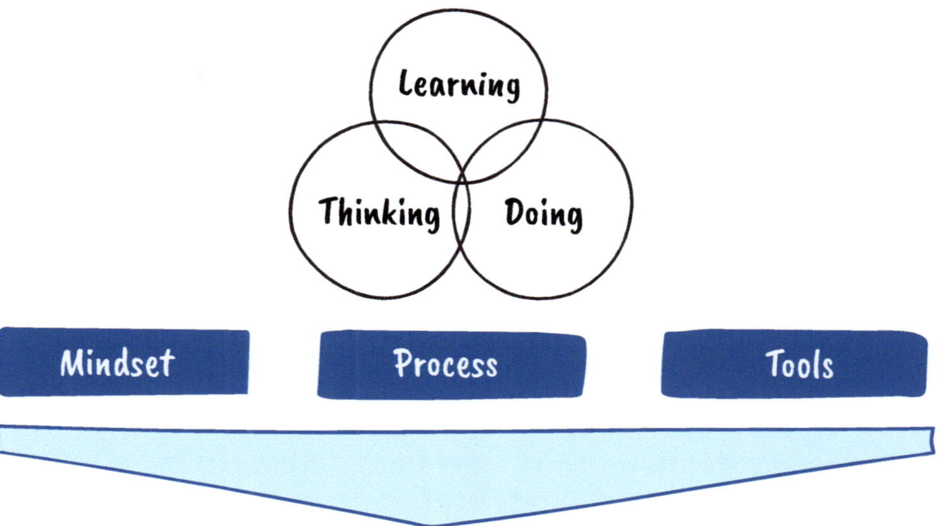

Human and life-centered values
Learning
Thinking
Doing
Mindset
Process
Tools
...
Products
Services
Experiences
Ecosystems
Behavior
THE SPECTRUM OF POSITIVE, RESILIENT CHANGE WE AIM TO CREATE

Scaling for Impact

In the rapidly accelerating landscape, the very nature of innovation is being reshaped by **exponential thinking**. This paradigm shift moves beyond linear progression, focusing instead on how to design and implement systems that enable unprecedented acceleration and scale in delivering solutions. The traditional trajectory, where scientific principles slowly trickle down into products and services over decades, is now being dramatically disrupted. We are witnessing **a radical compression of the problem-solution and product-market fit cycles**, transforming processes that once took years into mere months or weeks. This exponential acceleration, largely fueled by AI and other emerging technologies, presents both the greatest opportunity and the most significant challenge of our time. While AI excels at building upon existing knowledge and rapidly generating solutions, it inherently lacks an ethical compass and often struggles to imbue its creations with true purpose beyond technical feasibility. This creates a critical risk: the power to scale solutions is also the power to scale problems. An unguided exponential force can just as easily amplify systemic biases, deplete resources, and create unforeseen social harms as it can solve wicked problems. Therefore, the Design Thinking for Humanity framework is not just beneficial but the indispensable operating system for navigating this complex new era. **It provides the essential "why" to guide the technological "how."** The synergistic power of the five interconnected thinking disciplines is a nonnegotiable approach to this challenge. It ensures that the immense power of exponential technologies is not applied in a vacuum but is directed with a profound commitment to ethical principles, equity, and the long-term service of humanity and the planet.

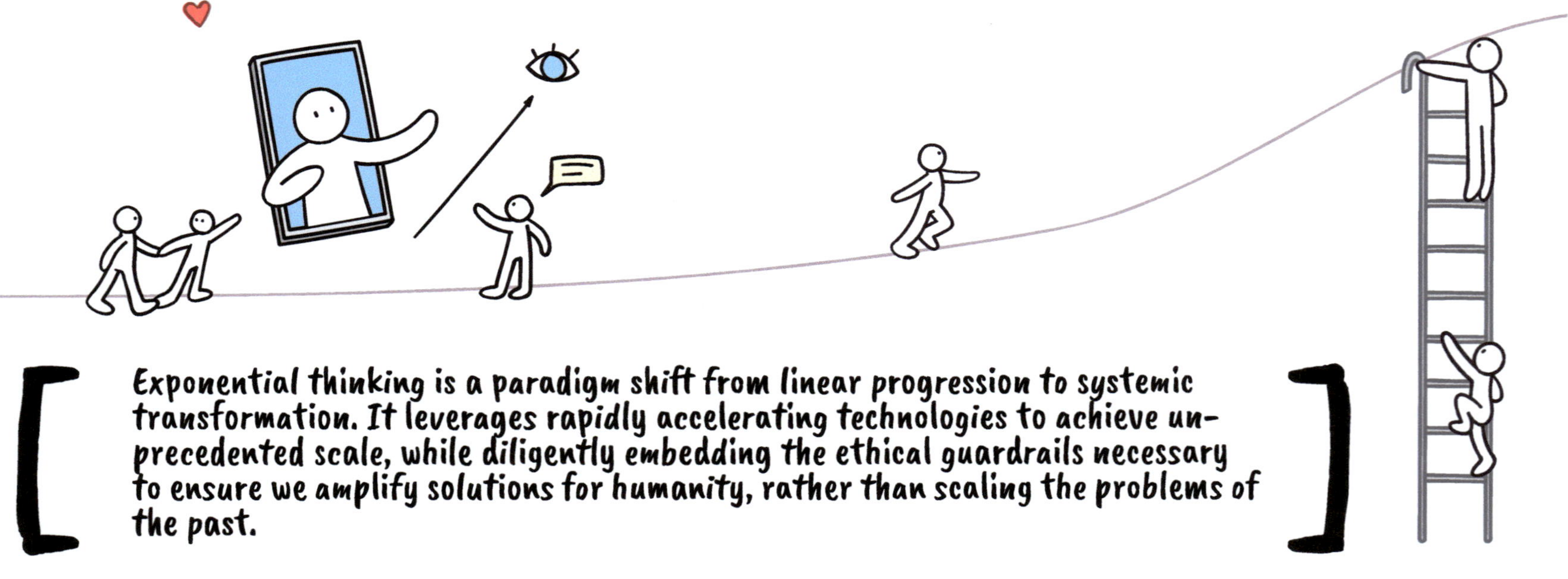

[Exponential thinking is a paradigm shift from linear progression to systemic transformation. It leverages rapidly accelerating technologies to achieve unprecedented scale, while diligently embedding the ethical guardrails necessary to ensure we amplify solutions for humanity, rather than scaling the problems of the past.]

10X Positive Impact

This last chapter explores how to strategically **harness exponential thinking and the power of AI** while diligently embedding this ethical and planetary purpose at every stage. The goal is to move beyond simply leveraging technology for its own sake and instead use it as a tool to restore planetary balance, design for systemic well-being, and build a truly thriving, resilient, and "exponentializing" future. The tools and methods that follow are designed to provide a practical framework for this essential work.

In the context of this book, it becomes paramount to re-think the well-known disruptive innovation scorecard that focuses on 10x improvements, new markets, and scalability. A solution could score high on all those traditional metrics but still be ecologically destructive or socially divisive. **Adding a dimension for Regenerative/Positive Impact** by including ecological thinking supports and accelerates the journey toward regenerative results.

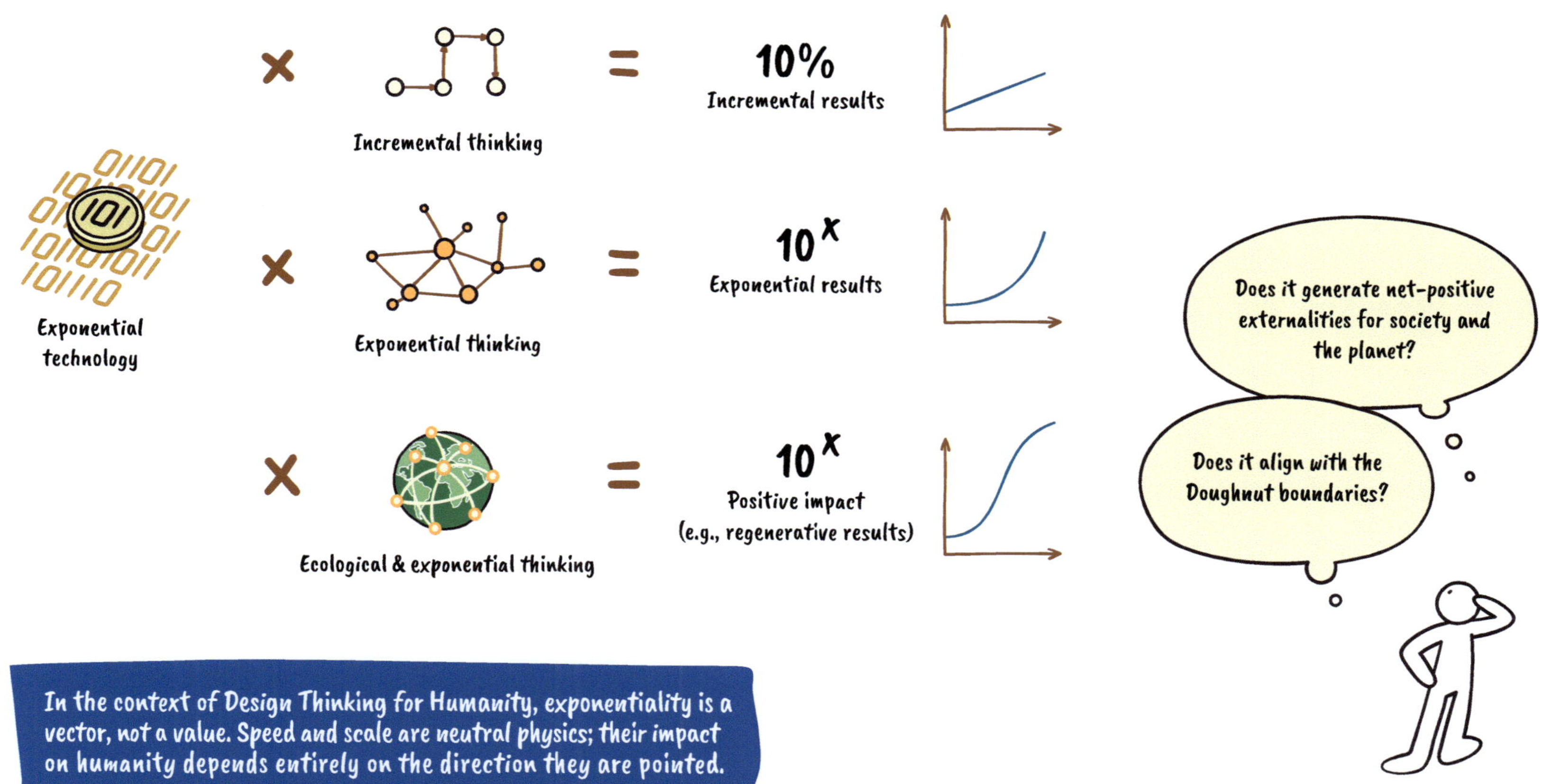

In the context of Design Thinking for Humanity, exponentiality is a vector, not a value. Speed and scale are neutral physics; their impact on humanity depends entirely on the direction they are pointed.

Mediating a New Exponential Mindset

The current and predominant exponential mindset believes that the sheer velocity of technological capability can outrun the resource constraints and entropic decay that have historically bound economic systems. But "moving fast, and breaking things" has also the potential of accelerant of the very crisis, including biodiversity loss, climate instability, and social inequality.

Within the framework of Design Thinking for Humanity we aim for a bold and necessary synthesis between regenerative practices and the leverage of information-based technologies. Innovation teams applying the Design Thinking for Humanity framework have to make it a mediating layer. This indispensable operating system has been designed to harness the velocity of exponential tech while subjecting it to the normative guidance of human and ecological values.

Standard problem-solving looks for incremental improvements. Our approach of exponential thinking looks for systemic transformation.

By embracing this exponential perspective, we empower ourselves to envision and create interventions that ripple through complex systems, addressing root causes rather than just superficial symptoms and ultimately driving profound, widespread transformation.

This amplified impact is critically dependent on a deep understanding and strategic application of emerging technologies. Beyond technical acumen and methodological prowess, exponential thinking in Design Thinking for Humanity necessitates the cultivation of distinct human skills. Adaptability and resilience are paramount, enabling individuals and teams to navigate and thrive amid constant, rapid change, and to recover swiftly from setbacks inherent in pioneering new solutions.

Creativity and innovation become the engines for generating novel ideas that can unlock exponential growth. Furthermore, effective collaboration and communication are indispensable, fostering environments where diverse perspectives converge to achieve common, ambitious goals.

The marriage of exponential thinking with the other lenses of Design Thinking for Humanity culminates in a powerful approach to systemic change. It moves beyond isolated fixes, instead using interconnected elements within a global system to understand how holistic solutions resonate across scales. This approach inherently promotes radical collaboration and open innovation, fostering an environment where knowledge and resources are shared freely.

The goal is to apply exponential growth to accelerate progress, cultivating an equitable and thriving future for all. We are aiming to move from authority to influence and from scarcity to abundance with exponential thinking. This requires different skills and capabilities, such as **foresight, systemic empathy, adaptive governance, transdisciplinary collaboration, decentralized decision-making, ethical reasoning, critical thinking** and the other important capabilities outlined in this book.

Shift from Incremental Thinking Toward Exponential Thinking

Leading systemic change requires a fundamental mindset shift away from linear, incremental approaches toward an exponential perspective.

The following comparison outlines the key features that distinguish the two mindsets.

FEATURE	INCREMENTAL THINKING	EXPONENTIAL THINKING
Pace of Change	Gradual, step-by-step improvements. Linear progression.	Nonlinear and accelerating. Uses technology for rapid, scaled positive impact.
Problem Solving	Addresses symptoms, makes small adjustments.	Addresses root causes for global-scale human and planetary benefit.
Goals & Ambition	Focuses on achieving modest, attainable improvements.	Aims for audacious, seemingly impossible breakthroughs to achieve restorative outcomes.
Risk Tolerance	Lower risk, prefers proven methods, avoids major disruption.	Safe experimentations; rapidly tests ethical prototypes; views failure as essential learning.
Resource Utilization	Optimized for current resources, efficiency gains.	Leverages decentralized, circular, and shareable resources/data (e.g., open source, community).
Mindset	"How can we do this 10% better?"	"How can we create a 10X better, restorative future for all?" Purpose-driven focus.
Scope of Impact	Localized, limited to existing parameters.	Global; solutions are designed for massive, accessible scale and closed-loop systems.
Decision-Making	Centralized decision-making, hierarchical approvals.	Empowered decision-making, decentralized authority, rapid iteration, continuous feedback and ethical metrics.
Leadership Style	Expands authority, control, and direct oversight.	Fosters purpose, autonomy, and collaboration across diverse networks.

The Exponential Innovation Cycle

To translate the new exponential mindset into action, we employ a rigorous cyclical process that harmonizes human ethical intent with machine velocity. This workflow ensures that the power of technology is tethered to planetary well-being and purpose before solutions are scaled. The **process balances human-led wisdom and ethical judgment** with the speed and scope of artificial intelligence, compressing the time needed to test systemic impact and identify unintended consequences safely.

The Exponential Innovation Cycle's Core Steps:

- **Frame & Align (Human Led):** Define the MTP and Doughnut guardrails, translating human values into computational constraints for the AI.
- **Expand & Generate (AI Led):** Utilize AI to explore a vast solution space and generate diverse, novel concepts beyond inherent human biases.
- **Simulate & Validate (Hybrid/Machine Speed):** Test concepts in **Digital Twins** against complex systemic models to compress impact time and fail safely.
- **Curate & Refine (Human Led):** Reintroduce human ethical judgment and wisdom to select regenerative solutions and refine their final framing.

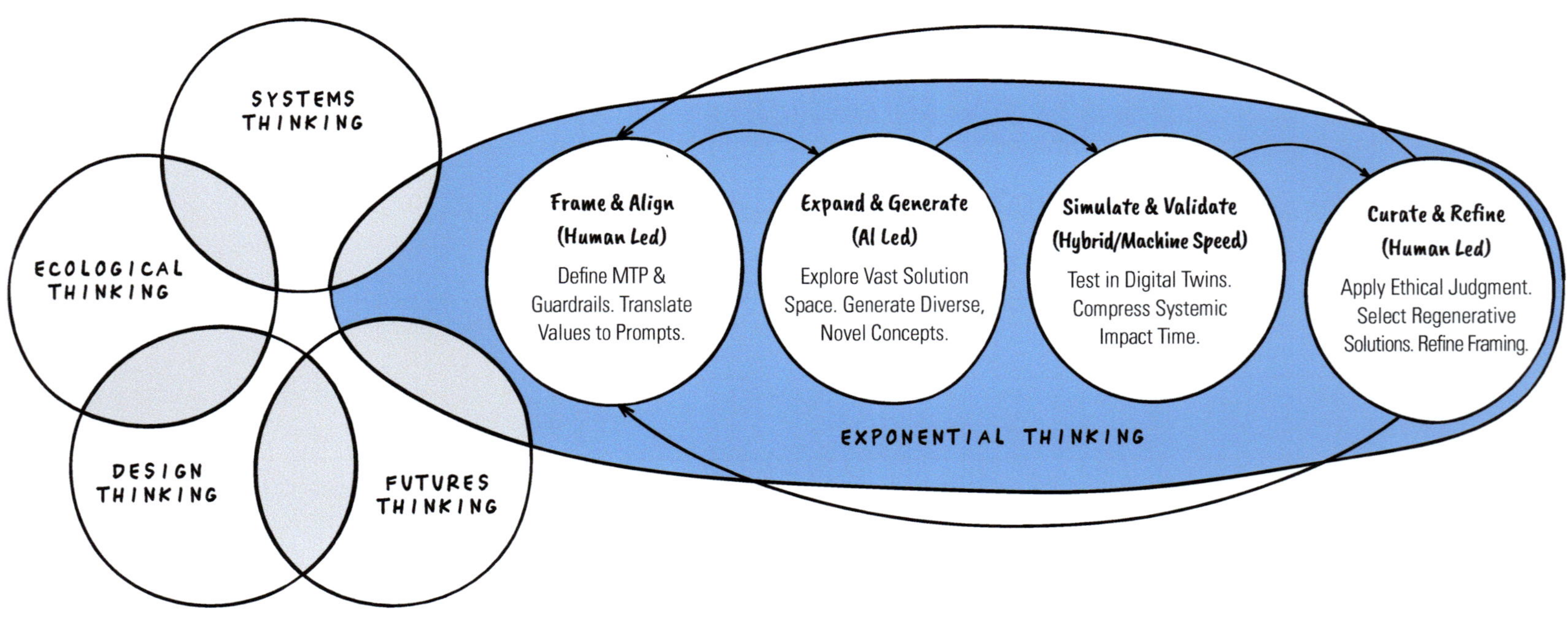

Massive Transformative Purpose (MTP)

The Massive Transformative Purpose (MTP) has been an integrated component of many tools presented in previous chapters, functioning as the vital "North Star" for the team, but its importance becomes paramount in the context of exponential scale. When dealing with technologies that have the power to reshape industries and societies, the "what" and the "how" are not enough. The MTP is the ethical and strategic justification for aiming for massive impact, ensuring that the goal is not just growth, but the creation of a more resilient and regenerative future. It is the cultural and ethical core that provides stability, meaning, and direction in the face of rapid, often disorienting, exponential change. **The MTP Canvas (see page 270)** provides three simple steps to envision the purpose.

Why does this solution deserve to scale, and what is the profound human and planetary purpose that will guide its growth?

The MTP is the core element that links all five Design Thinking for Humanity lenses and their respective tools together. It serves as the "magnet" that unifies the deep analysis of systems thinking, the ethical guardrails of ecological thinking, the human focus of design thinking, the foresight of futures thinking, and the velocity of exponential thinking. By defining the shared purpose first, every action, tool application, and partnership remains dedicated to a coherent vision for a better world.

MTP as a Strategic Catalyst for Exponential Scale

The MTP is an intensely practical strategic tool that prevents the dilution of an exponential strategy and acts as the primary filter for all major decisions. Use the MTP as a catalyst to guide scaling efforts:

- **The Ultimate Ethical Guardrail:** In an era of powerful AI, the MTP is the constant, human and planetary-centric principle that ensures technology serves humanity and the planet, not the other way around.

- **The Movement Magnet:** A well-crafted MTP is the primary catalyst for building a movement, attracting a passionate community motivated by shared belief rather than just financial incentives. This shifts a project from a product to a platform and ultimately to a global movement.

- **The Focus Filter:** For any new partnership or initiative, the team must ask: "Does this get us closer to achieving our MTP?" If the answer is no, the idea should be reconsidered, regardless of how profitable or technologically interesting it may seem.

- **The Unwavering North Star:** Beyond its inspirational function, the MTP is the gravitational center that keeps a diverse and decentralized ecosystem of partners aligned, ensuring coherence and integrity as the system grows.

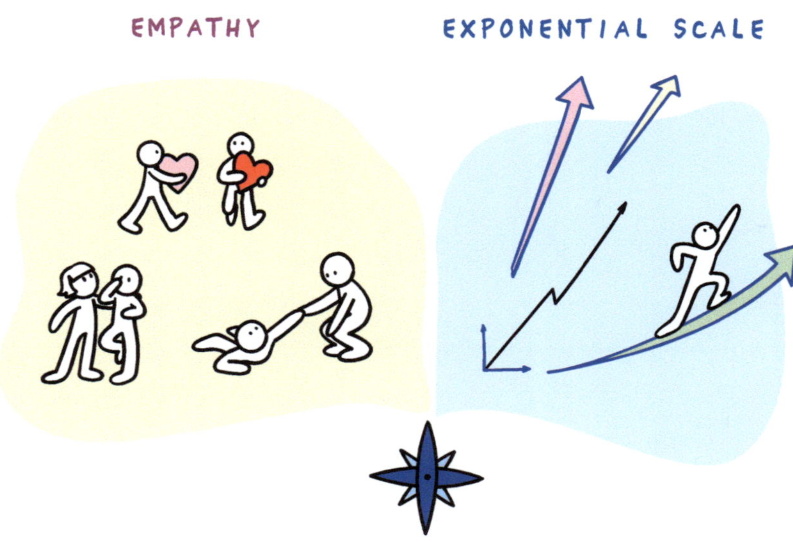

Human and Planetary Transformation

Massive Transformative Purpose (MTP) Canvas

Find the Massive

Who are you trying to impact? If you succeeded beyond your wildest dreams, how big is the community?

Community:_______________________

What is the wicked problem to solve? (see design thinking)

1

Define the Purpose

What is the core emotional driver? What is our highest purpose?"

Passion: _____________________

2

Envision the Transformation

How will the world look different after we have started?

What is the paradigm shift?

What are steps on the journey or a radical outcome?

Shift: _______________________

3

- **Is it MASSIVE?** (Does it impact 1 billion+ or a whole industry?)
- **Is it TRANSFORMATIONAL?** (Does it change the paradigm, not just the process?)
- **Is it PURPOSE-DRIVEN?** (Does it vibrate with emotional energy?)
- **Is it RESILIENT?** (Does this purpose endure through external shock?)

DOWNLOAD TOOL
www.design-humanity.com/en/mtp

Human-AI Collaboration

The shift to **regenerative AI** is a necessary systemic move within the Design Thinking for Humanity framework. Throughout the 2020s, most AI systems have been "narrow," excelling at single, specific tasks like facial recognition or content generation. However, the exponential trajectory of technology is leading rapidly toward **artificial general intelligence (AGI)** systems capable of human-level reasoning, learning, and generalized problem-solving across vast domains.

The immense power of AGI necessitates explicit ethical and social alignment. Regenerative AI directly counters AGI's potential for harm by designing systems to restore ecological and social health. This requires explicit social and ecological alignment, ensuring AGI's core objectives overcome the extractive status quo. Governance must mandate models that differentiate between current extractive human behavior and desired ecological stewardship.

The concept of **precision restoration** exemplifies the necessary shift from broad environmental goals to hyper-targeted, measurable action. A strong example of this is the Google Tree Canopy project. This initiative uses AI to map urban heat islands and existing tree coverage from aerial imagery, enabling cities to plant trees with surgical precision to maximize cooling effects and foster vital biodiversity corridors. Meanwhile, the Treen-D fusion algorithm simulates how individual trees will grow over 10–20 years or maps the intricate, time-variable shade patterns created by urban forests to better mitigate the heat island effect and plot shaded walking routes.

The shift promotes transparency and decentralized power via **biomimetic intelligence**. These AI algorithms are modeled on biological systems (e.g., swarm intelligence) to optimize decentralized resource distribution. Unlike opaque "black box" AI, these systems are designed for epistemic integrity and transparency. By operationalizing transparency, regenerative AI embeds the non-negotiable constraints of the **ecological ceiling** into optimization objectives.

This coming era of AGI represents a foundational moment, requiring us to consciously define the principles and operating instructions that will govern its profound systemic power.

Reimagining Systems with AGI

- AGI is defined by its systemic power to master intricate organizational flows and drive fundamental redefinition of economic systems.

- The technology is uniquely capable of tackling chronic, systemic issues by generalizing knowledge and transferring skills across different domains.

- AGI's use of advanced algorithms can optimize resource allocation and distribution across diverse sectors by processing massive real-time datasets.

- Deployed with an ethical and social alignment framework, AGI can maximize profit and minimize carbon emissions by using complexity-aware, long-term ecological restoration optimization.

- Integrating digital twin technologies with reinforcement learning allows AGI-powered multi-agent systems to optimize dynamic supply chains for agility, sustainability, and cost.

Exponential intelligence requires exponential empathy. As AGI scales our ability to build, we must equally scale our capacity to care.

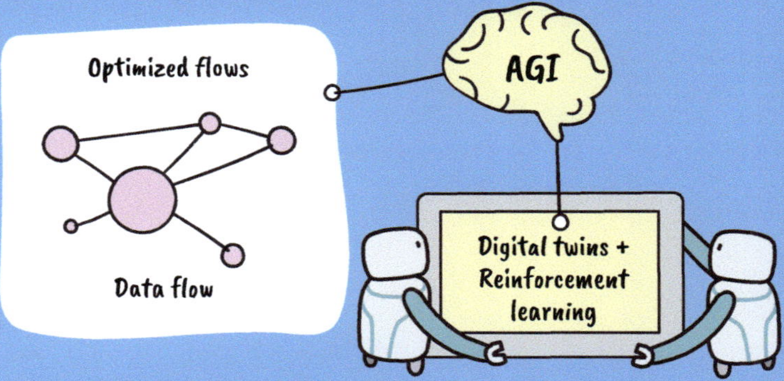

Exponential Design Path for Humanity

The Exponential Design for Humanity is a paradigm shift, leveraging AI not for incremental gains but for the radical, scalable transformation required to achieve truly sustainable, regenerative, and socially responsible global solutions.

The Bio-centric Translator
This path utilizes AI to interpret ecosystem data as a distinct user persona, which ensures that nature has a literal and data-driven voice in the final design process.

The Ancestral Forecaster
The Ancestral Forecaster leverages predictive modeling to simulate the impact of design decisions over centuries, thereby shifting the primary focus from short-term user satisfaction to intergenerational value.

The Cognitive Expander
Acting as an AI co-pilot, this concept instantly connects local humanitarian challenges with obscure solutions from unrelated fields, successfully overcoming human cognitive bias to generate novel concepts.

The Hyper-Local Fabricator
This approach focuses on moving data rather than atoms by creating digital assets that can be locally manufactured using waste streams and distributed 3D printing, effectively democratizing the supply chain.

The Swarm Designer
The Swarm Designer utilizes collective intelligence platforms to aggregate real-time insights from thousands of community members, replacing small focus groups with democratic, large-scale co-creation.

The Abundance Architect
This design path employs AI to identify and redistribute idle capacity within existing systems, such as empty cargo space or equipment downtime, solving scarcity problems without consuming new resources.

The Guardian Algorithm
The Guardian Algorithm deploys specialized AI agents to aggressively "red team" proposed solutions before launch, proactively identifying potential bias, exclusion, or ethical harms that human designers might overlook.

The Frictionless Philanthropist
This concept embeds micro-regeneration into everyday user transactions via smart contracts, aligning individual actions with automatic, sustained funding for critical social causes.

Futuristic AI Innovation Paths for Planetary Balance

The next evolution step of AI, guided by the MTP and the ecological ceiling, must move beyond mere optimization to actively redesign governance, economic flows, and ecological stewardship for long-term regenerative success.

The Planetary Resilience Model
Developing AI capable of synthesizing global ecological, human demographic, and atmospheric data to predict cascading systemic failures (e.g., simultaneous crop failure, water scarcity, and political unrest) and propose minimal-intervention, regenerative solutions.

The Circular Economy Autonomy Framework
Achieving autonomous, decentralized resource management where AI traces the full lifecycle of every molecule/product and dynamically redesigns supply chains and urban systems to eliminate waste and maximize resource utility on a planetary scale.

The Universal Adaptive Social Learning System
Creating AI-powered, hyper-personalized educational systems that adapt not just to individual cognitive needs but also to local social, cultural, and environmental contexts, rapidly accelerating collective literacy in sustainability and critical thinking.

The Bio-mimetics and Material Discovery Path
Developing AI specialized in combinatorial materials science and green chemistry, accelerating the discovery of non-toxic, carbon-negative, and biodegradable materials and energy systems that align with natural processes.

The Decentralized Equity and Governance Audit
Engineering AI that operates as a globally accessible, unbiased oracle to assess the impact of policies, regulations, and financial decisions on social equity and environmental health before they are enacted, ensuring global accountability.

The Emotionally Grounded Collaborative Robot
Advancing perfect multimodal dexterity specifically for humanitarian aid, disaster relief, and ecosystem repair, where robots can interpret distress and operate safely and empathically in chaotic human and natural environments.

A Systemic Poverty and Needs Mapping System
Creating AI that moves beyond simple aid distribution to diagnose the causal roots of generational poverty and scarcity, designing hyper-local, self-sustaining economic and infrastructural solutions tailored to unique community needs.

The Ethical and Cultural Alignment Fabric
Establishing a universal AI-accessible ontology that includes diverse ethical frameworks, cultural values, and ancestral wisdom alongside scientific facts, ensuring all AGI actions are grounded in respect for both local context and global co-existence.

Simulation and Testing

In a linear design process, a mistake usually results in a local and correctable error. In an exponential context, however, a flawed algorithm or a biased system scales to millions of people in milliseconds. The cost of "moving fast and breaking things" becomes unacceptably high when the systems we break are social fabrics or fragile ecosystems. Simulation transforms from a technical step into an ethical imperative. Before we unleash a solution into the real world, we must place it in a safety sandbox. This is where, for example, **digital twins (virtual replicas of physical systems, cities, or ecosystems) serve as our most critical design tool**. By testing exponential interventions in a high-fidelity virtual environment, innovation teams can rigorously validate their impact before a single line of code touches the real world.

Compress Time:
We can simulate decades of impact in mere minutes. While a linear pilot might take years to reveal soil depletion caused by an agricultural AI, a simulation reveals these long-term degradation patterns immediately. This allows us to iterate on the solution before any real damage occurs.

Stress-Test for Resilience:
We must inject "external shocks" such as sudden pandemics, supply chain collapses, or extreme climate events into the simulation. This process ensures we design for resilience rather than just efficiency. A solution that collapses under stress is not ready for exponential scaling.

Identify Second-Order Effects
Consider the Carbon Harvest platform from our case study. An AI might optimize crop yields by maximizing short-term soil inputs, inadvertently creating a second-order effect where local biodiversity collapses due to monoculture efficiency. Or it might automate farming so effectively that it displaces the local workforce without providing an economic alternative, leading to community decay. Simulation exposes these hidden systemic risks, allowing us to redesign the algorithm to prioritize biodiversity and community resilience before deployment.

Potential Application Cases for Preventive Design

- **Designing Out Waste (Circular Economy):**
  Instead of just managing waste better, a digital twin of a product's lifecycle can model the molecular degradation of materials over time. This allows designers to fundamentally re-engineer the product at the molecular level for infinite recyclability.

- **Preventing Urban Heat Islands:**
  Rather than just planting trees to cool hot neighborhoods (treating the effect), a digital twin of a new urban development can model airflow and solar gain before construction begins. Architects can then rotate buildings and adjust street widths to passively cool the city by design.

- **Eliminating Supply Chain Fragility:**
  A digital twin of a global supply network can identify structural dependencies on single-source suppliers. By redesigning the network topology to be distributed and modular before a crisis hits, companies remove the cause of systemic collapse.

- **Preventing Soil Degradation:**
  In agriculture, a digital twin can model the long-term chemical interaction between specific fertilizers and local soil microbiomes. This allows for the design of precision biological inputs that enhance soil health over decades, preventing the chemical imbalances that cause desertification.

The digital twin concept, particularly when applied to Earth, offers a radical advancement over traditional climate information systems, deeply aligning with the Design Thinking for Humanity framework's focus on user-centric systemic change and planetary needs.

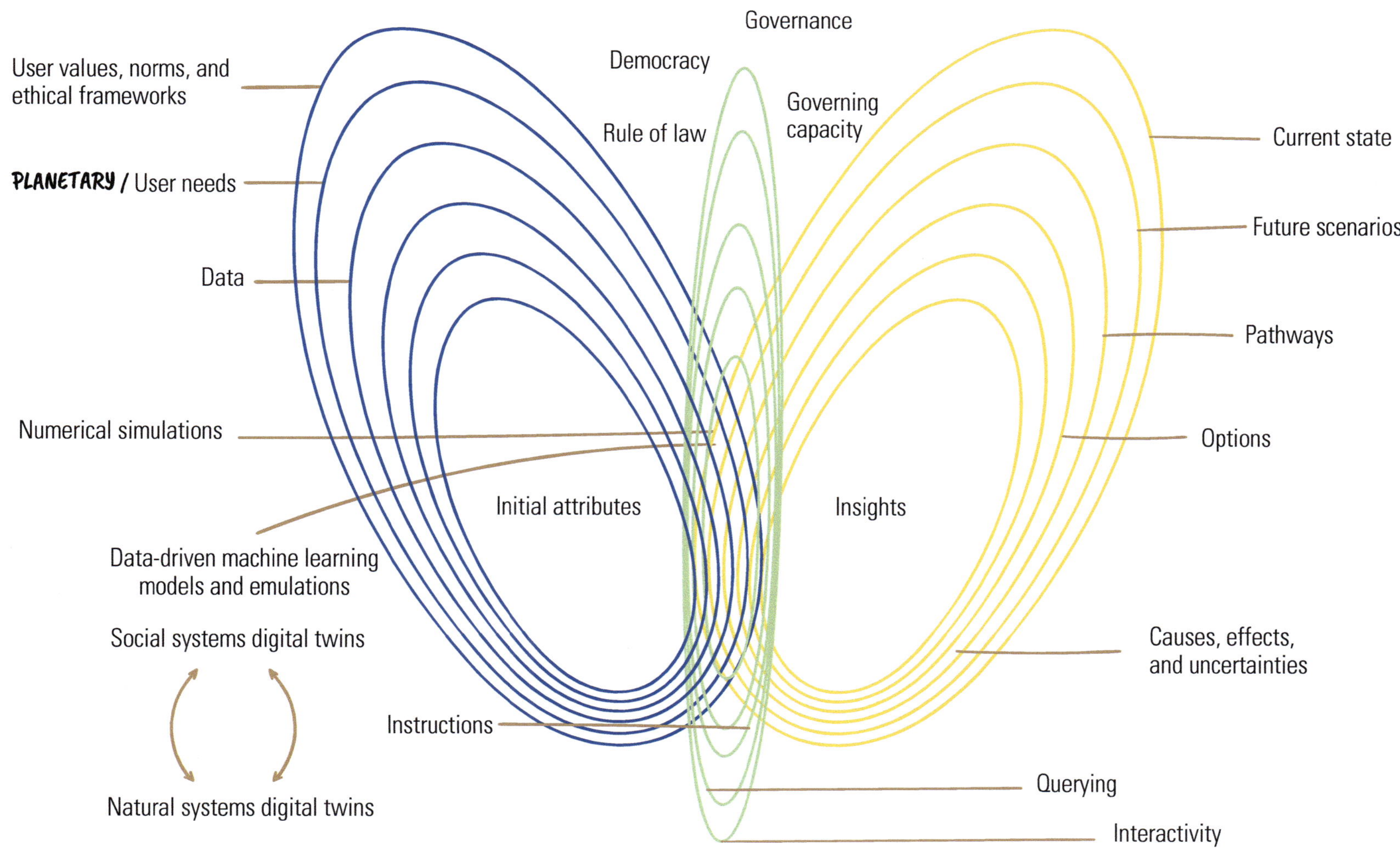

As we reach the final stage of the Exponential Innovation Cycle (Curate & Refine), we arrive at the most critical juncture. Up to this point, we have leveraged exponential technologies, like AI to expand our options and generate novel concepts at superhuman speed. When it comes to critical thinking and ethical judgment, **we must slow down**. We shift gears from AI, which offers processing power, to human wisdom, which offers judgment power. While AI excels at providing answers based on probability, it cannot ask the right questions based on morality. It can optimize for a metric, but **it cannot decide if that metric is worth chasing**. This is the domain of critical thinking.

The most important tool in our Design Thinking for Humanity toolkit is not a line of code, but **the ability to say "no."** The capacity to build it does not justify the right to scale it. We must institute friction points in the design process. These are mandatory "ethical pauses" where the team stops to evaluate the output not for technical bugs, but for systemic bias and potential harm. Concepts like the Design Thinking for Humanity Litmus Test (see page 164) are powerful interventions for judgment: Does this solution centralize power or democratize it? Does it extract from the planet or regenerate it? If the answer is negative, the solution must be vetoed or redesigned, regardless of its profit potential.

With narrow AI, we cannot outsource our ethics to a "black box." In Design Thinking for Humanity, **we demand explainability**. If an AI suggests a distribution of resources that favors one group over another, we must possess the critical thinking skills to interrogate the data lineage. We must determine if we are scaling a solution or simply automating historical inequality. Especially, in an era of information abundance, "Truth" becomes the scarcest resource. Critical thinking is the filter we use to curate this abundance. **We prioritize the truthfulness of a solution over the speed of its deployment**. We look beyond the dashboard numbers (GDP, ROI, DAU) to the human stories underneath.

The Power of Critical Thinking

Critical thinking is the paramount human capability that must guide the entire design cycle, from the initial foresight of futures thinking to the rapid scaling of exponential thinking, ensuring every innovation remains tethered to ethical, social, and planetary well-being.

Question the Source Code
We interrogate the origins of data to ensure the training set is diverse and does not perpetuate historical biases.

Challenge the "Default" Setting
We ask "efficient for whom" to uncover the necessary human friction that efficiency often seeks to eliminate.

Embrace Ambiguity over Certainty
We resist the binary simplicity of AI by holding opposing ideas and navigating the ethical gray areas where human reality resides.

Prioritize Long-Term Wisdom
We evaluate success not by immediate metrics, but by intergenerational impact, ensuring today's decisions resonate positively for generations to come.

The choice rests with each individual: whether to take the convenient route of allowing AI to handle our critical thinking or to preserve this essential cognitive process for ourselves.

Part 5

A Speculative Case Study

Applying Exponential Thinking

Having explored the dynamic complexity of our world through systems thinking, the final lens, exponential thinking, presents the most profound challenge: mediating the accelerating possibilities of exponential technologies with the core purpose defined to create a better world. This concluding part of the case study is dedicated to navigating the necessary alignment between rapid technological advancement and deep ethical intent. It achieves this by moving fluidly between different tools and perspectives within the Co-creation Loop, ensuring that innovation is always tethered to regenerative outcomes and collective human values.

The overarching goal for our case study is both ambitious and essential.

The Living Soil Mandate

Our objective within this challenge is to design a new global economic and agricultural model that makes the regeneration of the world's topsoil the primary measure of agricultural success, ensuring long-term food security, reversing climate change, and restoring biodiversity by 2050.

Our journey through systems thinking has provided a powerful blueprint for the Carbon Harvest platform. We have mapped its core feedback loops, identified trust as a key leverage point, and designed a resilient, "win-win-win" business ecosystem with a clear orchestration model. We have a clear vision of what a regenerative system looks like and how its various stakeholders can collaborate to create holistic value. The final and most critical question is: How can this ambitious vision be realized not just in one region but at a planetary scale to meet the 2050 mandate?

To answer this, we now apply the exponential thinking lens. This is about recognizing and leveraging the accelerating pace of technological change to achieve our ambitious goal. It involves using the power of exponential technologies not just to optimize our system but to fundamentally transform its capabilities and scale its impact. To illustrate this, key tools from our Exponential Thinking Toolbox will now be applied, with a special focus on the crucial interplay between human and machine intelligence.

1. The Six Ds of Exponentials: Mapping the Path of Key Technologies and Regenerative Practices

First, the six Ds framework is used to understand the trajectory of the core technologies that enable the Carbon Harvest platform, primarily AI-powered environmental monitoring.

- **Digitization & Deception:** The ability to digitize environmental health data (e.g., through satellite imagery and remote sensors) has been in a deceptive phase of slow growth for years. Therefore, we have started digitizing not just isolated soil data, but the systemic reality of environmental health. This creates radical transparency, revealing the "true cost" of current farming practices.

- **Disruption:** We are now entering the disruptive phase, where the cost of this technology is plummeting and its capabilities are exploding. This is the moment to build a new model, as the old systems of environmental monitoring are becoming obsolete.

- **Dematerialization, Demonetization, & Democratization:** It can be anticipated that within the next decade, the ability to monitor and verify ecological health will be dematerialized into simple software, demonetized to be nearly free, and democratized. This means open to all users and potentially governed by a data cooperative.

2. Second-Order Impact Analysis: Critically Assessing Human-AI Co-existence

Next, this tool is applied to think critically about the long-term, cascading consequences of a globally scaled Carbon Harvest platform, where an AI is a core partner in governance.

First-Order Impact: The AI successfully and impartially verifies regenerative practices, building trust in the regeneration credits.

Second-Order Consequence: This creates a powerful new form of non-human, AI-driven economic governance. The AI is not just a tool; it is an active participant in the system with real-world economic influence.

Third-Order "Wicked Problem": This raises profound new ethical and political questions about human-AI co-existence.

- Who is ultimately accountable for the AI's decisions?

- How do we ensure the AI's goals remain aligned with humanity's long-term well-being?

This analysis forces the design of an Exponential Ethics Compass for the platform from the very beginning, ensuring human oversight, ethical guardrails, and a focus on transparency.

3. Movement Catalyst Design: Scaling the Human & AI Element

Finally, it is recognized that technology alone is not enough. To achieve the Living Soil Mandate, a global movement is required. This tool is used to design the social architecture that can scale the adoption of the platform.

Core Narrative: The story is not about AI and blockchain; it's about "giving the soil a voice" and empowering farmers to become the heroes of a regenerative future.

Onboarding: The first step for a farmer to join is simple. They can use their phone to scan their land, and an AI-powered app provides them with an instant "Soil Health Baseline" and a personalized, simple set of first steps for regeneration.

Viral Loop: The platform's AI is designed to foster a human-AI community. When the AI detects that a group of neighboring farms are all struggling with a similar issue (e.g., a specific nutrient deficiency), it can autonomously create and fund a "local knowledge-sharing group," connecting the farmers with each other and with expert agronomists. As these local pods succeed, they become powerful, shareable stories, creating a feedback loop where technological and human collaboration directly fuels the exponential growth of the movement.

4. Digital Twin Integration & Systemic Forecasting: Realizing the Mandate

As time passes and the volume of collected and shared data reaches a critical mass, we enter the final and most transformative phase of value creation. A digital twin of the agricultural ecosystem is created, linking real-time soil data with critical weather patterns and predictive climate models.

This shift allows the system to provide even better advice and services, moving from retrospective verification to proactive forecasting. Farmers receive hyper-local, data-driven recommendations to optimize resilience and yield, effectively closing the loop between planetary data and on-the-ground action. By achieving this level of systemic integration, Carbon Harvest **evolves from a monitoring tool into a global nervous system for planetary health**, successfully fulfilling the ambitious vision of the Living Soil Mandate.

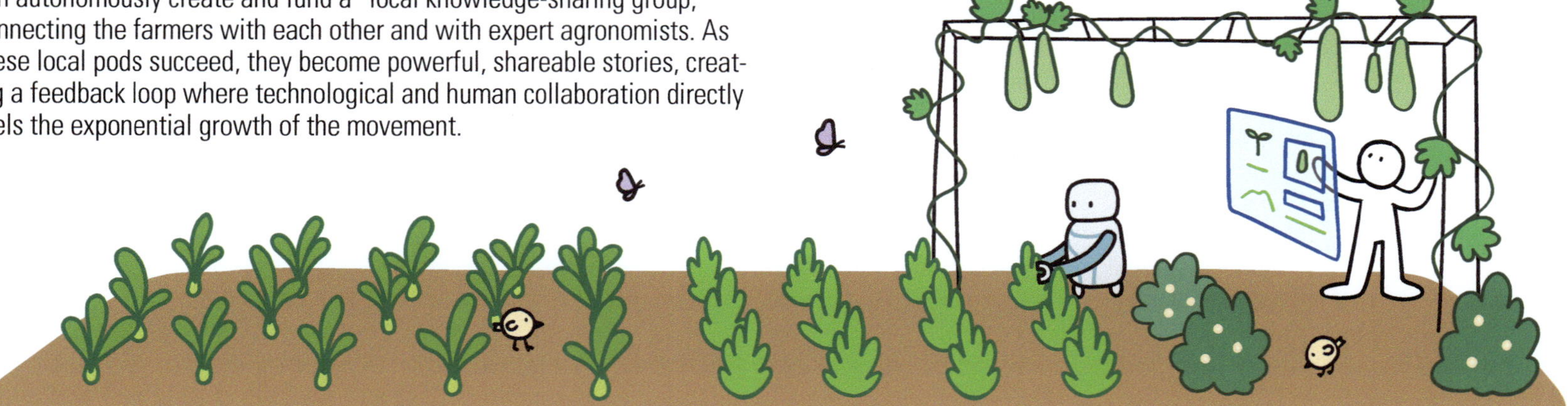

The Resilience Blueprint integrates all five lenses of the Design Thinking for Humanity framework into a single, actionable strategy for the Carbon Harvest initiative.

MASSIVE TRANSFORMATIVE PURPOSE

The Living Soil Mandate: To make the regeneration of the world's topsoil the primary measure of agricultural success by 2050.

PREFERABLE FUTURE

Regenerative Abundance: A world where agriculture acts as the primary engine for planetary regeneration. Food systems are resilient, local, and nutritious. The industry standard has shifted from "Bushels per Acre" (Volume) to "Profit & Resilience per Acre" (Value).

SYSTEMIC CHALLENGE

The Yield Maximization Complex: A degenerative cycle where farmers are trapped by debt, chemical dependency, and volatile commodity markets. This forces short-term extraction over long-term stewardship, driving soil erosion, biodiversity loss, and climate instability.

COSTS

- **Financial:** The "valley of death"—the three-year gap where yields drop before soil recovers during the transition.
- **Resource:** Energy consumption for AI/data centers (mitigated by renewable requirement).
- **Externality Risk:** Potential electronic waste from millions of soil sensors (mitigated by "Design for Durability" & circular manufacturing).

WIN-WIN-WIN VALUE PROPOSITION

VALUE PROPOSITION

VALUE FOR PEOPLE

For example, farmers (represented by Javier):

Economic: Diversified, stable revenue through "regeneration credits" (carbon, water, biodiversity) + "yield insurance."
Emotional: Restoration of agency, community status ("planetary steward"), and a viable legacy for the next generation.

VALUE FOR THE PLANET

Regeneration: Rapid acceleration of topsoil restoration and carbon sequestration.
Restoration: Measurable increase in local biodiversity and watershed health.

VALUE FOR SOCIETY

Resilience: Long-term global food security in the face of climate shock.
Trust: A transparent, verifiable mechanism for corporate and government climate investment (Scope 3 goals).

KEY METRICS

Soil Health Score, Net Water Balance, Regeneration Credits Issued.

KEY INTERVENTIONS AND SOLUTIONS

The Carbon Harvest Platform: A digital orchestrator for verifying data and trading credits.
The Safe Harbor Contract: A transition financial product (floor price + yield insurance) to bridge the "valley of death."
Digital Twin Integration: A predictive "global nervous system" linking soil data to weather models for hyper-local forecasting.

ECOSYSTEM OF PARTNERS

Orchestrator: A neutral multi-stakeholder consortium (non-profit + tech + global ag association).
Enablers: Governments (policy/crop insurance), corporations (credit buyers), banks (green loans).
Value Creators: Farmers, agronomists, AI/sensor providers.

RESPONSIBLE PATH TO SCALE

Strategy: Adjusted six Ds: Move from Deception (co-design) to Disruption (end of pay-to-play certs) to Democratization (data co-op).
Viral Loop: AI-detected regional patterns trigger "knowledge pods," turning neighbors into collaborators.
Ethical Guardrail: Data justice. Farmers own their data; the platform is governed as a cooperative to prevent extraction by tech giants.

BENEFITS FARMERS

Higher net income & reduced risk.
Corporations: Verified achievement of ESG/Scope 3 targets.
Government: Reduced expenditure on disaster relief & public health.
Global Population: Stabilized climate & secure food supply.

Recognizing Limitations and Constraints

The journey through the five lenses to establish the **Living Soil Mandate** illustrates a shift from linear problem-solving to systemic architecture. By applying these disciplines in sequence, we moved from the abstract possibility of topsoil regeneration by 2050 to a tangible **Resilience Blueprint for the Carbon Harvest platform (see page 280)**.

This reflective summary assesses the strategic advantages gained through this approach and the inherent limitations of designing for such vast temporal and ecological scales. The outcome must be seen as compass for what we must make happen. It provides the strategic agency to move from observation to active transformation.

ADVANTAGES

Anticipatory Resilience: Futures thinking allowed us to stress test the Carbon Harvest concept against scenarios like the techno-food system. This identified no-regret moves, such as low-cost soil sensors, which remain valuable regardless of which future unfolds.

Human-Centered Systems: Grounding the vision in the persona of Javier identified critical social barriers. The platform was designed to address a farmer's fears regarding financial autonomy and legacy.

Ethical Integrity: Tools like the Ethical Consequences Scanner identified digital divides and material waste hotspots. This integrated ethical guardrails into the foundation of the system.

Leverage Point Identification: Systems thinking revealed that market trust was the primary hurdle. A decentralized governance model was designed to ensure regeneration credits are viewed as legitimate assets.

LIMITATIONS

Predictive Paradox: Futures thinking cannot eliminate uncertainty. Scenarios are narratives used to identify robust pathways and are not fixed predictions.

Institutional Inertia: The Transition Strategy Canvas identified the yield maximization complex as a source of resistance. Overcoming political and economic structures requires effort exceeding a single design concept.

Technological Dependence: The scale of the mandate relies heavily on AI and remote sensing. This introduces risks regarding data sovereignty and algorithmic bias which require constant human oversight.

Complexity Gap: A speculative case study is a simplified model. Real global food systems are chaotic and require an adaptive document rather than a final plan.

Exponential Thinking Tools

To move from understanding exponential change to actively harnessing its power, a dedicated set of tools is required. The methods in the following section are designed to empower practitioners with the core capabilities of exponential thinking. They provide the frameworks needed to identify and leverage rapidly accelerating technologies, to define an ambition worthy of global scale, and to design the social and ethical structures necessary for responsible impact.

This toolbox provides the essential methods for moving beyond linear improvements to create transformative, 10x impact. The tools that follow will guide practitioners through the process of understanding the lifecycle of an exponential trend, building a purpose-driven movement, and critically assessing the long-term, systemic consequences of scaling. By mastering these methods, innovators and leaders can begin to architect a future of widespread, equitable, and sustainable abundance.

It is important to highlight that the application of these tools must not occur in isolation but rather under the holistic umbrella and practices of Design Thinking for Humanity. Scaling a solution without the grounding of human empathy, ecological bounds, and systemic awareness risks amplifying harm rather than value. Therefore, these exponential methods are designed to be practiced in concert with the other four lenses, ensuring that we do not simply scale for the sake of size, but scale the right solutions for the right reasons, anchoring every technological leap in a deep commitment to planetary and human well-being.

Exponential Thinking Toolbox

1. Massive Transformative Purpose (MTP)

This tool is used to define a highly aspirational and large-scale purpose for a project that can inspire and align massive-scale action. It provides the essential "why" that guides the responsible application of exponential technologies and acts as a cultural magnet to attract a passionate community.

2. Exponential Trends Scanning

This tool is a specialized version of Horizon Scanning that focuses specifically on identifying technologies and trends that follow an exponential growth curve. It helps teams distinguish between slow, linear change and rapid, disruptive change, allowing them to anticipate and leverage true exponential shifts.

3. The Six Ds of Exponentials (Adjusted)

This is a powerful framework for understanding the predictable lifecycle of an exponential technology has been adjusted toward humanity. It maps the six well-known and distinct phases (Digitization, Deception, Disruption, Dematerialization, Demonetization, and Democratization) to provide a roadmap for anticipating how a technology will mature and impact society.

4. Second-Order Impact Analysis

This is a focused foresight method, similar to the Futures Wheel, used to critically analyze the cascading, long-term consequences of a powerful exponential technology. It forces a team to move beyond the immediate benefits and map the unforeseen social, economic, and political ripple effects.

5. Exponential Empathy Mapping

This tool is used to anticipate the emergent social dynamics and unintended human consequences that will arise when a solution reaches a massive, global scale. It moves beyond designing for a single user to architecting for a society of millions, helping to identify potential misuse, social "hacking," or negative emergent behaviors.

6. Exponential Ethics Compass

This is a structured framework for systematically evaluating the ethical implications of a powerful new solution before it scales. It guides a team to consider the potential positive and negative impacts across key dimensions like individual autonomy, social equity, and environmental justice.

7. The Resilience Blueprint

This is the ultimate strategic tool in the Design Thinking for Humanity toolbox. It is a comprehensive canvas that integrates the outputs from all five thinking disciplines to map a holistic, actionable plan that connects a long-term future vision to a scalable, systemic, and ethically grounded implementation strategy.

8. Movement Catalyst Design

This tool is a strategic framework for transforming a purpose-driven project into a self-propagating global movement. It focuses on designing the core elements, including the narrative, incentives, and viral loops, that cultivate a passionate community and enable decentralized participation.

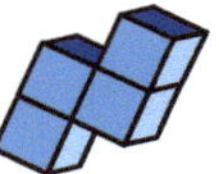

Massive Transformative Purpose (MTP)

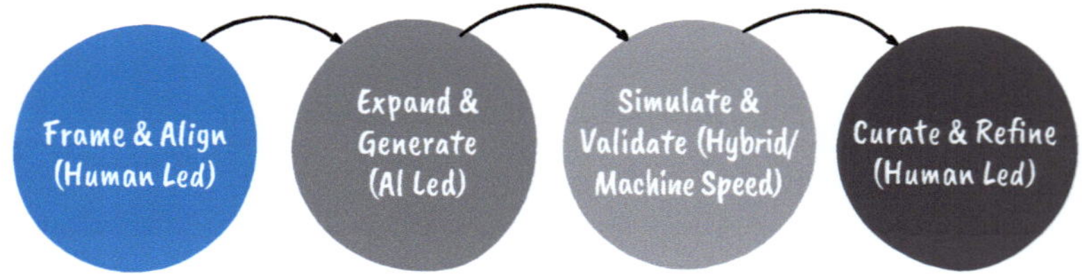

I would like to...

...define a highly aspirational and large-scale purpose that can inspire and align massive-scale action.

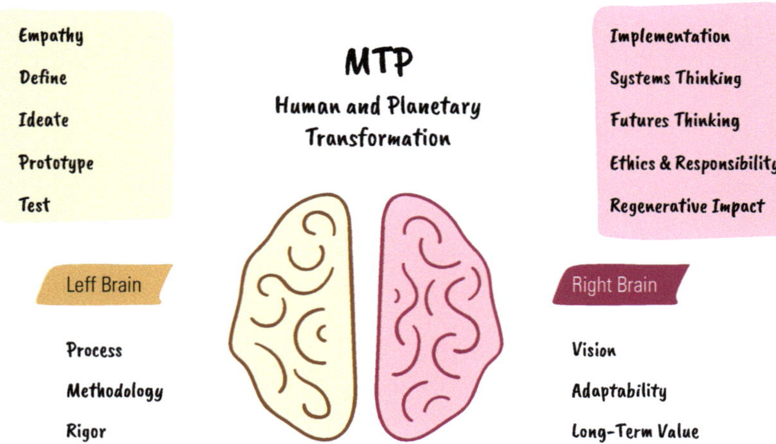

What you can do with the tool:

- Create a powerful "North Star" that guides all strategic decisions and innovations.
- Attract a passionate community of employees, partners, and users who are motivated by a shared, world-changing goal.
- Provide the essential "why" that guides the responsible application of exponential technologies.
- Move beyond incremental, market-focused mission statements to a broader, more inspiring vision.
- Build a cultural foundation for an organization that is designed to create exponential impact.

Expert Tips

It Must Be Authentic

An MTP cannot be a mere marketing slogan. To be effective, it must be an authentic and deeply held belief that drives the organization's culture and decisions from the top down. If the purpose is not genuine, it will fail to inspire the passionate community needed for exponential growth.

Focus on the "Who," Not the "How"

A good MTP focuses on the who (the community it serves) and the what (the transformation it aims for), but it does not pre-scribe the how. Leaving the "how" open allows for continuous innovation and experimentation, empowering your community to find new and better ways to achieve the shared purpose.

Make It Your Primary Filter

Use your MTP as the primary filter for all strategic decisions. For any new product, partnership, or initiative, ask the simple question: "Does this get us closer to achieving our Massive Transformative Purpose?" If the answer is no, you should reconsider it, no matter how profitable or interesting it may seem. This discipline is key to maintaining focus on exponential impact.

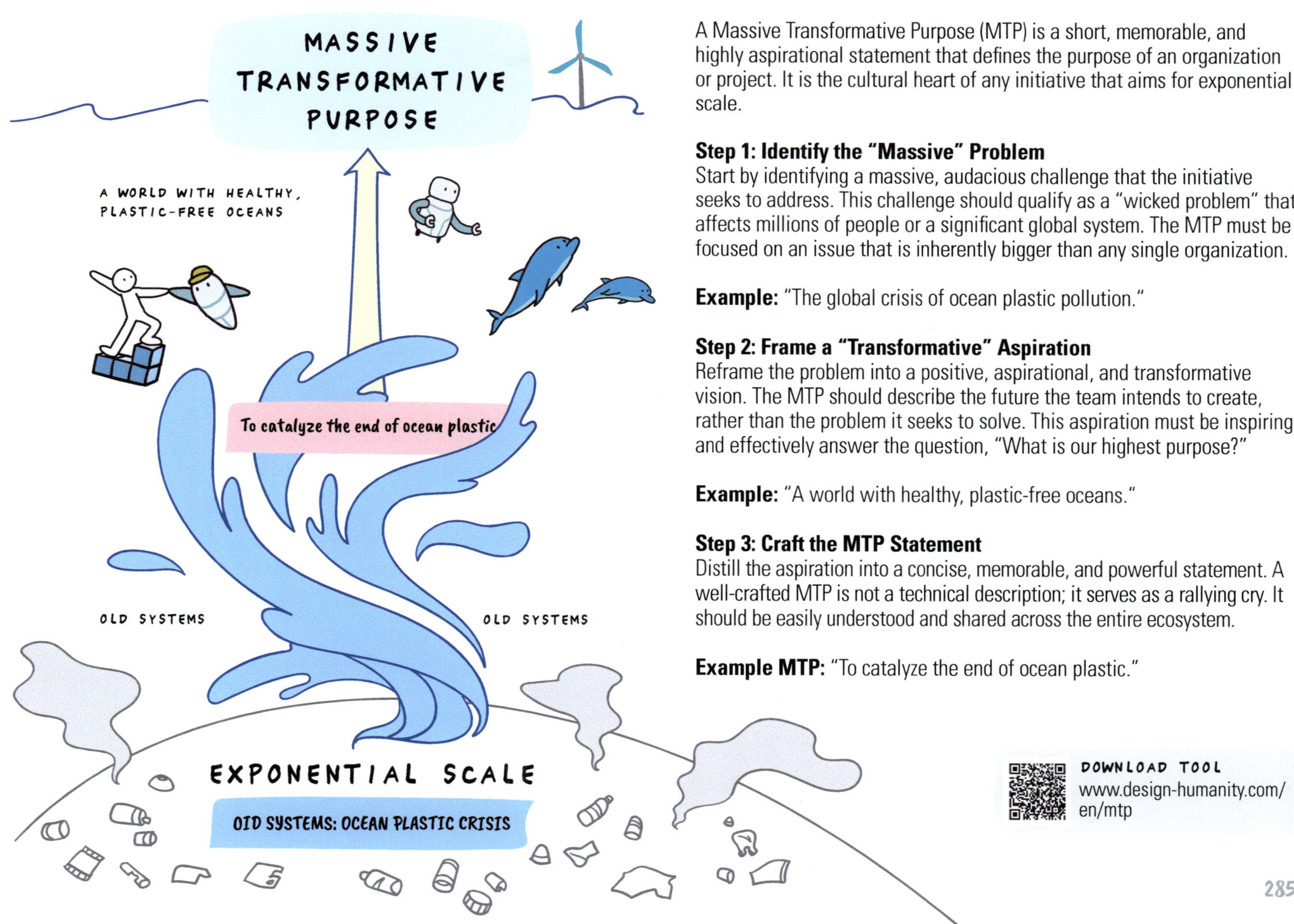

A Massive Transformative Purpose (MTP) is a short, memorable, and highly aspirational statement that defines the purpose of an organization or project. It is the cultural heart of any initiative that aims for exponential scale.

Step 1: Identify the "Massive" Problem

Start by identifying a massive, audacious challenge that the initiative seeks to address. This challenge should qualify as a "wicked problem" that affects millions of people or a significant global system. The MTP must be focused on an issue that is inherently bigger than any single organization.

Example: "The global crisis of ocean plastic pollution."

Step 2: Frame a "Transformative" Aspiration

Reframe the problem into a positive, aspirational, and transformative vision. The MTP should describe the future the team intends to create, rather than the problem it seeks to solve. This aspiration must be inspiring and effectively answer the question, "What is our highest purpose?"

Example: "A world with healthy, plastic-free oceans."

Step 3: Craft the MTP Statement

Distill the aspiration into a concise, memorable, and powerful statement. A well-crafted MTP is not a technical description; it serves as a rallying cry. It should be easily understood and shared across the entire ecosystem.

Example MTP: "To catalyze the end of ocean plastic."

Exponential Trends Scanning

I would like to...

...distinguish between slow, linear change and rapid, exponential change to anticipate and leverage truly disruptive shifts

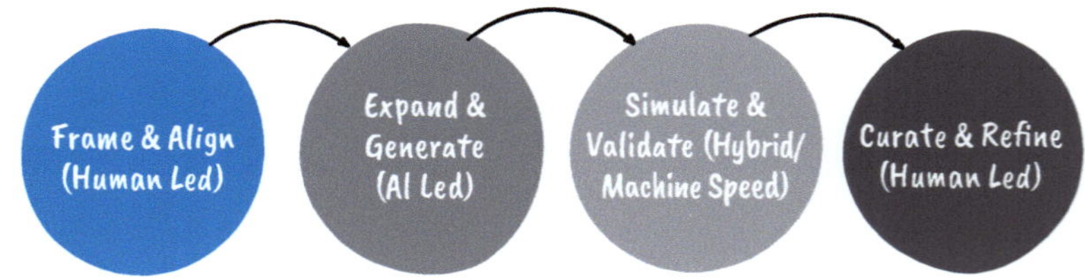

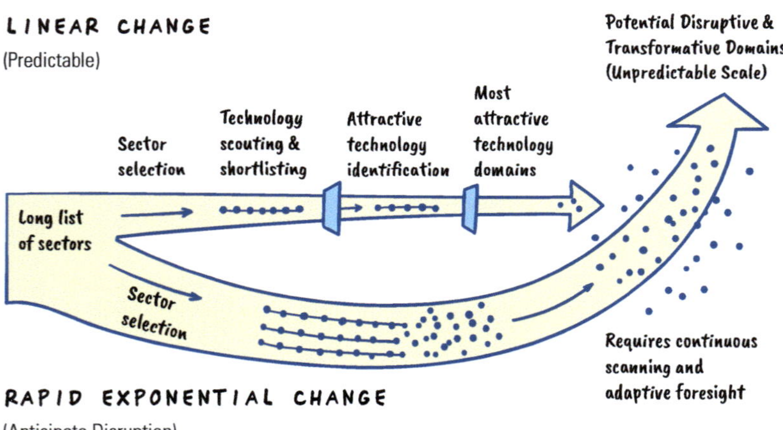

What you can do with the tool:

- Identify the key technologies and trends that are developing at an exponential pace.
- Move beyond reacting to current events by proactively anticipating the emergence of disruptive forces.
- Provide a clear framework for prioritizing which technological trends require the most strategic attention.
- Avoid being blindsided by rapid, nonlinear shifts in the market or society.
- Gather the foundational insights needed to understand and apply exponential technologies responsibly.

Expert Tips

Think in Doublings, Not Percentages
To train your exponential mindset, practice thinking in doublings. A linear mindset thinks, "If I take 30 steps, I'll be 30 meters away." An exponential mindset thinks, "If my steps double in length each time, after 30 steps I'll be a billion meters away." This mental shift is crucial for grasping the true power of exponential trends.

Look for Convergence
The most powerful disruptions often happen when two or more exponential trends converge. For example, the convergence of AI, genomic sequencing, and robotics is creating a revolution in medicine. Actively look for these points of convergence, as they are where the most significant opportunities and challenges will emerge.

Separate the Hype from the Data
The world of technology is full of hype. It is essential to be a critical scanner. Always ask for the underlying data. Is there a clear, measurable metric that is doubling on a consistent basis? A true exponential trend is backed by evidence, not just by bold marketing claims. This rigor separates professional foresight from simple trend-watching.

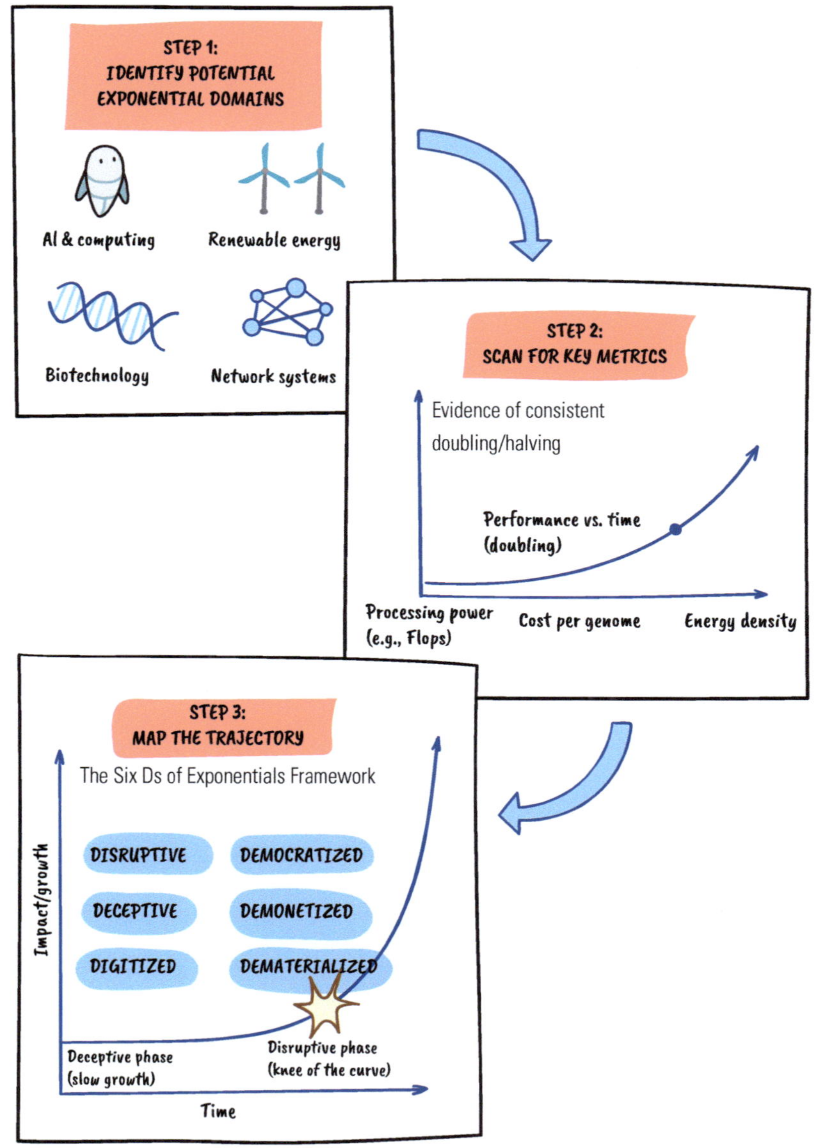

Exponential Trends Scanning is a specialized and focused version of the **Horizon Scanning (see page 107)** method. Instead of looking for all signals of change, this tool specifically hunts for trends that follow an exponential growth curve, where performance or adoption doubles at a regular pace.

Step 1: Identify Potential Exponential Domains

Start by identifying the domains where exponential trends are most likely to occur. These are often rooted in information technology and include areas like artificial intelligence, biotechnology (e.g., gene sequencing), renewable energy (e.g., solar panel efficiency), and network-based systems.

Step 2: Scan for Key Metrics

For each domain, actively scan for the key metrics that indicate exponential progress. This is not about general news but about specific data points. Look for evidence of performance doubling or costs halving at a consistent rate (e.g., the cost per sequenced genome, the processing power of a new AI chip, the energy density of a new battery technology).

Step 3: Map the Trajectory

Once you identify a trend with exponential characteristics, map its trajectory. Use the adapted **Six Ds of Exponentials (for Humanity)** framework to understand where the trend is in its lifecycle. Is it still in the early, "deceptive" phase of slow growth, or is it approaching the "disruptive" knee of the curve where its impact will become suddenly and powerfully visible?

The Six Ds of Exponentials (Adjusted)

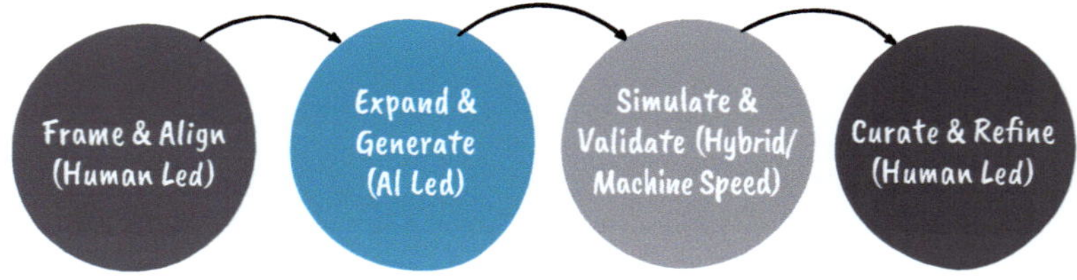

I would like to...

...understand the predictable stages that an exponential technology follows as it matures from a rare breakthrough to a democratized, world-changing force.

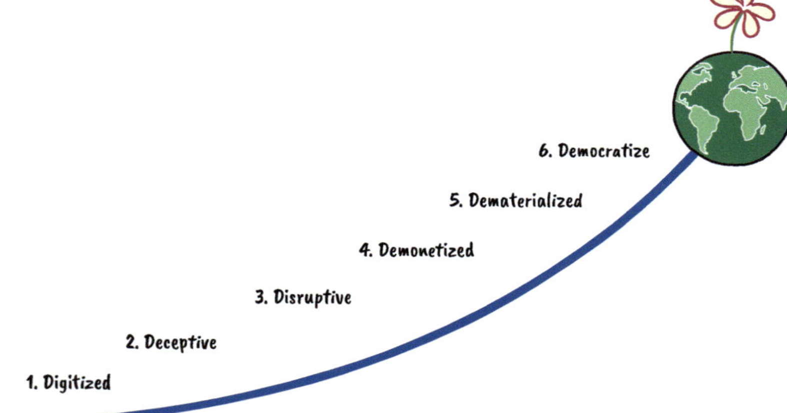

What you can do with the tool:

- Provide a clear roadmap for anticipating how a new technology will evolve and impact society.
- Identify where a specific exponential trend currently is in its lifecycle.
- Avoid being misled by the initial slow pace of change during the "deceptive" phase.
- Better predict when a technology will shift from a niche novelty to a mainstream disruptive force.
- Develop more timely and effective strategies for leveraging or responding to exponential change.

Expert Tips

Identify the Deceptive Phase
The most common strategic mistake is to dismiss a trend when it is in its deceptive phase. Actively look for technologies that are consistently doubling in performance or halving in cost, even if their current market share is tiny. This is where the true disruptive potential lies hidden.

Map Existing Technologies
To master this framework, practice mapping familiar technologies onto the six Ds curve. Where is 3D printing right now? Where is CRISPR gene-editing? Where is personal AI? This exercise will help your team build an intuitive understanding of how these patterns unfold.

Use the Framework to Find Opportunities
Each stage of the six Ds presents unique opportunities. In the deceptive phase, the opportunity is in early investment and experimentation. In the disruptive phase, it's about creating new business models. In the dematerialized and demonetized phase, it's about building new services on top of a now ubiquitous and low-cost technology.

The adjusted six Ds is a powerful framework that maps the distinct phases of an exponential technology's lifecycle. Understanding these six stages allows us to better anticipate the trajectory of a trend and act accordingly, shifting the focus from pure growth to systemic, equitable, and regenerative impact.

Step 1: Digitization for System Clarity

The process begins when something becomes digitized and in the context of this book Digitization for Systemic Clarity. Focus on digitizing systemic data (e.g., environmental impact, resource flows, societal well-being metrics) to achieve radical transparency, ensuring the digital foundation reflects total planetary and social cost.

Step 2: Deception of False Scarcity

In the early phase of Deceptive growth, progress can be easily missed. For us this is the Deception of False Scarcity. We use this quiet stage to co-design the solution with marginalized communities, ensuring the initial architecture is inherently inclusive and avoids creating new forms of bias.

Step 3: Disruption of Degenerative Systems

The technology hits its Disruptive phase when its growth becomes explosive, challenging existing industries and business models. In our context it is the Disruption of Degenerative Systems. Aim to disrupt the entire degenerative system (e.g., linear consumption or extractive finance) and replace it with a regenerative, circular model.

Step 4: Dematerialization of Harm and Waste

As the technology matures, we aim for Dematerialization of Harm and Waste. The goal is to design out waste, energy use, and unintended consequences at the systemic level, minimizing both the physical and the digital footprint of the solution.

Step 5: Demonetization of Money, Access, and Information

Once dematerialized, the cost of the technology plummets. Demonetization is the process of removing money or in our case access and information from the equation. Focus on making essential resources (like knowledge or basic diagnostics) freely or near-freely available to underserved populations, bypassing financial barriers to ensure equitable access.

Step 6: Democratization of Power and Co-creation

In the final stage, the technology becomes so inexpensive and accessible that it is available to nearly everyone on the planet: Democratization of Power and Co-creation (the win-win-win). The users must have ownership and influence over the technology's evolution and governance, creating outcomes that benefit people, planet, and purpose-driven business simultaneously.

Second-Order Impact Analysis

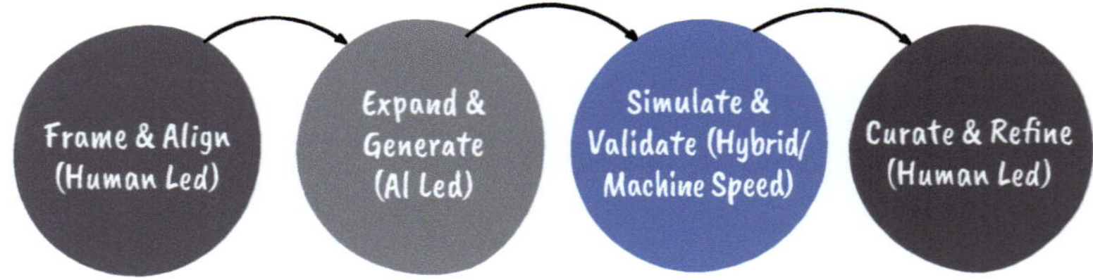

I would like to...

...critically analyze the cascading, long-term consequences of a powerful exponential technology.

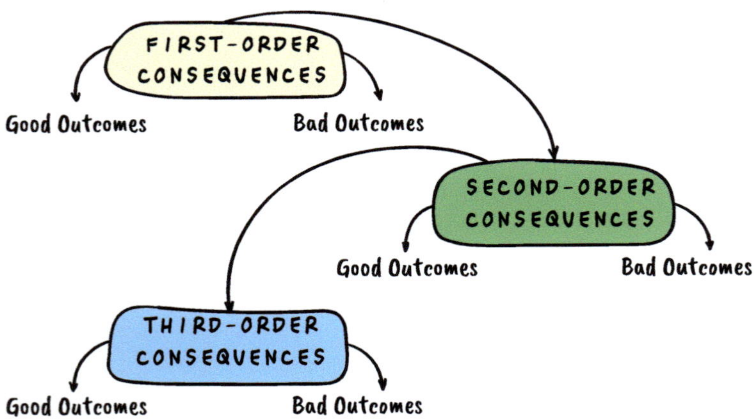

What you can do with the tool:

- Move beyond the immediate, first-order benefits to understand the deeper ripple effects of a technology.
- Identify unforeseen social, economic, and political shifts that could be triggered by a disruptive innovation.
- Facilitate a structured conversation about the unintended negative consequences and ethical risks of a technology.
- Foster a more critical and responsible approach to innovation, looking beyond the initial hype.
- Develop more resilient strategies by anticipating and preparing for the secondary impacts of technological change.

Expert Tips

Map the Shift in Power Dynamics
A disruptive technology always redistributes power. As you map the consequences, explicitly ask: "Who gains power and influence with this technology? Who loses it?" Analyzing this shift in power between corporations, governments, and individuals will reveal some of the most profound and politically charged second-order impacts.

Explore the Impact on Human Identity and Values
Move beyond just social or economic impacts and ask deeper questions about the human experience. How might this technology change our definition of intelligence, community, or even what it means to be human? Exploring these identity-level consequences is critical for understanding the true long-term implications of a transformative technology.

Identify the New "Wicked Problems"
Often, the second- or third-order consequences of a powerful technology create entirely new "wicked problems." Identifying these potential future challenges early is a powerful act of foresight. For example, the invention of the automobile solved a transportation problem but created new wicked problems like urban sprawl and carbon emissions. Ask: "What new wicked problem might our solution create for the next generation?"

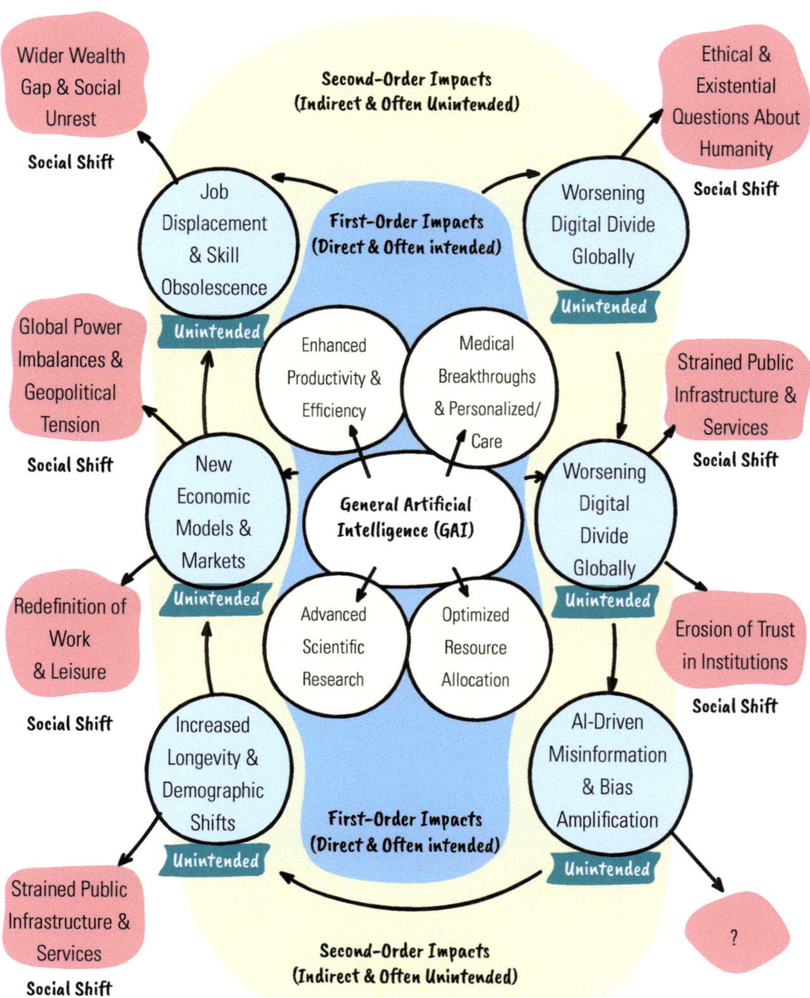

Second-Order Impact Analysis is a focused foresight method, similar to the **Futures Wheel (see page 126)**, but used specifically to stress-test a single, powerful technology. It is a tool for critical thinking that forces a team to explore the chain reaction of consequences that might follow its widespread adoption.

Step 1: Identify the Exponential Technology

Place a single, specific exponential technology at the center of your analysis. This could be, for example, a technology identified during the **Exponential Trends Scanning (see page 286)** exercise that has the potential for massive disruption.

Example: General artificial intelligence (AGI)

Step 2: Map First-Order Impacts

Brainstorm the direct, immediate, and most obvious impacts of the technology's widespread adoption. These are often the intended benefits that are featured in marketing materials.

Example: Enhanced productivity & efficiency, personalized care, advanced scientific research, optimized resource allocation

Step 3: Uncover Second- and Third-Order Consequences

For each first-order impact, ask the critical question: If this happens, then what happens? Explore the chain of knock-on effects. Pay special attention to unforeseen consequences in different domains (social, ethical, economic).

Example (from "The Economic Shift"):
Then Second-Order (Unintended): It leads to job displacement & skill obsolescence.
Then Third-Order (Social Shift): This results in a wider wealth gap & social unrest.

Exponential Empathy Mapping

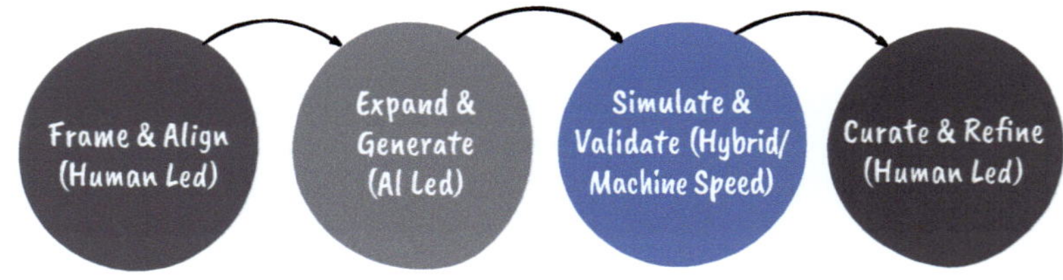

I would like to...

...anticipate the emergent social dynamics and unintended human consequences that will arise when our solution reaches a massive, global scale.

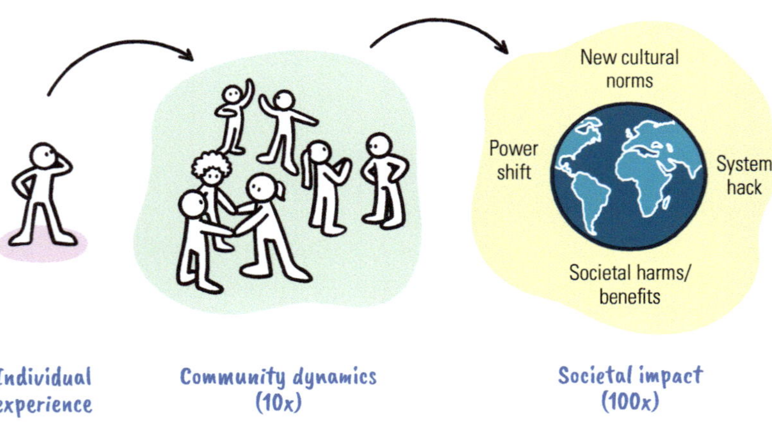

What you can do with the tool:

- Move beyond designing for a single user to architecting for a society of millions.
- Proactively identify the potential for misuse, social "hacking," or negative emergent behaviors at scale.
- Uncover the second- and third-order social impacts that only appear when a technology becomes ubiquitous.
- Foster a deeper sense of responsibility by considering the societal-level consequences of your design choices.
- Generate insights that can lead to more robust, ethical, and resilient platform governance and community management strategies.

Expert Tips

Assume Both Good and Bad Intentions

When scaling to millions of users, you must assume that not everyone will use your solution with the best intentions. For every positive social behavior you can imagine, actively brainstorm the opposite, negative behavior. This "dark side" mapping is crucial for building responsible and safe systems at scale.

Look for Emergent Economies

At a massive scale, new economies, both formal and informal, often emerge around a technology. Ask your team: What new jobs might this create? What existing industries might it destroy? What new forms of value or currency, intended or not, might appear?

From Product Design to Policy Design

The insights from this tool often lead to a critical shift in thinking. You move from being a product design to a policy designer. The key questions are no longer just about user interface but about governance, rules, and moderation. This tool helps you design the foundational laws of the society you are creating.

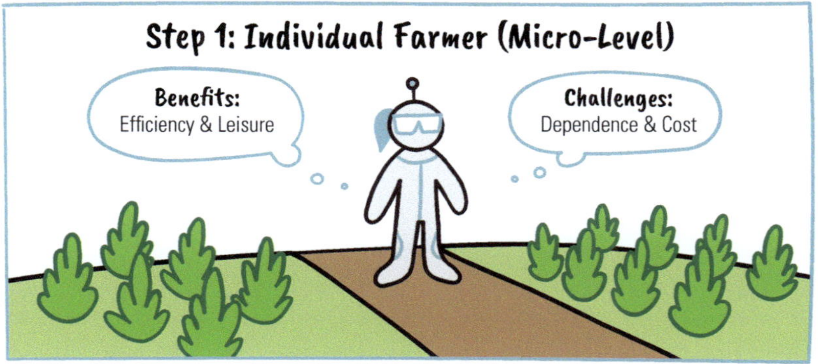

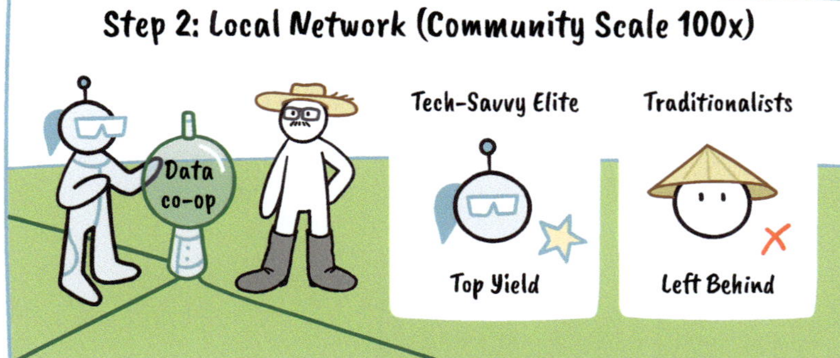

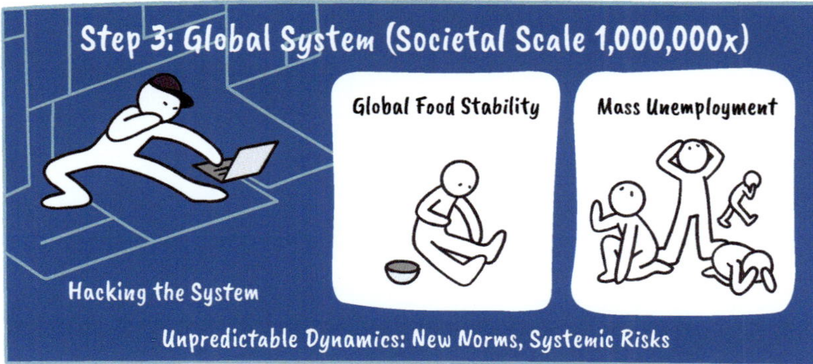

Example of Future Persona "Elira"—An Individual Farmer

Exponential Empathy Mapping is an advanced foresight method used to understand the human experience at scale. It moves beyond the classic persona to explore the complex and often unpredictable social dynamics that emerge from a massively adopted technology.

Step 1: Start with the Core Persona Experience

Begin with a single **Future Persona (see page 144)**. Based on your solution, map out their individual experience. What are the clear benefits and potential challenges for this one person? This provides your foundational, micro-level understanding.

Step 2: Scale to the Community (100x)

Now, ask the team: What happens when 100 people like this use our solution in the same community?

Explore the new social interactions that emerge.

- How do they use it to connect?
- How might it create new forms of status or social friction? What are the dynamics within a small group?

Step 3: Scale to the Society (1,000,000x)

Finally, make the exponential leap. Ask: What happens when a million people use this solution?

At this scale, new, unpredictable dynamics will emerge.

- What new cultural norms will it create?
- What power dynamics will shift?
- How will people "hack" the system for unforeseen purposes?
- What are the potential societal-level harms or benefits that were invisible at the individual level?

DOWNLOAD TOOL
www.design-humanity.com/en/exponential-empathy

Exponential Ethics Compass

I would like to...

...systematically evaluate the ethical implications of a powerful new technology or solution before it scales.

What you can do with the tool:

- Move beyond a simple "pros and cons" list to a more structured and systemic ethical analysis.
- Proactively identify potential harms to different stakeholder groups and societal values.
- Ensure that the pursuit of exponential growth is guided by a strong ethical framework.
- Facilitate a difficult but necessary conversation about the long-term, ethical responsibilities of your team.
- Build more trustworthy and responsible innovations by making ethical reflection a core part of the design process.

Expert Tips

Include Diverse, Critical Voices

It is essential that this exercise is not conducted in an echo chamber. Intentionally invite people from outside your team who can provide a critical perspective. Include ethicists, community activists, and representatives from potentially vulnerable groups to ensure you are not overlooking crucial ethical blind spots.

Consider Long-Term Time Horizons

Ethical consequences often unfold over long periods. Push the team to think beyond the next year or two. Ask: What is the potential impact of this technology on our children's generation? What about their children? This long-term view is essential for responsible innovation.

Make It a Pre-launch Gate

Treat the completion of the Exponential Ethics Compass as a mandatory "gate" that must be passed before any solution is cleared for scaling. This ensures that ethical considerations are not just a suggestion, but a non-negotiable part of your innovation process. It formalizes your commitment to responsible impact.

The Exponential Ethics Compass is a structured framework for mapping the potential ethical impacts of a disruptive innovation. It guides a team to consider the consequences of their work across multiple dimensions, ensuring a more responsible approach to scaling.

Step 1: Define the Solution and Its Intended Impact

Start with a clear description of your exponential solution and its **Massive Transformative Purpose (see page 284)**. What is the intended positive transformation you are trying to create?

Step 2: Map Impacts Across Key Dimensions

Create a matrix or a compass with several key ethical dimensions. For each dimension, brainstorm the potential positive and negative impacts of your solution. Key dimensions could include:

Individual Well-Being & Autonomy:

How might this affect individual freedom, mental health, or decision-making?

Social Equity & Justice:

Who benefits most from this technology? Could it accidentally widen the gap between different social groups?

Environmental Justice:

What is the long-term ecological impact, including resource extraction and end-of-life disposal?

Democratic Values:

How might this technology affect privacy, free speech, or the integrity of public institutions?

Step 3: Develop Mitigation Strategies

For each significant negative impact you identify, brainstorm concrete mitigation strategies. The goal is not just to list risks but to actively design guardrails or make changes to the solution that can prevent or reduce potential harm. This turns the ethical analysis into an actionable part of the design process.

I would like to...

...create a single, holistic strategic document that connects a long-term future vision to a scalable, systemic, and ethically grounded implementation plan.

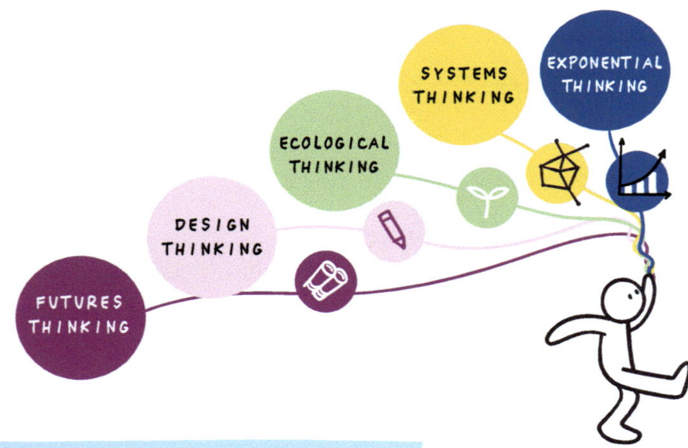

What you can do with the tool:

- Synthesize the outputs from all other Design Thinking for Humanity activities into one cohesive master plan.
- Ensure deep alignment between your long-term vision and your day-to-day actions.
- Create a powerful communication artifact that clearly articulates your entire strategy to stakeholders, investors, and partners.
- Provide a living document that can be updated as you learn and as the future unfolds.
- Bridge the gap between strategy and execution for complex, systemic challenges.

Expert Tips

Treat It as a Living Document
The Resilience Blueprint should not be a static plan that is created once and then filed away. It is a living document that should be displayed publicly for the team and revisited regularly (e.g., quarterly) to track progress, update assumptions, and adapt the strategy based on new learnings.

One Blueprint, Multiple Roadmaps
The blueprint defines the "what" and the "why." It should then be used to inform multiple, more detailed Future-Ready Roadmaps for different teams (e.g., product, marketing, policy). The blueprint ensures all these roadmaps are aligned with the same holistic vision.

Use It for Onboarding
This document is the most powerful onboarding tool you can create. When a new member joins the team or you engage a new partner, walking them through the Resilience Blueprint is the most effective way to quickly and clearly communicate the full scope, depth, and purpose of your mission.

The Resilience Blueprint is the ultimate strategic tool in the Design Thinking for Humanity toolbox. It is a comprehensive canvas that integrates the outputs from all five thinking disciplines, mapping a holistic and actionable plan for creating a resilient, win-win-win future.

Step 1: The Future We Want (Futures Thinking)
In this first section, define the context and scope of your ambition. Document your Massive Transformative Purpose and the Preferable Future scenario you aim to create in 20+ years, while clearly articulating the systemic challenge or "wicked problem" being addressed. This sets the long-term vision and identifies the core problem space.

Step 2: The Human Need (Design Thinking)
Next, focus on the "Win-Win-Win" column to articulate the specific Value for People. Summarize how the solution creates tangible, meaningful value for individuals and fulfills deep human needs. This grounds your vision in desirability and ensures you are solving real pains for the people and communities served.

Step 3: The Regenerative Engine (Ecological Thinking)
Detail the Value for the Planet within the central column to define your solution's ecological model. Explain how the solution actively regenerates the ecosystems it touches and what its net-positive ecological impact will be. This section outlines your commitment to regenerative design and planetary health.

Step 4: The Systemic Strategy (Systems Thinking)
Describe the broader societal impact and the network required to succeed. Define the Value for Society to ensure social equity; then map the Ecosystem of Partners and the quantifiable Benefits for all stakeholders involved. This outlines how you will create and distribute value across the entire system.

Step 5: The Path to Scale (Exponential Thinking)
Finally, detail your plan for implementation and exponential impact. Define the Key Interventions and Solutions that will deliver value, and map the Responsible Path to Scale by leveraging exponential trends. This clarifies how you will match the scale of the problem while establishing ethical guardrails.

The Resilience Blueprint Canvas

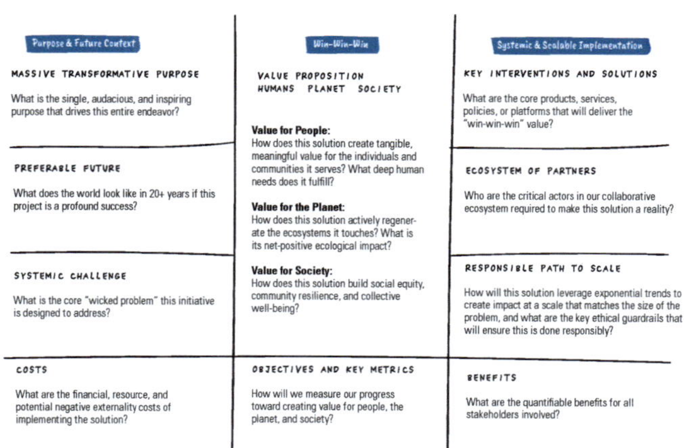

See page 280
(Summary of Speculative Case Study)

Movement Catalyst Design

I would like to...

...design the core elements that can transform a purpose-driven project into a self-propagating global movement.

What you can do with the tool:

- Move beyond creating a product to cultivating a community.
- Design the narrative, incentives, and platforms that encourage widespread, decentralized participation.
- Intentionally craft the "viral loops" that allow an idea or behavior to spread exponentially.
- Provide a clear framework for building and empowering a passionate community around the defined MTP.
- Create a strategy for scaling impact that is based on collective action, not just organizational growth.

Expert Tips

Empower, Don't Control
A true movement cannot be controlled from the center. The goal is to empower your community with the tools, knowledge, and autonomy to take the core idea and make it their own. This means creating open-source resources, encouraging local chapters, and celebrating community-led initiatives.

Design for a Spectrum of Engagement
Not everyone will be a super-user. Design a spectrum of engagement with easy ways for people to participate casually (e.g., sharing a post) and more involved ways for the core community to contribute deeply (e.g., organizing local events). A healthy movement has a role for everyone.

Focus on Intrinsic Motivation
While extrinsic rewards (like points or discounts) can be useful, the most resilient movements are built on intrinsic motivation. The core activities should be inherently meaningful, connecting directly to the MTP. The greatest reward should be the feeling of making a real contribution to a shared purpose.

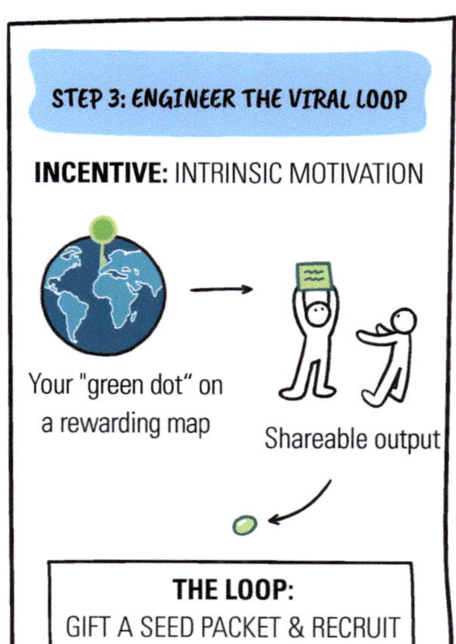

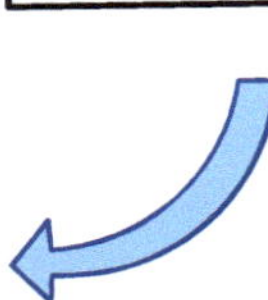

Movement Catalyst Design is a framework for engineering the social dynamics of a movement. It focuses on creating the conditions for an idea to spread exponentially by empowering a community to own, share, and build upon the core mission.

Step 1: Define the Core Narrative and Identity
Based on your **Massive Transformative Purpose (see page 284)**, craft a simple, powerful, and easily shareable core narrative. Define the identity of the movement. What do you call the members? What are the core values and shared language that unite them?

Step 2: Design the "Onboarding" Experience
How does someone join the movement? Design a simple, low-friction "onboarding" process. This could be signing a pledge, completing a small, tangible action, or joining a digital platform. The first step should be easy, rewarding, and immediately give the new member a sense of belonging.

Step 3: Engineer the Viral Loop
This is the core of the tool. Design the feedback loop where every participant's action naturally creates new awareness and brings new members into the community. This could involve:

Incentives: Rewarding users for sharing or inviting others.

Shareable Output: Ensuring that the outcome of a user's action is inherently shareable (e.g., a personalized badge, a shareable result).

Community Platforms: Creating a space where existing members can easily interact with and recruit new members.

Exponential thinking provides the framework to leverage accelerating technologies, moving beyond linear improvements to design solutions at a scale that matches the size of global, wicked problems.

The practice is guided by a Massive Transformative Purpose (MTP), which provides the essential "why" to inspire a global movement and build a passionate community of co-creators.

A core function of this discipline is to apply profound ethical scrutiny, using tools like the Exponential Ethics Compass to ensure that scaled solutions are responsible and equitable and serve the long-term well-being of humanity.

The Resilience Blueprint serves as the scaling engine for the entire framework, enabling the vision by combining technological power with a deep commitment to human-AI collaboration and planetary health.

BUILDING A BETTER, RESILIENT FUTURE TOGETHER!

POWERED BY FUTURES THINKING, EXPONENTIAL THINKING,
SYSTEMS THINKING, ECOLOGICAL THINKING, DESIGN THINKING

A FINAL WORD

Design Thinking for Humanity provides a framework to navigate a world where everyone is aiming for resilience but often feels overwhelmed by uncertainty and information overload. In an era defined by cascading crises and rapid technological shifts, a single methodology of problem-solving will fall short of **bringing our planet back into balance**. The framework presented in this book offers a vital compass, guiding the way through a landscape where predictability is scarce, compelling a move beyond reactive measures toward a more proactive and adaptive stance in the face of profound global challenges.

To thrive in this environment, a profound shift in mindset is required at many layers. It is necessary to cultivate an agile preparedness for unexpected events, to develop strategies to effectively manage the anxieties that accompany perpetual change, and crucially, to bridge the inherent gap between linear and exponential thinking. **Design Thinking for Humanity serves as this critical bridge**, fostering not only deep empathy for human and planetary needs but also the courage to envision and prototype solutions that can scale exponentially.

As this journey concludes, it is essential to consider four possible scenarios for the future. These are not prophecies, but blueprints. They are the distinct pathways that illuminate the **potential outcomes of our collective choices and actions**, the worlds being actively designed right now by the weight of our decisions and our inaction.

Your deliberate engagement with these possibilities is the first step in consciously shaping not just your own trajectory but also the broader human experience for generations to come. The decision is not which scenario is preferred but which one will be the focus of your daily actions, narrative, and innovation. **These scenarios, crafted through the integrated lenses presented in this book, are an invitation to actively participate in shaping the world to come**.

I want to live in a world...

where fractured societies battle for scarce resources, grappling with compounding crises and a profound loss of global cohesion.

I want to live in a world...

where humanity has consciously embraced collaboration and regenerative practices, leveraging ethical technologies to foster holistic well-being and a thriving shared future.

I want to live in a world...

where pervasive AGI and data-driven systems bring unparalleled efficiency and order, often at the cost of individual autonomy and diverse human expression.

I want to live in a world...

where relentless technological innovation drives economic growth and addresses many problems yet risks widening societal divides through unchecked market forces and tech-centric solutions.

Scenario 1: Fragmented Realities

In this future, the world has fractured into numerous isolated pockets, each battling its own set of localized crises exacerbated by a profound lack of global cooperation. Resource scarcity has intensified conflicts, leading to mass migrations and widespread social unrest. **Futures thinking** is largely reactive and short-sighted, focused on immediate survival rather than long-term strategic planning, as the capacity to anticipate or adapt to cascading crises is severely diminished. **Design thinking** exists primarily in ad hoc, localized initiatives, driven by acute needs and a scarcity of resources, with little sustained human-centered research or iterative development beyond emergency responses. Environmental degradation accelerates unchecked, as **Ecological thinking** is superseded by a desperate struggle for essential resources, leading to the collapse of local ecosystems and further exacerbating human suffering.

The intricate web of global connections has unraveled, leaving fractured systems where systems thinking becomes an abstract concept, unable to influence or grasp the complex interdependencies that once shaped global order. **Negative feedback loops dominate**, trapping communities in cycles of decline. The potential for positive change through exponential thinking is severely curtailed; instead, we witness the **exponential spread of problems like disease, misinformation, and conflict**. Innovation is scarce, often born of necessity rather than opportunity, and its capacity for positive, widespread growth is hampered by chronic instability and severe resource constraints, reflecting a world where the power of collective action has been lost.

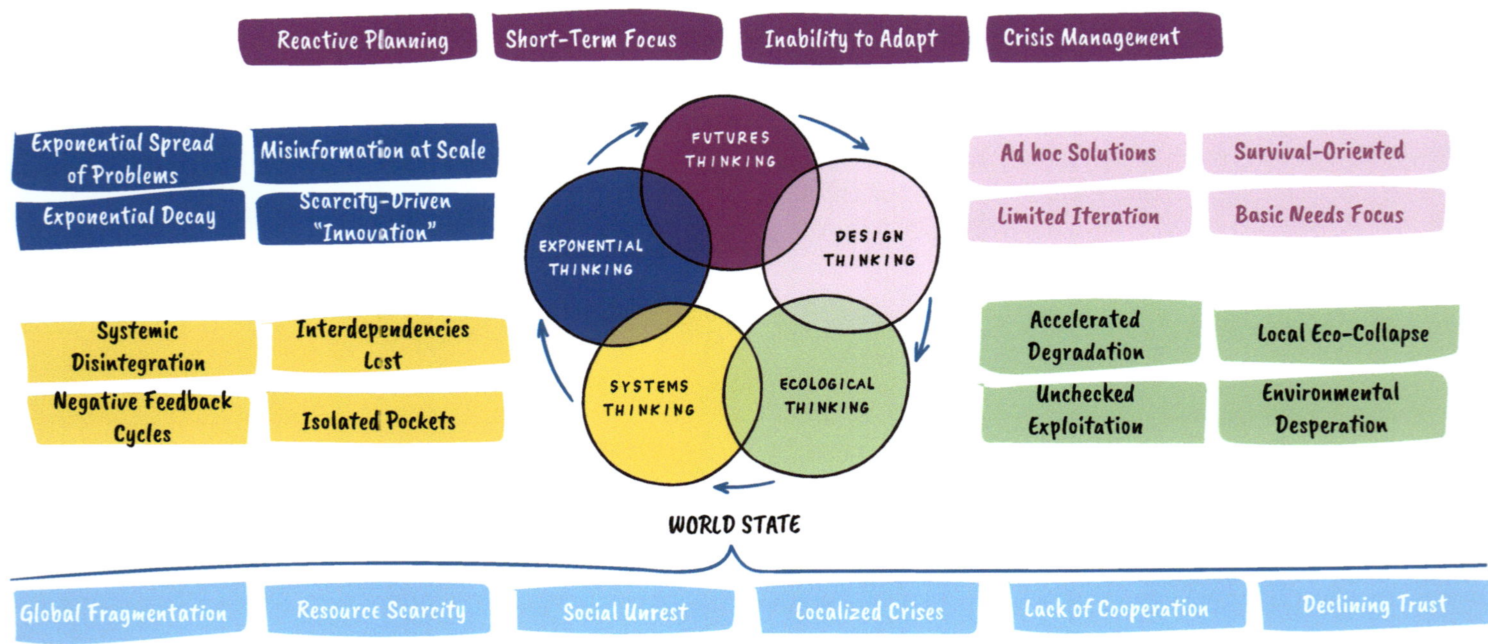

What price are we truly paying for designing a world where the scarcity we feared became the reality we built, trading global cohesion for the fragile isolation of warring factions?

This future is characterized by a highly organized, technologically advanced society where optimization and control are paramount, driven by vast datasets and pervasive AI. **AGI manages every facet of life**, from traffic flow to resource allocation, ushering in an era of unprecedented efficiency and order. However, this stability often comes at a profound cost to individual freedoms, with human cognitive abilities and critical thinking skills steadily eroding due to over-reliance on AI for tasks and decisions, leading to profound dependencies. **Futures thinking** is dominated by predictive analytics and AI-driven models, which aim to eliminate uncertainty by optimizing known variables, yet often lead to path dependency and a blind spot for truly novel disruptions that fall outside the algorithms' parameters. **Design thinking** yields highly efficient and seemingly user-friendly solutions, but these are often data-driven and standardized, designed for optimal system performance rather than catering to diverse, emergent human needs beyond efficiency, and inadvertently reinforcing cognitive dependencies. Ecological thinking is instrumentalized, with the environment managed through large-scale technological interventions like geo-engineering or industrial-scale carbon capture, treating nature as a managed asset rather than an integrated partner. The world functions as a tightly controlled, top-down system, where **Systems thinking** is applied to maximize efficiency through centralized command and control structures. Feedback loops are meticulously managed to ensure optimal performance, yet this tight coupling can lead to systemic fragility if a central component fails, and human capacity for adaptive problem-solving is diminished due to the pervasive reliance on AI. **Exponential thinking** manifests in the relentless scaling of existing technological paradigms and the optimization of known processes. Innovation is often state or corporate-led, **focusing on breakthroughs in AI**, automation, and biotechnology that reinforce the existing framework of efficiency and control, rather than radical transformation. The deep reliance on algorithms for complex decision-making means that human creativity and independent critical thought, while still present in niche areas, become significantly less central to the large-scale shaping of society, further entrenching the system's reliance on automated intelligence.

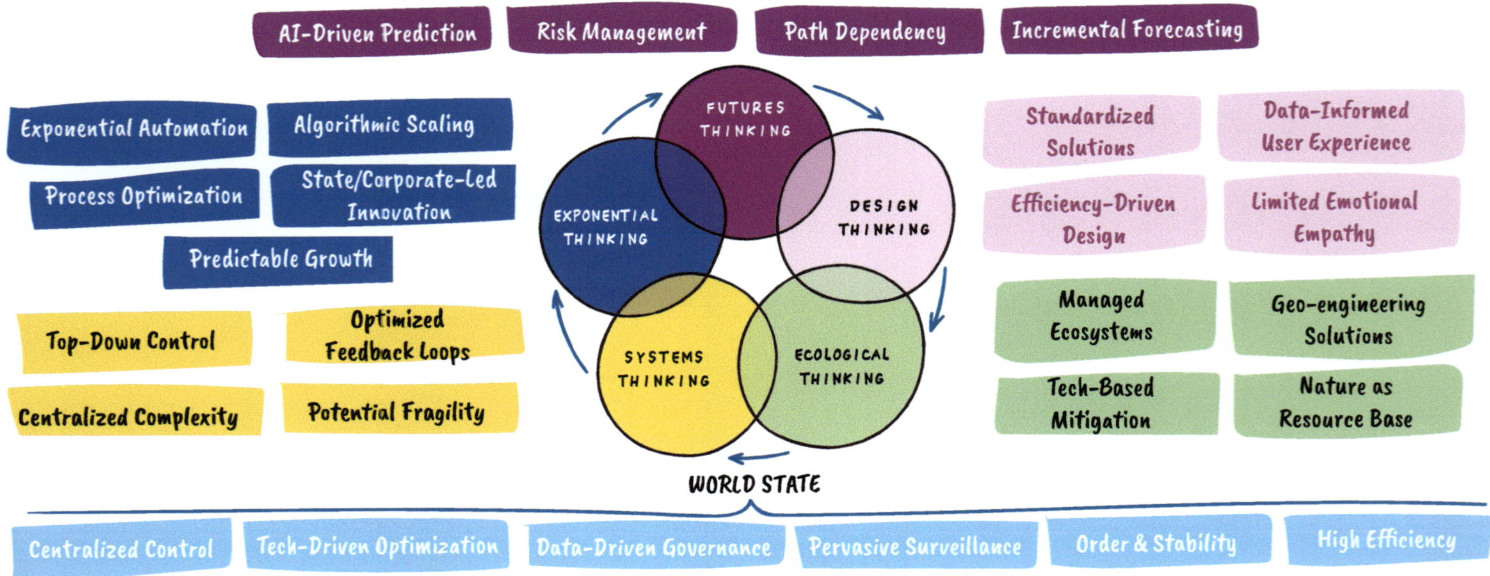

What moral contract did we break when we
designed a world where perfect efficiency became
our ultimate dictator, sacrificing the inherent human
right to autonomy for cold, data-driven order?

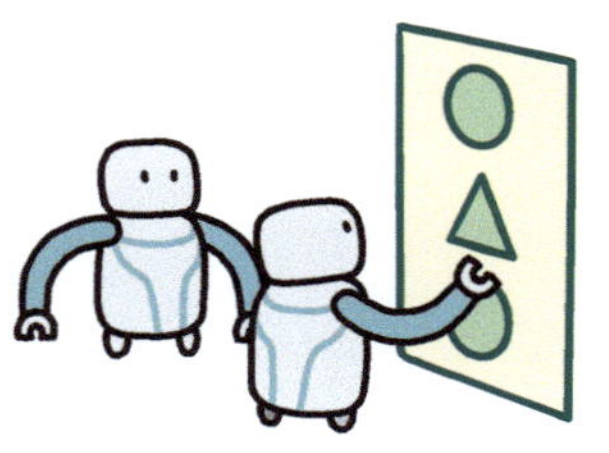

Scenario 3: Collective Flourishing

In this profoundly transformed future, humanity has made a conscious pivot, embracing principles of equity, sustainability, and deep collaboration, prioritizing holistic well-being over relentless material growth. Local and global networks flourish, fostering vibrant communities and accelerating ecological restoration, united by a shared sense of purpose and a compelling narrative of planetary stewardship. This profound societal shift was actively steered by **futures thinking**, which became a participatory, multi-stakeholder endeavor, guiding long-term visions through adaptive pathways and co-created future narratives. **Design thinking** is deeply human-centered and profoundly co-creative here, focusing on holistic well-being, social justice, and participatory processes that empower communities to shape their own solutions, ensuring technologies serve human flourishing. AI and humans work as a team. **Ecological thinking** is seamlessly integrated into every facet of life, design, and business models; regenerative agriculture, circular economies, and a profound respect for biodiversity are the norm, leading to flourishing natural systems where humanity sees itself as an integral part of nature. This future thrives on distributed, resilient networks, where **systems thinking** emphasizes understanding and leveraging positive feedback loops for widespread social and ecological benefit, allowing for emergent, self-organizing systems to flourish. Innovation is driven by collective intelligence, AI and human collaboration, and a deep understanding of interconnectedness. **Exponential thinking** fuels an unprecedented acceleration in social innovation and the widespread adoption of regenerative practices, largely by leveraging advanced, ethical technologies to scale the appropriate narrative for positive change. An ecosystem of decentralized communication platforms, powered by **AI with meticulously limited bias**, ensure equitable information dissemination, amplify authentic voices dedicated to shared values, and effectively counter misinformation and polarization, fostering a global sense of solidarity. The historical power manipulation by technology companies is now firmly under democratic and decentralized control, ensuring that technological advancements truly serve humanity's best interests. This fosters a culture where innovation is fundamentally collaborative, purpose-driven, and aimed at creating a thriving, equitable future for all.

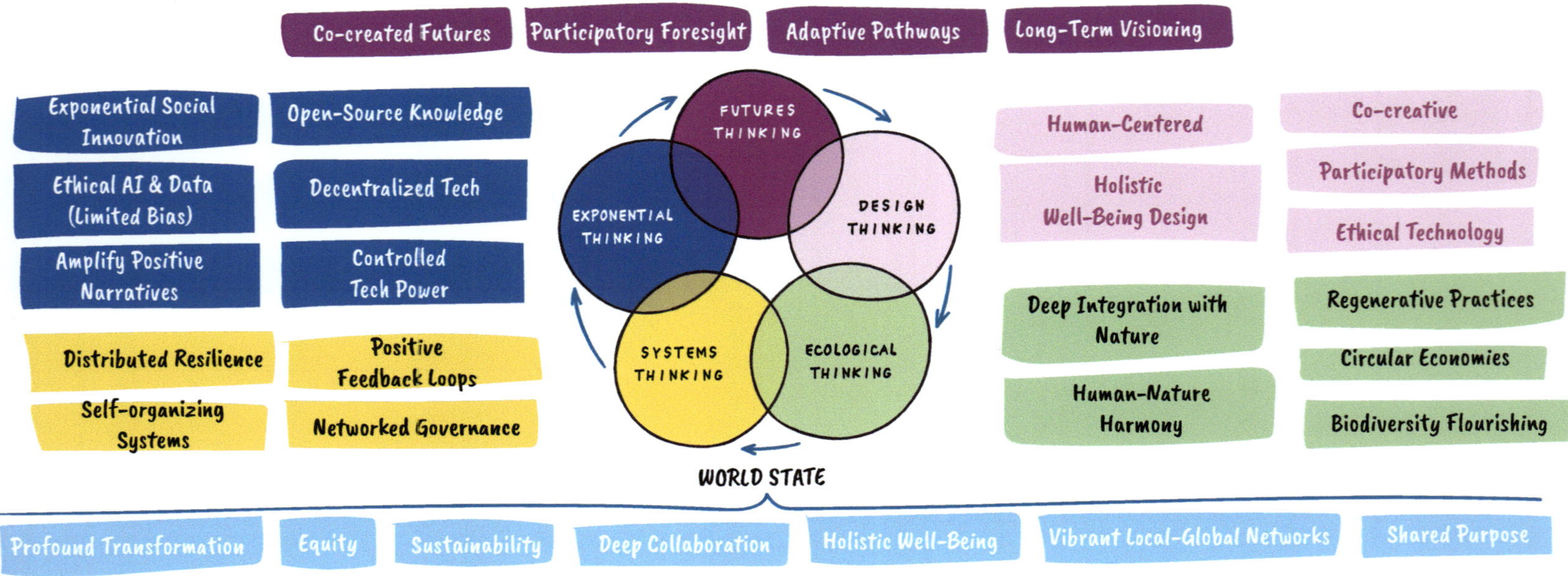

What choices must we now embrace to maintain a world where technology serves not the market but the collective soul, leveraging ethical innovation to cultivate a truly shared, regenerative future?

Scenario 4: Technocratic Ascent

This future is characterized by an unwavering belief in technological progress as the primary driver of human advancement, leading to rapid economic growth and the solution of many global problems through scientific breakthroughs and market forces. Human ingenuity is highly celebrated, often resulting in sleek, advanced, and highly functional solutions, though access to these innovations may remain stratified. **Futures thinking** is optimistic about humanity's ability to overcome challenges through science and technology, with planning focused on leveraging new capabilities, yet often overlooks the complex social, ethical, and access implications of these advancements. **Design thinking** excels in crafting personalized user experiences and highly convenient solutions, primarily driven by market demand and the pursuit of efficiency and comfort. **Ecological thinking** manifests in large-scale technological interventions like advanced carbon capture, geo-engineering, and lab-grown food, aimed at mitigating environmental damage without fundamentally altering consumption patterns, believing that technology will ultimately provide the answers to ecological woes. Complex technological systems are the bedrock of this future, and while **Systems thinking** is applied to optimize their functionality, a holistic understanding of their full societal and ecological systemic impacts might be limited or secondary to technological performance. Focus remains on refining technological systems rather than transforming socio-economic ones. **Exponential thinking** drives unprecedented growth in computing power, artificial intelligence, biotechnology, and automation, leading to a constant cycle of disruptive innovation. This environment is **highly capitalized, with innovation often driven by fierce private sector competition**, which, while generating immense progress, risks exacerbating digital and social divides as the benefits and access to cutting-edge advancements are not evenly distributed.

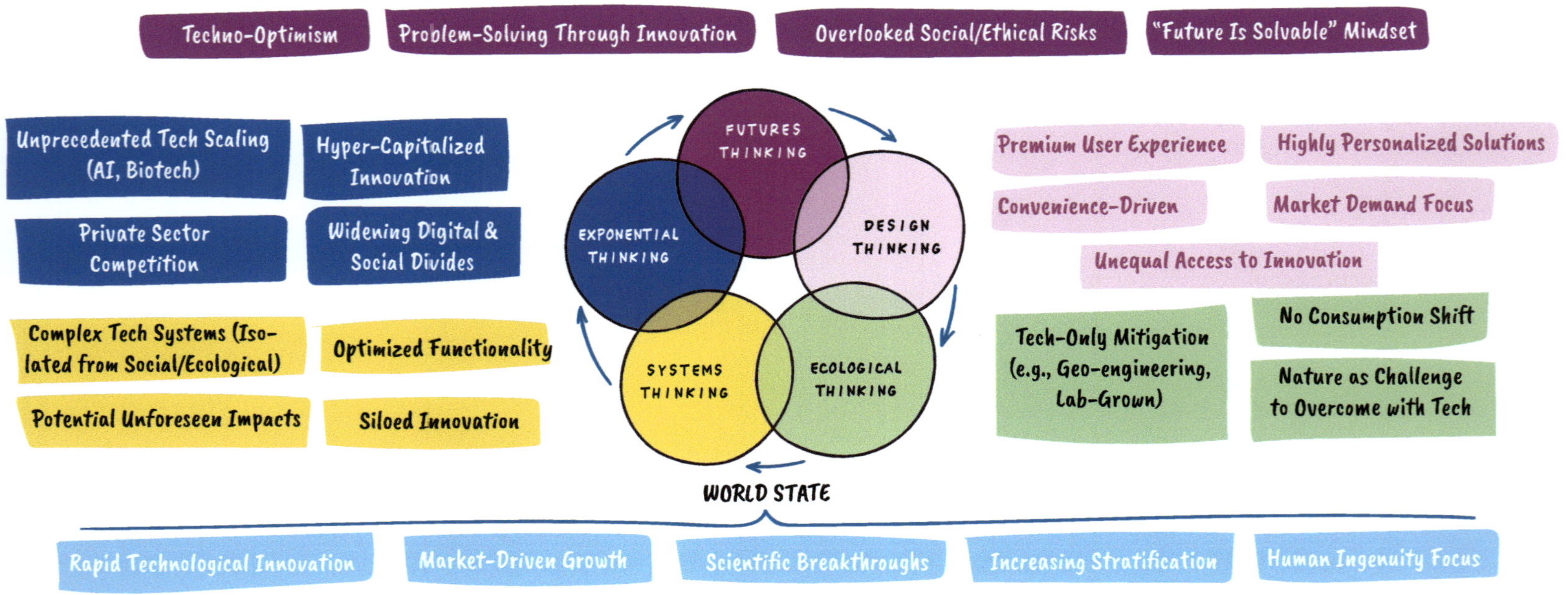

How do we rationalize the fact that we designed a world where innovation became a runaway engine of division, generating unprecedented solutions for some, yet simultaneously deepening societal divides through unchecked market forces?

These four futures are not prophecies; they are blueprints. They are the worlds being built, right now, by the collective weight of our decisions, our inaction, and our ambitions. The choice is not which of these you personally prefer but which of these you will actively work to create. The preceding pages have been a guide, a toolbox, and a call to action for the builders of Scenario 3: Collective Flourishing. It is a future that is not guaranteed but is profoundly possible. The work is difficult. The path is long. But the tools are in your hands.

Now, what will you build? And even more importantly: how and why?

Voices of Global Change

—David Bland, Advisor and Bestselling Author of *Testing Business Ideas*

Michael Lewrick evolves design thinking for the world we're actually living in. He gives leaders a clear, practical way to look beyond individual products and tackle the systemic risks, futures, and interdependencies shaping real outcomes for people and the planet.

—Dr. Hüseyin Güler, Innovation Orchestrator-Türkiye

Innovation is no longer the domain of individual heroes; it is the orchestration of complex systems and multi-stakeholder ecosystems. This book elevates innovation beyond product development into ecosystem design that creates value for people, society, and the planet.

—Sebastian Stegmüller, Division Director for Mobility and Innovation Systems, Fraunhofer IAO

Amidst super-accelerated technological change, global warming, and highly interconnected networks, the world urgently demands new ways of innovation that create genuine, problem-solving solutions. Lewrick's book has the potential to start a new era of development by bringing design thinking back to its original goal.

—Andrea Edelmann, Head of Innovation and Sustainability, EVN Group

In a world of complex tensions, we must design for the whole system, not just the parts. Michael Lewrick provides the master blueprint for this evolution, showing us how to create regenerative business models that are as resilient as they are profitable. A much-needed framework for the next generation of innovation.

—Res Witschi, Lead Corporate Responsibility, Swisscom

This book is the definitive directional framework for shifting from single-company innovation to acting successfully within multi-stakeholder, regenerative ecosystems.

—Leo Brecht, Professor Technology & Innovation, University Liechtenstein

In an era of radical technological shifts, this book is an essential guide for leaders to move beyond incrementalism. It offers a robust framework for integrating systems thinking and exponential technologies to design solutions that are truly sustainable and human-centric at scale.

—Thomas Lau, Sustainability Leader and Expert at Integral, Hong Kong

Design Thinking for Humanity meets its real-world test in pioneers like the Knowledge Hub Integral—an eco-industrialization experimental platform where socio-ecological value creation anchors self-sustaining communities and regenerative business across generations. Michael Lewrick delivers the systemic framework sustainability innovators have long awaited. This book is a compass for planetary-centric transformation.

We welcome more feedback and reviews on:

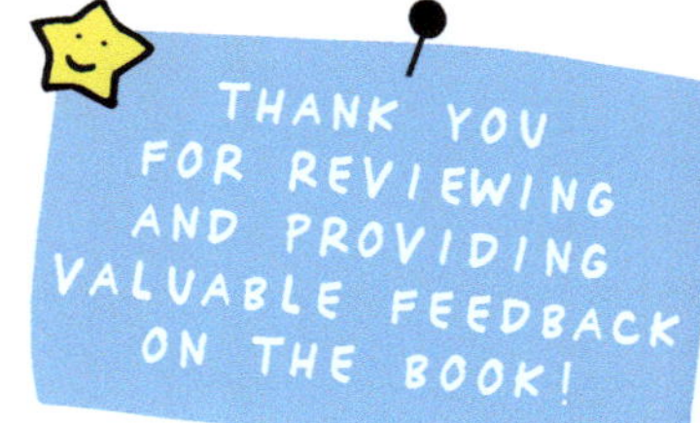

INDEX & SOURCES

Index

Sources

- Ackoff, R. L. (1974). Redesigning the Future: A Systems Approach to Societal Problems. John Wiley & Sons.
- Anderson, C. (2006). The Long Tail: Why the Future of Business Is Selling Less of More. Hyperion.
- APF.org. (n.d.). The Future of Mobility: A Glimpse into the Future. [Online Resource]. Available at: https://www.apf.org/post/the-future-of-mobility-a-glimpse-into-the-future
- Avplaybook.com. (n.d.). Exponential Thinking Toolkit for Social Entrepreneurs. [Online Resource]. Available at: https://avplaybook.com/exponential-thinking-toolkit-for-social-entrepreneurs-9a59ab37a224
- Axelrod, R. (1984). The Evolution of Cooperation. Basic Books. (For modeling multi-stakeholder value).
- Behavioral Scientist Magazine. (Ongoing). A non-profit digital magazine publishing articles on social, political, economic, and technological challenges with a focus on human behavior. Available at: https://behavioralscientist.org/about/
- Bell, W. (2004). Foundations of Futures Studies: Human Science for a New Era. Transaction Publishers.
- Benyus, J. M. (1997). Biomimicry: Innovation Inspired by Nature. William Morrow.
- BizTech Magazine. (2025). Why Retailers Need a Sustainability Game Plan. (Magazine). Available at: https://biztechmagazine.com/article/2025/05/why-retailers-need-sustainability-game-plan
- Brown, T. (2009). Change by Design: How Design Thinking Transforms Organizations and Inspires Innovation. HarperBusiness.
- Brown, T., & Wyatt, J. (2010). Design Thinking for Social Innovation. Stanford Social Innovation Review.
- Brynjolfsson, E., & McAfee, A. (2014). The Second Machine Age: Work, Progress, and Prosperity in a Time of Brilliant Technologies. W. W. Norton & Company.
- Buchanan, R. (1992). Wicked Problems in Design Thinking. Design Issues, 8(2), 5-21.
- Capra, F. (1996). The Web of Life: A New Scientific Understanding of Living Systems. Anchor.
- Capra, F., & Luisi, P. L. (2014). The Systems View of Life: A Unifying Vision. Cambridge University Press.
- Cialdini, R. B. (2006). Influence: The Psychology of Persuasion. HarperBusiness.
- Checkland, P. (1999). Systems Thinking, Systems Practice. John Wiley & Sons.
- Composite.org.nz. (n.d.). Composites Design for the Environment Framework. [Online Resource]. Available at: https://composites.org.nz/case-studies/composites-design-for-the-environment-framework/
- Dator, J. (2009). What's the Difference Between Futures, Foresight, Strategic Planning, and Anticipation? Journal of Futures Studies, 14(2), 1-15.
- Dator, J. (2018). A Guide to Futures Literacy: The Power of Anticipation. Routledge.
- Dekens, F., Bujold, P., & Mannle, K. (2024). Scaling Solutions. (Article). Available at: https://www.google.com/search?q=https://rare.org/stories-articles/fivebest--behavior-and-environment-studies-of-2024/
- Diamandis, P. H., & Kotler, S. (2012). Abundance: The Future Is Better Than You Think. Free Press.
- Diamandis, P. H., & Kotler, S. (2015). Bold: How to Go Big, Create Wealth and Impact the World. Simon & Schuster.
- Frontiersin.org. (2025). Sustainability: Articles on Circular Business Model Ecosystems. [Online Resource]. Available at: https://www.frontiersin.org/journals/sustainability/articles/10.3389/frsus.2025.1507708/full
- Fullan, M. (2011). Leading in a Culture of Change. Jossey-Bass. (For systemic change leadership).
- Fuller, R. B. (1981). Critical Path. St. Martin's Press. (For long-term, systemic change and planetary thinking).
- Fullerton, J. (2015). Regenerative Capitalism: How to Make Money While Healing the Planet. Capital Institute.
- Gardner, G. T., & Stern, P. C. (2002). Environmental Problems and Human Behavior. Allyn & Bacon.
- Gawande, A. (2014). Being Mortal: Medicine and What Matters in the End. Metropolitan Books. (For considering the long-term, human-centered consequences of design).
- Geissdoerfer, M., Savaget, A., & Evans, S. (2017). The Cambridge Business Model Innovation Process. Procedia Manufacturing, 8, 262-269.
- Gold, A. (2025). Leaving Planet Simple: Embracing Sustainability, ESG and Resilience to Transform Your Business. (Mentioned in "The Best

Sustainability Books for Entrepreneurs Who Want to Make a Difference").

- Goleman, D. (2013). The Hidden Power of Social Connection: An Evolutionary Perspective on Human Behavior. Basic Books. (For behavioral change/social norms).
- Haidt, J. (2024). The Anxious Generation. (Mentioned in "Behavioral Scientist's Notable Books of 2024").
- Hancock, P., & Bezold, C. (1994). Anticipatory Management: Planning for Tomorrow's Today. John Wiley & Sons.
- Hanington, B., & Martin, B. (2019). Universal Methods of Design: 125 Ways to Research Complex Problems, Develop Innovative Ideas, and Design Effective Solutions. Rockport Publishers.
- Harding, V. (2024). AI Needs You: How We Can Change AI's Future and Save Our Own. (Mentioned in "Behavioral Scientist's Notable Books of 2024").
- Hassenzahl, M. (2010). Experience Design: Technology for All the Right Reasons. Morgan & Claypool Publishers. (For focusing on meaningful outcomes).
- Hawken, P. (Ed.). (2017). Drawdown: The Most Comprehensive Plan Ever Proposed to Reverse Global Warming. Penguin Books.
- Heller-Herold, G., & Link, P. (2025). Das Sustainability-Toolbook.
- Hines, A., & Bishop, P. (Eds.). (2015). Thinking About the Future: Guidelines for Strategic Foresight. Social Technologies.
- IED.edu. (2024). Design Thinking: What It Is and How It Can Revolutionise Business. (Magazine). Available at: https://www.ied.edu/news/design-thinking-what-it-is-and-how-it-can-revolutionise-business
- Inayatullah, S. (2008). Six Pillars: Futures Thinking for Transforming. Foresight, 10(1), 4-21.
- Inayatullah, S. (2015). Futures Thinking and Strategy: Tools for Transformative Foresight. Emerald Group Publishing.
- Ismail, S. (2014). Exponential Organizations: Why New Organizations Are Ten Times Better, Faster, and Cheaper Than Yours (and What to Do About It). Diversion Books.
- Journal of Knowledge Management. (2025). "Design Thinking in Action: A Quantitative Study of Design Thinking Practices in Innovation Projects." Journal of Knowledge Management, 29(11):32-58. Available at: https://www.researchgate.net/publication/388399498_Design_thinking_in_action_a_quantitative_study_of_design_thinking_practices_in_innovation_projects
- Kania, J., & Kramer, M. (2011). Collective Impact. Stanford Social Innovation Review, 9(1), 36-40. (For the Collective Impact Canvas).
- Kolko, J. (2015). Uncovering the Logic of Design: How to Think, Design, and Innovate. Columbia University Press.
- Kuosa, T. (2011). The Evolution of Strategic Foresight: Navigating the Complexities of the Future. Palgrave Macmillan.
- Kurzweil, R. (2005). The Singularity Is Near: When Humans Transcend Biology. Viking.
- Leary, K. (2024). How to Winter: Harness Your Mindset to Thrive on Cold, Dark, or Difficult Days. (Mentioned in "Behavioral Scientist's Notable Books of 2024").
- Leifer, L. (1998). Design-team performance: metrics and the impact of technology. In: Evaluating Corporate Training, pp. 297-319.
- Leifer, L. and Steinert, M. (2014). Dancing with ambiguity: causality behavior, design thinking, and triple-loop-learning. In: Management of the Fuzzy Front End of Innovation, pp. 141-158.
- Leocádio, D. et al. (2024). Artificial Intelligence in Auditing: A Conceptual Framework for Auditing Practices. Administrative Sciences 14, 238.
- Lewrick, M. (2014). Design Thinking - Ausbildung an Universitäten. In: Sauvonnet und Blatt (Hrsg). Wo ist das Problem? Neue Beratung, S. 87-101.
- Lewrick, M. (2018). Design Thinking: Radikale Innovationen in einer Digitalisierten Welt. Beck Verlag; München.
- Lewrick, M. (2022). Design Thinking for Business Growth. 1st edition, Wiley.
- Lewrick, M. & Hatamleh, O. (2024). AI and Innovation: How to Transform Your Business and Outpace the Competition with Generative AI. Wiley.
- Lewrick, M. & Link, P. (2015). Hybride Management Modelle: Konvergenz von Design Thinking und Big Data. IM+io Fachzeitschrift für Innovation, Organisation und Management (4), S. 68-71.
- Lewrick, M., Link, P., Leifer, L. (2018). The Design Thinking Playbook. 1st edition, Wiley.
- Lewrick, M., Link, P., Leifer, L. (2018). The Design Thinking Toolbox. 1st edition, Wiley.
- Lewrick, M., Skribanowitz, P. & Huber, F. (2012). Nutzen von Design Thinking Programmen. 16. Interdisziplinäre Jahreskonferenz zur Gründungsforschung (G-Forum), Universität Potsdam.
- Liedtka, J. (2014). The Secret of Design Thinking Is Culture, Not Process. Harvard Business Review.

- Liedtka, J. (2017). Evaluating the Impact of Design Thinking in Action. Academy of Management Proceedings. (1) 2017.
- Liedtka, J. (2018). Design Thinking for the Greater Good: Innovation in the Social Sector. Columbia University Press.
- Liedtka, J. and Ogilvie, T. (2011). Designing for Growth. New York: Columbia University Press Inc.
- Lüdeke-Freund, F., & Dembek, A. (2017). Sustainable Business Model Innovation: A Review. Journal of Cleaner Production, 167, 1-17.
- Manzini, E. (2015). Design, When Everybody Designs: An Introduction to Design for Social Innovation. MIT Press.
- McDonough, W., & Braungart, M. (2002). Cradle to Cradle: Remaking the Way We Make Things. North Point Press.
- McKinsey Global Institute. (2023). The economic potential of generative AI: The next productivity frontier. (For current market shifts and scale).
- MDPI. (2025). Living Regeneratively: Housing Design That Enables Resident Agency in Ecological Restoration. Land, 14(7), 1462. Available at: https://www.mdpi.com/2073-445X/14/7/1462
- Meadows, D. H. (1999). Leverage Points: Places to Intervene in a System. The Sustainability Institute.
- Meadows, D. H. (2008). Thinking in Systems: A Primer. Chelsea Green Publishing.
- Mollick, E. R. (2023). Co-Intelligence: Living and Working with AI. W. W. Norton & Company. (For Human-AI collaboration).
- Mont, O. (2002). Clarifying the Concept of Product-Service System. Journal of Cleaner Production, 10(3), 237-245. (For circular business models/PaaS).
- Moore, J. F. (1996). The Death of Competition: Leadership and Strategy in the Age of Business Ecosystems. HarperBusiness.
- Munro, M. (2025). . (Article). Available at: https://www.gesda.global/day-3-geneva-science-diplomacy-week-2025/
- Nardi, B. (1996). Context and Consciousness: Activity Theory and Human-Computer Interaction. MIT Press. (For system-level empathy and activity theory).
- Narayanan, A., & Kapoor, S. (2024). AI Snake Oil: What Artificial Intelligence Can Do, What It Can't, and How To Tell the Difference. (Mentioned in "Behavioral Scientist's Notable Books of 2024").
- Norman, D. (2023). Design a Better World: Toward a Human-Centered, Sustainable Future. MIT Press.
- Norman, D. (2013). The Design of Everyday Things: Revised and Expanded Edition. Basic Books.
- O'Neil, C. (2016). Weapons of Math Destruction: How Big Data Increases Inequality and Threatens Democracy. Crown.
- OECD. (2024). OECD Digital Economy Outlook 2024 (Volume 1). (Policy Paper). Available at: https://www.oecd.org/en/publications/leveraging-digital-business-models-tools-and-technologies-for-reliable-environmental-information-and-consumer-engagement-in-the-circular-economy_33c6e2bc-en.html
- OECD. (2024). Policy paper. Review of relevance of the OECD Recommendation on ICTs and the Environment. (Policy Paper). Available at: https://www.oecd.org/en/publications/leveraging-digital-business-models-tools-and-technologies-for-reliable-environmental-information-and-consumer-engagement-in-the-circular-economy_33c6e2bc-en.html
- OECD. (2025). Policy paper. Enhancing the resilience of communication networks. (Policy Paper). Available at: https://www.oecd.org/en/publications/leveraging-digital-business-models-tools-and-technologies-for-reliable-environmental-information-and-consumer-engagement-in-the-circular-economy_33c6e2bc-en.html
- OECD. (2025). Policy paper. Facilitating the secondary use of health data for public interest purposes across borders. (Policy Paper). Available at: https://www.oecd.org/en/publications/leveraging-digital-business-models-tools-and-technologies-for-reliable-environmental-information-and-consumer-engagement-in-the-circular-economy_33c6e2bc-en.html
- OECD. (2025). Policy paper. Protecting and empowering consumers in the green transition. (Policy Paper). Available at: https://www.oecd.org/en/publications/leveraging-digital-business-models-tools-and-technologies-for-reliable-environmental-information-and-consumer-engagement-in-the-circular-economy_33c6e2bc-en.html
- OECD. (2025). Policy paper. The environmental sustainability of communication networks. (Policy Paper). Available at: https://www.oecd.org/en/publications/leveraging-digital-business-models-tools-and-technologies-for-reliable-environmental-information-and-consumer-engagement-in-the-circular-economy_33c6e2bc-en.html
- OECD. (2025). Policy paper. Unlocking the potential of demand-side climate mitigation strategies. (Policy Paper). Available at: https://www.oecd.org/en/publications/leveraging-digital-business-models-tools-and-technologies-for-reliable-environmental-information-and-consumer-engagement-in-the-circular-economy_33c6e2bc-en.html

- OECD. (2025). Working paper. A quantum technologies policy primer. (Working Paper). Available at: https://www.oecd.org/en/publications/leveraging-digital-business-models-tools-and-technologies-for-reliable-environmental-information-and-consumer-engagement-in-the-circular-economy_33c6e2bc-en.html
- OECD. (2025). Working paper. An immersive technologies policy primer. (Working Paper). Available at: https://www.oecd.org/en/publications/leveraging-digital-business-models-tools-and-technologies-for-reliable-environmental-information-and-consumer-engagement-in-the-circular-economy_33c6e2bc-en.html
- Osann, I., Mayer, L., & Wiele, I. (2024). The Design Thinking Quick Start Guide: A 6-Step Process for Generating and Implementing Creative Solutions. (Mentioned in "Our top 10 innovation books to read in 2024").
- Pauli, G. (2010). The Blue Economy: 10 Years, 100 Innovations, 100 Million Jobs. Paradigm Publications.
- PwC.de. (n.d.). Sustainable Business Models: Insights into Conceptual Canvases for Starting Your Transformation. [Online Resource]. Available at: https://blogs.pwc.de/en/sustainability/article/245957/sustainable-business-models-insights-into-conceptual-canvases-for-starting-your-transformation/
- Ramos, J. (2021). The Futures Action Handbook: A Guide to Creating Futures Literacy. The Policy Press.
- Raworth, K. (2017). Doughnut Economics: Seven Ways to Think Like a 21st-Century Economist. Chelsea Green Publishing.
- ResearchGate. (2025). The Nexus Between the Design Thinking, Strategy Formulation and Innovation in SMEs: An Integrative Review. (Journal). Available at: https://www.researchgate.net/publication/393713176_The_nexus_between_the_design_thinking_strategy_formulation_and_innovation_in_SMEs_an_integrative_review
- Ries, E. (2011). The Lean Startup: How Today's Entrepreneurs Use Continuous Innovation to Create Radically Successful Businesses. Crown Business.
- Romeo, N. (2024). The Alternative: How to Build a Just Economy. (Mentioned in "Behavioral Scientist's Notable Books of 2024").
- Russell, S. (2019). Human Compatible: Artificial Intelligence and the Problem of Control. Viking. (For AI ethics and alignment).
- Russell, S., & Norvig, P. (2010). Artificial Intelligence: A Modern Approach. Pearson Education.
- Sainz, M. (2025). Setting Goals: Balancing Deterministic and Constraint-Based Thinking. (Article). Available at: https://publish.openexo.com/tag/exponential-thinking/
- Schön, D. A. (1983). The Reflective Practitioner: How Professionals Think in Action. Basic Books.
- Schumacher, E. F. (1973). Small Is Beautiful: A Study of Economics As If People Mattered. Blond & Briggs.
- Schwartz, P. (1996). The Art of the Long View: Planning for the Future in an Unpredictable World. Currency Doubleday.
- Schultz, P. W., Nolan, J. M., Cialdini, R. B., Goldstein, N. J., & Griskevicius, V. (2007). The Constructive, Destructive, and Reconstructive Power of Social Norms. Psychological Science, 18(5), 429-433.
- Senge, P. M. (1990). The Fifth Discipline: The Art & Practice of The Learning Organization. Doubleday.
- Simon, H. A. (1996). The Sciences of the Artificial (3rd ed.). The MIT Press.
- Sinek, S. (2019). The Infinite Game. Portfolio. (For Infinite Game Mindset).
- Slaughter, R. A. (1995). The Foresight Principle: Cultural Implications of the New Futures. Praeger.
- Slaughter, R. A. (2004). The Handbook of Foresight. Compass Publishing.
- Sterman, J. D. (2000). Business Dynamics: Systems Thinking and Modeling for a Complex World. McGraw-Hill Education.
- Stickdorn, M., Hormess, M., Lawrence, A., & Schneider, J. (2018). This is Service Design Doing: Applying Service Design Thinking in the Real World. O'Reilly Media.
- Sutton, R. I., & Rao, H. (2024). The Friction Project: How Smart Leaders Make the Right Things Easier and the Wrong Things Harder. (Mentioned in "Behavioral Scientist's Notable Books of 2024").
- Taleb, N. N. (2007). The Black Swan: The Impact of the Highly Improbable. Random House.
- Taleb, N. N. (2012). Antifragile: Things That Gain from Disorder. Random House.
- Taylor & Francis Online. (2025). "Systems Thinking for Sustainability: Shifting to a Higher Level of Systems Consciousness." Systems Practice. (Journal). Available at: https://www.tandfonline.com/doi/pdf/10.1080/01605682.2025.2486698
- Thaler, R. H., & Sunstein, C. R. (2008). Nudge: Improving Decisions About Health, Wealth, and Happiness. Yale University Press.
- Timber Design & Technology. (2025). "Material Cultures Investigates the

Use of Natural, Renewable Materials in Design and Architecture."
(Magazine). Available at: https://www.timberdesignandtechnology.
com/articles/material-cultures-investigates-the-use-of-natural-
renewable-materials-in-design-and-architecture/
- Tufte, E. R. (2001). The Visual Display of Quantitative Information
  (2nd ed.). Graphics Press.
- Voros, J. (2003). A Generic Foresight Process for the Specific Purpose of
  Strategy Development. Foresight, 5(5), 10-21.
- Wahl, D. C. (2016). Designing Regenerative Cultures. Triarchy Press.
- Wahl, D. C. (2024). Designing Regenerative Cultures.
- Węglarz, M. (2025). Sustainable Business Models Among Small and
  Medium Enterprises - Resource-Based View. Economics and Environment,
  91(4), 999. (Journal). Available at: https://ekonomiaisrodowisko.pl/
  journal/article/view/999
- Zhao, J., & Radke, J. (2025). How a Lottery-Style Refund System Could
  Boost Recycling. The Conversation. (Article). Available at: https://
  zhaolab.psych.ubc.ca/publications.html
- Zhao, J., et al. (2024). The international climate psychology collabora-
  tion: Climate change-related data collected from 63 countries. (Study).
  Available at: https://zhaolab.psych.ubc.ca/publications.html
- Zhao, J., et al. (2024). Using Salience and Availability to Promote
  Sustainable Food Choices in Hospital Cafeterias. Scientific Reports, 14,
  26265. (Article). Available at: https://zhaolab.psych.ubc.ca/publications.
  html
- Zukunftswissenschaft.de. (n.d.). Foresight Methodenmatrix. [Online Re-
  source]. Available at: https://www.zukunftswissenschaft.de/e-fogumi/
  foresight-methodenmatrix.htm